RENEWALS 458

MENDING FENCES

The Evolution of Moscow's China Policy
from Brezhnev to Yeltsin

WITHDRAWN
UTSA Libraries

MENDING FENCES

The Evolution of Moscow's China Policy from Brezhnev to Yeltsin

ELIZABETH WISHNICK

UNIVERSITY OF WASHINGTON PRESS

Seattle and London

This publication was supported in part by the
Donald R. Ellegood International Publication Endowment

Copyright © 2001 by the University of Washington Press
Printed in the United States of America

All rights reserved. No part of this publication may be reproduced or transmitted in any form
or by any means, electronic or mechanical, including photocopy, recording, or any information
storage or retrieval system, without permission in writing from the publisher.

Library of Congress Cataloging-in-Publication Data

Wishnick, Elizabeth.
    Mending fences : the evolution of Moscow's China policy from Brezhnev to Yeltsin /
Elizabeth Wishnick.
        p.   cm.
    Includes bibliographical references and index.
    ISBN 0-295-98128-8 (alk. paper)
    1. Soviet Union—Foreign relations—China.   2. China—Foreign relations—Soviet Union.
    3. Russia (Federation)—Foreign relations—China.   4. China—Foreign relations—
    Russia (Federation)   5. Soviet Union—Foreign relations—1953–1975.   6. Soviet Union—
    Foreign relations—1975–1985.   7. Soviet Union—Foreign relations—1985–1991.   8. Russia
    (Federation)—Foreign relations.   9. China—Foreign relations—1949–1976.   10. China—
    Foreign relations—1976—I. Title.
    DK68.7.C6 W57   2001
    327.47051'09'045—DC21

                                                                                  2001017476

The paper used in this publication is acid-free and recycled from 10 percent post-consumer and
at least 50 percent pre-consumer waste. It meets the minimum requirements of American
National Standard for Information Sciences—Permanence of Paper for Printed Library
Materials, ANSI Z39.48–1984.⊗♻

Library
University of Texas
at San Antonio

For my parents,

and

in memory of Henry Shapiro (1906–1991)

Contents

Acknowledgments

Writing a book about Moscow's China policy turned out to be a good pretext for travel and adventure. My research took me to Moscow, Vladivostok, Khabarovsk, Birobidjan, Blagoveshchensk, Beijing, Harbin, Taipei, Oxford, Boston, Palo Alto, and Washington, D.C., and provided opportunities along the way to meet many interesting colleagues all over the world. Conferences organized by Sherman Garnett, Thomas Lahusen, Stephen Kotkin, Gilbert Rozman, and David Wolff played a big part in introducing me to a international network of scholars who study similar issues.

I would like to thank all of the institutions that assisted me, including the Institute of Asia and Africa at Moscow State University, the Institute of the Far East (Moscow), the Archives of the Central Committee of the CPSU (Moscow), the Carnegie Moscow Center, the Institute of History, Archeology and Ethnography of the Peoples of the Far East (Vladivostok), the Institute for Economic Research (Khabarovsk), the State Archives of Khabarovskii Krai, the Research Institute on Contemporary China (Beijing), the Research Institute for East European and Central Asian Studies (Beijing), Heilongjiang University (Harbin), the Research Institute for Siberian Studies (Harbin), the Institute of Modern History (Taipei), St. Antony's College (Oxford University), the Harriman Institute and the East Asian Institute (Columbia University), the Davis Center for Russian Studies (Harvard University), the Hoover Institution (Stanford University), the National Archives (Washington, D.C.), the National Security Archives (Washington, D.C.), and the Library of Congress (Washington, D.C.).

Research trips proved fruitful only because of the generous assistance of my colleagues in Russia, the People's Republic of China (PRC), Taiwan, the United States, and England, who consented to be interviewed, helped me to identify sources, and challenged my assumptions. By taking the time to study Russian and Chinese and to travel to both countries to consult experts and sources, I have tried to be balanced in my assessments. While I take full responsibility for any errors, the history of Moscow's China policy remains controversial, and I expect that this book will stimulate debate rather than put an end to it. In my view, a more open discussion of the history of relations between

Beijing and Moscow can only be a positive development, both for the stability of their bilateral relations and for Asia as a whole—in their rush to move forward with a new Sino-Russian relationship based on strategic partnership, many of the underlying sources of their earlier conflict were not addressed and contribute to distrust, especially on the regional level.

A special thank you to Gilbert Rozman, whose great enthusiasm for my project, consistent support, and considerable assistance throughout have been invaluable. I am particularly grateful to colleagues, including Gilbert Rozman, who commented on various drafts, especially Evgenii Bazhanov, Lev Deliusin, Bruce Elleman, Valere P. Gagnon, Jr., Li Jingjie, Li Zhuanxun, Ni Xiaoquan, Allen Lynch, Cynthia Roberts, and Sarah Paine. I am indebted to my Chinese language teachers at the Taipei Language Institute, who helped me prepare for my field research in the PRC in record time. The idea for the book emerged from my doctoral dissertation, and I would like to thank my advisers at Columbia University, Thomas Bernstein and Robert Legvold.

My research was funded by a research exchange grant from the American Council of Teachers of Russian (ACTR), a postdoctoral fellowship from the Davis Center (Harvard University), a Title VIII postdoctoral fellowship from the Hoover Institution (Stanford University), short-term grants from the International Research and Exchanges Board (IREX) (with funds from Title VIII and the National Endowment for the Humanities), and research grants from the Pacific Cultural Foundation (Taipei) and the Smith Richardson Foundation. Many thanks to all of these organizations for their financial support.

Keeping pace with all of the changes in Russia and China in the 1990s and taking advantage of the increasing variety of sources have been major challenges in completing a book about Moscow's China policy. I am very grateful to Michael Duckworth, acquisitions editor at the University of Washington Press, for his patience with the twists and turns of my project, his unflagging interest in the topic, and his considerable editorial assistance with my revisions. It was a pleasure working with him, and I am grateful to John Stephan for referring my name to him.

Four anonymous reviewers provided many helpful comments. I also would like to thank Bruce Acker and Barbara Roesmann for their careful editing of the final draft, and Marilyn Trueblood and Xavier Callahan at the University of Washington Press for stewarding the manuscript through the production process.

My friends and family were a great source of support, especially my parents, who had to cope with my periodic disappearances to far-flung locations. This book is dedicated to my parents and to the memory of Henry Shapiro, whose stories about his life as a journalist in Moscow from the Stalin years to the Brezhnev era helped inspire this enterprise.

I would like to thank the editors of the following publications for allowing me to include material and photographs from my previously published articles:

"Chinese Perspectives on Cross-Border Relations," in Sherman Garnett, ed., *Rapprochement or Rivalry?* (Washington, D.C.: The Brookings Institution Press, 1999).

"Prospects for the Sino-Russian Partnership: Views from Moscow and the Russian Far East," *Journal of East Asian Affairs,* vol. 12, no. 2 (Summer/Fall 1998), pp. 418–51, published by the Research Institute for International Affairs, Seoul, Korea.

"Where the Grass Seems Greener: Russia's New Chinese Immigration Problem," *The Asia-Pacific Magazine,* no. 6 and 7 (1997), pp. 54–60, published by the Institute of Advanced Studies, Research School of Pacific and Asian Studies, Australian National University.

"Soviet Reactions to the Sino-Soviet Border Rift, Introduction and Translations," *Cold War International History Project Bulletin,* Winter 1995/1996, pp. 194–201.

"Sino-Soviet Tensions, 1980: Two Russian Documents, Introduction and Translations," *Cold War International History Project Bulletin,* Winter 1995/1996, pp. 202–7.

The cover art is based on a poster by Iurii Shibanov, and I would like to thank him for permission to use it.

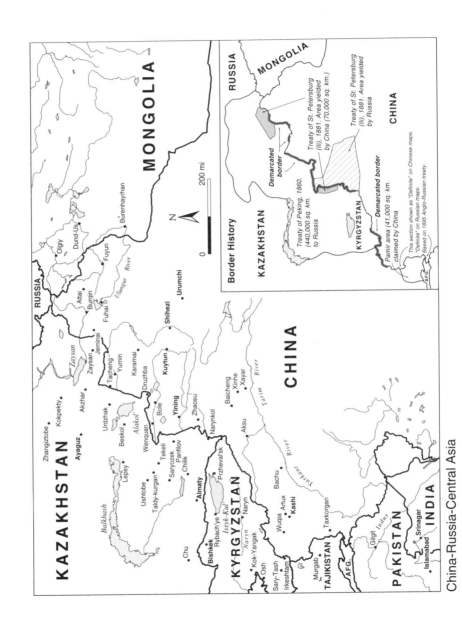

Border History

Treaty of St. Petersburg (III). Area yielded by China (70,000 sq. km.).

Treaty of St. Petersburg (III), 1881. Area yielded by Russia

Demarcated border

Treaty of Peking, 1860. (440,000 sq. km.) to Russia

Demarcated border

Pamir area (41,000 sq. km. claimed by China

This section shown as "Definite" on Chinese maps. "Definite" on Russian maps. Based on 1895 Anglo-Russian treaty.

RUSSIA

MONGOLIA

KAZAKHSTAN

CHINA

KYRGYZSTAN

AFG.

N

0   200 mi

MONGOLIA

RUSSIA

KAZAKHSTAN

CHINA

KYRGYZSTAN

Zhangiztobe
Kokpekty
Ayaguz.
Akzhar
Urdzhak
Beskol
Lepsy
Ushtobe
Taldy-kurgan
Tekeli
Saryozek
Panfilov
Chilik
Wenquan
Bole
Yining
Zhaosu
Narynkol

Olgy
Dund-Us
Altai
Zaysan
Burqin
Fuhai
Jeminai
Tacheng
Yumin
Karamai
Druzhba
Kuytun

Ulungur River

Fuyun

Bürenhayrhan

Shihezi

Urumchi

Baicheng
Xinhe
Xayar
Aksu

Tarim River

Balkhash

Alakol

Zaysan

Issyk-Kul

Almaty

Przhevalsk

Bishkek
Rybach'ye
KYRGYZSTAN
Naryn
Chu
Kok-Yangak
Osh
Sary-Tash
Irkeshtam

Naryn

Bachu
Artux
Kashi
Wuqia

Taxkorgan

Murgab
TAJIKISTAN
AFG.

Yarkand River

CHINA

PAKISTAN

Gilgit
Islamabad
Srinagar
INDIA

Indus

China-Russia-Central Asia

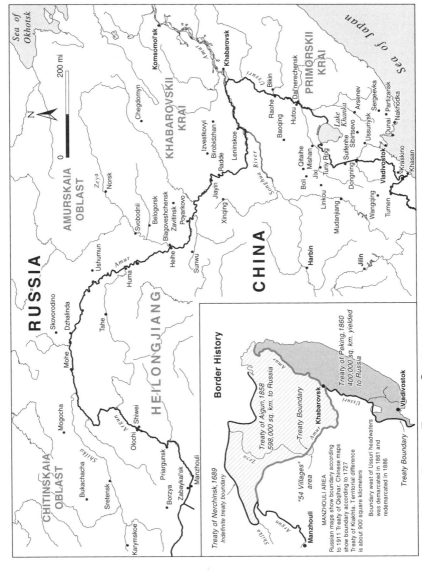

China-Russia Border: Eastern Sector

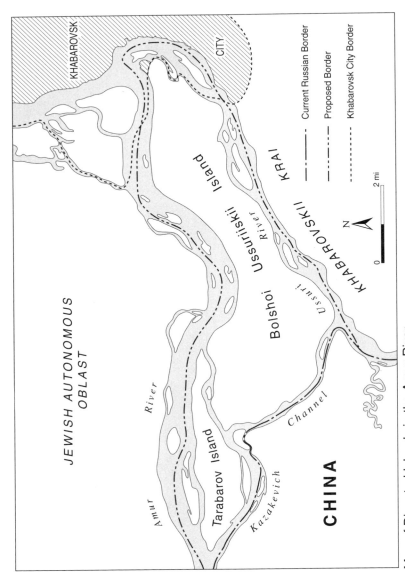

Map of Disputed Islands in the Amur River

MENDING FENCES

The Evolution of Moscow's China Policy
from Brezhnev to Yeltsin

1 / Introduction

Relations between Moscow and Beijing have gone full circle in the past half century—from alliance to containment and now back to strategic partnership. Moscow's part in this dynamic is the subject of the present study, which seeks to resolve some of the remaining mysteries about the slow evolution of the Soviet Union's, and now Russia's, China policy since 1969.[1]

While highlighting the importance of the foreign policy process for policy outcomes (in Russia and more generally), the book tells the tale of relations between the two great neighbors from border confrontation in 1969 to strategic partnership in 1999, and explains the persistence of conflict during the Brezhnev era and the sources of change in relations in subsequent periods. Although a key focus of the study is on post-1991 developments, discussion of the post-1969 history of relations is crucial to understanding the contemporary relationship. Historical grievances continue to cast a shadow on Sino-Russian relations today, especially in the border regions.[2] Thanks to the availability of new documentary evidence, recent scholarship on both sides of the Amur River has begun to reexamine many contested issues, and the publication of new historical analyses has fueled debates on current developments.[3]

To understand the ebbs and flows in Moscow's China policy, it is necessary to look within the Soviet and post-Soviet political process. Although international developments, especially interaction in the Sino-Soviet-American strategic triangle, have exerted an important influence on Moscow's relations with China, the main sources of stasis and change have come from within. As Robert Putnam has shown, two sets of negotiations often take place to resolve international problems—one in the international arena, and another at home.[4] Leadership change in Moscow played a key role by bringing into power new coalitions of political leaders with different interests in China policy.

This study reconstructs the strategic environment facing the top decision-makers in Moscow during the Soviet period and shows how they formulated China policy in response to three audiences that were instrumental in legitimating Soviet power: the international communist movement, political and military officials in Moscow, and leaders in the Russian border regions.

Motivated by concerns specific to their constituent members, the three audiences elaborated divergent historical narratives of relations between Moscow and Beijing and used these accounts to press their interests in China policy.[5]

Above all, Soviet leaders aspired to present a united front to the world on China policy. Because China's alternative vision of socialist development challenged the Soviet Union's leadership of the communist movement as well as the validity of its own path to socialism as a model for other ruling parties, Soviet leaders made sure that officials in Moscow and the border regions spoke with one voice and sought to coordinate a unified response by socialist bloc countries.

While researchers typically have confined their analyses of the influence of policies on specific constituencies to democratic states, this study shows that Soviet leaders continuously sought the support of officials in Moscow, the border regions, and the international communist movement.[6] New evidence from archives and interviews shows that these three audiences were hard to please. Often the means used by Soviet leaders to maintain the appearance of unity within these three spheres, especially in the international communist movement, worked at cross-purposes with Moscow's strategic goals in the US-USSR-PRC triangle.[7]

By the early 1980s, the crisis in Poland over the Solidarity movement and the rise of Eurocommunism created new obstacles for the achievement of united responses within the socialist community regarding China and many other central questions. As border tensions receded from memory, Soviet regional officials pressed for reopening Sino-Soviet border trade.[8] Meanwhile, in Moscow, different views on China policy became more apparent, although proponents of retaining the previous policy of containing China held the upper hand until Mikhail Gorbachev came to power.

Gorbachev's commitment to the reform of the Soviet model led to the promotion of reformers who had long favored a reassessment not only of China's post-1979 reform model but also of the USSR's China policy. Gorbachev's reform program called for involving the Soviet Union in new forms of economic cooperation, and in the mid-1980s, the Soviet leader finally acceded to the wishes of regional leaders to reopen border trade with China. Moreover, as Gorbachev sought new approaches to socialist development, he encouraged fellow socialist leaders to do the same while admitting the possibility of different roads to socialism. No longer was unity on China policy an essential component of intra-bloc relations.

The demise of communism and then the collapse of the Soviet Union itself coincided with the rise in centrifugal tendencies within the Russian Federation. The demands of the regional audience began to influence national policy more than in earlier decades. Similarly, by the early 1990s, the factional politics under-lying the formulation of Russia's foreign policy became more apparent and the range of perspectives on Russia's China policy began to be defined more sharply. The Yeltsin administration quickly became disenchanted with Russia's initial pro-West foreign policy orientation and began to pursue a strategy more balanced between East and West. Sino-Russian partnership became the Yeltsin team's new watchword, although this new policy faced criticism, especially in the Russian border regions. In Moscow as well, moderates who favored closer ties with the West and nationalists who feared China's rise in power criticized increased Sino-Russian cooperation.

DOMESTIC-INTERNATIONAL LINKAGES IN THE STRATEGIC TRIANGLE

While there is a voluminous literature on the US-USSR-PRC strategic trian-gle,[9] the Chinese side of the Sino-Soviet dispute has received the lion's share of attention. As Donald Treadgold pointed out, there are few attempts to explain the specific configuration of international and domestic developments influenc-ing Moscow's behavior in the triangle.[10]

According to realist theories of international relations, less powerful states respond to threats from a greater power by balancing against that power.[11] In the context of a strategic triangle, however, balancing becomes a matter of degree. When one of the three states perceives at least one of the other two as a threat, that state tries to avoid having simultaneously poor relations with the other two and endeavors at all cost to prevent collusion between them.

The term "collusion" simplifies reality—when two of the three sides share parallel interests, the third may perceive collusion between the side it consid-ers to be its main enemy and the secondary adversary. The aim of each is to avoid collusion of the two others, and to blackmail one's main enemy by threat-ening collusion with the third.[12] The way one state avoids collusion by the other two depends on the patterns of alignment in the triangle.

Analysts of triangular interaction typically look for patterns of tactical flexi-bility, whereas Brezhnev-era China policy—with a few exceptions in the early 1970s and early 1980s—was remarkably consistent and largely unresponsive to change in the international environment. While Soviet leaders had a compelling interest in fashioning an international environment that would enable them to achieve their foreign policy goals, the pressures generated by American and Chinese actions in the triangle were by no means determining.[13] To fully under-stand Soviet behavior, it is necessary to examine the choices made by policy-makers in Moscow.

Balancing behavior typically includes increasing military capabilities as well as seeking allies against the threatening state. From the mid-1960s to the early 1980s, however, the strategy employed by Soviet policymakers focused on two main tasks, which often worked at cross-purposes. Because Soviet policymakers saw Chinese policies as a military threat and a challenge to Soviet preeminence in the communist movement, building up Soviet capabilities had an important political component.[14] While Soviet leaders devoted considerable resources to shoring up the USSR's defenses against China, especially in the border area, they mounted an equal effort to respond to China's political challenge to Soviet leadership of the communist movement by coordinating a countervailing strategy with allied parties, the Moscow policy community, and regional communist party officials in the Russian border regions.

The second component of Soviet strategy involved efforts to prevent China from increasing its security through an alliance with the United States. However, the measures the Soviet leadership employed to meet China's political-military challenge created a security dilemma for the Chinese leaders and drove them to seek closer relations with the United States.[15] These measures also limited the ability of the Soviet Union to balance the Chinese threat with closer ties to the United States because they reinforced American views of a Soviet threat.

By the 1980s, however, the domestic-international linkages in Moscow's China policy began to evolve. As tensions emerged in Sino-American relations and Soviet-American relations reached an unprecedented low point in the early 1980s, China sought a more independent foreign policy stance and simultaneously embarked on a major program of economic modernization. Within a few years, the Soviet Union, too, began a program of domestic reform. As the differences in Soviet and Chinese domestic strategies narrowed and the Soviet Union under Gorbachev's leadership became more tolerant of diversity in the international communist movement, China's challenge to Soviet domestic interests was reduced greatly.

After the disintegration of the Soviet Union, however, domestic factors once again began to work at cross-purposes with Moscow's goals in the triangle. Once President Boris Yeltsin decided on a foreign policy balanced between the West and the East, the Russian leadership focused on the development of a strategic partnership with China to offset perceived pressures from the United States. However, the Russian border regions, which initially favored the improvement of Sino-Russian relations, especially in the economic sphere, soon began to express their opposition to what some regional leaders saw as a one-sided orientation toward China. While policymakers in Moscow viewed China as the centerpiece of Russian foreign policy, in some of the border regions China was regarded as a potential threat, and regional leaders expressed their preference for a foreign economic strategy directed at a broader range of states, including the United States, South Korea, and Japan.

POLITICAL STRUCTURE, COALITION POLITICS, AND BREZHNEV'S CHINA POLICY

Ever since George Kennan's pioneering analysis of the impact of Soviet totalitarianism on Soviet foreign policy, analysts of the domestic sources of Moscow's foreign policy have noted that the nature of the regime influences foreign policymaking.[16] In particular, the Soviet Union's adherence to a Leninist conception of party and bloc structure played a key role in its China policy.

The limited de-Stalinization of Soviet ideology begun in the Khrushchev era had profound implications for Moscow's relations with its socialist neighbors in Eastern Europe and China and raised questions about the legitimacy of the Soviet system itself. When Chinese departures from the Soviet model began to coincide with mounting challenges in Eastern Europe in the 1950s and 1960s, Soviet leaders, especially in the Brezhnev era, formulated a China policy premised on the need to maintain the legitimacy of the Soviet model of socialism as well as the Soviet Union's leadership of the communist movement.[17]

Many scholars have examined the deterioration of the Sino-Soviet relationship in the 1950s, which ultimately led to sharp public exchanges of ideological polemics in the early 1960s.[18] By 1966, the Chinese Communist Party refused to send representatives to the Twenty-third Party Congress of the Soviet Communist Party and the split between the two parties became official. The extremism of the Cultural Revolution deepened the ideological fault lines between the two neighbors. Tensions between the two countries were reflected in periodic border skirmishes in the 1960s, which escalated to actual exchanges of fire on Damanskii/Zhen Bao Island in the spring of 1969 and in other border areas throughout the summer.

While the September 1969 meeting between Zhou Enlai and Aleksei Kosygin diffused the military confrontation in the border regions, the Soviets and the Chinese maintained a Cold War of their own for another fifteen years. From the early 1970s to the early 1980s, the Brezhnev leadership advocated normalizing Sino-Soviet relations while pursuing a containment policy towards China.[19] Soviet strategy, involving a massive military build-up in the Far East and interference in Third World conflicts to counter Chinese interests, not only confirmed Chinese fears of a Soviet threat but also undermined détente with the United States.

The Soviet leadership selected this course of action to defend their vulnerable border, ensure military superiority in case of hostilities with China, and compensate for the foreign policy costs of continued ideological differences with China over issues such as relations with the West, socialist states, and the international communist movement.[20] These ideological differences led key Soviet policymakers to overestimate the military threat posed by China, particularly to the Russian border regions, although military observers proved more sober in their analysis of the limitations of Chinese military power.

Soviet political leaders used ideological concepts to justify their policy choices in an effort to legitimate their own political power.[21] Because only they had the authority to set the ideological parameters of debate on key issues, adherence to the party line became the prerequisite for a role in the policy process and the main criterion for membership in the communist movement.[22]

Marxist-Leninist ideology served as a rationale for policy in that it functioned as a conceptual framework, which influenced the choice of alternatives, provided a sense of purpose, and facilitated agenda-building.[23] This framework presented barriers to policy innovation, since there was no real provision for responding to problems that departed from accepted doctrinal concepts, barring revision of the concepts themselves.[24] A Soviet leader's decision to revise the ideology could undermine his own power (as happened with Gorbachev) because ideological concepts endowed his rule with legitimacy.[25]

As long as Marxist-Leninist ideology justified Soviet policy, the Soviet Union required that other socialist states legitimate its preeminent role in the communist world and mirror Soviet policy choices. According to Ken Jowitt, this is because the structure of the socialist bloc paralleled that of the Leninist party. In Jowitt's view, Leninist parties are novel in that they combine modern and traditional elements. While providing a framework for addressing contemporary problems such as class struggle, he argues, Leninist parties are structured according to status considerations typical of traditional peasant societies: (1) insiders (i.e., party members) are distinguished from outsiders (non-members); (2) security is derived from membership in a closed group; and (3) the personal role of the (party) leader is emphasized.[26] As the bloc leader, the Soviet Union provided security and a sense of belonging for other bloc members, and established the criteria for membership.[27]

Although Soviet policymakers always considered China to be a socialist state, even during periods of hostility between the Soviet Union and China, Chinese behavior did not always conform to Soviet expectations of the way socialist states should act.[28] When Soviet leaders observed that China's actions failed to coincide with policies expected of socialist states, they perceived a political challenge to the Soviet Union's leadership of the bloc.[29] It became difficult to predict Chinese behavior and to find a suitable response within their ideologically defined conception of relations between socialist states.

Jowitt contends that the superimposition of China's political challenge to the Soviet Union's leadership of the bloc with the rapprochement between China (an insider) and the United States (an outsider) proved doubly threatening to Soviet leaders.[30] As a consequence, they overreacted to Chinese policies and relied on a political and military containment strategy to bolster Soviet positions. Since the Chinese leadership interpreted these measures as aggressive and responded in ways that further hurt Soviet positions, a security dilemma was created.

China's political challenge affected different interests within the Soviet Union, and a coalition of key party, military, KGB, and government leaders formed in response.[31] Recent memoir literature puts Yuri Andropov, Andrei Gromyko, Mikhail Suslov, and Dmitrii Ustinov at the center of this coalition.[32] Although their interests in China policy were different in many respects, they came together to resist China's political challenge and to address the concerns of the three audiences outlined previously.

These leaders played a key role in China policy during the Brezhnev period because of the general secretary's deference to their foreign policy expertise. Brezhnev was a leader who knew his own limitations, once telling his long-time foreign policy adviser, Andrei Aleksandrov-Agentov, that the best position he ever held was that of *obkom* first secretary.[33] Moreover, Brezhnev had better personal relations with each of these top policymakers than they enjoyed with each other. Brezhnev could benefit from their foreign policy advice without fearing that the foreign policy coalition in the Politburo would pose a more fundamental challenge to his authority.[34]

Mikhail Suslov. Brezhnev, who recognized that he was no innovator in Marxist-Leninist theory, relied on Suslov's analyses of theoretical issues. Apparently, Suslov's dogmatism and caution suited Brezhnev, despite the fact that the former's views exacerbated the Soviet Union's relations with many of the more reform-minded communist parties, such as the Yugoslav and Italian parties.[35] Indeed, right after Khrushchev's ouster, Brezhnev began looking to Suslov to advise him on China policy.[36]

Brezhnev also highly valued Suslov's work in administering the party and state *apparat.*[37] With Suslov, the Communist Party's Central Committee secretary in charge of ideology and the *apparat* until 1982, and Oleg Rakhmanin managing relations with Asian socialist states in the Department for Liaison with Socialist Countries until 1986, the Central Committee became the headquarters of opposition to any major changes in Soviet China policy.[38] Because it enjoyed a near monopoly of control over information and analysis on China, the Central Committee was able to maintain its hold over China policy and resist any changes that would threaten its purview.[39]

Dmitrii Ustinov. Ustinov, Gromyko, and Andropov formed the main triumvirate on foreign policy issues during Brezhnev's rule.[40] Ustinov, who became defense minister in 1976, was known for his cautious stance on disarmament, a confrontational approach to the United States, and his support for military action in defense of socialist gains.[41] Ustinov reportedly favored Soviet intervention in Czechoslovakia in 1968 and was one of the key proponents of the invasion of Afghanistan.[42]

Andrei Gromyko. Gromyko served as foreign minister of the Soviet Union for almost thirty years. Gromyko was lauded for his professionalism and devotion to his work, yet his long-time colleague, former Ambassador to the United States Anatolii Dobrynin, noted that, like many leaders of his generation, he proved a captive to "old thinking."[43] This involved both a determination to preserve the gains made by the Soviet Union in the aftermath of World War II and a paternalistic view of Soviet relations with other bloc countries.[44] In China policy, this led to a certain "anti-Chinese inertia" in the Foreign Ministry, as well as in the Central Committee *apparat.*[45]

Yuri Andropov. The memoir literature portrays Andropov as the most "pragmatic" member of the small group of top leaders who played a central role in Soviet foreign policy.[46] Andropov—who had been the Ambassador to Hungary during the Soviet invasion of Hungary in 1956, who was the former head of the Central Committee Department on Ruling Socialist Parties during the time of the Sino-Soviet polemics, who went on to head the KGB in 1967, and who then succeeded Brezhnev as general secretary—clearly was no liberal thinker.

Yet Andropov was a leader who repeatedly recruited consultants who had fundamentally different political views, but who could be counted on to provide him with objective analyses of current events. As a consequence, Andropov, unlike his fellow Politburo members, appears to have had a clear understanding of the negative contribution of the Sino-Soviet conflict to the Soviet Union's global position, especially in the strategic triangle.[47]

Nonetheless, the benefits of an improved relationship with China were outweighed by other interests, which overlapped with those of Andropov's colleagues in the Politburo. Like Suslov, the number two man in the Brezhnev Politburo who viewed Andropov as a rival for the general secretary position, the KGB chief was concerned about the impact of China on the Soviet Union's leadership of the communist bloc.[48] If Suslov approached the problem from the point of view of Marxist-Leninist dogma, then Andropov was more concerned about the stability of the bloc itself. Suslov, as head of the party *apparat,* also faced the task of coordinating a unified rebuttal to Chinese heresies by party officials in Moscow, the border regions, and other socialist bloc countries.

Gromyko, like Andropov and Ustinov, was disquieted by the adverse influence of Chinese policies on the political-military balance of power. For Gromyko, this led to great caution on the expansion of economic ties with China, lest this boost China's wherewithal. For Ustinov, these concerns necessitated building a substantial military capability, especially in the border regions, to ensure that a political challenge would not escalate into a military one.

As Jack Snyder has argued, the existence of a coalition such as the one noted above, based on overlapping interests, constrains the ability of the top leader to adjust policy and reinforces rigidities.[49] In formulating Moscow's China policy, key Soviet policymakers used concepts relating to the ideological struggle with Beijing both to justify the importance of continued containment of China and to maintain their own hold over China policy.[50]

LEADERSHIP CHANGE AND SOURCES OF CHANGE IN CHINA POLICY

Although the existence of a powerful coalition of leaders with overlapping interests created barriers to change in China policy, there were several opportunities in the period under study for a shift in strategy: 1964–69, 1982–84, 1985–89, and 1992–99. Scholars have long debated the sources of foreign policy innovation in the Soviet Union and have noted the central role of leadership succession in opening up opportunities for change. Archie Brown has argued, for example, that in every case of leadership change since Stalin's day, succession "altered the balance of forces among the different political tendencies, opinion groupings and institutional interests which compete for the attention of power-holders and for influence in the policy process."[51] In Valerie Bunce's view, however, while leadership change is an important precondition for major reform, in order to precipitate a shift in policy, the transition must occur at a time of crisis that threatens the survival of the regime.[52] While the importance of leadership succession for policy change has been demonstrated, numerous studies of international crises make the case for the opposite viewpoint, that on such occasions the likelihood of innovation is reduced.[53]

In the case of Soviet China policy, the role of crisis in propelling a shift in strategy is inconclusive. The first opportunity for change (1964–69) took place during a time of crisis, but no improvement in Sino-Soviet relations resulted, and indeed the Sino-Soviet border clashes led to a hardening of Soviet positions on China. During the period right after Khrushchev's ouster and continuing through the resolution of the crisis over the border clashes in September

1969, Brezhnev's main rival for the general secretary position, Aleksei Kosygin, attempted to play a more active role in China policy in an effort to improve relations. There was little support for Kosygin's approach, however, either within the top leadership or in the *apparat*. While Chinese sources allege that he succeeded in attaining a resolution of the border clashes, which would have led to greater improvement in Sino-Soviet relations, Soviet sources deny such claims. Until a complete archival record is available, what can be concluded with certainty is that Kosygin's strategy failed, although the degree to which his colleagues in Moscow undermined it remains unclear.

While this first opportunity for change in China policy coincided with a foreign policy crisis, the second one took place in March 1982, when there were no unusual developments in Sino-Soviet relations but when Soviet-American relations had reached their nadir. At this time, Brezhnev gave a speech in Tashkent that provided momentum for the limited rapprochement with China that unfolded during Andropov's rule.

Similarly, the two major periods of improvement in relations with China— in the latter half of the 1980s and in the 1990s—took place in the absence of any crisis in relations. The third occasion for change occurred when Gorbachev became general secretary. By making key personnel changes, the new Soviet leader was able to end the inertia in China policy, resolve outstanding issues, and ultimately normalize relations during a summit meeting in Beijing in May 1989.

The last major phase in the improvement of relations between Moscow and Beijing began in 1992, as Yeltsin sought greater balance between East and West in his foreign policy.

EXPLAINING CHANGE IN MOSCOW'S CHINA POLICY

Although crises may not drive policy change, external events often play an especially important role in the reshuffling of domestic alliances at a time of leadership transition. In his study of Khrushchev's foreign policy, James Richter has shown that international pressures are more likely to influence the configuration of domestic coalitions during periods of leadership change. Richter explains that while the succession process is unfolding, interests that had been ignored or suppressed may gain a hearing and compete for political support.[54]

While a foreign policy crisis was not a necessary precondition for change in Moscow's China policy, periods of leadership change in the 1980s and 1990s provided opportunities for the expression of competing strategies in response to signals from China. When accompanied by personnel change, as in the case of the Gorbachev period, the reorganization of the ruling coalition resulted in fundamental change in China policy.[55]

In the early 1980s, several researchers called attention to a correlation between the evolution of Soviet images of China and changes in Soviet policy toward the People's Republic of China (PRC).[56] However, from the beginning, scholars who looked for different images in the writings of the Soviet foreign policy elite were clear about the limitations of this approach. Franklyn Griffiths, who pioneered the study of Soviet images, was quick to point out that these were "transactional perceptions" but argued that policy tendencies could be inferred from them.[57]

In the early 1990s, American scholars began offering another type of explanation for the evolution of Soviet China policy—they attributed change to learning by the Soviet foreign policy elite.[58] The identification of patterns of learning in Soviet society presents serious problems. Because of censorship and self-censorship by writers to avoid sanctions, it would be tenuous to argue that a reading of published speeches and articles was evidence of the beliefs of particular officials. Kremlinology has always been limited to detecting nuances which would establish the existence of different positions, not beliefs.[59] Unfortunately, even since the opening of the Central Committee archives, few documents are available that would reveal the thinking of individual Soviet leaders during the period under study.[60]

Apart from the difficulties involved in applying the learning approach to Soviet foreign policy in general,[61] it does not seem to explain Moscow's China policy very well. According to this approach, policy should have responded to Soviet setbacks in the 1970s and changes in China in the early 1980s.[62] Despite major changes in Chinese domestic policies signaling rejection of many of the Maoist policies that Soviet leaders had found objectionable, only a limited rapprochement developed in the early 1980s. Soviet policy towards China, however, resulted in the Soviet Union's international isolation by the end of the decade.

Chinese reformism, coinciding with the Soviet leadership's grave concern about the Polish crisis of 1980–81, called into question the failing policies that characterized the twilight of Brezhnevism.[63] When Chinese policies began to change beginning in the late 1970s, and Chinese leaders began to focus on domestic modernization and the pursuit of an independent foreign policy, reformist voices in the Soviet foreign policy elite saw Chinese policies as less of a challenge.[64] During this period, however, most Soviet officials continued to claim that the new leadership in Beijing continued Maoism without Mao.

The rapprochement achieved in the early 1980s was a limited one due to obstruction by conservative Soviet officials in charge of China policy. These officials had no interest in resolving the obstacles to normalization because their careers were linked to the perpetuation of the Sino-Soviet conflict. They also relied on doctrinal orthodoxy to discount the changes in China and oppose reform in the Soviet Union. For example, they interpreted the Four Modernizations program—the comprehensive reform of agriculture, industry, science and technology, and defense, which Deng Xiaoping began implementing in the late 1970s—as evidence of China's return to the capitalist path.

While conservative officials dominated China policy from the mid-1960s through the mid-1980s, even in that period there were significant differences of views on China policy among scholars and policymakers, although disagreements were a matter of nuance rather than the subject of open debate. Reformers promoted the improvement of relations with China and supported reform in the Soviet Union. This group included scholars who had an interest in separating the academic field of Chinese Studies from the ideological confrontation with China, as well as officials who believed that Soviet interests would best be furthered by détente with the United States and a more liberal approach to diversity in the communist movement.

Reformist voices painted a more complex picture of Sino-Soviet relations than the ideologically uncompromising view prevailing in the Soviet foreign policy elite. They admitted the possibility of conflict in the communist movement and tried to understand domestic sources of Chinese policies, while the conservatives focused on condemning Chinese departures from Soviet foreign and domestic policy positions.[65]

The learning explanation would link efforts to normalize relations with China in the late 1980s to a reevaluation of Soviet China policy in response to setbacks or changes in China.[66] Interviews with Soviet officials and scholars and recently published accounts reveal that in the 1970s and early 1980s, a minority already was well aware of the drawbacks of the Soviet policy of containing China, had identified changes in post-Mao China, and advocated improving relations with Beijing, but censorship and self-censorship constrained their analyses to fit within the procrustean bed of the Soviet ideological framework.[67] Moreover, some officials in charge of China policy had an interest in perpetuating the conflict with China to maintain their positions. They claimed to detect deviations from the orthodox ideological framework—for example, accusing China of returning to the capitalist path in the late 1970s—and used these "findings" to avoid changes in Soviet policy towards China as well as to oppose domestic reform in the USSR. As a consequence, reformist academics and officials who were critical of the Soviet leadership's self-defeating policy towards China and who favored reform in the Soviet Union had little policy input until the Gorbachev leadership replaced doctrinal orthodoxy with reformist concepts and promoted reformers to advisory and policy positions in the mid-1980s.

The coalition in the Brezhnev-era Politburo had developed a lasting consensus on the need for political and military containment of China and these leaders were able to harness the resources of the *apparat* in Moscow, the international communist movement, and party officials in the border regions in support of their conception of China's behavior and the required Soviet response.[68] Thus, rather than responding to changes in China, Soviet leaders required their subordinates to look for signs of continuity in Chinese behavior which would justify continuing existing Soviet policy.[69] According to Karen Brutents, a longtime Central Committee official, this behavior was pervasive in the *apparat*. He recounted a joke about a bureaucrat telling his boss: "I have an opinion, but I don't agree with it."[70]

In the early 1980s, however, Soviet leaders began playing on Sino-American differences. One could argue that this is evidence that the Soviet leadership was attempting to end the USSR's isolation by learning the rules of interaction in the Sino-Soviet-American strategic triangle.[71] This shift can also be attributed to domestic changes in the Soviet Union and China, however. The reciprocal abandonment by the Soviet Union and China of ideological polemics, beginning in 1979, as well as Suslov's death in January 1982, gave the Soviet leaders an opportunity to adjust policy, if only to a limited extent. Nonetheless, despite the new independent foreign policy espoused by the Chinese leadership, Soviet policies continued to provide China with an incentive to maintain closer ties with the Unites States than with the Soviet Union. Soviet leaders maintained previous policies towards Afghanistan and Vietnam as well as the military build-up along the Sino-Soviet border.

It was only once the Gorbachev leadership reexamined the Soviet ideological framework and made personnel changes that the majority of the new team of policymakers arrived at a new assessment of China's policies.[72] The general secretary promoted officials and sought out advisers who both favored reform at home and the normalization of relations with China. It was leadership turnover that led to change in China policy, not learning.[73]

Some recent studies of Soviet foreign policy have focused on the role of so-called policy entrepreneurs: leading scholars who were credited with playing a key role in bringing about policy change. These "entrepreneurs" supposedly took advantage of "policy windows," created during a period of foreign policy crisis, to press for the revision of policies.[74] Contrary to this assertion, however, the most significant crisis in Sino-Soviet relations, the border clashes of 1969, led to a strengthening of the coalition in the Politburo favoring containment of China and resulted in the discrediting of proponents of improving relations with China, such as Kosygin. No crisis in Sino-Soviet relations coincided with the period of limited rapprochement in the early 1980s or with normalization later on in the decade, although during this period reformist scholars and officials increasingly were able to make their voices heard.

A more interesting question is how certain scholars reached a position in which they had a voice on foreign policy matters. Rather than portraying these individuals as successful impersonal lobbyists, it would be more appropriate to view them in terms of traditional patronage networks. In Jowitt's discussion of the charismatic-traditional features of the Soviet political system, he notes that ties of reciprocity (*blat* in Soviet parlance) based on personalized relationships characterize social exchanges.[75]

Indeed, the reformist scholars who were able to whisper their views on the need for change in Soviet China policy into Andropov's ear, and later into Gorbachev's, were able to do so because of their preexisting relationships. Andropov was the first top Soviet official to depend on outside consultants when he headed the Central Committee department on ruling socialist parties in the early 1960s.[76] At that time he recruited a group of highly qualified, reform-minded individuals, including Georgii Arbatov, Aleksandr Bovin, Fedor Burlatskii, Lev Deliusin, and Georgii Shakhnazarov, whom he could count on for objective analysis of events.[77] When Andropov became general secretary, he recalled this group into government service and, as a result of their preexisting relationships, they were able to take advantage of their proximity to the seat of power to press for changes in China policy.[78]

Gorbachev, whose rise to power to a large extent was due to Andropov's support, later promoted many of his patron's former consultants. Georgii Shakhnazarov, for example, was to become a foreign policy advisor to Gorbachev and traveled with him to the Beijing summit in May 1989.

GORBACHEV AND NORMALIZATION

Despite Andropov's reliance on the advice of reformist advisers who favored improving relations with China, only a limited rapprochement was achieved during his tenure. As Burlatskii recalled, Andropov may have been a more pragmatic leader than many in his cohort, but his views were contained within certain ideological parameters. According to Burlatskii, for example, Andropov's support for Soviet intervention in Hungary in 1956, Czechoslovakia in 1968, and Afghanistan in 1979 could be explained by the Soviet leader's adherence to conceptions regarding the ideological confrontation between the Soviet Union and the United States and the need to preserve socialist gains.[79] Moreover, even by promoting a limited rapprochement with China, Andropov encountered the opposition of his colleagues in the ruling coalition, as well as in the Central Committee *apparat*.[80]

Unlike his powerful patron, Mikhail Gorbachev belonged to a new generation of Soviet leaders, who built their careers entirely during the post–World War II period. Moreover, at age 54, he was the youngest Politburo member ever to accede to the position of general secretary.[81] Gorbachev's position as a young newcomer to Kremlin politics initially worked against him.[82] While he had a staunch ally in Andropov, Gorbachev had a substantial number of opponents, too, who objected to his unusually swift promotion to the number two position once Chernenko succeeded Andropov.[83] When Gorbachev ultimately became general secretary in 1985, his political support rested largely with provincial party officials with independent power bases.[84]

Thus Gorbachev, who came to power with a longstanding determination to improve the life of Soviet citizens,[85] faced the crucial first task of assaulting entrenched interests that perpetuated counterproductive policies. Once this process was successful, Gorbachev opened a far-reaching discussion of previous policy failures, but his initial motivation was a political one.[86]

After Gorbachev became general secretary in 1985 and brought on board a new team of reformers committed to improving relations with China, the new leadership substantially modified the ideological framework of foreign policy to bring about a more benign international environment conducive to domestic reform. Changes included distinguishing between the spheres of interstate relations and the global class struggle, emphasizing cooperation among states with different social systems, and allowing for diversity in the models of socialism adopted by socialist states. Once these changes were made, the Soviet leadership no longer saw the Sino-American rapprochement as a threat to the Soviet Union's international position or interpreted Chinese policies as a challenge to Soviet leadership of the communist movement. The revision of the Soviet ideological framework paved the way for a new level of cooperation. The responsiveness of Soviet China policy to changes in Chinese behavior, then, is closely linked to changes in Soviet domestic politics.

Moreover, Soviet policymakers saw less of a challenge from China when China's role fit the revised model of socialism and began to address the problems in relations on their own terms. When Gorbachev launched *perestroika*, similar in many ways to Deng Xiaoping's Four Modernizations reform strategy, the coincidence in their approaches to reform reinforced the need for the two states to explore their common interests as well as to resolve outstanding differences. While in the 1950s commitment to the Marxist-Leninist orthodoxy shaped Sino-Soviet relations, from 1985 to 1989 a common stake in the reform of socialism became a new ideological stance binding the two states together.

Unlike the 1950s, when China was supposed to emulate "older brother," the parallels in development in the Soviet Union and China in the 1980s were arrived at independently.[87]

However, just as differences in views of socialism contributed to the undermining of the relationship in the 1960s and 1970s, so too have diverging concepts of reform—revealed in the aftermath of the Tiananmen events in June 1989 and the onset of far-reaching political reform in the Soviet Union—called into question whether a common commitment to reform is a stable basis for relations. Although dogmatic assertions about the correlation of forces and Soviet leadership of the communist movement no longer impeded the Sino-Soviet relationship, differences in reform strategies persisted and continued to influence relations between the Soviet Union and China and even between Russia and China in the first year after the USSR's collapse.

POST-SOVIET CHINA POLICY

Once the Soviet Union disintegrated, Russian proponents of the Chinese model of reform became the strongest supporters of close ties to China. Initially a position advocated by a minority in Yeltsin's government, today the stable growth of relations with China generally is perceived as one of Yeltsin's few foreign policy successes. Ever since the summer of 1992 when Yeltsin moved away from a pro-West orientation, there was considerable consensus within his government about the need to achieve greater balance in Russia's relations with East and West. Moreover, disenchantment with rapid market-oriented reforms has reinforced interest in alternatives, particularly the Chinese model.

Nonetheless, while most officials in Moscow emphasize the political, economic, and security benefits of the newly achieved strategic partnership with China, moderates emphasize its limitations and contend that greater attention to relations with the West and Japan would provide more long-term benefits. Ultra-nationalists are equally cautious about China because of their greater distrust of Chinese intentions.

THE REGIONAL FACTOR IN MOSCOW'S CHINA POLICY

The subtext of the conflict between Moscow and Beijing always has been geopolitical. Throughout history, Russia and China have been wary neighbors, sharing a lengthy but poorly marked border, and the balance of power between them has defined their relations. Beginning in the 1960s, ideological issues exacerbated feelings of vulnerability in the Russian border regions. Tensions in Sino-

Russian relations were felt most acutely in the border regions, and regional concerns in the dispute at times differed from Moscow's, even in the 1970s and 1980s. Recently released documents from the Khabarovskii Krai Party archive show that regional party leaders were often caught between two different constituencies with divergent interests in relations with China. On the one hand, regional leaders had to address the concerns of Khabarovskii Krai residents about the security of the border and the impact of tensions with China on the economy of the region. Central party authorities, however, expected regional party officials to legitimate their policies, and, consequently, the regional leaders had to be cautious in airing their differences with Moscow.

After the collapse of the USSR, however, regional leaders in the newly decentralized Russia began to criticize Moscow's China policy quite vocally when regional concerns were affected. Officials in the border regions called attention to new problems such as illegal immigration from China and uncontrolled border trade and urged the central authorities to address these issues in bilateral discussions with Beijing.

Increasingly, developments in the Russian border regions are making their mark on Sino-Russian economic and political relations. The challenge for Moscow today is not so much to maintain the strategic partnership with Beijing—the top leaders of both countries agree about this—but in finding common cause with regional leaders in the Russian Far East regarding China's place in Russia's overall strategy in Asia.

NEW SOURCES ABOUT MOSCOW'S CHINA POLICY

Now that new sources of information about relations between Moscow and Beijing are available and the relationship has gone full circle to a sometimes uneasy coexistence of neighboring powers, it is a particularly propitious moment to reexamine the causes of conflict and cooperation. This study relies on some newly available sources,[88] including some fifty recently declassified documents from the Tsentr Khraneniia Sovremennykh Dokumentov (TsKhSD, the archive of the Central Committee of the Communist Party of the Soviet Union) and the Khabarovsk Regional Communist Party Archive (within the Gosudarstvennyi Arkhiv Khabarovskogo Kraia), as well as individual documents from the Soviet Foreign Ministry and KGB archives, made available by the National Security Archive in Washington, D.C. Material from several sets of interviews with scholars and officials (Moscow, 1991, 1993, 1999; Vladivostok, 1994, 1995, 1998, 1999; Khabarovsk, 1995, 1998, 1999; Blagoveshchensk, 1999; Beijing, 1996, 1999; and Harbin, 1996, 1999) and recently published memoirs of key officials are also included. While Chinese documents for the period under study were not available, published accounts by Chinese scholars with access to such documents were used and some scholars with access to the documents were interviewed. Finally, American documents from the Nixon archive and the State Department Central Files regarding the 1969 Sino-Soviet border clashes were consulted.

All Chinese sources are transliterated according to the Pinyin system. Russian sources are transliterated according to the Library of Congress system, with a few exceptions. More commonly used Western spellings are used for well-known figures, such as Yuri Andropov, Georgi Arbatov, and others.

PART I
BREZHNEV'S CONTAINMENT POLICY

2 / The Soviet Union's China Strategy, 1969–79

At their summit meeting in May 1989, Deng Xiaoping and Mikhail Gorbachev agreed to "close the past and open the future," yet the history of Sino-Soviet relations—especially of their common border—remains a contested one. Even today, as leaders in Beijing and Moscow hail the achievement of a Sino-Russian strategic partnership, Chinese officials remain acutely sensitive to the history of what they view as Russian and Soviet imperialism in relations with China. As recently as the summer of 1998, for example, officials in Beijing refused to allow a conference on the 100th anniversary of the founding of Harbin—a date connecting the birth of the city to the building of the Chinese Eastern Railway and consequently to Russian imperialism in China—to take place in Harbin. Even once the meeting was relocated to Khabarovsk, the Chinese authorities prevented Chinese participants from attending.[1] Meanwhile at the conference, their Russian counterparts used the occasion to deny vigorously that the nineteenth-century treaties that are the basis for the current border demarcation were ever forced upon China and to promote a revisionist vision of a friendly relationship historically grounded in principles of equality.[2]

The decision by Soviet and Chinese leaders in 1989 to put aside any differences emerging from their divergent understanding of the history of their relations in hope of achieving a firmer basis for normalization has produced exactly the opposite effect and has left an undercurrent of mutual suspicion. Indeed, contemporary Russian critics of Moscow's China policy, both at the center and in the border regions, still raise many of the unresolved questions that have plagued relations between China and Russia for decades. For this reason, the history of relations between the two great neighbors is just as important for understanding their contemporary relations as for comprehending the evolution of their relationship from the border clashes in 1969 to normalization and then to partnership.

The Sino-Soviet border clashes represented the clearest expression of China's challenge to the USSR. As the ideological conflict between the Soviet Union and China began to take a dangerous new turn, a new coalition of Soviet leaders

fashioned a two-pronged strategy: (1) negotiations to achieve Chinese acqui-
escence to Soviet positions on the border conflict and (2) military containment.

Sino-Soviet border talks spanned a decade, but very little progress was made
because of the incompatible objectives of the two sides. China was prepared to
accept the status quo as a starting point for discussion of border problems, but
insisted that the Soviet Union recognize that the border demarcation resulted
from "unequal treaties" which Russian tsars imposed on China in the nineteenth
century. The USSR, on the other hand, preferred to deal with the border issue
in the context of broader discussions on the overall Sino-Soviet relationship.
Despite these differences, the border talks served as an important channel of
communication between the Soviet Union and China throughout the 1970s.[3]

The military aspect of Soviet strategy worked at cross-purposes with these
negotiation efforts. The Soviet Union's efforts to contain China militarily
spurred the Chinese leadership to seek a rapprochement with the United States.
Although Soviet-American détente kept the threat of Sino-American collusion
at bay in the early 1970s, U.S.-China relations would become a matter of great
concern to Soviet policymakers later on in the decade when détente with the
United States began to derail.

HISTORICAL BACKGROUND

China and the former Soviet Union shared one of the world's longest borders—
stretching some 4,150 miles, separating Central Asia from Xinjiang, and ultimately following the Amur and Ussuri Rivers all the way to the shores of the
Sea of Japan. This border has been a source of friction between Russia and China
for centuries, and when the Sino-Soviet conflict developed in the early 1960s,
tensions were reflected in a pattern of border incidents, culminating in military clashes in the spring and summer of 1969.

In the nineteenth century, Russia took advantage of a weakened Manchu
empire to extend the Russian imperial reach to areas of Central Asia, Siberia
and the Far East occupied by the Chinese.[4] The Russians then forced the
Manchus to sign the treaties of Aigun (1858) and Peking (1860) legitimating
this fait accompli and ceding a vast territory north of the Amur and east of the
Ussuri Rivers.[5] The Chinese have since referred to these treaties as unequal.

Following the Russian Revolution, the Bolshevik regime made an effort in
some instances to adhere to revolutionary principles in foreign policy.
Renouncing agreements which codified Russian imperialist privileges was one
way to distinguish the Bolshevik approach to foreign affairs from that of Tsarist
Russia. On July 25, 1919, Deputy People's Commissar for Foreign Affairs Lev

Karakhan informed Beijing that the Bolshevik government "declared null and void all treaties which were to enable the Russian government of the Tsar and his Allies to enslave the peoples of the East, and principally China. . . ."[6] The 1919 declaration also included a pledge to return the Chinese Eastern Railway and other concessions to China, but in a second version, issued more than a year later on September 27, 1920, Karakhan omitted this promise.[7] Thus the Bolshevik government, which came to power pledging to abolish foreign relations altogether now proved adept in realpolitik.[8]

The Bolsheviks turned out to be equally reluctant to depart from the Tsarist position on navigation in the border rivers, treating the Chinese shore as the boundary and claiming possession of the entire Amur River.[9] The border treaties of 1858 and 1860 left sovereignty over the border rivers unclear, and this issue had been a constant source of friction in the nineteenth century. During the Revolution and Civil War, Chinese merchant ships took advantage of the weakening of Russian control over navigation and began sailing on the lower Amur. In 1923, once the Bolsheviks had solidified their control over Russia's eastern regions, they began to enforce Russia's claim to the lower Amur and used gunboats to prevent Chinese ships on the Sungari River from entering the lower Amur.[10]

Meanwhile, Karakhan was made ambassador plenipotentiary to China, and in early 1924 opened negotiations with the Beijing government on several outstanding issues in Sino-Soviet relations in anticipation of a conference where a Sino-Soviet treaty would be signed. On March 14, 1924, however, Karakhan negotiated a secret protocol with his counterpart in Beijing, Wang Zhengting, which would sow confusion in Sino-Soviet border negotiations for years to come. According to this protocol, all former treaties, conventions, contracts, and protocols would continue to be enforced only until they would be annulled at the upcoming Sino-Soviet conference, where new agreements would be negotiated.[11] These terms proved to be quite disadvantageous for China, for the Soviet Union subsequently refused to renegotiate the border treaties and had a basis to claim that previous border treaties remained valid.[12] China, on the other hand, was loathe to admit that it had accepted the continued validity of treaties it considered unequal.

Two months later, on May 31, 1924, the Chinese government in Beijing and the Soviet Union signed a treaty governing their relations. The Soviet government restated the language of the second Karakhan declaration and the two sides agreed to hold a conference within a month and renegotiate the border treaties then.[13] This conference was delayed for more than a year, during which time the USSR regained full control over the Chinese Eastern Railway by signing a secret agreement with the Manchurian warlord, Zhang Zuolin.[14] When the conference finally took place, the Soviet Union refused to renegotiate the border treaties.

China's political fragmentation in the 1920s left it wide open to territorial encroachment by neighboring countries, such as Japan and the Soviet Union.[15] And the Soviet Union under Joseph Stalin proved willing to defend its interests in Manchuria, even by force. For example, when Manchurian warlord Zhang Zuolin seized control of the Chinese Eastern Railway (CER) in 1929, Soviet forces briefly invaded Manchuria. The Soviet position in the CER was restored by the December 1929 Treaty of Khabarovsk.[16]

In 1933, the Politburo affirmed that it was the Soviet Union's position that control over the border islands would be based on the Treaties of Aigun and Peking,[17] and that the boundary was the Chinese bank of the Amur River. In May 1995 testimony to the Duma, Genrykh Kireev, the head of the Russian delegation to the current Sino-Russian border demarcation commission, confirmed that in the 1930s the Soviet Union unilaterally occupied many of the border islands belonging to China, including Damanskii/Zhen Bao Island, which was to become the locus for the 1969 border clashes.[18]

Civil war in China and then World War II put the border issue on hold, and Stalin had no intention of reopening it. The Soviet Union emerged from World War II with a stronger foothold in north China, however. As a precondition for the Soviet Union's participation in the war against Japan, Stalin requested the restoration of territories lost to Japan in 1904, including southern Sakhalin, all the Kurile Islands, the Chinese ports of Dairen (Dalian) and Port Arthur (Lüshun), and control over the Chinese Eastern Railway. The Soviet leader also demanded the recognition of the People's Republic of Mongolia (Outer Mongolia) as an independent state. U.S. President Franklin Roosevelt acceded to Stalin's demands for control over southern Sakhalin and the Kurile Islands, but urged the Soviet leader to negotiate separately with the Chinese nationalists about the other issues.[19]

On June 30, 1945, the Soviet Union began talks with the nationalists. Stalin explained to the nationalist Foreign Minister T. V. Soong that Soviet rights in Dairen and Port Arthur, as well as an independent People's Republic of Mongolia in the Soviet security sphere, were essential for Soviet defenses against Japan.[20] By August, Soviet forces were fighting the Japanese in Manchuria. Fearing that if they balked at Stalin's demands the Soviet leader would increase cooperation with the Chinese communists, the nationalists ultimately accepted them. According to the Sino-Soviet Treaty of Friendship and Alliance, signed on August 14, 1945, the Soviet Union received a 30-year lease on Dairen and Port Arthur, as well as joint ownership of the Chinese

Eastern Railway. The nationalists also acquiesced to a "plebiscite" on Mongolian independence.[21]

Meanwhile Mao Zedong had long cherished hopes that the communist victory in the Chinese Revolution would lead to a return of Outer Mongolia to Chinese control.[22] When Politburo member Anastas Mikoyan traveled to China in January 1949, for example, Mao proposed the reunification of Inner and Outer Mongolia within the PRC. Mikoyan opposed the idea, claiming that the independence of Outer Mongolia had already been decided long ago.[23]

The signing of the Sino-Soviet Friendship Treaty of 1950 modified the 1945 treaty only slightly, as Stalin reportedly refused Mao's request to repeal it altogether.[24] After protracted negotiations, Stalin agreed to return Port Arthur and the Chinese Eastern Railway to the PRC by 1952, but stated that Dairen would only be returned after the conclusion of a peace treaty with Japan.[25] Moreover, an additional protocol committed China to forbid citizens of third countries to reside in or carry out any economic activities in Manchuria, thereby ensuring that Manchuria (as well as Xinjiang) would remain the buffer zone Stalin deemed necessary for Soviet defense. Due to the political sensitivity of the protocol for his regime, Mao decided to keep it secret and won Stalin's agreement not to divulge its contents.[26]

The Sino-Soviet Border Dispute

Recently released documents portray Sino-Soviet relations in the 1950s as beset with many difficulties from the very beginning, despite concerted efforts by each country to emphasize their enduring friendship.[27] In their attempt to underscore the positive, many contentious issues (including border questions) were swept aside.[28]

Differences soon emerged regarding sovereignty over the riverine islands. The 1951 Sino-Soviet treaty on border river navigation added to the existing confusion by stating that ships of either country should follow the main river channel, regardless of where the boundary lay. The Soviets chose to interpret this as confirming their view that the boundary was not the main river channel, while the Chinese stated that this treaty in no way defined the location of the boundary.[29] In 1960, however, a new Soviet law on the protection of state borders declared that the Talweg, or main river channel, constituted the border on navigable rivers.[30]

When Sino-Soviet relations deteriorated in the late 1960s, the border demarcation issue resurfaced. Chinese Prime Minister Zhou Enlai first raised the territorial question in a 1957 visit to Moscow, but Soviet Communist Party first secretary Nikita Khrushchev refused to discuss it.[31] As the two countries became embroiled in ideological disputes, they began to refer to the disorderly border crossings that had been going on for years as border violations and each side kept a running tally.[32]

Ultimately it was Khrushchev who opened Pandora's box in a December 1962 speech. Bridling at Chinese criticism that the Soviet Union had caved in to U.S. pressure during the Cuban Missile Crisis, Khrushchev noted that the Chinese seemed to be in no hurry to evict the imperialists from Macao and Hong Kong. The Chinese riposte came in a March 1963 article in *Renmin Ribao*, which listed the border treaties negotiated with Russia in the nineteenth century among the "unequal" treaties imposed by the imperialist powers on a weak China through intimidation.[33]

As the two countries traded allegations of increasing numbers of border violations, in August 1963 the Chinese government proposed that frontier patrols belonging to each side refrain from crossing the Talweg, prompting the Soviet side to object to an implied retreat.[34] Tensions continued, leading Khrushchev to propose bilateral talks. The talks began in February 1964 but ended inconclusively in August, and their content remains disputed.

In a recently published history, Vladimir Miasnikov, a prominent scholar at Moscow's Institute of the Far East, claims that the Soviet Union wanted to clarify the boundary, while the Chinese side pursued a dual strategy. The Chinese delegation contributed practical proposals for border demarcation, but at the same time engaged in ideological polemics and raised the issue of very substantial "disputed areas."[35] Despite the contentious tone of the negotiations, the two sides were able to agree on most of the eastern boundary, with the exception of disputed islands across from Khabarovsk and two other places.[36] In fact, the 1991 border demarcation agreement is based largely on the points agreed to in 1964.[37]

What impeded the signing of an agreement on the eastern boundary in 1964? According to Kireev, the Soviet Union refused to initial the treaty in the absence of agreement about the islands near Khabarovsk, but in Miasnikov's view, Mao's interview with Japanese socialists on July 10 torpedoed the negotiations.[38]

Mao complained to the Japanese that "there are too many places occupied by the Soviet Union. . . . Some people have said that Xinjiang province and the territory north of the Amur River must be included in the Soviet Union. . . . China has not yet asked the Soviet Union for an account about Vladivostok, Khabarovsk, Kamchatka, and other towns and regions east of Lake Baikal, which became Russian territory about 100 years ago." The Soviet Union replied to these allegations in a *Pravda* editorial on September 2, 1964, which warned that any attempt to enforce such territorial claims would have "the most dangerous consequences."[39]

The Chinese contend, however, that at the 1964 talks they specifically stated they were not asking for the return of the territories acquired by Russia as a result of the "unequal treaties."[40] According to the Chinese account of the 1964 talks, the Soviets recognized the validity of the main river channel as the river boundary, a position the Soviet Union subsequently denied, and indeed rejected publicly until 1986.[41]

The 1964 talks did little to dispel the fundamental disagreements between the two countries, and soon the border dispute began to take an ominous turn. One month before his ouster, Khrushchev issued a veiled nuclear threat in response to Chinese claims about the illegitimacy of the Sino-Soviet border. The Chinese upped the ante when they exploded their first nuclear bomb in October 1964.[42]

A Leadership Coalition in Flux, 1964-69

After Khrushchev was removed from office in October 1964, Communist Party First Secretary Leonid Brezhnev, Prime Minister Aleksei Kosygin, Yuri Andropov (then a Central Committee secretary), and Konstantin Rusakov (the head of the Central Committee department for ruling socialist parties) reportedly discussed options for the Soviet Union's China policy.[43] Kosygin, who at the time was positioning himself as a reformist alternative in the post-Khrushchev succession struggle, pressed for a new conciliatory approach to negotiations.[44]

In November 1964, Kosygin met with Zhou Enlai, who presented impossible preconditions for any improvement in relations, including a Soviet disavowal of the decisions of the Twenty-second Congress of the Communist Party of the Soviet Union and the CPSU Party program. The Soviet side did its share to inflame relations, too, when a drunk Defense Minister Rodion Malinovskii reportedly came up to Zhou at a reception and told him: "So, we did our job and threw out our old shoe—Khrushchev. Now you get rid of your old shoe—Mao—and then things will work out for us." After that remark, an infuriated Zhou left the banquet and returned to Beijing.[45]

Brezhnev, perhaps sensing an opportunity to maneuver his principal political rival into staging his own downfall, soon encouraged Kosygin to travel to Beijing to resume the dialogue with China. February 1965 meetings with Zhou and then with Mao failed to repair relations, as the Chinese side continued their attacks on Khrushchev's revisionism and insisted that they would never be the Soviet Union's "younger brother" again.[46]

Kosygin's approach to China was further discredited as both sides hardened their positions. In early 1966, Brezhnev traveled to Mongolia to sign an agreement on military cooperation, which allowed for a Soviet military presence some 500 kilometers from Beijing. Meanwhile as the Cultural Revolution unfolded in China, Chinese ideological attacks on the Soviet Union became more frequent. The Chinese leadership refused to attend the Twenty-third Party Congress in 1966, further confirming for Soviet opponents of Sino-Soviet normalization the view of continued Chinese intransigence.[47]

The Soviet Military Buildup in the Far East

In 1965, when border issues became a flashpoint in a rapidly deteriorating relationship, the Soviets began a military buildup in the border region.[48] As a result of the force increase ordered in 1965, the USSR from 1969 to 1973 tripled its manpower on the Sino-Soviet border from 1965 levels and deployed 37 to 42 divisions (approximately 370,000 men), 11 of which were at or near combat strength.[49] The construction of barracks, accommodations for families, rail spurs, roads, and training grounds suggests that these Soviet forces were there to stay, a "garrison force."[50] Almost all of the Soviet divisions were equipped with nuclear-capable tactical rockets, and four brigades had 160-mile-range tactical ballistic missiles. Soviet forces also deployed 500-mile-range Scaleboard and 300-mile-range Shaddock mobile missiles with their ground forces.[51]

The Soviets had the advantage in technology, mobility, and training, factors for which the Chinese numerical superiority could not compensate.[52] Some of the technology the Chinese moved into the border regions in the late 1960s, for example, dated back to the war against Japan.[53] Moreover, Chinese nuclear capabilities were minimal at the time.[54] While research and development on an intermediate-range ballistic missile (IRBM) capable of hitting Moscow (DF-4) and an intercontinental ballistic missile (ICBM) (DF-5) began in 1965, these missiles were not deployed until 1980.[55]

In a 1989 interview, Lev Deliusin, a distinguished Sinologist, recalled that at the time he had argued against the military buildup, which he viewed as "an instance of unparalleled squandering" that was justified by Soviet officials who inflated China's "enemy image."[56] Despite the gap between Soviet and Chinese military capabilities, in the late 1960s the image of the Chinese multitudes sweeping across the vulnerable Siberian steppes was fairly widespread, even among reform-minded scholars and officials in Moscow as well as in the border regions.[57] This view was linked to the Soviet perception of Chinese irrationality, derived from Mao's statements in the late 1950s on the utility of nuclear weapons in advancing the socialist cause, China's willingness to provoke border incidents with a superior opponent, and Chinese actions during the Cultural Revolution—especially the demonstrations by the Red Guards near the border and the harassment of Soviet diplomats in Beijing.[58]

While some Soviet officials noted that the Soviet Union could take advantage of instability in China,[59] for example if a pro-Soviet faction within the PRC requested Soviet support, for the most part they followed domestic developments in China with increasing concern. In conversations with their American counterparts, Soviet diplomats expressed their bewilderment at Beijing's "illogical" policies, which they feared could lead to dangerous and provocative actions.[60] Soviet first deputy foreign minister Vasilii Kuznetsov, for instance, told an American official that the Soviet Union viewed Sino-Soviet tensions seriously because of China's large population and "adventuristic" leadership.[61]

The length of the border, the difficulty in maintaining lines of communication with the area in case of hostilities, and the much larger population on the Chinese side of the border all contributed to a sense in political and military circles that the Soviet Union was vulnerable to a possible Chinese attack.[62] According to an officer in the Far Eastern Military district, although Soviet forces were technologically superior to the Chinese forces, the Chinese people were viewed as being better prepared for war and more willing to fight. They were also seen as actively preparing for war in light of Mao's campaigns to build tunnels in case of a Soviet attack.[63]

Beginning in the mid-1960s, the militarization and mobilization accompanying the Chinese government's Third Front policy—a massive investment program to create an industrial reserve in China's interior to guard against a possible U.S. attack—was expanded to prepare for possible Soviet aggression.[64] Anticipating a long-term confrontation with the Soviet Union, the Chinese launched a sustained propaganda campaign and built air-raid shelters (although no drills were observed).[65] Minority peoples were displaced from the Sino-Soviet border region in Xinjiang, which then was colonized with Han youth.[66]

Czechoslovakia: Prelude to Clashes

The Soviet Union's military intervention in Czechoslovakia in August 1968 to forestall Aleksander Dubček's attempt to depart from the Soviet model and institute a new type of "socialism with a human face" served as a clear warning to the Chinese leadership that ideological confrontation with the Communist Party of the Soviet Union (CPSU) could lead to military conflict.[67] After the Soviet invasion, the factional struggle within the Chinese Communist Party (CCP) over the nature of the main threat to China intensified. The position of the radicals, championed by Defense Minister Lin Biao, who saw a "dual adversary" threat from both the Soviet Union and the United States, began to lose ground to the moderates, led by Zhou Enlai, who viewed the United States as the lesser challenger to Chinese interests. While the radicals urged a continuation of China's strategy of self-reliance, the moderates attempted to take advantage of Soviet-American contention by improving relations with

Washington, and then to use the new relationship with Washington to deter potential Soviet military action against China.[68]

The Brezhnev leadership justified the invasion of Czechoslovakia as necessary to defend socialism there, a rationale that observers in the West dubbed the "Brezhnev Doctrine." As Brezhnev explained: ". . .when the internal and external forces hostile to socialism seek to reverse the development of any socialist country toward the restoration of the capitalist order, when a threat to the cause of socialism emerges in that country, a threat to the security of the socialist community as a whole emerges, this is no longer a problem of the people of that country but also a common problem, a concern for all socialist states."[69]

China reacted to the Soviet invasion with alarm for several reasons. First, there was reason to believe that the Brezhnev Doctrine could apply to China as well as to Eastern Europe.[70] Second, China perceived a certain symmetry in the Soviet Union's invasion of Czechoslovakia and the U.S. intervention in the Vietnam War. In the Chinese view, the two superpowers were trying, at all costs, to preserve the bipolar structure of the international system, an effort that was detrimental to Chinese security and interests in Asia.[71] Finally, the Chinese feared that the Soviets would next threaten Romania and Albania—the two states in Eastern Europe that maintained good relations with China.[72]

China immediately reacted to the Soviet invasion of Czechoslovakia by calling the Soviets "social-imperialists," a new term for socialists who pursued imperialist policies.[73] Zhou Enlai denounced Soviet "fascist aggression" in a September 1968 speech in Hanoi, a message that was also directed at those who harbored illusions about Soviet motivations (i.e., the Vietnamese).[74] Renouncing the Soviet concept of the socialist community, China announced its support for Romania and Albania in the event of a Soviet threat.[75] In late 1968, Zhou Enlai also expressed China's interest in renewing ambassadorial talks with the United States and a meeting was set for February 1969 in Warsaw.[76] Despite these moves towards rapprochement with the United States, the Chinese abruptly canceled the February 1969 meeting and the shift in Chinese policy toward the United States did not occur for another year.[77]

THE ERUPTION OF BORDER CLASHES

While the Chinese leaders debated the merits of improving relations with the United States, military skirmishes on the Sino-Soviet border in March and August 1969 brought the two countries to the brink of war.[78] Soviet and Chinese border patrols had harassed each other increasingly throughout the 1960s, but on March 2, 1969, tensions escalated to the shooting level, precipitated by a Chinese ambush.[79]

The predominant view in Soviet analyses of the clashes has been that they were planned deliberately by the Chinese government and could not be attributed to local error on either the Chinese or Soviet sides.[80] While some scholars in the West and in China have argued that the chaotic conditions prevailing in the border regions during the Cultural Revolution culminated in China's initiating the exchange of fire on Damanskii/Zhen Bao Island in March 1969, new evidence from an authoritative Chinese source provides a different picture. According to a book on the history of the People's Liberation Army (PLA), published in Beijing in 1989 by the CCP Party School Press, Heilongjiang Province's excessive zeal in carrying out Mao's instructions to combat revisionism at home and abroad brought about the Sino-Soviet border clashes in the spring of 1969.[81]

Ever since the Sino-Soviet split in the early 1960s, the Chinese Communist Party had referred to Soviet leaders as "modern revisionists." With the onset of the Cultural Revolution in 1966, Chinese leaders went beyond ideological polemics and began to take a series of concrete steps to counter Soviet revisionism, including demonstrations in front of the Soviet embassy in Beijing.[82]

The means to combat revisionism proposed by Heilongjiang Province in 1969—initiating a "defense" of Damanskii/Zhen Bao Island—resulted in an escalation of violence in the border clashes and exacerbated the Soviet security threat to China. One of the enduring mysteries of the Sino-Soviet conflict has been why China initiated the border clashes with the USSR on Damanskii/Zhen Bao Island and risked igniting a war with a much stronger opponent. Was it a calculated Chinese effort to show resolve after the Soviet invasion of Czechoslovakia?[83] Was it an instance of the Cultural Revolution spiraling out of control and allowing an unsanctioned military engagement?

According to the PLA study, on January 25, 1969, the Heilongjiang Province military district proposed a plan for the "defense" of Damanskii/Zhen Bao Island in response to years of Soviet harassment of Chinese border personnel. The authors cite 4,189 border incidents between October 1964 and March 1969 and 18 intrusions on the island from October 1967 to January 1969, resulting in the deaths of 5 Chinese guards, and the wounding of 122 Chinese and 10 Soviet border personnel.[84]

Although Heilongjiang initiated the plan that led to the March 2 border clashes, on February 19 it was approved by the Chinese General Staff and the Foreign Ministry, as well as by Zhou Enlai personally. The General Staff subsequently provided guidance about the rules of engagement.[85] The authors suggest that top officials supported this plan despite its inherent risks because at the time of the Cultural Revolution the Chinese people could not tolerate revisionism internally or externally.[86]

During the Cultural Revolution, Heilongjiang was a hotbed of revolutionary activity. Massive strikes took place in Harbin, paralyzing transportation. Red Guards from Harbin participated in revolts in other cities. During the late 1960s, Heilongjiang was considered to be a model for other provinces, being the first province in China to form a revolutionary committee based on the tripartite rule of the revolutionary rebels, the PLA, and party cadres.[87] In this context, it is not surprising that the province also would try to play a leading role in using military means to counter what was then perceived as the Soviet ideological threat on its border.

Still, the March 2 clashes created a real risk of escalation. According to the rules of engagement outlined by the General Staff, Heilongjiang forces were supposed to strictly observe "tit for tat," but this assumed that the Soviet forces would not respond by using excessive force. The clashes continued sporadically in the eastern and western border regions throughout the spring and summer of 1969 with more prepared and better-equipped Soviet forces.

The border incidents also raised Sino-Soviet recriminations to a fever pitch. After the March 2 border clashes, the Chinese government organized 250 million people in four days of anti-Soviet demonstrations all over China,[88] an enormous level of mobilization which only served to confirm Soviet fears of Chinese irrationality. The Soviets organized similar demonstrations in Moscow, Vladivostok, and Khabarovsk, albeit on a much smaller scale.[89]

In a March 12 statement, the Chinese government justified its aggressive patrolling on Damanskii/Zhen Bao Island by claiming that the island was on Chinese territory.[90] Two weeks after a second border incident, when a more extensive Soviet force inflicted heavy casualties on the Chinese, the Soviet government issued a statement proposing the resumption of border talks, suspended in 1964.[91] China failed to respond but agreed to reopen border river navigation talks in June.[92] On June 12, after another border incident, the Soviet government reiterated its call for border talks.[93] Nevertheless, border incidents continued throughout the summer and no plans were made to resume talks on the border issue, although the two sides managed to sign a protocol on river navigation on August 8.

DID THE SOVIET UNION PLAN
AN ATTACK AGAINST CHINA?

During the tense summer of 1969, Moscow authorized dependents of personnel stationed at the Soviet embassy in Beijing to evacuate.[94] Although the evacuation never took place, the suggestion reportedly unnerved the Chinese.[95] According to a CIA analysis of Soviet border deployments, there were clear signs that the Soviet Union was "preparing for the possibility of tactical nuclear warfare against China due to the presence of nuclear-capable tactical rockets in almost every division."[96] While American observers remained concerned about the possibility of a wider Soviet assault against China in the spring and summer of 1969, they saw no signs of massive redeployment of Soviet forces from other theaters that would have been an indication of the USSR's immediate mobilization against the Chinese threat.[97]

The Soviet air force, much of which was capable of delivering both conventional and nuclear weapons, was put on alert nationwide.[98] In June 1969, Soviet bomber units were redeployed from Eastern Europe to the Far East, where they participated in an exercise designed to practice hitting targets in northwest China (where Chinese nuclear facilities are located). According to Allen Whiting, a former State Department official, the Soviet Union may have been bluffing to intimidate the Chinese leadership into making territorial concessions, but the army's military exercise demonstrated that the Soviet Union had the capability to hit Chinese targets.[99]

American diplomats and their allies carefully monitored the Sino-Soviet border clashes for signs of escalation. They were concerned by indications that Soviet officials were sounding out possible international reactions to a preemptive attack on Chinese nuclear facilities.[100] One such report even reached President Richard Nixon's desk.[101]

Not long after this, in a meeting with National Security Advisor Henry Kissinger, Whiting argued that the real threat was not a Soviet nuclear attack against China, but a conventional air strike against Chinese nuclear facilities. Whiting urged Kissinger to signal to the Chinese that the United States would not condone such an attack, an effort which might have been rewarded with Chinese concessions on issues of importance to the United States, especially Taiwan.[102] Such signals were sent in late August to early September, a step which Kissinger later termed "revolutionary," given the legacy of Sino-American hostility.[103]

Meanwhile, Soviet diplomatic probing in the summer of 1969 was reinforced by a pattern of menacing official statements and newspaper articles. After a clash on July 8 on an island in the Amur River, the Soviet Foreign Ministry issued a note threatening to take unspecified additional measures in response to continuing Chinese provocations, a statement which the U.S. State Department took as an indication of possible plans for further military action.[104] One month later, on August 13, after a clash along the border between Xinjiang and Kazakhstan involving several hundred Soviet and Chinese troops, an editorial in *Pravda* warned that any attempt to violate Soviet frontiers would be rebuffed.

In a veiled nuclear threat, the editorial stated: "If a war were to break out under present conditions, with the armaments, lethal weapons and modern means of delivery that now exist, no continent would be unaffected."[105] In case Chinese officials had any doubts about Soviet capabilities, two prominent Soviet generals took advantage of the anniversary of the end of World War II in Asia to write an article in which they reflected on the crushing blow delivered by Soviet forces against the Japanese in Manchuria. Any attempts to encroach on Soviet territory in the Far East would be "doomed to scandalous failure," they asserted.[106]

Chinese fears of all-out war intensified in the summer of 1969. As Mao's doctor, Li Zhisui, recalled, "In August 1969, the remaining [Beijing] city residents were mobilized to 'dig tunnels deep' in preparation for aerial, possibly nuclear attack. In Beijing, the underground tunnels, crisscrossing the length and breadth of the city, were to serve as air-raid shelters in which the entire population could live for weeks."[107]

THE KOSYGIN-ZHOU MEETING

Fearing a Soviet attack, the Chinese leadership finally acquiesced to the USSR's request for a high-level meeting.[108] On September 11, 1969, Zhou Enlai received Kosygin at the Beijing airport on his way home from Ho Chi Minh's funeral.[109] Although a transcript of this important meeting is not yet available, existing reports reveal that Kosygin and Zhou each came away with a different interpretation of the oral agreement they reached on that occasion.

Zhou proposed that the two sides maintain the status quo on the border, withdraw their forces from the disputed areas, avoid confrontation there in the future, and begin consultations between border authorities regarding the dispute.[110] According to authoritative Chinese accounts, Kosygin agreed to Zhou's proposals.[111] However, a Soviet Central Committee report to the East German Communist Party described these four points in different terms. There was no mention of a border dispute or of a withdrawal of forces from disputed areas. Instead, Zhou and Kosygin were portrayed as agreeing to the "observance of the existing border, the inadmissibility of armed confrontations, the withdrawal of troops of both sides from direct contact in controversial sectors . . . " and the referral of decisions about economic activity of citizens of both countries in controversial sectors to representatives of the border authorities.[112] Although Zhou and Kosygin may have agreed to four points, they turned out to have divergent interpretations of their content—especially the meaning of the status quo on the border and the creation of a demilitarized zone.[113] Zhou repeatedly urged that the two sides recognize the fact that the present border demarcation represented the outcome of unequal terms forced on China by Tsarist Russia.[114] In Kosygin's view, rehashing the history of the Tsarist demarcation would only lead to "chaos." The Soviet Prime Minister suggested several times that demarcation details and use of border resources be resolved in expert-level negotiations.[115]

According to Aleksei Elizavetin, a counselor at the Soviet embassy in Beijing, Zhou called attention to the increasing Soviet forces in the border region and noted that there had been rumors of a preventive Soviet attack against Chinese nuclear installations.[116] Zhou explained that China had acquired nuclear weapons only to prevent the superpowers from having a monopoly over them.[117] Kosygin replied that the Soviet Union was not preparing for war, but emphasized that tensions persisted in Soviet-Chinese relations.[118]

Did Kosygin agree to any type of withdrawal of forces? In another account of the talks by Mikhail Kapitsa, a Foreign Ministry official who accompanied Kosygin, Zhou restated his view that military forces should be removed from all disputed territories.[119] Kapitsa remembers Kosygin's reply as somewhat equivocal, while in Elizavetin's recollection Kosygin flatly refused to entertain the idea of a mutual withdrawal of forces from the border region.[120] He reportedly stated: "As far as a withdrawal of forces is concerned, the Soviet side cannot accept that, since we have people in the border regions and we cannot leave them defenseless."[121] Instead he suggested that forces be withdrawn from the islands where fighting had occurred and that all measures be taken so that "there would be no further military confrontation on the border."[122]

According to Kapitsa's version, Kosygin agreed to forbid Soviet aircraft from flying over the border to the Chinese side. Kapitsa recalls that, at the conclusion of the meeting, Kosgyin made other proposals for improving relations, including a resumption of exchanges of ambassadors and contacts between Soviet and Chinese planning authorities. While Zhou agreed to take up the former, he rejected the latter as untimely.[123] In Kapitsa's recollection, the meeting that diffused the border clashes ended in a festive dinner, complete with Peking duck and *maotai,* hosted by Zhou.[124]

A Chinese scholar with access to the Chinese Foreign Ministry archives recounted that after the meeting the two leaders exchanged letters regarding their understanding of the oral agreement reached on September 11. In his letter, Kosygin reportedly failed to include two of the four points which the Chinese side claimed had already been agreed to in Beijing: the Soviet leader did not recognize the existence of disputed areas on the Sino-Soviet border and did not agree to withdraw Soviet forces.[125] Zhou later told the Chinese delegation to the October 1969 border talks that the Soviet letter of reply did not mention "the mutual understandings that had been reached."[126] Many Chinese scholars have since claimed that by the time the Soviet delegation arrived in Beijing for a new round of border talks in October 1969, the Soviet side had retreated from the agreement reached between Zhou and Kosygin.[127]

Indeed, Kapitsa recalled that Zhou had proposed an exchange of notes through diplomatic channels one week after the meeting to confirm their "agreement."[128] It is not surprising that China and Russia thus far have been unable to reconcile their accounts of events at the September 11, 1969, meeting, since even Kosygin and his assistant, Kapitsa, apparently came up with different versions of the meeting on their flight home from Beijing as they collaborated on a summary for the Politburo. In his memoir, Kapitsa implied that he was more suspicious than Kosygin of Zhou's intentions in calling for a withdrawal of forces from disputed areas. Kapitsa saw this demand as a trap and argued that the Chinese side would have interpreted Soviet agreement as recognition of the validity of China's territorial claims prior to any negotiations.[129]

While it is possible, as the Chinese allege, that Kosygin may have retreated from an agreement reached in the airport talks, it is more likely that he understood "withdrawal of forces" in much narrower terms, indicating areas where fighting had taken place, rather than a removal of troops from areas where China disputed the location of the border. Upon Kosygin's return, the Soviet leadership may have felt that even to refer to the sites of the border clashes as "disputed areas" would give credence to China's territorial claims and saw the need to remove from their official note any mention of "disputed areas" or withdrawal of forces from such areas.[130]

The controversy over the Zhou-Kosygin meeting would have important consequences, which went well beyond the confines of Sino-Soviet relations. For example, Goncharov and Usov raised the possibility that Kosygin's attempt to achieve a breakthrough at the Beijing airport meeting may have contributed to the subsequent decline in his political fortunes within the Brezhnev leadership.[131] Indeed, Brezhnev's increased visibility in foreign affairs coincided with Kosygin's continuing eclipse. By first opposing his rival's economic reform program and then allowing him to go out on a limb on China policy, Brezhnev was able to neutralize his political challenge. When his proposals for economic reform met with resistance, Kosygin reportedly sought an expanded portfolio in foreign affairs.[132] In China policy, certainly, Kosygin's efforts to improve relations through high-level meetings had met with no demonstrable results. As a consequence, interests within the Politburo began to converge over containment of China. A new containment coalition was born and would prove difficult to dismantle, even when circumstances began to change.

POST-SUMMIT THREATS

If the Chinese had wavered initially over their interest in border talks, the Soviets soon gave them an extra prod. Zhou's repeated comments to Kosygin that the

Soviet Union's forces were more technologically advanced and questions about rumors of a Soviet attack against China led the Soviet leaders to believe that they could use the threat of force to apply greater pressure on China.[133] Five days after the Zhou-Kosygin meeting, Viktor Louis, a Soviet journalist suspected of KGB connections,[134] published an article in the *London Evening News* arguing that a Soviet attack on Chinese nuclear facilities could not be discounted. According to Louis, there was no reason why the Brezhnev doctrine could not be applied to China, despite its size and the likelihood of active resistance. "Whether or not the Soviet Union will dare to attack Lop Nor, China's nuclear center, is a question of strategy, and so the world would only learn about it afterwards," Louis said.[135]

Not long after the Zhou-Kosygin meeting, the *New York Times* reported that the Soviet leadership had sent a letter to East European leaders suggesting a preemptive strike against Chinese nuclear facilities. The Chinese leadership responded to this war of nerves by moving some of their nuclear installations from Lop Nor to northern Tibet, farther from the Sino-Soviet border, and by agreeing on October 7 to hold border talks with the USSR.[136] In mid-October 1969, Lin Biao issued Order Number One, which called for the evacuation of the top leadership from Beijing and essentially put China on a full military alert.[137]

According to Arkadii Shevchenko, a defector who served at the time as an adviser to Foreign Minister Andrei Gromyko, Defense Minister Andrei Grechko had advocated a nuclear strike against China in response to the 1969 clashes.[138] Shevchenko recounted that a report from the Soviet ambassador to the United States, Anatolii Dobrynin, dissuaded the Politburo from adopting this course of action. Dobrynin reportedly warned that the United States was seeking to improve relations with China and that a Soviet nuclear attack might result in a U.S.-Soviet confrontation.[139]

Soviet nuclear threats may not have succeeded in reducing the threat from China, however, since the border crisis made the development of the then rudimentary Chinese nuclear program more urgent—it would eventually prevent the Soviets from gaining any advantage from intimidation in the future.[140] Moreover, the Soviet threats against China led the United States to accelerate contacts with Beijing.[141]

In the spring and summer of 1969, the Nixon administration requested a series of policy reviews on Sino-American and Sino-Soviet relations.[142] In late July to early August, while Nixon traveled on an overseas tour, he met privately with President Yahya Khan of Pakistan and President Nicolae Ceaușescu of Romania, countries friendly to the PRC, and reportedly told the two leaders that the United States would not condone a Soviet attack against Chinese nuclear facilities.[143] Soon after, Kissinger set up a back-channel to Beijing via Pakistan.

On September 9, the U.S. ambassador to Poland, Walter Stoessel, was asked to initiate contacts with his Chinese counterpart.[144] By the end of 1969, American efforts to reach out to China began to bear fruit. Harry Haldeman wrote in his diary on December 10, 1969, that Kissinger "was all excited" when he heard that the Chinese ambassador agreed to a meeting in Warsaw. He believed that "something's breaking" because there was "a real probability" of a Soviet attack against China by April 15, 1970."[145]

The Chinese leadership was making similar reassessments of their security environment. In the summer of 1969, an influential group of marshals, assembled by Zhou Enlai in mid-March to provide guidance on international matters, advised that the Soviet Union posed a greater threat to China than the United States.[146] One of the marshals, Chen Yi, went so far as to suggest that China should agree to a meeting with the United States in Warsaw.[147] As the Sino-American rapprochement unfolded from 1969 to 1971 and threat of a military conflict with the Soviet Union gradually diminished, by 1971 the Chinese leadership ended the Third Front policies.[148]

Soviet leaders failed to understand that they created a security dilemma for China—the measures they used to increase their security along the Sino-Soviet border had a negative impact on China's security.[149] Reflecting on this turn of events, Georgi Arbatov wrote in his memoirs that the Soviet leadership had made serious mistakes, including "a faulty assessment of the threat from China, which forced us to concentrate very large forces in the Far East. This, in turn, was interpreted by the Chinese as a threat forcing them to increase both their nuclear and their conventional forces and their political and military cooperation with the West."[150]

BORDER NEGOTIATIONS

The Sino-American rapprochement provided new incentives for renewed diplomatic efforts to improve Soviet-Chinese relations,[151] but little progress was achieved. In diplomatic initiatives after 1969, the Soviets offered general normalization proposals to preclude Chinese discussion of "unequal treaties" and "disputed areas," but the Chinese refused to reply to most of the Soviet proposals.[152] In a reflection of the continuing hold of the containment coalition over the USSR's China policy, the Soviets may have hoped to gain a propaganda advantage by publicly proposing agreements they knew the Chinese would reject and making China look intransigent.[153]

As before, the two sides remained at an impasse over the border issue—the Soviet Union was only willing to discuss modifications of the border, not question the basis for its demarcation, a point on which China insisted. On several occasions, Soviet negotiators suggested that the USSR and the PRC sign a non-use-of-force treaty and a nonaggression treaty.[154] Insisting that a withdrawal of forces from disputed areas would have to occur before any broader agreement could be signed, the Chinese side rebuffed Soviet proposals.

Although China and the Soviet Union remained at a tense stand-off on border issues, their bilateral relationship began to stabilize during this period. In 1970, the two countries finally exchanged ambassadors after a three-year lapse.[155] Trade between the two countries slowly improved. In 1971, the Soviet Union and China signed a trade protocol involving a 300 percent increase in trade over the previous year, from 41 million rubles to 138.7 million.[156]

By the spring of 1972, the Soviet leadership appeared to be coming to terms with a long-term freeze in Sino-Soviet relations when Brezhnev made public a conciliatory Soviet proposal to base relations with China on peaceful coexistence, rather than proletarian internationalism—which was the basis for relations between socialist states.[157] The Soviet leader in effect was stating that the USSR would not interfere in Chinese internal affairs, a concern for China since the development of the Brezhnev Doctrine.[158]

In his speech, Brezhnev also expressed frustration with years of fruitless diplomacy. He asserted that since the Soviet Union had already presented the Chinese with several proposals dealing with a range of issues in their relationship, the ball was now in China's court.[159] The Chinese did not respond.

The Soviet leadership carefully watched the Tenth Congress of the CCP in August 1973 (the first congress since the border clashes) for signs of change in the Chinese attitude towards the Soviet Union. Zhou's report gave no such indications. In fact, the Chinese leader accused the Brezhnev leadership of trying to subvert the CCP, even linking the Soviet leaders to Lin Biao.[160]

At the congress, Zhou appeared to respond at last to Brezhnev's 1972 speech by stating that political differences between the two countries should not impede normalization based on the principles of peaceful coexistence. The main obstacle remained the disagreement over the interpretation of the September 11, 1969, meeting with Kosygin. Zhou reiterated the Chinese position that the "Sino-Soviet border question should be settled peacefully through negotiations free from any threat."[161] In other words, the border issue could be resolved only once the Soviets withdrew their forces from the border area.

After the Tenth Congress of the CCP, the Soviet leadership concluded that the Maoist hold over Chinese foreign policy remained strong and that change was unlikely. Rather than make any new proposals to improve bilateral relations, the Soviets opted to wait for signs of movement from Beijing.[162]

Bilateral relations advanced little in the mid-1970s as intermittent tensions continued to interrupt any forward movement.[163] On January 7, 1974, the

Chinese issued a pamphlet outlining the provisions of twelve unequal treaties, including those signed with Tsarist Russia.[164] The next day the Chinese media came out with an analysis describing the struggle of the Soviet people against the "fascist dictatorship" of the "Brezhnev clique."[165] In mid-January 1974, the Chinese arrested five employees of the Soviet embassy in Beijing on charges of espionage. The Soviets retaliated by expelling a Chinese diplomat from the Soviet Union.[166] During the same week, the Chinese military wrested control of the Paracel Islands from Vietnam, in a show of force designed in part to demonstrate to the Soviets that the PRC would back up its territorial claims with military muscle.[167]

Then on March 14, 1974, the Chinese arrested the three-member crew of a Soviet helicopter that had crashed in Chinese territory while allegedly on a medical mission near the border. The Chinese authorities claimed that the members of the helicopter crew were being held under arrest because they were guilty of espionage, while the Soviets contended that the Chinese were using the incident to further exacerbate USSR-PRC relations.[168] On May 2, 1974, Leonid Il'ichev, the head of the Soviet delegation to the Sino-Soviet border talks, warned the Chinese ambassador that by continuing to detain the crew, the PRC would have to assume "full responsibility for the inevitable consequences of such a provocational position."[169] The three Soviet members of the helicopter crew were ultimately released in late December 1975.[170]

The border river navigation talks ended in late March 1974—after the shortest session in four years—without agreement.[171] This occurred when Beijing rejected a Soviet proposal to allow Chinese ships to navigate in the Fuyuan channel, running along the southern coast of Bolshoi Ussuriiskii/Heixiazi Island, from the Amur River to its confluence with the Ussuri. The Soviets had blockaded this channel since the border clashes, but their price for reopening it proved unacceptable to China: it would have involved acknowledging that the channel was a Soviet waterway.[172] China continued to insist on its right to navigation on its side of the main river channel.[173] In 1974, Sino-Soviet trade talks proved equally nettlesome and negotiations were drawn out to the extent that the annual protocol was delayed, resulting in a decrease in trade in 1975.[174]

On the occasion of the fifty-seventh anniversary of the October Revolution in 1974, the Chinese stated publicly for the first time that, based on the 1969 understanding reached between Aleksei Kosygin and Zhou Enlai, they wanted to conclude an agreement with the Soviets on nonaggression, non-use of force, and the maintenance of the status quo on the border, and then move on to the resolution of border questions in general.[175] The Soviets did not consider this anything more than a reiteration by the Chinese of what Moscow considered to be an obstructionist position: namely that the issue of the "disputed areas" on the border must be linked to the negotiation of a nonaggression treaty.[176]

In January 1975, China unveiled a new Constitution, which deleted earlier references to Sino-Soviet friendship.[177] Although the Soviets sharply criticized it, in October the Soviet leadership struck a conciliatory note in their greetings to the Chinese leaders on the anniversary of their revolution, omitting any threats and expressing their hopes for normalization.[178] During the fall, however, a serious border incident was reported.[179]

In early 1976, Mikhail Kapitsa, then chief of the Foreign Ministry's Far Eastern Department, published an article under a pseudonym in which he suggested that the Soviet Union would be justified in breaking diplomatic relations with China because of Chinese anti-Soviet propaganda and policies.[180] An April 28, 1976, *Pravda* article, written by I. Aleksandrov, a pseudonym for the Soviet leadership, again called for the direct examination of border issues without preconditions.[181] In June, the Soviet Foreign Ministry reiterated its earlier proposal to hold a summit meeting and resume talks on border issues.[182]

THE SOVIET MILITARY BUILD-UP IN THE 1970S

By the early 1970s, the Soviet military build-up on the Sino-Soviet border had begun to slow and the Soviets focused on improving existing capabilities.[183] From 1974 to 1976, the number of Soviet divisions in the Far East military district declined from forty-five to forty-three and the number in Mongolia held steady, as did their level of readiness.[184] In 1974, Brezhnev announced the building of the BAM (Baikal-Amur magistral') railway parallel to the Trans-Siberian to enhance the USSR's ability to reinforce Soviet troops on the border and provide an alternate line of defense against China. In mid-July 1975, the Soviets held large-scale conventional force maneuvers in Mongolia in conjunction with naval exercises in the East China Sea,[185] and one year later, naval exercises were held near Japan. At this time, the Chinese also were concerned about the Soviet Union's completion of a fourth naval yard on the Sea of Japan, at Sovetskaia Gavan', and the possibility of Soviet assumption of former U.S. basing rights in Vietnam.[186]

Although Brezhnev claimed in a November 1977 speech that the USSR wanted to improve relations with China, Soviet actions during the late 1970s gave a different impression. From March 28 to April 9, 1978, Brezhnev and Ustinov made a widely publicized tour of the Far East command posts in Khabarovsk and Vladivostok to emphasize Soviet military preparedness against China.[187] Despite Soviet saber-rattling, Sino-Soviet border talks were held in early May 1978, although they were interrupted by a border incident which seems to have been provoked by the Soviets.[188]

Moreover, the Soviet military buildup against China continued in the late 1970s, as some 250 of the Soviet Union's medium- and intermediate-range nuclear missiles (SS-4, SS-5, and the highly accurate SS-20s) and some of its newest bombers, Tu-22M Backfires, were specifically deployed against China.[189] In addition, Far Eastern ground forces were increased by two divisions in 1979 and received new hardware.[190]

According to a recently declassified CIA analysis, Soviet military preparations incorporated fixed fortifications all along the border with China, and particularly in Primorskii Krai. The CIA report noted: "The Soviets seem convinced that their powerful military position versus the Chinese is essential to prevent major trouble on the border and to inhibit anti-Soviet actions by China in other regions of Sino-Soviet rivalry."[191] Consequently, the Soviet leadership intended "to retain indefinitely the clear preponderance of military capability the USSR enjoys over China by continuing steadily to modernize the forces deployed in the Far East."[192] To improve the coordination of Soviet forces in the Far Eastern, Siberian, and Transbaikal military districts, as well as in Mongolia, a new Far Eastern command structure was established in the region by 1979.[193]

The increased Soviet military presence in the Far East was extremely expensive and did not necessarily improve Soviet security against China. The Soviet Union's policy of confrontation led the Soviet leadership to squander billions on building the BAM, while leaving the Russian Far East underdeveloped—resulting in its greater vulnerability.[194]

By 1978, both the USSR and the PRC had activated their search for allies in Asia. In August, the Chinese and the Japanese concluded a treaty which contained an anti-hegemony clause, directed against the Soviet Union.[195] The Soviet Union countered by signing a treaty of friendship and cooperation with Vietnam in November 1978. The treaty emboldened the Vietnamese, who subsequently invaded Cambodia, a Chinese client. China then invaded Vietnam in February 1979 to punish the Vietnamese for their actions in Cambodia. During these hostilities the Soviet Union assisted Vietnam with air and coastal support.

Vietnam suffered heavy casualties, as did China, and one month later the People's Liberation Army (PLA) withdrew. The Soviet Union subsequently held a large-scale military exercise in the Russian Far East, Siberia, and Mongolia in an attempt to dissuade the Chinese from undertaking any further military adventures.[196] Their poor performance against Vietnam, a much weaker adversary, may have led the Chinese leaders to reevaluate their position on relations with the Soviet Union and decide to begin political discussions with Moscow in September 1979.[197] The Soviet invasion of Afghanistan in December, however, postponed any progress in political relations for several years.

THE CONTAINMENT COALITION
AND THE END OF THE MAO ERA

According to Aleksandrov-Agentov, after Mao's death in 1976, Brezhnev expressed greater interest in finding a way to improve relations with China, but his efforts were thwarted by entrenched opposition in the Foreign Ministry and Central Committee, especially by Suslov and Boris Ponomarev, who headed the CPSU's International Department.[198] The Chinese leadership, still reeling from the Cultural Revolution, did nothing to encourage any change in Soviet policy either.[199]

Right after Mao's death, the Soviet government reissued its earlier proposal to hold talks about specific border issues, without preconditions.[200] But once more the Soviet Union sent a mixed message. On October 14, Viktor Louis was used again to warn that Soviet patience was limited. If the PRC did not make some conciliatory gesture within a month, Louis wrote in a French newspaper, the USSR might do something "irreversible."[201] No such gesture was forthcoming. According to one Chinese leader, no improvement in Sino-Soviet relations would take place unless the Soviet Union renounced the revisionist policies undertaken since Khrushchev's day.[202] On October 25, at the Twenty-fifth Congress of the CPSU, Brezhnev harshly condemned Maoism and reiterated his 1972 proposal to normalize relations with China on the basis of peaceful coexistence, though he added that the Soviet Union advocated resuming relations according to the principles of socialist internationalism.[203]

Soviet-Chinese relations were a mixed picture during the late 1970s, partly because the Chinese leadership, still involved in a factional struggle, was sending confusing signals to the Soviet Union. The Chinese publication of the fifth volume of Mao's collected works led to a spate of polemics. This volume dealt with the period of Sino-Soviet cooperation, but the editors (who included all of China's Politburo members) omitted most positive references to the USSR and prefaced the volume with a hostile editorial.[204] Nevertheless, in September Foreign Minister Huang Hua gave a speech at the UN in which he left the door open for improved relations with both the Soviet Union and the United States.[205]

The Soviet Union also sent confusing signals to the new Chinese leadership, reflecting disagreement within policy circles. Aleksei Brezhnev, a diplomat, recalled that after Mao's death analysts at the Soviet embassy in Beijing reported that greater pragmatism would characterize post-Maoist foreign policy and pave the way for a possible improvement in Sino-Soviet relations. After an initial positive response from Rusakov, more optimistic reports soon proved unwelcome to high-ranking CPSU officials, who had staked their careers on a worsening of relations with China.[206]

Thus, in an April 1977 conference, Central Committee Secretary Mikhail Zimianin asserted that there were "no changes of late" in Chinese policies.[207] Just six months later, in a *Pravda* article on the occasion of China's national day, the Soviet leadership's assessment appeared optimistic by comparison. "There are no questions in relations between the USSR and the CPR [PRC] that could not be resolved in a spirit of good-neighborliness," the article stated.[208] Relations actually did show some signs of progress, when in the beginning of October the USSR and the PRC announced an agreement on border navigation. According to this agreement, the Soviet Union lifted the blockade it had imposed in 1967 on Chinese navigation on the Amur River.

In 1974, the Soviet Union had agreed to allow Chinese navigation on the Amur in exchange for Chinese recognition of Soviet sovereignty over Bolshoi Ussuriiskii/Heixiazi Island, situated at the confluence of the Amur and Ussuri Rivers, across from Khabarovsk. After the Soviet channel between Bolshoi Ussuriiskii/Heixiazi Island and their bank of the Amur dried up and the Soviets began navigating the Chinese channel, the Chinese warned the Soviets at the 1977 talks that they could not continue to enjoy this privilege without allowing China navigation rights on the Amur. Ultimately, the Soviets agreed to allow Chinese ships to navigate through the confluence of the Amur and Ussuri Rivers, as long as they gave the USSR prior warning and sailed during the daytime.[209]

Despite such progress, in mid-October 1977 Deng Xiaoping suggested for the first time to a French correspondent that the United States (as well as the West European countries) could participate in a united front against the Soviet Union.[210] Still, the Chinese message in honor of the 60th anniversary of the October Revolution was fairly moderate in tone and Foreign Minister Huang Hua even attended the Soviet embassy reception, the first time a Chinese foreign minister had attended a function at the Soviet embassy in eleven years.[211] In their statement, the Chinese leadership suggested normalization on the basis of the discussions at the 1969 meeting between Zhou Enlai and Kosygin, which, the Chinese alleged, involved a military withdrawal from the border.[212]

When the Soviets proposed to the Chinese in February 1978 that the two sides draw up a general statement on the principles of their relations, based on peaceful coexistence, the Chinese refused, insisting that improvement in relations would require that the two sides sign the agreement on border issues already reached in October 1969.[213]

Citing changes in the international situation and claiming violations by the Soviet Union, on April 3, 1979, the PRC announced it would not renew the 1950 Sino-Soviet friendship treaty, which was due to expire the following April. Once again the Chinese sent contradictory messages, as they also indicated their interest in holding talks with the Soviets to settle outstanding issues and improve relations in a wide range of spheres, including science, technology, and culture.[214] The Soviet Union responded somewhat defensively in a note, calling attention to the fact that the Chinese had rejected a series of Soviet proposals to improve bilateral relations, but asserting that the "Soviet Union is convinced that a document about the principles of relations between the USSR and China . . . would be a suitable starting point for improving relations between them."[215]

The Chinese replied on May 5 that they would be interested in discussions concerning a wide range of questions, including political, economic, and cultural relations.[216] As in the border talks, during the preliminary discussions the Chinese insisted that the agenda for the political talks include "questions obstructing normalization of relations," namely the Soviet military presence along the border.[217] Although the Soviet and Chinese negotiators failed to agree to an agenda, ultimately they decided to hold talks at the deputy foreign minister level in alternating capitals.

Much had changed since the negotiation of the 1950 friendship treaty—the Chinese refused to regard the Soviet Union as the elder brother in the socialist movement and insisted on equal relations, while the Soviet Union had demonstrated in 1956 and 1968 its unwillingness to accept any significant departures from the Soviet model of socialism. Noting this difference, a Chinese radio commentary stated that the Soviets "find it difficult to change their bad habits and still regard themselves as teachers, vainly attempting to teach the Chinese people how to think and live and what road to choose. If the Soviet side adopts such an attitude to handle state relations and conduct negotiations, it assuredly will not work."[218]

After a fifteen-year hiatus in political talks, a first round actually was held in Moscow from October 12 through November 30, 1979, and talks were expected to continue.[219] The Chinese reportedly restated their long-standing position that the two sides should sign the agreement allegedly reached between Kosygin and Zhou Enlai in 1969 and also proposed that the Soviet Union reduce its border forces to 1964 levels, remove its troops from Mongolia, and stop supporting Vietnam's occupation of Cambodia. According to a Chinese account of the talks, the Soviet Union objected to involving third countries in Sino-Soviet discussions, refused to reduce its force levels, and proved willing to sign only hollow agreements.[220] A senior Chinese official told Japanese journalists that although the political discussions with Moscow would be difficult, they might produce some benefits for China, such as increased trade.[221] According to Kapitsa, who was present at the talks, the Chinese insistence on introducing issues concerning third countries (i.e. Vietnam and Mongolia), as well as China's territorial claims, anti-Sovietism, expansionism, and military buildup, derailed

Soviet attempts to achieve a new agreement on the principles of Sino-Soviet relations.[222] The Soviet invasion of Afghanistan led the Chinese to abandon the border talks for another three years.

CONCLUSION

In the 1960s and 1970s, Sino-Soviet differences proved extremely difficult to resolve. Kosygin's September 1969 effort to restore Sino-Soviet friendship met with defeat at the hands of Chinese leaders increasingly focused on the ideological struggle with the Soviet Union. Moreover, Kosygin's failure to achieve a breakthrough in relations gave Brezhnev further evidence with which to discredit his most serious rival for power, and China policy soon became a victim of Kremlin politics. By the mid-1970s, overlapping interests in containing China had cemented a coalition of top leaders (Brezhnev, Gromyko, Suslov, and Andropov) that ultimately deprived the General Secretary of any flexibility in China policy.

3 / The Sino-Soviet Conflict in Perspective

In the 1970s, Soviet strategy regarding the border conflict with China developed simultaneously on two fronts—regular but largely fruitless diplomatic contacts and military containment. Brezhnev was able to sustain a foreign policy coalition supporting this dual approach to Soviet China policy because of the overlapping interests of three important audiences: the international communist movement, the policy community in Moscow, and regional officials in the Russian Far East. While Sino-Soviet talks were held, key Soviet policymakers (Brezhnev, Gromyko, Suslov, Andropov, and later Ustinov) simultaneously took steps to coordinate Soviet China policy with other socialist states, develop propaganda and research materials about the history of the border, and request the support of regional party organizations for Soviet policies on border issues.

Each of these audiences presented a different narrative about the Soviet-Chinese relationship. The CPSU, in conjunction with the international communist movement, sought to maintain the illusion of unity—long after the open break between the Chinese and Soviet parties—and promoted measures to isolate the CCP and prevent it from swaying the allegiance of other parties. Soviet policymakers, with the help of sinologists enlisted for the cause, initially portrayed the Maoist regime as a temporary distortion of the (formerly pro-Soviet) principles of the Chinese party-state. By the end of the decade, officials and scholars in Moscow braced for a more long-term challenge to Soviet interests, which they called Maoism without Mao, and warned of an emerging strategic alliance between China and the United States. As in the case of the communist movement, this narrative of Sino-Soviet relations had important policy implications and led Soviet leaders to embrace a political-military containment strategy directed against China.

As early as 1969, a third narrative began to appear—a regionalist narrative which, despite the centralization of Soviet politics, showed clear evidence of differences in views in Moscow and in the border regions about China policy. At the time of the border clashes, officials in the regions questioned whether Moscow was keeping them fully informed about the extent of the security threat from China. Only three years later, however, regional officials promoted a more

49

pragmatic view of Sino-Soviet relations. In contrast with officials in Moscow who promoted a containment strategy directed against China, by the early 1970s, regional officials urged a reopening of border trade.

THE SINO-SOVIET CONFLICT
AND THE COMMUNIST MOVEMENT

While showing greater understanding of general trends in international relations beginning in the 1960s,[1] by and large Soviet officials and academics remained unresponsive to changes in the communist movement that raised uncomfortable doubts pertaining to the viability of Soviet pretensions to a leading role within it. China did not pose an immediate military threat, but a strong and independent-minded China undermined both Soviet leadership of the communist movement and its unity by advancing an alternative model of development. Soviet attempts to pressure China to return to the fold only solidified the resolve of the Chinese leaders to defend the legitimacy of their own version of Marxist-Leninist ideology.[2]

Beginning in the late 1960s, the Soviet leadership tried to orchestrate a unified socialist response to China's challenge. The International Department of the CPSU Central Committee held regular meetings with its counterparts in the East European socialist countries and Mongolia to coordinate propaganda on the China question, including symposia, research, and media campaigns in third countries.[3] These efforts by Soviet party leaders to showcase socialist unity largely were ineffectual and increasingly revealed signs of a fractious community.[4]

A former Central Committee official who worked as a Soviet diplomat in Beijing in the late 1970s recalled that the Soviet embassy also tried to coordinate China policy with the embassies of the East European countries with only limited success. The East Germans, for example, preferred to maintain a solid economic relationship with Beijing, while Polish and Hungarian diplomats questioned Soviet criticism of Chinese agricultural reforms, given that the Soviet Union had nothing better to propose.[5]

The Soviet Union also expanded research cooperation with their East Europeans colleagues. According to Aleksandr Grigor'ev, head of the history department at the Institute of the Far East, high-level meetings of China specialists from the Soviet Union, Hungary, Poland, East Germany, and Bulgaria were held from the late 1960s to the early 1980s to coordinate research activities: the Soviet experts dealt with all aspects of Chinese politics, while the Hungarians and Poles focused on foreign policy questions, the East Germans covered the workers' movement, and the Bulgarians paid special attention to Chinese policy towards the Balkans.[6]

The Impact of the Sino-Soviet Border Clashes

The Sino-Soviet border clashes came at a critical moment for the communist movement—they flared up in the months leading up to the international communist conference in Moscow on June 7, 1969. Official Soviet statements in *Pravda* and *Kommunist* interpreted the clashes as an attack against socialism as a whole as well as against Soviet territory.[7] The border clashes, following the Soviet intervention in Czechoslovakia, led some communists to draw other conclusions, however. Giuseppe Boffa, Moscow correspondent for the Italian Communist Party newspaper *L'Unità,* wrote an article advocating a more decentralized system of relations among socialist states. While Boffa criticized China's position on the border dispute as irresponsible, he defended the possibility of dissension in the communist movement.[8]

It was up to the CPSU to counter such appeals as forcefully as possible. Addressing the international communist conference, Brezhnev bemoaned the CCP's "departure from Marxism-Leninism," "break with internationalism," and "organization of armed conflicts." The Soviet leader urged his fellow communists to close ranks against imperialism and cooperate in the defense of Marxist-Leninist ideas.[9] Brezhnev also raised the idea of creating an Asian collective security system, which later would symbolize Soviet efforts to create an anti-Chinese alliance in Asia.[10] Soon after the conference, the Soviet Union recalled its ambassadors from Asia, signaling a rethinking of Soviet policy toward the region.[11]

China's Challenge to Communist Unity

As Lev Deliusin later commented, "The Soviet-Chinese conflict represented above all the expression of the crisis of socialist ideology, the defeat of Marxism-Leninism as a universal truth, capable of unifying the working masses of all countries around the common goal of building communism."[12] In the 1970s, the CPSU still refused to admit defeat, and Brezhnev continued to urge closer ties among communist parties and joint efforts to defend Marxist-Leninist positions.

The yearly meetings of Central Committee officials from the East European socialist states on the China question attempted to contain the damage caused by the CCP. A 1971 CPSU Central Committee preparatory report, for example, highlighted a new threat to socialist unity—China's attempt to pursue a "differentiated" approach by targeting certain socialist states as potential partners while maintaining hostility toward the USSR. The CPSU urged the fraternal parties to be as vigilant as ever and oppose Chinese efforts to break the unity of the "ideological front for the criticism of Maoism."[13] By differentiation, Soviet analysts referred to Beijing's efforts to strengthen relations with individual countries while remaining hostile to the socialist community as a whole;[14] for example, by offering some socialist states lower prices in trade agreements, thereby undermining socialist unity on economic matters.[15]

In the 1970s, Soviet analysts worried about the rise of Eurocommunism and efforts by states such as Yugoslavia and Romania to gain more autonomy within the socialist community. The Sino-Soviet conflict tended to accentuate Soviet problems in Eastern Europe because China's diatribes against the USSR echoed criticism from the West, and the Chinese emphasis on national communism reinforced Eurocommunist (French, Spanish, and Italian communist parties) and autonomist (Yugoslav and Romanian) positions.[16] The Soviet leadership handled this unlucky coincidence of views by urging like-minded communist parties to criticize Maoist policies, making a show of communist unity through meetings, and warning fellow socialists of Maoist subversion. According to Soviet party officials, there could be no "neutral position" in the struggle against Maoism.[17]

The Czechoslovak, East German, and Bulgarian media (and to a lesser extent the Hungarian and Polish press) were the most amenable to providing the Soviets with a mouthpiece for their condemnations of China's apostasy.[18] The Soviets were somewhat less successful in using communist meetings to gather support against Chinese positions. While it was easier to gain support in bilateral meetings with individual parties, larger gatherings were more important for providing an appearance of unity.[19]

Unity became harder to maintain throughout the 1970s, however. Instead of holding a major international communist party conference such as the 1969 Moscow meeting, which showcased criticism of Chinese policies, due to opposition by many Asian parties and some European parties, the CPSU had to settle for a smaller event for the Communist and Workers' Parties of Europe, held in June 1976 in East Berlin. Not only did the East Berlin conference not condemn China, but even Brezhnev purported to uphold the concept of autonomy—paradoxically achieving a show of unity by recognizing polycentric trends within the movement. The West European communists, particularly Santiago Carillo of Spain, elaborated on this theme to an extent that was unpublishable in the pages of *Pravda*.[20]

Autonomist communist parties irked the Soviets by offering fairly balanced appraisals of Chinese policies. For example, the foreign editor of TANJUG, the Yugoslav press agency, writing in the *Review of International Affairs*, criticized both the Soviet Union and China for engaging in polemics, which he said could only have a negative impact on the international situation.[21] The Romanians went even further. Disregarding the chill in Sino-Soviet relations, President Nicolae Ceauşescu, in a speech to the Eleventh Congress of the Romanian Communist Party, expressed his "great joy" over the improvement in Sino-Romanian relations and promised to "do everything to develop these relations."[22]

By the late 1970s, China's deliberate attempts to break socialist ranks greatly alarmed Soviet policymakers. Despite the impasse in Sino-Soviet relations, China made an effort to restore party-to-party ties with Romania and Yugoslavia and supported their positions, which deviated from Soviet policies.[23] CCP Chairman Hua Guofeng's visit to Romania in August 1978, for example, buttressed the Romanian claim to a more independent foreign policy.[24] He went on to Yugoslavia, where Tito's conception of Yugoslavia's special role in the nonaligned movement resonated with China's claim to leadership of the Third World. *Pravda* described the Chinese leader's trip to the Balkans as a series of "hit-and-run attacks on the USSR" in which China pursued "the goal of sowing seeds of discord among the socialist countries."[25] A March 1980 Central Committee analysis noted that Chinese tactics were achieving a degree of success in that some of the socialist states resisted coordinating all aspects of China policy.

The polemics between the Italian Communist Party (PCI) and the CPSU during the late 1970s, culminating in a 1981 split, also had far-reaching implications for the communist movement. The PCI and CCP found common cause in asserting that the Soviet leadership of the communist movement had outlived its utility. While the Chinese presented their revolution as an alternate path to follow, the Italians criticized proletarian internationalism as excessively restrictive, advocating instead cooperation between communist, socialist, and social-democratic forces.[26] Beginning in 1978, the PCI criticized Soviet foreign policy, particularly Soviet intervention in Third World conflicts, for aiming to establish spheres of influence.[27] Although this criticism was more measured in tone than the Chinese claims, the two parties soon decided to formally normalize relations, a step that the Soviet Union repeatedly tried to forestall. Ultimately, in April 1980 PCI chairman Enrico Berlinguer visited Beijing.[28]

The mounting Soviet inability to control demands for greater autonomy in the communist movement was apparent at the April 1980 conference of European communist parties. The PCI's refusal to attend came as no surprise, but this time the Yugoslavs, the Romanians, and several other parties from the smaller European countries also declined to participate. Although at the 1976 Berlin conference the Soviet Union paid lip service to demands for greater equality in the movement, in 1980 the CPSU reasserted the importance of unity.[29] This outmoded approach to an increasingly diverse communist movement only aggravated tensions within it and further challenged Soviet authority, as the rise of Solidarity in Poland later that summer soon demonstrated.

THE POLICY COMMUNITY IN MOSCOW
RESPONDS TO CHINA'S CHALLENGE

While CPSU Central Committee officials sought the support of their counterparts in other socialist states for Soviet China policy, Moscow's spin doc-
tors worked the local crowd. In 1963, members of the Politburo instructed the
Central Committee to restrict the availability in the Soviet Union of Chinese
sources that propagated "the well-known special views of the CPC [CCP]."[30]
Three years later, the Central Committee created a new closed department in
the Institute of the Economy of the World Socialist System to research issues
and prepare reports on contemporary China for party and government authorities. In the open press, this institute would be known as the Institute of the
Far East of the Soviet Academy of Sciences.[31]

The development of Soviet sinology was a matter of national security. Soviet
scholars were required by party authorities to defend Soviet positions in the
Sino-Soviet conflict. Periodically, Central Committee officials asked Soviet journalists and sinologists to outline the Soviet Union's policies on Mao's "anti-
Soviet and anti-Marxist ideology."[32]

To better coordinate the Soviet response to China's ideological challenge,
the Politburo established a special experts group on China. The group was
headed by Oleg Rakhmanin, the Central Committee official in charge of China
policy, and included other key party officials (Rostislav Ul'ianovskii and
Mikhail Titarenko), foreign ministry officials in charge of China policy (Ivan
Arkhipov and Sergei Tikhvinskii), as well as institute directors, including
Mikhail Sladkovskii (Institute of the Far East), Nikolai Inozemstev (Institute
of World Economic and International Relations), and Oleg Bogomolov
(Institute of the Economy of the World Socialist System).[33]

However, as Gilbert Rozman noted in a pioneering article on Soviet sinology, despite attempts by the CPSU to coordinate Soviet responses to China's
ideological challenge, there were diverse views about Chinese policies within
the Moscow policy community.[34] To be sure, hard-liners such as Mikhail
Sladkovskii and Oleg Rakhmanin set the uncompromising tone which dominated Soviet China policy until Andropov's tenure as general secretary, but
even in the 1970s some voices for change could be heard, albeit faintly, on key
issues such as Sino-American relations and recent Chinese policies.

The Territorial Question

Once the border question resurfaced as an issue in the Sino-Soviet conflict in
1964, top Soviet officials became concerned about the "inaccurate" portrayal

of the history of the Sino-Soviet border treaties and border relations in Soviet textbooks and scholarly literature written in the heyday of Sino-Soviet friendship. Soviet officials feared that these works unwittingly gave credence to Chinese positions, for example, by arguing that Tsarist Russia had contributed to imperialist seizure of Chinese territory in the nineteenth century, ignoring evidence of Chinese expansionism in the eighteenth and nineteenth centuries, showing Chinese ownership of land that never belonged to China, and exaggerating Chinese cultural influences in the Russian Far East and Central Asia.[35] In the aftermath of the border clashes, in September 1969 the Soviet leadership decided to enlist the aid of prominent Soviet scholars to refute Chinese (and Western) positions on the territorial question in journal and newspaper articles as well as in textbooks and scholarly works.[36]

In a March 1973 decree, the Soviet government required that several cities in the Russian Far East be renamed. These cities lost their original Manchu and Han names and were given new Russian names in a further bid to downplay the credence of Chinese territorial claims. Thus "Iman" became "Dal'n-erechensk," "Suchan" became "Partizansk," and "Tetiukhe" became "Dal'n-egorsk." A subsequent decree also renamed some 250 rivers and mountains which had Chinese names.[37]

The Chinese territorial claims and border clashes led many Soviet observers to conclude that expansionism was a central objective of the Maoist leadership. They attributed this to the nationalist essence of Maoist policies. Some saw evidence of "two lines" within the CCP: Mao's nationalistic grouping and the temporarily subdued internationalists—the "healthy core" of communists who favored cooperation with the Soviet Union. Other authoritative analysts highlighted the domestic sources of Chinese anti-Sovietism and militarization, which they viewed as a tactic by Chinese leaders to distract the people from failed economic policies.[38] Fearing Chinese propaganda on territorial claims would exert an adverse influence on scholars in some socialist states and in the West, the CPSU Central Committee advocated preparing more open materials outlining Soviet positions and publishing and distributing them in foreign languages.[39]

The Consequences of the Sino-Soviet Conflict for World Communism

The Sino-Soviet border clashes, the first instance of an attack by a socialist country against the Soviet Union, challenged Soviet dogma about the unity of the communist movement. In light of the escalation of the Sino-Soviet conflict from ideological sparring to outright military clashes, even veiled attempts by prominent scholars, such as Aleksei Rumiantsev[40] to interpret Chinese departures from the Soviet model as an effort to build socialism with national specifics disappeared from print as the Soviet foreign policy elite struggled to respond to a seemingly irrational Chinese leadership.

Soviet policymakers viewed the Ninth CCP Congress in April 1969 as a watershed in Chinese politics because the meeting officially approved the Maoist deviations from Marxism-Leninism that had been accruing.[41] After the congress, Soviet officials discussed their options. An authoritative discussion concluded that "contemporary China should not be 'excommunicated' (*nel'zia otluchat'*) from socialism, for the rule of Maoism in the country is a temporary phenomenon."[42] Most Soviet officials and scholars contended that the internationalist line in the CCP would ultimately triumph once the Chinese people recognized that internationalism and normalization of relations with the USSR represented their true interests, a view which precluded the need for serious negotiation with the present leaders and linked any improvement in relations to changes in China.[43]

While the prevailing view was that the socialist community was uniting further in response to the Chinese challenge, some Soviet scholars questioned this position, albeit obliquely. According to Anatolii Butenko, when the concept of the socialist system was first formulated, it assumed the absence of contradictions among socialist states. Butenko cited the 1969 meeting of communist parties as evidence that socialist states were not closing their eyes to problems and contradictions caused by differences in development, international positions, and, above all, nationalism.[44] Vladimir Gantman even envisaged the possibility of conflict between socialist states breaking out in the particular case when "there are nationalistic, chauvinistic, and anti-Soviet attitudes in the ruling forces of a socialist state, as there are in China."[45]

Politicheskii Dnevnik, a *samizdat* publication read by the more reform-minded intellectuals, made a more striking critique.[46] The piece, "Notes on Some Problems of Soviet Foreign Policy," faulted Soviet foreign policy-makers for failing to recognize changes in the international system, such as the virtual break-up of the socialist camp.[47]

Due to their reluctance to recognize changing conditions, particularly in the socialist camp, Soviet leaders opted to continue previous policies, and when faced with crises, as in the case of the Sino-Soviet border clashes, the leadership directed additional resources to the struggle against real or imagined enemies without reducing commitments elsewhere—an approach that eventually drained Soviet economic resources.[48] A few Soviet scholars urged reevaluation of intra-socialist relations in light of the Chinese challenge, but the predominant response among Soviet officials was to resist China's detrimental initiatives.[49]

By the 1970s, the Chinese leadership had articulated an alternative vision of the world that ran counter to Soviet postulates on proletarian internationalism—the ties binding the socialist community with the leftist liberation movements in developing countries. In an April 1974 speech that marked China's reemergence in world affairs, Deng Xiaoping outlined China's view of international relations, the "theory of the three worlds." According to this theory, international relations proceeded from three groups of states: the superpowers (first world), the West and East European states and Japan (second world), and the developing states (third world, including China). This theory was a further elaboration of the earlier concepts of the "intermediate zone" (the locus of the contention between the two superpowers) and the "struggle against the two superpowers." According to the theory of the three worlds, the main trend in international politics was the growing resistance by the developing countries, supported by developed countries of Western and Eastern Europe and Japan, against the hegemonism of the two superpowers (the Soviet Union continuing to be viewed as the more dangerous of the two).

In May 1975, the PRC established relations with the European Economic Community, while the Soviet Union continued to refuse to recognize it. Support for European integration was viewed by the Chinese leadership as a means of diminishing the potential for control by the superpowers over the "second world."[50] During the mid-1970s, the Chinese began to emphasize the Soviet threat to Western Europe and came out in support of NATO's role in Europe.[51] Normalization of China's relations with various West European states developed during the mid-1970s, as French President Georges Pompidou, German Chancellor Helmut Schmidt, and former British Prime Minister Edward Heath all visited Beijing between 1973 and 1975. The Soviet leadership was wary of such contacts, fearing that they would enhance the position of European conservatives, who were suspicious of détente from the beginning.[52]

Many Soviet officials and academics said that the theory of the three worlds, which explicitly denied the existence of a socialist community and overlooked the special bonds between the national liberation movements and the USSR, represented a new dangerous expression of China's geopolitical aims, dramatizing that Maoist policies posed a danger to all socialists.[53] They also criticized the theory because they claimed that it justified policies towards socialist states, developing countries, and Western Europe which ran counter to Soviet interests.

Soviet analysis emphasized that the Chinese were trying to create a bloc of their own with developing states. For example, in a critique of the theory of the three worlds, Soviet observers noted that "The Chinese leaders calculate that 'deideologization' of international relations and a non-class approach to world events enable them to resort to unprincipled maneuvers, draw any force to their side and perform any zigzag in foreign policy, and to sponsor a bloc spearheaded in the first place against the USSR and world socialism."[54] By feigning to be a developing country while pursuing hegemonic aims, the PRC became what one Soviet observer termed "the Trojan horse of imperialism within the national liberation movement."[55] Many Soviet commentators stressed that the Chinese were willing to form alliances with anyone in the Third World to create a sphere of influence and increase China's bargaining position in the newly created US-PRC relationship.[56] Others believed China's influence in the Third World would decline as a result of its rapprochement with the United States.[57]

U.S.–China Relations

The stalemate in Sino-Soviet relations was in stark contrast to the rapid improvement in U.S.–Soviet and U.S.–China relations from 1969 to 1972.[58] The Soviet leadership, fearing that the United States would take advantage of Sino-Soviet difficulties, repeatedly raised the issue in diplomatic meetings and urged American officials against such a course of action. Such attempts backfired, as the Soviet Union's obvious display of anxiety on the China issue only served to make the China card more attractive to U.S. policymakers.

Former Soviet ambassador to the United States Anatolii Dobrynin recounted that in his first official discussion with President Nixon in October 1969, he warned the American leader against taking advantage of problems in Sino-Soviet relations, although he later regretted this display of apprehension.[59] Nonetheless, he disputes Kissinger's claim that the Soviets pressed the United States for an anti-Chinese alliance as the price of an early summit meeting. In Dobrynin's view, the Soviet leadership was not so naive as to hold out hopes of an alliance with Nixon, whose anti-Soviet positions were well known.[60]

The Kissinger visit to Beijing in August 1971 and subsequent announcement of a Sino-American summit in 1972 came as a big shock to many in the Soviet leadership. As Arbatov recounted in his memoirs, "The almost hysterical response to the summit seemed to me almost incomprehensible: why should this political step by the Americans come as such a complete surprise to so many people? There had been plenty of clear signals—for example, the 'Ping-Pong Diplomacy,'. . . . Long before *glasnost,* the official press had written endlessly about the possibility of 'an alliance between the Chinese leadership and world imperialism,' and had accused the Chinese and the West of planning such a thing. In our panic-stricken deliberations we may have been telling the Americans where they could hurt us most."[61]

Arbatov viewed the Sino-American rapprochement as a blessing in disguise for its role in prodding the Soviet leadership to seek détente with the United

States,[62] but most Soviet officials and scholars believed that China's interest in improving relations with the United States stemmed from the Chinese leadership's desire to create a united front against the Soviet Union.[63] The official commentary following Kissinger's secret visit to Beijing and the announcement of the US-PRC summit tersely warned against using Sino-American contacts against the Soviet Union.[64]

Right after Kissinger's visit to Beijing in 1971, Arbatov argued that "one cannot draw the conclusion that all Americans who favor improving the relations of the USA with China pursue aims that are hostile to other socialist countries."[65] Those Soviets who saw the Sino-American rapprochement as a long-term trend focused on the U.S. side of the question and maintained that the United States sought to improve relations with China to compensate for the growing weakness of imperialism vis-à-vis socialism. Vladimir Lukin, in a subtler version of this argument, contended that the American reassessment of China's role in international affairs stemmed in part from Chinese anti-Sovietism but also from the American perception of a change in the international system from a bipolar to a multipolar configuration.[66]

In the prevailing Soviet view, socialist development in China required normalization of relations with the Soviet Union, and Soviet commentary emphasized that the United States was a false friend to China.[67] According to Central Committee officials Oleg Rakhmanin and Boris Kulik (writing under the pseudonyms Borisov and Koloskov), the PRC's new relationship with the United States represented "a decisive step on the path to the reorientation of the foreign policy of China to the capitalist camp."[68]

Authoritative Soviet sources stressed that the emerging US-PRC relationship was more than just normalization, and represented a rapprochement on an antisocialist and nationalistic basis. As evidence, these sources posited Sino-American concurrence on disarmament and regional problems and cooperation in the ideological struggle against the Soviet Union.[69] A few Soviet policymakers feared that by teaming up with the Maoists, the United States was appeasing Chinese expansionism. As Rakhmanin (writing as Vladimirov) warned, "In the nuclear age, the Munich policy of appeasing a potential aggressor can turn against, above all, those who pursue it."[70]

Soviet policymakers watched closely to see what impact the Sino-American rapprochement would have on China's growth as a military power. Political observers warned that China would try to use an alliance with the United States to develop its military potential,[71] but military analysts, writing in the semi-classified journal *Voennaia Mysl'* in the early 1970s, called attention to the limitations of Chinese military capabilities.[72] Those military writers who seemed most concerned about the Chinese threat focused on political factors, such as the development of a Sino-American rapprochement directed against the USSR.[73] Lukin, however, expressing a minority view in the academic community, called attention to the discrepancy between actual Chinese capabilities and the resources the PRC would need to carry out its aims, even considering the rapprochement with the United States and the Chinese nuclear potential.[74]

The majority in the academic community highlighted the potential for conflict in the Sino-American relationship owing to the instability in the Chinese leadership, American disappointment regarding trade opportunities with the PRC, and the possibility of US-PRC competition in Asia for spheres of influence. According to Boris Zanegin, a scholar at the USA and Canada Institute, China would be unable to realize its political aims in an alliance with the United States and would be relegated to the status of a "junior partner."[75]

Still, U.S. officials expected that the Soviet leaders would continue to probe the United States about its intentions vis-à-vis China.[76] And that is exactly what Brezhnev did at the 1972 U.S.–Soviet summit meeting. As Dobrynin recalls, "Brezhnev pointedly told Nixon that the Chinese leadership was out to sow discord in international relations and exploit the differences between the Soviet Union and the United States, and other countries as well."[77] Indeed, Brezhnev requested a personal meeting with Nixon devoted mainly to China, in which he warned the American president against concluding any military agreements with the Chinese.[78] He even told Kissinger that the Soviet Union and the United States had a "joint obligation" to prevent China from becoming a major nuclear power.[79]

As U.S.-Soviet détente unfolded in the early 1970s, most officials and scholars blamed the Chinese leadership for seeking to improve relations with the United States on an anti-Soviet basis.[80] One striking characteristic of Soviet commentary on U.S.–China relations during this period is the belief that détente was an irreversible process and that sober-minded leaders in the United States would be unwilling to sacrifice détente for closer relations with the Chinese. Still, Soviet leaders criticized the Nixon Administration for failing to condemn Chinese diatribes against détente.[81]

Despite emerging tensions in the U.S.–Soviet relationship over trade and Third World conflicts that were leading American policymakers to reevaluate détente, Brezhnev's remarks at the Twenty-fifth Party Congress in February 1976 were almost effusive. The Soviet leader stated, for example, that: "The world is changing before our eyes and changing for the better"[82] because the prospects for avoiding war and achieving peaceful cooperation were greatly improved.[83] This view was corroborated in an article appearing in the authoritative *Opasnyi Kurs,* which stated: "World reality and world development do not hinge on prescriptions from the Forbidden City, but on the radical change in the balance of forces in the world scene in favor of socialism and revolutionary movements."[84]

While in the mid-1970s Soviet commentators continued to have faith in the enduring nature of détente and the shift in the correlation of forces in favor of socialism, by the end of the decade it was no longer possible to ignore the deteriorating international climate. Soviet officials began discussing the negative impact of the "China problem" on international relations. According to the official view, Chinese policies in the late 1970s contributed to the development of new complications and instability in the international arena.[85] In the only vaguely optimistic assessment of the situation in the late 1970s, an unsigned article in *Kommunist* noted that the changes in Chinese policies influenced the military situation but that this had no impact on the basic tendencies of world development.[86] Other official and academic analysts, however, saw the need to consider the possibility that Chinese policies could result in a change in the balance of power between socialism and capitalism.[87]

During the heyday of détente, Soviet officials warned their American counterparts against getting pulled into China's plans for global confrontation. By the late 1970s, as U.S.–Soviet relations soured, Gromyko told President Carter that collusion with China against the Soviet Union would be "a great mistake." Despite Carter's assurances that the United States was not attempting to create an anti-Soviet alliance with China, the Soviet Foreign Minister seemed less than convinced. Gromyko noted that the Soviet leadership "would like to hope that the USA does not intend to play the Chinese card against the Soviet Union."[88]

Almost a year later, the Soviet embassy in Washington reported back to Moscow that the Carter Administration (especially National Security Advisor Zbigniew Brzezinski) yearned "for a plot with China against the interests of the Soviet Union."[89] The embassy suggested that the Foreign Ministry continue to emphasize in its dealings with the Carter Administration that the creation of an anti-Soviet alliance with China would have negative consequences for U.S.–Soviet relations.[90]

Against the background of mounting problems in Soviet-American relations over arms control and human rights, the United States and China normalized relations during Deng Xiaoping's visit to Washington in January 1979. In an analysis of the Chinese leader's visit, KGB Chief Yuri Andropov downplayed its practical significance, but warned that Soviet toleration of U.S. attempts to play the China card would have its limits.[91]

Many Soviet scholars viewed the US-PRC normalization as destabilizing because they interpreted it as an anti-Soviet political-military alliance.[92] The Soviet Union had good reason to make this charge, as the PRC leaders openly called for a united front against the USSR. Soviet observers were also on the mark in contending that some circles in the United States wanted to apply pressure on the Soviet Union by playing the China card.[93] From the vantage point of the Chinese and Americans, however, such a partnership was necessary to maintain stability in the international system, in view of increases in the Soviet Union's military might and Soviet interventionism in the Third World.

Recently released transcripts of meetings between Kissinger and Chinese leaders show their initial reluctance in the first half of the 1970s to move too quickly with strategic cooperation.[94] Much like their Soviet counterparts, the Chinese leadership also harbored suspicions about the possibility of a Soviet-American condominium against China.[95]

By the end of the decade the Soviet leaders' worst fears were confirmed: American and Chinese leaders spoke of their long-term strategic relationship, their parallel interests, and the desirability of military relations between their two countries. According to the Soviet leadership, the US-PRC relationship did not represent a formal military alliance, but nonetheless represented a dangerous situation in the international arena.[96]

This view was reinforced by the overestimation of the military threat from China in both military and political circles. Speculation regarding Chinese military cooperation with the West fueled Soviet fears. Soviet officials, for example, stressed that the Chinese reforms placed a high priority on increasing the PRC's military potential.[97] Some observers noted in more balanced but nonauthoritative analyses that China was relatively weak but nonetheless posed a threat.[98] Military and civilian writers in *Voennaia Mysl'* also mentioned China's backwardness, but warned of the potentially dangerous implications of Chinese military ties with the West.[99]

An analysis of secondary sources on China's military deployment and acquisition patterns in the late 1970s does not reveal evidence of a mounting Chinese military threat during that period. According to Jonathan Pollack, the Chinese portrayal of the Soviet Union as the more dangerous superpower did not translate into fear of an imminent Soviet attack against China.[100] The Chinese military tended to concentrate on preparing for border and theater warfare, rather than strategic war. Conventional forces were massed near but not right at the border so as to avoid provoking an attack.[101] The one and a half million men facing the Soviet Union in seventy-five divisions (a 3:1 numerical advantage) were supposed to provide a numerical deterrent, given the low level of Chinese weapons technology.[102] Force comparisons between the Soviet Union and China lead to the conclusion that Chinese conventional forces were inferior to the Soviet forces in all indicators except number. Given that the Soviet Union was unlikely to undertake an all-out invasion of China, a situation where the Chinese numerical advantage would be key, more limited assaults on strategic areas such as Xinjiang or Northern Manchuria with air power would reveal the vulnerability of the Chinese "people's war" strategy.[103] In addition to technical inferiority, Chinese forces had limited mobility and were deficient in some types of weapons. Lacking the facilities and logistics for operations outside China, they served primarily as a defensive force.[104]

Chinese military modernization, the last component of the Four Modernizations plan, seemed to be a long-term aim due to a range of constraints. Although the Chinese purchased some foreign systems, these were to be used to improve tactical defense. Chinese military shopping trips involved much more looking than buying, however, and represented an effort to give direction to the home defense industry.[105] Military modernization had to follow industrial modernization, above all for reasons of cost.[106] In addition, the revolutionary ethic of the Chinese People's Liberation Army also provided an impediment to the revision of strategy to emphasize weaponry.[107]

Despite the Soviet military's grasp of Chinese capabilities, many thought that as long as there was no guarantee that an irrational China would not attack, the Soviet Union had to be prepared for this eventuality.[108] Many Soviet analysts accused the United States of naively appeasing China.[109] Yet some Soviets continued to have faith that sober forces in the West would foresee that a strong China could turn against them in the future.[110]

Soviet analysts pointed to the Chinese intervention in Vietnam in 1979 as a clear indication that the new Chinese leaders continued to pursue Maoist hegemonic aims.[111] The Chinese action was disconcerting for several reasons. Soviet officials noted that the PRC's aggression against Vietnam was evidence of a new stage in its approach to socialist states.[112] It also showed that the Chinese leaders were willing to put their warmongering slogans into action.[113] Contending that Deng's visit to the United States just prior to the intervention demonstrated America's tacit approval, Soviet observers became more alarmed about the consequences of the US-PRC normalization.[114] An unsigned article in *Kommunist* warned against the "bloody fruits of playing the China card," which could ultimately "engulf the whole world into the abyss of destructive war."[115]

Just after the Chinese invasion on February 17, 1979, Brezhnev and Carter spoke on the hot line, but this communication did nothing to reduce Soviet suspicions regarding U.S. tacit support for the Chinese military action. Carter subsequently asked Dobrynin to reassure the Soviet leadership that the United States had no advanced knowledge of the Chinese attack and in fact had warned

Deng Xiaoping against taking such an action. The Soviet ambassador noted, however, that it would be difficult to disabuse Brezhnev of the notion that the timing of the invasion, immediately following the Sino-American summit, was mere coincidence.[116]

Thus, the confidence displayed by the Soviet foreign policy elite in the early 1970s that the United States set greater store in détente than in a rapprochement with China turned out to be misplaced. As détente unraveled later in the decade due to Soviet interventionism in the Third World, relations with China became more important to the American effort to counter what was perceived as a growing Soviet threat. Soviet policymakers maintained an uncompromising position in relations with the Chinese, resulting in the USSR's increasing isolation in the international arena.

Chinese Domestic Politics

By the mid-1970s, most Soviet observers saw signs of increasing crisis within the PRC as a result of Maoist policies.[117] They continued to discuss Chinese domestic politics in terms of the struggle between Maoist and socialist forces in the Chinese leadership, although the latter were considered to be removed from the forefront of policymaking. Some Soviet observers presented a more complex picture of events in China, however. For example, Vilia Gel'bras noted that "the CPC [CCP] is not a party of like-minded people." In his view, diminishing support for the Maoist regime reflected its inability to present a coherent theoretical framework as an alternative to socialism.[118]

While most Soviet analysts attributed the predominance of the Maoist line to the Chinese leadership's appeal to nationalistic feelings among the population and to the isolation of the PRC from the rest of the socialist community, one alternative posited that Maoist dominance was due to the impact of the difficult domestic conditions in China, particularly the need to overcome economic backwardness and eradicate feudal vestiges. According to V. Larev, Lenin foresaw the possibility of mistakes and even backsliding in the process of the transition to socialism by backward countries. In Larev's view, Mao used these difficulties as a pretext to lead the PRC away from the socialist path and fulfill his hegemonic aims.[119] Fedor Burlatskii also linked Maoist policies to social conditions, emphasizing the continued influence of Taoism, Confucianism, and populism in Chinese political culture. Unlike Larev, however, Burlatskii concluded that this blend of Chinese traditions and Maoist power produced a particular type of ideological regime, which merited study on its own terms.[120] Efforts like Burlatskii's to make sense out of the Chinese case in its own terms were few and far between. At times, scholars and officials asked hard questions, but then expended little effort to find any real answers.[121]

How did these analysts propose to deal with this new phenomenon? They ruled out the excommunication of the CCP, and advocated struggle against Maoism on the one hand, and normalization of Sino-Soviet relations on the other.[122] If the Chinese leaders were deluded about the main trends in international politics, such as the shift in global balance of power in favor of socialism and the need to pursue policies in line with the Soviet Union's leadership of the socialist community, the prevailing Soviet view argued that sooner or later they would come to their senses.[123] The only thing the Soviet Union could do in the meantime would be to encourage the socialist forces in the CCP. This they would do by holding out the possibility of Soviet-Chinese cooperation once the PRC returned to socialist positions, and wait for these socialists to emerge triumphantly in the succession struggle in the PRC. However, encouraging Chinese socialists would also involve struggling against the Maoists and rebuffing the latter group's attempts to split the socialist movement.

Maoism without Mao

For years, Soviet leaders counted on leadership change in China to remove the Chinese challenge to Soviet authority in the communist movement. After Mao's death, however, most Soviet policymakers saw no reason for optimism. They accused Hua Guofeng of pursuing Maoism without Mao and interpreted the new reform program, the Four Modernizations, as a continuation of previous economic policies.

Paradoxically, Soviet analyses in the late 1970s portrayed China as both posing a threat to Soviet gains in the world arena and as a crisis-ridden and weak state. Soviet observers closely monitored the leadership struggle taking place in China during Mao's last years; in analyzing the post-Mao succession, they grappled with the implications of instability in China. Would the weakened communist party and state institutions enable the military to strengthen its hold? Was there a viable opposition to Maoism? Soviet observers were divided on the meaning of the Tiananmen demonstrations in 1976 and the Democracy Wall movement in 1979, for example. Officials and academics interpreted these as evidence of mounting social tensions and discontent,[124] although some scholars saw signs of the development of a rather disorganized opposition to Maoism.[125]

Soviet officials and academics generally concurred that Mao's death exacerbated the factional struggle within the CCP, resulting in continued campaigns, such as the struggle against the Gang of Four.[126] They disagreed, however, over the sources of the leadership struggle. Some argued that Maoist politics was characterized by perpetual power struggle.[127] Burlatskii, on the other hand, attributed the instability at the top to the lack of a formal succession mechanism,[128] also a growing problem for the Soviet Union at the time due to Brezhnev's declining health. Most Soviet officials and academics agreed on one point: Mao's death did not immediately bring back to power the long-awaited pro-Soviet forces in the CCP.

Unlike Western officials who detected evidence of Chinese departures from Maoism, most Soviet policymakers argued instead that the Chinese leadership continued Maoism without Mao, an interpretation that gave credence to their hostile policy toward China.[129] Some Soviet officials genuinely believed that the CCP should be condemned for its deviation from the Soviet model, while others owed their positions to their support for the policy of containing China.

As a result, Soviet analysis continued to downplay evidence of departures from Maoism in the late 1970s. For example, most Soviet observers considered the Four Modernizations reform program to be a new strategy for achieving the same hegemonic aims.[130] In February 1978, when Hua Guofeng called for China to become a strong developed state with decisive geopolitical influence by 2000, many Soviet scholars concluded that economic reform was designed primarily to help China achieve superpower status more quickly.[131] Even Burlatskii, one of the most charitable of Soviet analysts of the Four Modernizations in the late 1970s, commented, "Without a doubt, the main aim of modernization consists of transforming China in the shortest possible time into a strong military power and in so doing to change its role in the contemporary world."[132]

After Deng's reform program prevailed over Hua's new Great Leap, some Soviet analysts still derided the continuity between Maoist voluntaristic economic methods and the overly ambitious Four Modernizations.[133] Ironically, Soviet criticisms of Chinese policies paralleled those of the Gang of Four. A change in Soviet evaluations of Chinese domestic politics would have to await leadership change and the launching of economic reform in the USSR in the mid-1980s.

REACTION IN THE BORDER REGIONS

In various ways, Soviet regional and republic party authorities reinforced Moscow's efforts to coordinate support for the CPSU's China policy.[134] At the center's request, the Khabarovsk party committee spearheaded the development of television and radio programs and the publication of materials that validated the history of Russia's claim to the Far East and refuted China's territorial pretensions.[135] Although officials in the Soviet border regions were situated on the front lines of the Sino-Soviet conflict, in the 1970s they had limited opportunities to suggest policy alternatives to their counterparts in Moscow. Documents in the Khabarovsk party archive do, however, show signs of differences in views on China policy between center and peripheries, even in this early period.

Tensions in Sino-Soviet relations had the most immediate impact on life in the border regions. The Sino-Soviet split in the 1960s led to the suspension of border trade in 1966, to the detriment of the economic health of these areas. At the same time, the Soviet military buildup in the border regions began. When armed confrontations erupted on the border, anti-Chinese violence reportedly broke out in Vladivostok.[136] Many local boys lost their lives in the border clashes in 1969, and their stories continue to be remembered even today in an exhibit at the Border Guard Museum in Vladivostok.

How did Communist Party activists in the Soviet border regions respond to the news of Aleksei Kosygin's September 11, 1969, meeting with Zhou Enlai in Beijing? On September 22, the regional and city party *aktiv* convened to discuss the Central Committee's account of Kosygin's discussion with Zhou.[137] The party committee then reported back to the Central Committee in Moscow.[138] The Khabarovskii Krai report to Moscow focused on the good news—many socialists applauded the meeting as a positive step towards resolving Soviet-Chinese differences through peaceful means.

To show support for Moscow's handling of the border clashes, Khabarovsk party officials left out the details of the local *aktiv*'s concerns about continued tension.[139] For example, during the September 22 meeting, the Secretary of the Khabarovsk City Committee of the CPSU, comrade Pasternak, described the state of relations as "increasingly tense" and observed that the anti-Soviet hysteria and propaganda in Beijing had not abated.[140] Comrade Bokan', the head of the political department of a military district in the region, noted that there were more than 300 incidents of incursions by Chinese citizens onto Soviet territory in his district in 1969 alone. Bokan' urged his comrades to be prepared for any provocation on the border, while his colleague in the military district, comrade Popov, noted that Chinese ideological positions were dangerous for the international communist movement "and cannot but evoke alarm" among the Soviet people.[141]

Because the region's reporting function served to legitimate the Center's policies, such comments by the regional *aktiv*, which showed that the Zhou-Kosygin meeting had done little to reduce alarm in Khabarovsk, were omitted. The Khabarovskii Krai committee was reluctant to address substantive problems or uncomfortable questions in reports to the Central Committee in Moscow—the Center only found out what it wanted to hear.[142]

At times regional and central government interests coincided, for example, on the subject of Bolshoi Ussuriiskii/Heixiazi and Tarabarov/Yinlong Islands across from Khabarovsk. In late 1972, the Khabarovskii Krai Party Committee authorized the city of Khabarovsk to promote economic development on the disputed islands.[143] A large farm and dachas were built on Bolshoi Ussuriiskii/Heixiazi Island, which indeed have bolstered the city's claim to the island, even to this day. The regional party committee also pledged to further encourage the publication of books upholding the Soviet Union's position on the history of Russia's settlement (*osvoenie*) in the Russian Far East.[144]

Meetings with ordinary Khabarovsk workers tended to provide a more faithful picture of center-regional differences on China policy. Typically the workers' most provocative questions were listed at the end of the Khabarovsk committee's report—without comment. At one meeting, for example, workers asked the regional party authorities: Is war between the PRC and the USSR possible? Could Mao use atomic weapons against the USSR? What is the military potential of the USSR? When will the civilian population of the *krai* receive military training? Why aren't Soviet borders fortified enough?[145] By mentioning the workers' concerns in this indirect way, Khabarovsk officials were able to convey to Moscow that in their region not everyone was satisfied with Moscow's response to the Sino-Soviet clashes. Although Khabarovsk officials affirmed their support for Soviet China policy, the inclusion of such questions by workers reveals signs of disagreement between the Khabarovsk and Moscow party officials over the adequacy of Soviet responses to the China threat.

Differences between Moscow and the region continued in the 1970s. As early as 1972, for example, the Khabarovskii Krai party secretary proposed reopening border trade between the Soviet Union and China because the region depended on this trade for access to otherwise unavailable goods and for a market for its excess production.[146] Despite this plea, however, Sino-Soviet border trade was not reopened until 1983. For the most part, in the early 1970s, the regional party continued to downplay dissatisfaction with aspects of Soviet China policy. At another party meeting, for example, participants suggested that one way to improve the security of the border regions would be to improve the standard of living of the Amur river workers. In the final version of the minutes of the meeting, however, this comment was crossed out.

Despite the interest in the regions in expanding economic ties with the Chinese, by the end of the decade, border areas were further militarized and integrated into Soviet contingency plans vis-à-vis China. A new military command structure was put in place and military exercises were held in the border zone in an effort to intimidate the Chinese. Thus, the lines of demarcation in the Sino-Soviet dispute became more entrenched in the 1970s, and the Russian border regions increasingly were cut off from their Chinese neighbors.

CONCLUSIONS

As a result of their overlapping interests in socialist unity, the primacy of the Soviet model of socialism, and the security of the border regions, Brezhnev's coalition on foreign policy elaborated a policy of containing China, which soon became entrenched in the Foreign Ministry and Central Committee bureaucracies and proved remarkably impervious to changes in either the international environment or in China itself. Nonetheless, despite the dominance of the containment coalition over Moscow's China policy, regional officials expressed interest in reopening Sino-Soviet border trade by the early 1970s, military officers objectively commented on Chinese military weakness, and voices for change in the academic community saw moderating trends in Chinese policies by the end of the decade. At the time, these countervailing pressures proved insufficient to reverse the momentum of the existing policy of containing China.

PART II
THE ROAD TO BEIJING

4 / Leadership Change in the USSR
and Sino-Soviet Relations, 1980–85

By the late 1970s, Soviet China policy was immobilized in a pattern of containment. As Soviet officials saw it, Mao's death had failed to produce the desired return to pro-Soviet positions and the post-Mao succession justified the continuation of the USSR's longstanding containment policy. Initially the prospects for improving Sino-Soviet relations looked bleak. Following Deng Xiaoping's January 1979 visit to the United States, when Sino-American relations were normalized formally, Chinese forces attacked Vietnam. While Beijing's attempt to "punish" Vietnam for its intervention in Cambodia failed and Chinese forces were forced to withdraw, the Chinese action accentuated Soviet fears of Sino-American collusion and confirmed Soviet hardliners' arguments for containing China.[1] As Brezhnev's health declined, more and more foreign policy and arms control decisions were deferred to the Politburo coalition favoring containment. But later Andropov, a key member of the coalition, would break the inertia in China policy once he achieved the top leadership position.

Nonetheless, even by the late 1970s there had been some indications of a thaw, beginning with signs of interest within China in reducing polemics with the Soviet Union. At the time, Chinese reevaluations of the Soviet Union were caught up in internal debates about Mao's legacy. Deng Xiaoping, championing the need to "seek truth from facts" rather than upholding whatever Mao said and did—the approach favored by his rival, Hua Guofeng—asserted in June 1978 that Marxism had been revised constantly since Marx's day.[2] In Deng's view this was a natural process of adjusting to changing realities. As Deng's view gained ascendance, the Communist Party of the Soviet Union was no longer termed "revisionist," which had been the mainstay of Maoist attacks for more than 15 years.[3] Instead the Chinese attacked the Soviets for their hegemonism.

In September 1979, at a conference on Soviet literature in Harbin, for the first time in decades a majority of the delegates called the Soviet domestic system "essentially socialist" although they continued to refer to Soviet foreign policy as hegemonic.[4] The conference report was published in a Heilongjiang provincial journal, *Wenyi Baijia* [*Cultural professional*], but provincial officials reprimanded the journal staff for their premature reinterpretation, and the issue was pulled off library shelves.[5]

A few months later, in a January 1980 speech to party cadres, Deng Xiaoping himself called the USSR a socialist country, albeit by paying the Soviet Union a backhanded compliment. Deng stated that "The Socialist system is one thing, and the specific way of building socialism is another. Counting from the October Revolution, the Soviet Union has been engaged in building socialism for 63 years, but it is still in no position to boast about how to do it." Even such faint praise as this remained controversial in China and did not appear in print until 1983.[6]

By April 1980, however, *People's Daily* was condemning articles published in 1963 and 1964 that had accused the Soviet Union of revisionism.[7] Confirming this shift, the street in Beijing where the Soviet embassy was located—called "Struggle against Revisionism Street" since the Cultural Revolution—regained its former nonpolitical name.[8]

Talks on outstanding political issues, proposed by the Chinese in lieu of extending the Sino-Soviet Friendship treaty, were scheduled to resume in early 1980. When the Soviets invaded Afghanistan in late December 1979, however, the Chinese cancelled the talks, declaring that the "Soviet invasion of Afghanistan menaces world peace and the security of China as well."[9]

Despite their condemnation of the Soviet intervention, the Chinese kept some lines of communication open. While political talks were broken off indefinitely, border river navigation talks were held on schedule, from February 5 to March 19, 1980.

Soviet policy towards China softened in 1982, as new personnel undertook a policy review, and differences between the Foreign Ministry and the Central Committee over China policy became more conspicuous.[10] While the Foreign Ministry saw some changes for the better in Chinese policies, the Central Committee—particularly Oleg Rakhmanin's Department for Liaison with Socialist Countries—continued to be highly critical of the Chinese reforms and rapprochement with the West. For example, when diplomats at the Soviet embassy in Beijing followed the Central Committee's lead in its 1982 annual report about China, their report was warmly received by the Central Committee. Foreign Ministry officials sharply criticized it, however, and sent a letter to the embassy tersely stating that "Nobody in Moscow thinks any longer in this stupid way about China."[11] This was not entirely true: following Mikhail Suslov's death in January 1982, another conservative official, Konstantin Chernenko, was given responsibility for ideology. Chernenko was equally unwilling to reassess Soviet positions on China.

Andropov's rise to power created some new momentum in Sino-Soviet relations, however, and he appears to have been the initiator of a more pragmatic approach to China that involved the expansion of economic relations even while political differences remained.[12] According to Dobrynin, Andropov's authority over foreign policy had been growing slowly and steadily throughout the 1970s as Brezhnev's health deteriorated.[13] Key issues such as China policy and arms control were handed over to specially formed commissions within the Politburo and by the end of the decade Andropov, along with Gromyko and Ustinov, became the key architects of Soviet foreign policy in the Politburo.[14] Of the three, Andropov was in the best position to exert influence: while Gromyko had expertise in foreign affairs and Ustinov in defense, Andropov was well versed in both.[15]

He also had considerable experience in dealing with socialist bloc relations, as he had served as ambassador to Hungary from 1954 to 1956 and then as head of the Central Committee Department for Liaison with Socialist Countries from 1957 to 1967. Since Suslov's job as ideology secretary involved overseeing relations with socialist countries, it is unlikely that Andropov's differences with Suslov were fundamental.[16] Nonetheless, when Andropov headed the Liaison Department, he hired a group of reform-minded consultants, including Georgy Arbatov, Fedor Burlatskii, Aleksandr Bovin, Lev Deliusin, and Oleg Bogomolov, all of whom consistently favored improving relations with China and implementing reforms at home. Andropov himself had been involved in China policy at the time of the worst polemics between the leaders of the Soviet Union and China in the early 1960s, but according to Burlatskii he never envisioned the conflict leading to war.[17] In fact, Andropov wrote an article in April 1964 in which he stated that China was a socialist country and that differences with the Chinese leadership were temporary.[18]

Brezhnev's March 1982 Tashkent speech marked the beginning of the Soviet Union's efforts to mend fences with China. The speech, drafted when the general secretary was very ill, reflected the ascendance of Andropov at the expense of Gromyko and others who opposed any softening of the anti-Chinese line.[19]

The speech included many conciliatory remarks and proposed that political talks be resumed. Brezhnev emphasized that despite Soviet criticism of Chinese policies for departing from socialist theory and practice, the Soviet Union never denied "the existence of a socialist system in China." He dismissed Chinese assertions of a Soviet threat to China and, playing on Sino-American tensions, stated that the Soviet Union never pursued a two-China policy.[20] Recalling friendlier days, Brezhnev expressed his hope for improved relations on the basis of mutual respect and noninterference, and without detriment to third countries (referring to Soviet interests in Afghanistan, Vietnam, and

Mongolia).[21] The Chinese reacted with reserve, contending that normalization depended on the resolution of what they called the three obstacles—the Soviet intervention in Afghanistan, the Vietnamese occupation of Cambodia, and the presence of Soviet troops along the Sino-Soviet border and in Mongolia—which the Soviet side refused to discuss until 1986.

The cautious Chinese reply to the 1982 Tashkent speech irked the Soviet leadership and weakened the position of those in Moscow advocating greater efforts to improve relations with China. On May 20, *Pravda* printed an editorial, "On Soviet-Chinese Relations," signed by I. Alexandrov, a pseudonym for the Soviet leadership. The main portions of Brezhnev's Tashkent speech were restated, but the thrust of the article criticized the wary Chinese reaction to the speech.[22]

Despite the reserved Chinese response, a major review of China's Soviet policy was taking place in the summer of 1982 as a result of a reassessment of the Soviet threat. In the Chinese leadership's view, a more resolved United States had succeeded in impeding Soviet expansionist aims in Afghanistan and elsewhere. These difficulties could account for Brezhnev's more conciliatory line in Tashkent. Foreign Minister Qian Qichen, at the time the Vice-Foreign Minister for Soviet affairs, recalled being summoned to a meeting at Deng's home, where the Chinese leader called for "a big move" toward improving relations with Moscow. Before any major policy change would be undertaken, however, Deng insisted that the Soviet Union would have to show good will by voluntarily resolving one of the three obstacles. On August 10, 1982, a high-level Foreign Ministry official was dispatched to Moscow to convey Deng's message. Ten days later the Soviets replied that they would be prepared to meet with the Chinese to discuss the bilateral relationship "at any time, at any venue, and at any level."[23]

In a September speech in Baku, Brezhnev reiterated that the Soviet leadership considered the establishment of normalized relations between the Soviet Union and China to be an important matter.[24] The Chinese responded somewhat more favorably; Zhao Ziyang told Japanese Prime Minister Zenko Suzuki that the normalization of Sino-Soviet relations would take time and required that the Soviet Union remove the threats to China posed by the three obstacles. Zhao further stated that the PRC had no intention of playing the Soviet card against the United States, nor would China tolerate being used as a card in any other country's hand. Political consultations between the two states resumed in October 1982, one month before Brezhnev's death, paving the way for gradual rapprochement.

When Andropov succeeded Leonid Brezhnev as general secretary in 1982, he immediately began repairing relations with China.[25] In a sign of Chinese interest in improving ties with the USSR, Foreign Minister Huang Hua attended Brezhnev's funeral, where Andropov had a long conversation with him.[26] Andropov maintained the momentum from Brezhnev's Tashkent speech, advocating Sino-Soviet normalization and improved relations with all socialist states, including China. One month later, the Soviet Union and China opened a new channel for dialogue on international questions, a means of ensuring regular high-level contacts. These meetings began in Beijing in 1983, when the Chinese Foreign Ministry invited Mikhail Kapitsa, who had just been promoted to Deputy Foreign Minister, to participate in yearly discussions of foreign policy issues with his Chinese counterpart.[27]

When Andropov took over as general secretary, he brought with him former consultants from his Central Committee days in the 1960s. They would play a key role as advocates for a shift in Soviet China policy.[28] Arbatov, for example, convinced Andropov to mention this as a priority in one of his first speeches.[29] Not surprisingly, the more conservative leaders in the Politburo, such as Chernenko and Ustinov, opposed the influence of liberal-minded outsiders and at times tried to poison relations between Andropov and his consultants.[30]

LIMITS TO THE SINO-SOVIET RAPPROCHEMENT IN THE EARLY 1980S

The Andropov interregnum was insufficient to achieve a fundamental break with the inflexible foreign and domestic policies that characterized the early 1980s, now termed the period of *zastoi*, or stagnation. A recently declassified transcript of a May 1983 Politburo meeting demonstrates the limits that the Andropov leadership imposed on any shift in China policy. Andropov and his colleagues focused mainly on expanding economic cooperation. Gromyko, though portrayed by several of his colleagues as caught up in the "anti-Chinese inertia," by this point was pragmatic enough to see the need for further steps to achieve diplomatic progress. During the meeting, however, Defense Minister Ustinov rejected Gromyko's suggestion to scale back the Soviet military presence along the border and in Mongolia. No Politburo member was prepared to contemplate a change of policy on Cambodia, and the issue of Afghanistan was not even on the table.[31]

> *Andropov:* I think that the Chinese will not go any farther in the negotiations with us than when they stopped. But all the facts show that they could expand their economic cooperation with the Soviet Union. In fact by their own initiative they proposed a trade agreement for this year which would significantly increase the trade turnover from last year's level. In connection with this, perhaps it would be a good idea to send comrade Arkhipov to conduct the requisite negotiations,

to sound them out. And if we are successful in expanding economic cooperation with China in line with [exchanges with] cultural, athletic, and other organizations, then this would be, in my opinion, a step forward. . . .[32]

Gromyko: . . . The People's Republic of China expresses the desire to expand economic ties. Even on a practical level, it is already taking some steps in this direction, for example, by expanding the trade turnover.

Andropov: We should explore this, as I said.

Gromyko: I think that the Chinese won't go any farther than this. One of the conditions for the normalization of relations that they put forward is the withdrawal of forces from the border. It seems to me that it would be possible to consider this. But then the Chinese began to insist that the Vietnamese withdraw from Cambodia.

Andropov: I think that it would evidently not be appropriate for us to raise this question.

Gromyko: Regarding Mongolia. Perhaps we should withdraw a portion of the forces from the border.[33]

Ustinov: . . . Regarding Mongolia, it must be said that if we withdraw the Soviet forces located there to our territory, then we will lose a good base, we will deprive ourselves of a forward defense area. Indeed, everything is built for us there. Therefore there's no sense in making any moves back to the Soviet border. Regarding Cambodia and Vietnam, we have discussed this many times. I suggest that we shouldn't lose the achievements of these military bases, we need to hold the positions gained there.[34]

Tikhonov: . . . All the initiatives for the expansion of trade turnover between the USSR and China come from China. This is very important. Therefore it is necessary to explore a basis for the expansion in the near future of economic and other relations with China and send comrade Arkhipov for negotiations. As far as the withdrawal of forces from the border, this seems unrealistic.[35]

Grishin: With China we can develop economic relations on a higher level. Of course, the Chinese won't give up Cambodia and we won't be able to reach any agreement on this with them.[36]

Deng Xiaoping commented in February 1984 that radical change in Sino-Soviet relations was unlikely as long as the three obstacles remained, but this need not impede the development of relations in other areas.[37] Thanks to the Chinese leadership's new receptivity to expanding bilateral relations with the Soviet Union, some progress did occur in the mid-1980s. Tourism and student and cultural exchanges started up again, and bilateral trade increased appreciably. The Sino-Soviet Friendship Society and its affiliates in the border regions restored contacts in 1983 and exchanges began again in 1984.

Progress was slow as Moscow continued to sidestep the underlying causes of the dispute—the three obstacles. On several occasions, for example, the Soviet Union proposed that the two sides engage in confidence-building measures on the border,[38] but the Chinese always preferred to wait until the resolution of outstanding border demarcation questions.[39]

CONTINUATION OF CONTAINMENT

Although there was some speculation about Soviet willingness to scale down their presence on the Sino-Soviet border,[40] in fact the number of troops there grew slightly. In the early 1980s, the Soviets increased ground forces in the Far Eastern strategic theater from forty-six divisions in 1981 to fifty-three in 1985.[41] In addition, the acceleration of Soviet deployments of SS-20 missiles in Siberia in 1982–83 further alarmed the Chinese, who added this to their list of grievances against the Soviet Union.[42] As Brezhnev's health failed and he began to play less of a role in international issues, Gromyko, and even Andropov, proved unwilling to challenge the Defense Ministry on key issues such as the SS-20 decision.[43]

Soviet military relations with Vietnam also expanded during this period. In November 1983, for example, the Soviet Union deployed TU-16 Badger medium-range bombers in Vietnam. Not surprisingly, Soviet policies toward Vietnam and the USSR's continued intervention in Afghanistan reinforced the rationale for China's tilt towards the United States, despite Deng's stated interest in equidistance.[44]

Soviet political leaders justified continuing their policy of containing China because of the military content of the Sino-American relationship in the early 1980s. An October 1980 Central Committee document warned, for example, that "the partnership between American imperialism and Peking hegemonism, a negative development in world politics, dangerous for all humanity, is more actively expanding into the military sphere."[45] Considering that Sino-American military ties were stalled from 1981 to 1983 because of tensions over U.S. arms sales to Taiwan, it is perplexing that at this time Soviet officials focused on the issue of military cooperation between the United States and China.

Secretary of State Alexander Haig's June 1981 trip to Beijing, occurring right after President Reagan's decision to make China eligible to purchase American weapons, alarmed Soviet leaders, who interpreted it as a dangerous new turn of events.[46] At the time, the Taiwan issue was the primary reason behind China's lack of enthusiasm for the expansion of military cooperation with the United States, and the Chinese were not prepared to contemplate arms purchases while the United States continued arms sales to Taiwan.[47] Since the Chinese leadership saw President Reagan as more committed than the previous administration to containing Soviet expansionism, they saw no reason to overlook U.S. policy toward Taiwan to sustain Sino-American strategic cooperation against the USSR.[48]

The lack of progress in Sino-American military cooperation failed to relieve Soviet concerns, however. Soviet policymakers viewed Defense Secretary Weinberger's September 1983 trip to Beijing with equal apprehension.[49] Although Chinese and American officials discussed sales of defensive weapons, in fact the Chinese government did not purchase any U.S. weapons until September 1985.[50]

Some commentators suggested that the United States had its own reasons for pushing forward China's military modernization—to alter the strategic balance in the U.S. favor,[51] disrupt the Sino-Soviet normalization process,[52] and achieve greater stability in Sino-American relations.[53] By late 1984 a few Soviet academics began calling attention to continued Sino-American differences despite the military relationship.[54]

Some Soviet academic analysts argued that the modernization of the military was the priority of the Chinese reform program.[55] Considering that modernization of the military was listed as only the fourth priority in the Four Modernizations policy and that Deng Xiaoping's main interest in the early 1980s was in trimming the size of the armed forces and in diminishing its role in Chinese society, this emphasis on Chinese militarization was misplaced.[56]

On April 15, 1985, Deng demonstrated the priority of economic reform by announcing that the PLA would be reduced by one million men, cutting the Chinese armed forces by one fourth. Although military modernization remained important, the Chinese party and military leaders reached a consensus on the necessity of emphasizing economic reform while streamlining the PLA to create a leaner and meaner force in the future.[57]

Unlike their civilian counterparts, who saw political advantage in continuing to label China a threat to Soviet security, Soviet military analysts understood that a modern military required an advanced level of economic achievement, which China had not yet reached. The Soviet Union was facing this dilemma as well, due to the challenge posed by the Reagan Administration's

Strategic Defense Initiative. The aim of the Chinese reforms, they claimed, was greater technological prowess but this would entail overcoming a problematic political and economic situation, the low level of general education and military training of the forces, and the negative impact of traditions.[58]

High-ranking Soviet military officers pointed to considerable obstacles facing China's military modernization, even if Western assistance were received, and noted that the Chinese defeat in Vietnam demonstrated the need for better training and command of ground forces. According to one military observer, the technological level of the relatively developed Chinese aviation industry still lagged behind that of the industrialized countries by ten to fifteen years. Chinese industry faced difficulties in producing engines, navigation equipment, and electronic guidance systems—problems compounded by the lack of qualified cadres.[59] Chinese officials tried to redress these shortcomings by copying foreign designs, often through third countries, or by purchasing Western technology, such as the British Spey jet engines.[60]

As another military observer noted, although Chinese naval forces currently lacked aircraft carriers and nuclear submarines,[61] by the end of the 1980s, China's naval capabilities could increase appreciably.[62] Thus, Soviet military experts envisioned a long-term threat from Chinese military modernization.

Although the Soviet political leadership remained preoccupied with Sino-American military ties, the issue was not discussed in *Voennaia Mysl'*. Moreover, while the Soviets noted in 1982 that the Chinese planned to freeze and eventually reduce the number of ground troops by 300,000 to 400,000 men, mostly in military administration,[63] there was no discussion of the 1985 announcement of cuts of 1,000,000 men in the PLA. In fact, from 1982 to 1985, no articles at all about the Chinese military forces were published in *Voennaia Mysl'*. The silence by the military on these issues may indicate that the Chinese military threat was being reevaluated at the same time the political leaders were reviewing China policy as a whole.

CHERNENKO AND CHINA POLICY

Andropov broke the torpor of the Brezhnev years by exposing pressing economic concerns[64] and linking Sino-Soviet normalization to the resolution of economic problems in both countries.[65] After Andropov died in early 1984, the momentum toward an improvement in relations with China stalled, though many of Andropov's initiatives were continued. As before, foreign policy responsibility largely rested in the hands of Gromyko and Ustinov—a situation that some critics dubbed the *dvoekratiia*, or "two-man rule."[66] In his first major address as general secretary, on March 9, 1984, Chernenko said that the

Soviet Union consistently advocated normalization of relations with China and noted that an improvement in relations would "facilitate the enhancement of the role of socialism in international life."[67]

Despite the continuity in Chernenko's China policy, Sino-Soviet polemics, which had virtually ceased since the time of the Tashkent speech in March 1982, resumed in January 1984, largely because of mounting Sino-Vietnamese tensions. In February 1984, CCP General Secretary Hu Yaobang made a highly publicized trip to the border with Vietnam and urged the Chinese to be ready to fight the Vietnamese. The Soviets responded by sending the aircraft carrier *Minsk* and the amphibious assault ship, *Ivan Rogov*, to the Gulf of Tonkin. The Vietnamese shelled the border with China, sparking Chinese border raids in April.

Sino-Vietnamese tensions and the Reagan summit meeting delayed Deputy Premier Ivan Arkhipov's visit to China by more than six months.[68] His December 1984 visit was the highest-level Sino-Soviet meeting in decades and, since Arkhipov had served as a senior economic advisor in China in the heyday of cooperation in the 1950s, reinforced the earlier trend toward a Sino-Soviet rapprochement. During his stay, important economic agreements were signed, including Soviet aid in renovating Soviet-built plants,[69] but the Chinese were quick to emphasize that the Arkhipov visit did not represent a breakthrough in Sino-Soviet relations. The Soviets and the Chinese resumed their polemics immediately after the meeting. A January 1985 article in *Beijing Review* blamed Soviet hegemonism for the deterioration of Sino-Soviet relations,[70] and the Soviets renewed their criticism of China after renewed Sino-Vietnamese border clashes that month.[71] Exchanges of media insults were to last until Chernenko's death.

CONCLUSIONS

Despite the pressures for continuity in Soviet China policy, the period of protracted succession in the Soviet Union in the first half of the 1980s created sufficient momentum for a slow process of Sino-Soviet rapprochement to unfold. In his speech in Tashkent in March 1982, one of his last, Brezhnev left the door open for an improvement in relations with China. Andropov took this even further, although he remained reluctant to address any of the substantive obstacles to a Sino-Soviet rapprochement. This momentum quickly abated once Chernenko assumed power, but Gorbachev and his new team ultimately would prove able to build on early efforts and achieve real progress in relations in the latter half of the decade.

5 / Pressures for Continuity and Change in Soviet China Policy in the Early 1980s

Soviet China policy in the early 1980s evolved very slowly away from containment and in the direction of a cautious rapprochement. The gradual change in official policy contrasted with the emergence in the three main policy audiences—the border regions, the Moscow policy community, and the international communist movement—of voices urging a more rapid shift. Regional officials in the Soviet Union as well as in China called for the resumption of border trade. They promoted a vision of Sino-Soviet cooperation well ahead of their colleagues at the center who still favored the containment option.

Meanwhile, in Moscow, policymakers and academics began expressing divergent views about the prospects for meaningful economic reform in China and the consequences for the USSR of the deepening Sino-American relationship. To be sure, censorship set parameters for any change in the official narrative of Soviet China policy, but Yuri Andropov's rise to power provided some new opportunity for alternative views about China policy to be heard. Similarly, increasingly obvious fissures in the international communist movement, due to the Polish crisis of 1980 and 1981 and open tensions between the CPSU and the Italian Communist Party, led to greater discussion within the movement of the contradictions impeding unity among parties. The reassessments proceeding among these three important policy audiences would prove crucial in providing a source of alternatives to the longstanding but increasingly counterproductive strategy of containing China.

THE BORDER REGIONS' PUSH FOR REOPENING BORDER TRADE

The resumption of cross-border trade heralded a change for the better in Sino-Soviet relations. In October 1982, as Sino-Soviet relations began to thaw, the two sides held negotiations in Khabarovsk on the resumption of border trade. Khabarovskii Krai had urged Moscow to reopen border trade as early as 1972, and when CCP General Secretary Hu Yaobang paid a visit to China's border provinces almost ten years later, he found local residents equally eager to resume trade. In a Heihe speech, Hu Yaobang urged opening the Chinese north to the outside world: "Shenzhen in the south, Heihe in the north—they should take off side by side" (*nan shen, bei hei, biyi qifei*). Residents of Heihe were enthusiastic about Hu's visit and speech. During the 1983 Chinese New Year celebration, when they hung the traditional red streamers on their front doors, instead of a couplet about prosperity they wrote the words from Hu's speech referring to Heihe as the next Shenzhen.

Two agreements were signed on April 10, 1983, restoring border trade between Heilongjiang Province and the Soviet Far East, as well as between Inner Mongolia and Siberia.[1] Border regions like Khabarovskii Krai especially welcomed the resumption of border trade. In a November 1984 report, the Khabarovsk regional party leadership restated its view that the expansion of border trade could facilitate the supply of scarce goods in the Russian Far East.[2]

Heilongjiang provincial officials were even more active in lobbying Beijing. Harbin officials held a series of high-level meetings on border trade. The State Council ultimately approved the province's recommendations, which served as the basis for the Chinese government's subsequent proposal to open four pairs of border ports to trade: Heihe/Blagoveshchensk; Suifenhe/Grodekovo; Tongjiang/Nizhneleninskoe; and Manzhouli/Zabaikalsk.[3]

While the Chinese and Russian border regions played an important role in the early 1980s in explaining the advantages of resuming border trade to their national leaders, and in the case of Heilongjiang in outlining the mechanisms to accomplish this aim, their efforts were constrained by events in Beijing and Moscow. Once Soviet and Chinese leaders gradually began to sanction a thaw in bilateral relations, regional officials had greater success.

THE MOSCOW POLICY COMMUNITY AND CHINA POLICY

At the beginning of the 1980s, the Soviet Union faced a grim picture in the international arena—Beijing and Washington had normalized relations at a time of mounting U.S.-Soviet tensions. Some progress in Soviet-Chinese relations had been achieved, mostly due to change in the Chinese foreign policy approach, but the rapprochement was very limited.[4] Instead of trying to reverse policies that were leading to the Soviet Union's deteriorating international and domestic positions, the ailing Brezhnev and his aged successors, Andropov and Chernenko, chose a damage-limitation strategy. They blamed the Soviet Union's mounting domestic and international problems on a U.S.–Chinese cabal.

Yet at the same time, moderating trends in Chinese foreign and domestic policies in the aftermath of Mao's death gave the Soviet Union an unprecedented opportunity to improve relations with China. A minority of reform-minded scholars and journalists believed that an improvement of Sino-Soviet relations could reinforce moderating trends in China.[5]

Despite these changes in China, however, the majority in the Soviet foreign policy elite contended that "Maoism without Mao" continued to prevail and saw few reasons for optimism regarding the possibility of any substantial improvement due to the continuity in Chinese policies. While this coalition of officials and scholars continued to exert considerable control over the content of discussion on China in the academic journals and the press, by the early 1980s reform-minded analysts and pragmatic foreign policy practitioners began to depart from the prevailing hard line to some extent.

The growing frustration within the Foreign Ministry over the Central Committee's stranglehold on China policy, for example, was evident in divergent interpretations in *Problemy Dal'nego Vostoka*, the main academic journal on China, as early as February 1982. While Rakhmanin (using the pseudonym Borisov), called relations "frozen" and placed the blame squarely on the Chinese side, Kapitsa (writing under the pen name Ukrainstev) spoke of "small steps" which the Soviet Union recently had been undertaking in hope of achieving some improvement in relations.[6] Nonetheless, despite his interest in moving forward on the diplomatic front with China, Kapitsa's views of Chinese politics remained much closer to Rakhmanin's than to those of reformist scholars such as Deliusin, who saw real signs of change in post-Mao China.[7]

Even after Brezhnev's March 1982 Tashkent speech, key proponents of containing China such as Rakhmanin found a platform for their views. This led to some controversy within the Central Committee between the Liaison Department and reform-minded specialists in the International Department, such as Anatolii Cherniaev, who would later become one of Gorbachev's foreign policy advisors. In his memoirs, Cherniaev recalled the time when the Party journal *Kommunist* proposed a laudatory review of one of Rakhmanin's books, which, despite Brezhnev's effort to develop a more conciliatory line on China, was full of anti-Chinese invective. According to Cherniaev, Rakhmanin remained extremely powerful, controlling a host of sinologists and thus much of the propaganda about China. Moreover, since he had built his career on the "exposure" of Maoism, normalization of relations would not do him any good.[8]

Cherniaev opposed the review of Rakhmanin's book, incurring the wrath of his boss, Boris Ponomarev, who was loathe to see open fighting between members of different Central Committee departments. Cherniaev refused to give up and even went so far as to write to Brezhnev, who was vacationing in the south. Upon his return to Moscow, Brezhnev issued an aide-mémoire to the Politburo (which Cherniaev called his "testament"), reminding his colleagues of the content of his Tashkent speech.[9] Andropov reportedly supported him fully, even if subsequently he too proved unable to silence the conservative opponents of normalization of relations with China.

During Andropov's brief rule, however, reformers who supported improving relations gained greater influence within the Soviet foreign policy elite. Andropov's former consultants, who worked for him during his tenure at the Central Committee in the 1960s and who were long-time advocates of improving relations with China, at last had the opportunity to discuss their views with a leader who would listen to them. These scholars and journalists had always been opposed to the Soviet Union's China policy and did not change their views over time. In the 1970s, their analysis tested the limits of Moscow's policy of containing China by providing a more balanced analysis of Chinese military power and the Sino-American relationship. When Andropov began a cautious opening to China, they still could not be openly critical because of the restraints of censorship, which required that analysis fit into the official ideological framework.

Arbatov reportedly suggested to Andropov that the Soviet Union had an opportunity to do something about China in light of the dramatic changes in Chinese polices since Deng Xiaoping embarked on a far-reaching economic program in 1978.[10] Growing indications of friction in Sino-American relations in the early 1980s provided an additional incentive for Soviet leaders to attempt to improve Soviet-Chinese relations and reduce Soviet isolation in the strategic triangle.

Bovin, a well-known journalist and one of Andropov's former consultants, was one of the first to take advantage—he paid a visit to China in February 1983 and commented subsequently that "regardless of the situation in the official talks on the normalization, life is bypassing this problem somewhat and normalization is progressing albeit slowly."[11] At this time, however, conservatives continued to occupy important posts and advocated caution in dealing with China, alleging that the Chinese reforms would lead to the restoration of capitalism and emphasizing that Sino-American cooperation posed a threat. Only after Gorbachev's assumption of power in 1985 were such conservative critics removed from positions of power.

Reactions to the Development of Sino-American Relations

The Soviet Union potentially gained room for maneuver vis-à-vis China when tensions developed in Sino-American relations as a result of the Reagan

Administration's contradictory China policy. Sino-American differences during this period are often attributed to the three "Ts": Taiwan, trade, and technology. Although President Reagan initially wanted to involve the PRC in a broad anti-Soviet alignment, he was reluctant to improve relations with Beijing at the expense of Taiwan. A proposed sale of advanced fighter-bombers to Taiwan resulted in friction with Beijing in 1981–82, and ultimately the sale was cancelled.[12] The Chinese leadership minced no words in its reaction to the incident. A Xinhua dispatch asserted that anyone who thinks that "China will have to swallow the bitter pill" because it needs "American support on the question of combating Soviet hegemonism" should remember the Sino-Soviet split.[13] At the time, Chinese policymakers had other complaints about U.S. policies, particularly American restrictions on imports of Chinese textiles and on sales of high-technology items to China.

With the Reagan Administration's commitment to reasserting the power of the United States, the Chinese felt that the Soviet threat was more manageable.[14] During the early 1980s, there was a growing perception in China that Soviet power was waning in light of Soviet difficulties in Afghanistan and Eastern Europe and the increasingly obvious economic crisis in the Soviet Union. Paradoxically, just when the Chinese saw less of a need to tilt towards the United States, the Reagan Administration became more interested in a close relationship with China. In fact, the Chinese leadership's reappraisal of the U.S.–Soviet balance of power in the early 1980s led them to shift to a more independent foreign policy.[15]

President Reagan's April 1984 visit to Beijing resulted in a turnaround in the Reagan Administration's China policy. It was Reagan's first visit to a communist country and he returned hopeful that the PRC would soon embrace capitalism. Reagan's anti-Soviet rhetoric proved too much for his Chinese hosts, however, who censored his speeches during his stay.[16] The Chinese leadership wanted the United States to provide a sufficient challenge to the Soviet Union on issues such as Afghanistan, but they were wary of getting drawn into a U.S.–Soviet conflict themselves. They also rejected American calls for strategic partnership, fearing it would reduce China's leverage in the international arena.

Despite the friction in U.S.–China ties in the early 1980s, the PRC continued to insist that any improvement in relations with the USSR depended on the resolution of the three obstacles (the Soviet Union's intervention in Afghanistan, support for the Vietnamese occupation of Cambodia, and military presence in Mongolia and along the Sino-Soviet border), which they viewed as symptomatic of the Soviet Union's expansionist strategy in Asia. As Zbigniew Brzezinski explained, "the Chinese used the three obstacles as a kind of measuring stick" to assess the kind of change they wanted in Soviet behavior.[17] From the Soviet vantage point, the costs to Soviet foreign relations with other countries outweighed the potential benefits of meeting Beijing's conditions. Indeed, the Chinese never explicitly stated what concessions, if any, they were prepared to make in exchange.[18] Yet the Soviet refusal to address the three obstacles confirmed the Chinese perception of a Soviet threat and reinforced the previous pro-Western tilt in Chinese foreign policy.

Although in the early 1980s the Chinese abandoned their policy of aligning with Soviet opponents, the Soviet leaders interpreted the problematic Sino-American relationship as hostile by definition. The Politburo instructed Soviet diplomats to expose the dangerous character of the rapprochement between the United States and China—particularly possible cooperation in the military sphere. Alleging that the United States dangled the prospect of military ties before the Chinese leaders to influence China in a "favorable direction," while China feigned a "peace-loving" foreign policy to gain time to improve its defense capabilities, the Politburo contended that the Chinese modernization strategy was in effect designed to achieve China's rapid transformation into a military superpower.[19]

In an article in *Voennaia Mysl'*, A. Kruchinin provided a particularly pessimistic view of the consequences of US-PRC cooperation. More alarmist than his military colleagues, he claimed that contradictions between the United States and China "did not predominate."[20]

In the early 1980s, many Soviet officials viewed the Sino-American alignment as a marriage of convenience—the West was using China to alter the balance of power and apply pressure against the Soviet Union, while the Chinese took advantage of Western aid to develop into a great power.[21] Rakhmanin commented that "comprehensive analysis allows one to affirm that a qualitatively important shift is taking place both in relations between the PRC and the US and in the distribution of power in the international arena as a whole."[22] However, Evgenii Primakov, then a prominent academic, criticized interpretations that saw evidence of polycentrism in international relations based on China's deviation from the socialist line. According to Primakov, just because China's leaders formulated policies that ran counter to socialism and the revolutionary process, this did not mean that any structural change was taking place in the international system or in the regularity of socialist development.[23]

In the early 1980s, the Chinese leadership finally began a process of reevaluating Maoist political and economic strategies, a development which Soviet leaders had long claimed was a precondition for any improvement in Sino-Soviet relations. In June 1981, the Sixth Plenum of the Eleventh Central Committee of the Chinese Communist Party passed a resolution criticizing aspects of Mao's record, particularly the Great Leap Forward and the Cultural Revolution.

When Deng Xiaoping returned to the Chinese leadership in 1978 and began to implement fundamental economic reform measures in the 1980s, far-reaching changes in Chinese foreign policy resulted. Because China needed a stable international environment to focus on pressing domestic tasks, Beijing wanted to reduce international tensions and establish good relations with a wide range of states.[24] Thus, in 1982 at the Twelfth CCP Congress, the Chinese leadership proclaimed that China would pursue an independent foreign policy and would refrain from alliance with either superpower. This move away from the quasi alliance with the United States of the late 1970s reflected both growing tensions in the U.S.–China relationship and the anticipation that Soviet economic difficulties would constrain the military buildup against China, obviating the need for an alignment with Washington to counterbalance the Soviet threat.

Despite the major shift in Chinese foreign policy announced at the Twelfth CCP Congress in 1982, authoritative Soviet commentators, following Brezhnev's lead, continued to emphasize the continuity in Chinese positions. Although by then the view in Moscow that "Maoism without Mao" persisted was on the defensive, highly placed Soviet observers noted the continued influence of Mao's legacy on Chinese foreign policy, especially in the PRC's pursuit of anti-Soviet and hegemonic policies, including efforts to split the communist movement.[25] Moreover, some official commentary denigrated the changes announced at the Twelfth CCP Congress as tactical.[26]

Concerned by a continuing Sino-American alignment directed against Soviet interests, Soviet analysts sorted out the similarities and differences in the Chinese and American positions on Sino-American relations. Some analysts stressed the contradictions in the Sino-American relationship, particularly differences over Taiwan and competing interests in Asia. Vladimir Lukin, then head of the China Department at the USA and Canada Institute, and Aleksandr Bovin alleged that such contradictions would preclude any parallel interests between the United States and the PRC in the long term.[27]

The majority of Soviet academic analysts, however, preferred to focus on the concrete differences.[28] As U.S.–Soviet relations deteriorated under Reagan, Soviet officials increasingly blamed the Reagan Administration for inveigling China into its anti-Soviet schemes. Many authoritative analysts asserted that China was being used by the United States and this form of cooperation ill-served Chinese interests.[29] Similarly, Soviet academics warned that the United States was trying to gain control over Chinese policies to ensure access to the Chinese market and erode socialist development in the PRC.[30] Soviet commentary played on Chinese fears regarding its independence and often stressed that the United States was trying to turn the PRC into a "junior partner."[31]

The Soviet Response to China's Economic Reforms

Throughout the 1970s and early 1980s, the Soviet leadership saw the development of China's market-oriented reforms as a challenge to the Soviet model of socialism. Coinciding with the increasingly apparent economic crisis in the USSR and the political crisis in Poland, the Chinese alternative figured prominently in Soviet debates in the early 1980s about socialist development.

Until the mid-1980s, Brezhnev's successors had attempted to forestall a Polish-type political crisis without instituting market-oriented reforms. Moreover, conservative officials in charge of China policy, whose careers had thrived on Sino-Soviet tensions for two decades, seized on China's alleged adoption of capitalism to justify a continued policy of hostility towards Beijing.[32] Rakhmanin, a leading proponent of this viewpoint, called the return to a mixed economy in the PRC "an obvious step backward in the socioeconomic sphere" and foresaw China's Western-oriented reforms leading to unemployment, political instability, and the undermining of socialist gains.[33]

Deliusin later commented that Soviet policymakers raised the specter of "China's turn to the capitalist path to strengthen the widespread view in Soviet society that it was impossible to overcome the Soviet-Chinese split. . . . In quarrels, as in friendship, some grow accustomed, some become subdued, and some extract advantage and therefore become interested, not in ending the conflict, but in perpetuating it."[34] Such officials continued to dominate China policy until the Gorbachev era.

Thus, in the early 1980s the prevailing view in the Soviet foreign policy elite was one of hostility to the Chinese modernization program. This stemmed from the Chinese decision to reject the development model based on the Soviet experience. In particular, Soviet academic commentary took the Chinese to task for failing to chart out economic policy through comprehensive planning. Many Soviet observers also interpreted China's piecemeal approach to reform as a failure to deal with problems systematically and as the precursor of new voluntaristic approaches similar to the Great Leap. These analysts criticized the Chinese for attempting to build socialism with Chinese characteristics (and Maoist underpinnings) because, in their view, this was tantamount to negating the value of Marxism as a universal teaching and denigrated the importance of the Soviet experience in socialist construction. Some Soviet scholars accused the Chinese of aiming to implement a nationalistic and "right-wing reformist type" policy, which posed a direct threat to socialist gains and represented a "deep strategic retreat along the socioeconomic front."[35]

Other commentators tried to defend the Soviet Union's policy towards other socialist countries, asserting that no rigid models were imposed on anyone.

These academics criticized the Chinese approach for misinterpreting the balance between the general and the specific: in other words, for downgrading the value of the Soviet experience and overemphasizing Chinese specifics.[36] Anatolii Butenko's explanation was more nuanced. In his view, the Soviet experience remained relevant because certain phenomena which reappeared in other countries (socialist revolution, power held by the working class, socialist transformation of industry and agriculture) first occurred in the USSR. He noted, however, that "the way of every country towards socialism represents an organic blend of the general, the particular, and the unique."[37]

Officials criticized China's receptivity to capitalism, but noted that this was not surprising given the distortions in socialist development in that country for the past twenty years. Brezhnev stated that "the experience of socioeconomic development in the PRC in the past two decades is a difficult lesson, showing what the distortion of socialist principles leads to. . . ."[38] According to one authoritative observer, since Maoist economic policies were framed in socialist terms, socialism had become discredited in China.[39]

Beginning in 1982, censorship of writing on China became stricter as a result of the struggle over China policy between conservatives and reformers within the Soviet foreign policy elite. After Brezhnev died, however, there was very little official Soviet commentary about the Chinese reforms, except to remark that the reform process was a stimulus to cooperation between the United States and China.[40]

Despite the continued dominance of conservative officials over China policy in the early 1980s, different perspectives on Chinese reforms within the Soviet foreign policy elite began to emerge more clearly during Andropov's tenure as general secretary. Under Andropov, a debate developed on Soviet China policy that pitted proponents of normalization, who also tended to favor reform in the Soviet Union, against officials who clung to the orthodox ideological framework to maintain their hold on China policy and preserve the status quo in the Soviet Union.[41] Given the Andropov leadership's commitment to limited reform in the Soviet Union, the conservative view, opposed to reform in the USSR and critical of Chinese deviations from Marxism-Leninism, largely disappeared from academic publications during this period. Because of the censored media in the Soviet Union, reformist academics and officials often veiled their criticism of Soviet problems in discussions of the Chinese reforms.[42]

A notable example is Fedor Burlatskii's article in *Novyi Mir* in 1982 about the succession process in China, which was widely interpreted as a critique of Stalinist as well as Maoist tyranny.[43] Burlatskii viewed the Chinese reforms as a sign of the reorientation of economic development along the socialist path and the rebuilding of institutions which had been corrupted by long years of tyrannical rule.[44] He later commented that in his writings he tried to express his great respect for the goals of Deng's reforms because he saw the need for similar structural economic reforms in the Soviet Union, as well as the development of a more pluralistic political system.[45]

Until the Andropov period, Soviet academics had tended to downplay any improvements in China's economic performance and ignored the positive consequences of the Open Door policy. As of 1983, however, some analysts began commenting on the benefits of China's Open Door policy—attracting foreign investment and developing joint ventures, particularly as a means of compensating for the weakness of the economic base. Nonetheless, China's economic links with capitalist states were seen as a threat to socialist gains.[46] Soviet scholars argued that the advantages of cooperation with socialist states, demonstrated in the 1950s, by far outweighed the potential benefits of Beijing's Open Door policy.[47]

At this time, Soviet scholars took more of an interest in the specific aspects of the Chinese reform program, although published analysis continued to find fault with it until the Gorbachev period. Grudgingly, Soviet academics conceded that some economic progress had been achieved in the PRC since 1978, but this was greatly understated—some Soviet analysts attributed the success of the Chinese reforms to the contrast between the 1978–1983 period and crisis conditions of the Mao years.[48] Still, Soviet commentary remained critical, for example, finding fault with agricultural reforms for involving the use of household contracts—which could lead to the resumption of private property relations and social stratification.[49]

During Chernenko's rule, debate continued both on Soviet China policy and on contradictions in socialist states. According to Marc Zlotnik, Chernenko was opposed to the dogmatic application of Marxism-Leninism and saw the need for the CPSU to be more responsive to the masses, if it was going to avoid the fate of Poland's party.[50]

The parameters of discussion of the ideological framework tightened somewhat during Chernenko's rule, despite the fact that Gorbachev became the new secretary for ideology. Although discussion of economic reform was allowed to continue, two reformist academics, Evgenii Ambartsumov and Anatolii Butenko, were censured for their views. In Zlotnik's view, Chernenko's need for political allies won out against his reformist leanings.[51] Further ideological innovation required personnel changes, and this only occurred when Gorbachev became general secretary.

During the first year of Gorbachev's rule, for the most part Soviet officials reserved comment about the Chinese reforms. However, Fedor Burlatskii's comments on Soviet television in the summer of 1985 about the reforms in China signaled greater official interest in them. He stated that "the results and problems of these major social experiments are being widely discussed in China itself and overseas." Burlatskii noted that it was "interesting and important" for the Soviet Union to know about the Chinese reforms."[52]

In the mid-1980s, the Soviet academic community began to direct more attention to the reform process in China. Objective economic analysis of aspects of the reforms became more common in the academic literature, and several analysts noted approvingly that the Chinese had made some radical innovations.[53] Soviet observers continued to criticize individual aspects of the Chinese reforms, however. For example, although Soviet discussion of the Open Door policy in 1985 lent itself to a more objective economic analysis of costs and benefits, there was a sense in the writings of some Soviets that an Open Door policy was somehow incompatible with the role of a socialist state. One Soviet scholar stated that "the movement to develop ties with the West in various spheres weakens China's international position."[54]

In 1985, there was also considerable criticism of the problems involved in loosening central controls and some doubts continued to be expressed regarding the ability of the Chinese approach to solve the country's considerable economic problems.[55] Moreover, at that time there was disagreement among Soviet analysts about whether the Chinese focus on building socialism in Chinese conditions was an excuse for abandoning the scientific theory of socialism used by the USSR and other socialist states or was in keeping with Marxism-Leninism's rejection of rigid models.[56]

Although critical analysis of events in China diminished significantly by the mid-1980s, the gradual rapprochement with China heightened the political sensitivity of any discussion of Chinese policies. As Gorbachev began to take concrete measures toward achieving normalization and implementing reforms in the USSR, discussions of Chinese reforms became more and more relevant, both to the development of Sino-Soviet economic relations and to the debates within the Soviet Union about reform.

CHINA AND SOCIALIST UNITY

In the early 1980s, China's policy toward communist parties began to evolve. As Beijing began moving toward an independent foreign policy, the CCP began to view a communist party's willingness to improve relations with the Chinese communists—rather than hostility toward the USSR—as the main reason to improve ties.[57] Even though anti-Sovietism would no longer be the litmus test for the CCP's relations with other communist parties, the CPSU continued to see a challenge from China's new approach to proletarian internationalism, which failed to perceive unity as a duty, but rather as a choice contingent on a party's approach to the CCP.[58]

In response to the CCP's new approach to communist parties, the normalization of Sino-American relations, and the Chinese reform alternative, the Soviet Union shored up its defenses and tried to summon communist unity behind Soviet international and domestic positions. For example, from the 1970s through the early 1980s, the Soviet Central Committee held regular talks with Central Committee members from the socialist countries in Eastern Europe to coordinate China policy.[59] At a May 1980 meeting, for instance, representatives of the International Departments from the Eastern European socialist states and the USSR noted that, in view of the PRC's attempt to split the socialist community by courting parties that sought greater autonomy, it was all the more important to create a broad front, agree on a course of action, and closely coordinate China policy.[60]

The crisis in Poland in 1980 and 1981 further challenged Soviet ideological assumptions about socialist development and colored Soviet evaluations of the Chinese reform alternative. In the first half of the 1980s, an important ideological debate took place largely in response to the Polish situation. Many Soviet officials who recognized the need to address the growing economic crisis in the Soviet Union—the consequences of ignoring severe problems being amply demonstrated by the Polish events—found the Chinese approach to reform too radical.

The debate appeared to focus on hair-splitting distinctions: whether or not there were contradictions under socialism, and if so whether they were antagonistic or non-antagonistic.[61] But this topic led to a discussion of pressing current issues, such as the causes of the unrest in Poland and the possibility of a similar socioeconomic crisis developing in Soviet society.[62]

Three positions in this debate can be distinguished. The first admitted to contradictions in socialism, of a non-antagonistic nature, in cases where socialism was not yet developed, as in Poland. According to the leading ideologists who espoused this view, crisis conditions arose in Poland due to the lingering presence of capitalist vestiges, such as private farming and cooperatives.[63] Since the Soviet Union was a developed socialist society, such a crisis could not happen there.[64] Supporters of this position also believed that departures from the orthodox approach to socialist construction undermined social cohesion. Adherents therefore considered the Chinese reform model—involving decollectivization and the introduction of some capitalist measures—to be heretical.

According to the second view, non-antagonistic contradictions may develop when the party loses touch with the masses. This perspective, espoused by Brezhnev in the aftermath of the Polish crisis, as well as by Andropov and Chernenko, conceded that problems existed even in a developed socialist society such as the USSR. Proponents of this view argued that the answer was control rather than structural reform. Andropov was more willing than his colleagues to examine the causes of problems, although he was still reluctant to embark on far-reaching changes either in domestic or foreign policy.[65] It is not surprising, then, that the prevailing view of the Chinese reforms during the first half of the 1980s was at best ambivalent, if not critical.

The third view, held by proponents of reform in academe such as Butenko and Ambartsumov, saw the possibility of antagonistic contradictions under socialism due to the perpetuation of conflicts of interest.[66] For example, Ambartsumov noted in his discussion of the crises plaguing socialist countries in Eastern Europe that Lenin had decided to implement a more liberal economic program, the New Economic Policy (NEP), in response to the crisis caused by the Kronstadt rebellion.[67] According to this view, the only possible response to a pre-crisis condition was reform, the position subsequently assumed by Gorbachev. If reform was necessary for socialist states to resolve social conflicts, then the Chinese reform model could be seen as a positive development, at least for Chinese conditions.

Ideological issues suffused Soviet China policy, and were reflected not only in the Soviet response to Chinese reforms and the impact of these reforms on Soviet domestic debates, but also in the tensions the imposition of martial law in Poland provoked in the communist movement. In the early 1980s, Soviet officials and scholars continued to emphasize the importance of unity in the socialist community and the communist movement. A 1981 editorial in *Kommunist* stated, for example, that China's return to the socialist path would involve fulfilling the following criteria: (1) enhancing the role of the working class in China; (2) adjusting the role of the peasantry; and (3) increasing the influence of the socialist community and the communist movement as a whole.[68]

In the early 1980s, some officials continued to attack the Chinese leaders for undermining socialist unity, although it was questionable to speak of unity in the communist movement in the wake of the Polish crisis and the split between the CPSU and the Italian Communist Party (PCI). Rakhmanin stated, for example, that "it was inadmissible to be neutral when principles are being destroyed by combining internationalism and nationalism."[69]

The imposition of martial law in Poland led to a public break between the PCI and the CPSU. The PCI's criticism of Soviet foreign policy echoed earlier Chinese claims about the similarity between Soviet and American aggressive efforts to maintain their spheres of influence. The Italian communists, like the Chinese, called the Soviet Union to task for its intervention in Afghanistan and accused the Soviets of interfering in the affairs of other socialist countries and parties.[70]

After Mikhail Suslov's death in early 1982, the Soviets toned down their attacks on the PCI. According to Joan Barth Urban, this decision coincided with Brezhnev's March 1982 overture to China. In her view, the Chinese would not have responded kindly to Soviet overtures had public polemics between the Soviet and Italian communists continued.[71] Nevertheless, relations between the CPSU and the PCI remained tense after 1982, in contrast with PCI-CCP relations, which had continued to improve since the last the late 1970s. The contrast was reinforced when, in the summer of 1983, Enrico Berlinguer spent his holiday in China.[72]

Cherniaev recalled that during Andropov's tenure the Soviet leadership displayed greater realism in bloc relations, exemplified by attempts to improve ties with both the PCI and the Chinese, although for the wrong reason—to perpetuate the myth of Soviet leadership of the communist movement.[73] It was a conciliatory Mikhail Gorbachev, however, who attended Enrico Berlinguer's funeral in June 1984, foreshadowing changes in Soviet policy towards the communist movement later in the decade.

During this period of polemics between the PCI and the CPSU, the Chinese found themselves on the same side as the Italian communists on many basic points, such as their evaluation of Soviet foreign policy and their unwillingness to follow blindly Soviet leadership in the communist movement. The coincidence in the Italian and Chinese positions reinforced the claims that each party had made about its right to seek its own path to socialism, what the Italians referred to as the *terza via* (third way) and the Chinese called "socialism with Chinese characteristics." By any name, the Soviets found this objectionable because of their own claim to leadership of the communist movement and the importance of this claim for Soviet legitimacy.

During the early 1980s, the Chinese also concurred with the Romanians and the Yugoslavs about the importance of the principles of independence and sovereignty in relations among socialist states. For the first time in years, the Chinese leadership expressed an interest in improving economic and political relations with the other East European countries.[74] Although the Soviet leadership had always castigated the Chinese for preferring relations with the West over ties with socialist states, the Soviet Union was faced with the prospect of Chinese relations with the East Europeans outpacing Soviet-Chinese relations—another challenge to Soviet leadership of the socialist community.

CONCLUSIONS

By 1985, China policy had become a lightning rod for a range of different interests. Deng's reform program emboldened autonomist sentiment in the socialist community and enabled China to find new allies among the Eurocommunists. Meanwhile, regional officials on both sides of the Sino-Soviet border regions seized on signs of a thaw in bilateral relations to call for the resumption of border trade in an effort to spur development in depressed border regions. In Moscow, reform-minded scholars and journalists, inspired by Deng's economic reforms and convinced that a diversity of paths to socialism was the only alternative in an increasingly fractious and unstable communist movement, pressed for further steps to improve relations with China. Foreign ministry officials remained critical of Chinese policies but saw the need for pragmatic measures to move Sino-Soviet relations forward.

While Andropov recruited reformist scholars and journalists to serve as his consultants once be became general secretary, the coalition favoring containment largely remained in place in the early 1980s. Still there were pressures from key coalition members such as Andropov and Gromyko to make adjustments in the anti-Chinese containment policy. Only Ustinov and Rakhmanin remained implacable in their opposition to dismantling the military and ideological defenses gradually put in place since the 1960s to address the Chinese political-military challenge. It would take Gorbachev's rise to power and new approach to security and bloc relations for fundamental change in Soviet China policy to occur.

6 / From Rapprochement to Normalization

One of Mikhail Gorbachev's top priorities upon taking office in March 1985 was to improve relations with China. To do so, he first had to neutralize the coalition of interests supporting the previous containment policy and put a new foreign policy team in place, a process which would take two years to complete. Beginning in 1986, Gorbachev took a series of steps that reversed the policy of containing China and culminated in the normalization of relations in May 1989. The advantages of normalization became very compelling because improved relations with China contributed to the Gorbachev leadership's revised international and domestic aims.[1]

NEW DIRECTIONS IN FOREIGN POLICY

In an effort to create an international environment conducive to domestic reform, the new general secretary spearheaded a full-scale reevaluation of the ends and means of Soviet foreign policy.[2] Drawing on the views of reform-minded academics, Gorbachev sought to discard the Stalinist dogma[3] that had resulted in the Soviet Union's increasing isolation in the international community. This "new thinking" led to a cooperative thrust in Soviet foreign policy involving a commitment to resolve outstanding regional conflicts peacefully, renewed enthusiasm for multilateral diplomacy, and reductions in military spending—goals served by reducing tensions with China. Since the Soviet Union also sought better relations with the United States, Soviet officials no longer equated China's desire for good relations with Washington with anti-Sovietism.

Gorbachev's China Policy Review

During his years in office, Gorbachev in effect overturned the Soviet Union's longstanding policy of containing China. In 1986, the Gorbachev leadership's policy reexamination found that the benefits of normalization with China far outweighed the anticipated costs. The new Soviet foreign policy agenda implicitly addressed the resolution of what the Chinese considered to be the three obstacles to normalization (the Soviet Union's intervention in Afghanistan, support for the Vietnamese occupation of Cambodia, and military presence in Mongolia and along the Sino-Soviet border).[4] Broader changes in Soviet foreign and domestic policy, such as the new Soviet willingness to play an active role in the resolution of the Cambodian question, the fulfillment of the Soviet pledge to pull out of Afghanistan completely by February 15, 1988, and planned conventional arms cuts, paved the way for the May 1989 Sino-Soviet summit in Beijing. The Chinese leadership recognized new congruences in Soviet and Chinese foreign policy positions and was impressed by Soviet admissions of past mistakes in relations with socialist countries.[5]

By the mid-1980s, Sino-Soviet relations had come a long way from the 1950s, when China was expected to imitate "older brother" in domestic and foreign policy. *Perestroika* heightened the Soviet interest in cooperation with China by creating a shared interest in economic reform. At first many Soviets asserted that the commitment of the two states to a common reform path facilitated their cooperation. However, by the end of the decade, when Soviet and Chinese reforms diverged more fundamentally, the two neighbors became invested in the normalization process itself because of its clear economic and security benefits.

Momentum for rapprochement accelerated when Gorbachev announced in a July 1986 speech in Vladivostok that six Soviet regiments would be removed from Afghanistan as would a "significant" number of troops from Mongolia.[6] He also publicly acceded to the Chinese position on the demarcation of their common river boundaries.[7] As a result of the Soviet proposal, the two sides agreed to reopen boundary talks at their ninth round of normalization talks in the autumn of 1986 in Beijing. Deng Xiaoping, interviewed on the American television program *60 Minutes* just after the Vladivostok speech, reiterated his position that the Vietnamese occupation of Cambodia (an issue which Gorbachev had stated was up to Cambodia and Vietnam to resolve) was the main obstacle to improving Sino-Soviet relations. If the Soviet Union would facilitate the Vietnamese withdrawal from Cambodia, Deng said he would be prepared to meet with Gorbachev anywhere in the world.

Impact of Personnel Changes

To spur the Soviet-Chinese normalization process, Gorbachev quickly disbanded the Politburo commission in charge of China policy and made some critical personnel changes in the China area.[8] Replacing Andrei Gromyko (who had been foreign minister throughout the long period of Sino-Soviet hostility) with Eduard Shevardnadze, an outsider with no diplomatic experience, gave Gorbachev more freedom in reassessing the Soviet approach to Asia.

Ustinov's death in December 1984 provided Gorbachev with the opportunity to select a much less powerful figure for Minister of Defense, Marshal Sokolov, who was not yet even a candidate member of the Politburo.[9] In January 1986, Anatolii Cherniaev supplanted the more conservative Aleksandrov-Agentov as Gorbachev's foreign policy adviser, and in March, Anatolii Dobrynin, the Soviet Ambassador to the United States for more than twenty years, was asked to take Boris Ponomarev's job as head of the Central Committee's International Department.[10] Under Ponomarev, a long-time party official convinced of the Soviet Union's leading role in the communist movement, this department had mainly supervised the CPSU's relations with communist parties. With Dobrynin in charge, the department began to take on a broader spectrum of foreign policy responsibilities.[11] A couple of months later, Oleg Troianovskii, another experienced diplomat, became the new Soviet ambassador to China.[12]

Also in 1986, Konstantin Rusakov, chairman of the Central Committee's Department for Liaison with Socialist Countries, retired from his position due to illness and was replaced by Vadim Medvedev. According to Evgenii Bazhanov, who worked under Oleg Rakhmanin in the section of that department dealing with Asian socialist states, Rusakov's poor health and frequent absences from his job in 1985 had given "the anti-China mafia" an opportunity to promote their views.[13]

Rakhmanin in particular took advantage of the power vacuum in the department to promote his own hardline opinions on key policy issues. According to Cherniaev, Gorbachev became incensed when Rakhmanin published an article in *Pravda* in July 1985—without clearing it with the Politburo first, not to mention with his own boss, Rusakov. In the article, Rakhmanin, using the pseudonym "Vladimirov," criticized the GDR, Hungary, and Romania for carrying out "unnecessary reforms" and for showing insufficient international "discipline."[14]

Rakhmanin had taken a hard line on reconciliation with China throughout the Brezhnev years, although his publicly stated views moderated somewhat when the Soviet Union and China made their first steps toward rapprochement in 1982–83. Bazhanov, in an anonymous memoir published in the *Far Eastern Economic Review*, described how Rakhmanin and others set about to frustrate Gorbachev's initial efforts to normalize relations with China without ever openly disagreeing.[15] Under Rakhmanin's instructions, for example, the Department prepared an analysis arguing that China had renewed its claims to Soviet territory. When no evidence could be found to back up such assertions, the department doctored Chinese statements and maps from the 1960s to suit its purpose.[16] According to Bazhanov, it took a year for Medvedev to rein in the opponents of Gorbachev's China policy within the Liaison department.[17]

Rakhmanin's star began to eclipse in October 1986 when Georgii Sha-khnazarov, a reform-minded scholar and party official, joined him as first deputy chief of the liaison department, an important position that directly addressed ideological questions between the Soviet Union and China.[18] Oleg Rakhmanin ultimately left his Central Committee position in early 1987.[19] At the same time, another leading supporter of containing China, Deputy Foreign Minister in Charge of Asian Affairs Mikhail Kapitsa, was replaced by Igor' Rogachev and transferred to the directorship of the Institute of Oriental Studies.[20]

Gorbachev's personnel changes and reorientation of Soviet foreign policy expanded opportunities for academics to offer policy advice and provided greater room for scholarly debate. Many Brezhnev-era sinologists had used their subject as a veil to discuss reform prospects in the Soviet Union. Since a reformist outlook went hand in hand with a positive assessment of changes in China,[21] at least until the brutal crackdown by the Chinese leadership against prodemocracy protesters in June 1989, the views of leading China specialists tended to reinforce Gorbachev's conciliatory policy.

Officials and academics who held reformist views were emboldened by *glasnost'* and Gorbachev's emphasis on reform to express themselves fully. Others who had opposed normalization with China in the past and were not favorably disposed to reform in general had to change their views or lose their jobs. Some went into academic exile, where much to the consternation of reformist scholars they tended to hinder scholarship but at least could no longer impede Gorbachev's normalization policy.[22]

Beginning in the early 1980s, antireform views faded from print. Erstwhile critics of Chinese policies, among them Mikhail Titarenko and Mikhail Kapitsa, reappeared later in the decade, propounding the need for cooperation with China. Ideological strictures and bureaucratic inertia tended to be mutually reinforcing, but thanks to Gorbachev's assault on Stalinist dogma and to personnel changes, supporters of the previous anti-Chinese containment strategy lost considerable influence over Soviet China policy in the late 1980s. One of Gorbachev's advisers, Aleksandr Iakovlev, commented on television in 1989 that he thought the opponents of Sino-Soviet normalization had renounced their views. Reflecting on his own situation, he stated: "Thank goodness, I was lucky; I was not involved in that. It was easy for me to start with a clean slate."[23]

THE ROAD TO BEIJING

By 1987, the Soviet Union was becoming increasingly frustrated by the economic burden posed by subsidies to Vietnam and began to pursue a more active diplomatic role in Southeast Asia. But there was still no evidence that the Soviets were pressuring Vietnam to withdraw from Cambodia, as demanded by China. Progress in Sino-Soviet relations continued in other areas, however, as the border talks, suspended since 1978, resumed in February 1987. They led to an agreement to discuss the entire border, beginning with the eastern portion, which had been the site of the bloody Sino-Soviet border clashes in the spring and summer of 1969. In August, the Soviet Union formally acknowledged that the main river channel constituted the boundary along the Amur and Ussuri Rivers and the Chinese recognized the validity of existing treaties regarding the demarcation of the eastern border. At this meeting, the two sides agreed to set up a working group to discuss particular issues concerning the eastern border, such as ownership of the disputed riverine islands.[24]

Beginning in late 1986, the Soviet leadership directed its attention to extricating the Soviet military from the deteriorating situation in Afghanistan. Subsequently, Foreign Minister Shevardnadze went so far as to term the intervention illegal and immoral,[25] and Gorbachev pledged to withdraw completely by February 15, 1988. Moreover, Gorbachev's commitment to sufficiency rather than numerical superiority in weapons deployments led him to endorse both the removal of SS-20s from Europe and Asia as well as substantial troop reductions along the Sino-Soviet border.[26] The marked improvement in East-West relations brought about by the Soviet decision to withdraw from Afghanistan and the signing of the Intermediate Nuclear Forces (INF) treaty in November 1987 contributed significantly to progress in Sino-Soviet relations.

In mid-November 1987, during a visit to China by Japanese Socialist leader Takako Doi, Deng restated his interest in meeting Gorbachev once the three obstacles were resolved. In December, Gorbachev was interviewed in the Chinese weekly *Liaowang*, the first time a Soviet leader's views had been solicited by the Chinese media in three decades. According to Gorbachev, who implicitly rejected Deng's preconditions, a Sino-Soviet summit would be the "logical component" of the dialogue between the two sides that had begun at the regular normalization talks.[27] The Chinese, firmly committed to achieving results on the Cambodian issue before agreeing to a Sino-Soviet summit, declined to respond to Gorbachev's overtures.

Finally, in 1988, substantial progress was made on ending the Vietnamese occupation of Cambodia. This resulted from the Gorbachev leadership's concern about the cost-effectiveness of Soviet aid to Vietnam, the USSR's more active diplomacy in Asia, and improved relations with nonsocialist states such as the members of the Association of Southeast Asian Nations (ASEAN). In mid-1988, Vietnam announced the withdrawal of 50,000 troops from Cambodia and reaffirmed its intention to withdraw the rest by the end of 1990. The real breakthrough occurred in August, however, at a special meeting on Cambodia between Deputy Foreign Ministers Igor' Rogachev and Tian Zengpei, when the Soviet side admitted for the first time that the Vietnamese withdrawal was the key to the resolution of Cambodia's problems.[28]

As the USSR demonstrated its serious intent to change its behavior in regional crises in Asia and reduce its military presence in the Far East, the PRC reassessed the possibility of a Sino-Soviet summit. After a visit by Chinese Foreign Minister Qian Qichen to Moscow in late December 1988, the two sides announced that their top leaders would meet in 1989.

ECONOMIC RELATIONS

Sino-Soviet economic relations gathered momentum long before the political differences between the two countries were ironed out. In the late 1980s, Sino-Soviet trade first rebounded to the level achieved during the years of friendship in the 1950s, then rose dramatically from $1.8 billion in 1988 to $3.8 billion in 1989, ultimately reaching $5.2 billion in 1990.[29] The development of border trade, increasing more than 4,000 percent between 1983 and 1988, played a key role in the expansion of bilateral relations.[30] Even in the late 1980s, Moscow continued to direct the pace of the development of border relations. For example, a document from the Khabarovsk regional party committee shows that it was up to the Central Committee of the CPSU to authorize ties between regional governments in the Soviet border regions and their Chinese counterparts.[31]

Despite the considerable progress in bilateral trade relations in the late 1980s, the Soviet Union continued to rank fifth among China's trading partners in 1990, accounting for 3.1 percent of China's total trade. Trade with China represented an equally small percentage of total Soviet trade.[32] Despite the shortfall in trade, the two states were able to make progress in economic relations in nontraditional ways.[33] The Soviets extended an $82 million loan to China for the completion of the railway connecting Urumqi in Xinjiang Province to the Turk-Sib Railway in Alma Ata. This railway, which became operational in 1991, was supposed to boost trade between China and Central Asia and facilitate the shipment of Chinese goods from inland areas to Europe.[34]

In addition, the Soviet Union began hiring Chinese laborers and paying them with Soviet manufactured goods. This mutually beneficial arrangement gave the Soviets a market for goods like refrigerators that could not be sold in the West and provided jobs for Chinese workers. By 1990, 20,000 Chinese laborers were employed in the USSR. The Soviet Union and China also entered into agreements for cooperation in nuclear energy, transport, communications, and peaceful uses of space.[35]

THE BEIJING SUMMIT

The Sino-Soviet summit in Beijing, May 15–18, 1989, represented the natural culmination of three years of steady progress in relations. During the opening banquet at the summit, Gorbachev gave the following explanation for the improvement: "Today we have the right to say that these relations are entering a qualitatively new stage, both because our two countries have changed and because the world around us is different."[36]

The Soviets reassured the West and such friends as India and Vietnam that neither the Soviet Union nor China had any intention of returning to the alliance of the 1950s, while Deng Xiaoping, inviting three American warships from the Seventh Fleet to pay a port call to Shanghai on the day that Gorbachev was to visit that city, emphasized that the visit by the Soviet leader would not change China's close relationship with the United States.[37] In the end, the naval visit was delayed by one day, but Deng's message still rang clear—China planned to continue its independent foreign policy and would not ally itself with either superpower.

During Gorbachev's visit, student protests broke out in Beijing, forcing the relocation of many summit events and taking a considerable amount of the limelight away from the Soviet leader. While Deng Xiaoping was trying to avoid an overly exuberant welcome for Gorbachev, the demonstrations were a source of embarrassment for the Chinese leader because some of the protestors were emboldened by Soviet reforms to press for political change in China.

The Chinese downplayed the political significance of normalization of party-to-party ties with the CPSU, just as they had done with the East European parties. But when Gorbachev and Deng Xiaoping shook hands, the bitter dispute between the Soviet and Chinese Communist Parties officially ended.[38] Deng told Gorbachev that the significance of the summit could be summed up with the phrase: "End the past, open up the future."[39] To avoid any repetition of past problems in relations, the two leaders agreed that there was no single model of socialist development and that international problems should be solved through political means.[40] Deng and Gorbachev were unable to settle all aspects of the Cambodian conflict and decided to refer the remaining questions to their respective foreign ministers.[41] Gorbachev's subsequent discussion with Zhao Ziyang on reform and socialist development in the two countries then marked the natural resumption of relations between the two communist parties.[42]

Gorbachev also met with Chinese Prime Minister Li Peng, and the two leaders explored future Sino-Soviet cooperation in a range of spheres. Renouncing any intention to return to the Sino-Soviet alliance of the 1950s, they agreed to base their relations on peaceful coexistence, which was meant to include respect for international norms such as sovereignty, noninterference, and peaceful resolution of disputes. Li Peng and Gorbachev called for raising the border talks to the foreign minister level. The two sides agreed to refrain from using arms against each other "by any means, including the use of territorial, land, water or air space of a third country bordering on the other side."[43] The Soviets and the Chinese also pledged not to seek "hegemony in any form" in Asia or elsewhere, thereby eliminating another phrase from the lexicon of the Sino-Soviet split.

In a televised address, Gorbachev offered a detailed picture of warmer relations, suggesting that the demilitarization of the border could be achieved through mutual and balanced force reductions. An article published in the Soviet military newspaper, *Krasnaia Zvezda*, at the end of the summit called for military contacts that "would not be confined only to questions of demilitarization of the border, but will assume a much broader scope."[44]

Despite lingering differences and the chaos caused by the student demonstrations, Gorbachev appeared satisfied with the results of the summit, which he considered of far-reaching importance (*rubezhnyi*). Although some problems remained unsolved, as *Izvestiia* commentator Yurii Bandura reported, these differences no longer impeded the development of Sino-Soviet relations.[45]

In view of the progress in the late 1980s in resolving bilateral problems, Gorbachev was concerned mainly that the three decades of hostility had inculcated the younger generation of Chinese with an unwillingness to resolve future differences. These fears proved groundless. When he met with Chinese young people during the summit, the Soviet leader was struck by their friendliness—a promising sign for the development of Sino-Soviet friendship and cooperation.[46]

SOVIET RESPONSES TO THE CHINESE CRACKDOWN

The interrelationship between the reforms in the Soviet Union and China became obvious during the Beijing summit, when prodemocracy protestors waved pictures of Gorbachev and posters advocating *glasnost'*. As his interpreter recalled, the demonstrations put Gorbachev in a tight spot. While he was sympathetic to the demands of the students, he knew that their actions put his Chinese hosts in a difficult position.[47]

Nevertheless, Gorbachev could not but comment on the unprecedented events in the Chinese capital, when demonstrations by thousands of students, intellectuals, and workers forced the rescheduling of several of the planned activities. Referring to the thousands of demonstrators, he told Zhao Ziyang: "We have our hotheads who want to change socialism overnight. But this does not happen in real life, only in fairy tales."[48] When pressed repeatedly to comment on the student demonstrations at the concluding press conference, Gorbachev welcomed the dialogue between the Chinese government and the students. He said that he could not discount the possibility of similar events occurring in the Soviet Union and, should this happen, the Soviet leadership would try to resolve them through negotiation.[49] Moreover, in his interview on Chinese television, Gorbachev had only warm words for the Chinese students who wrote to him expressing their support for *perestroika*.[50]

The students also pressed for a meeting with Gorbachev during his visit. Although the Chinese leaders left it up to him to decide, they made no effort to hide their opposition to the idea. In the end, Gorbachev diffused the issue by including some students in a larger gathering with Chinese intellectuals.[51]

The following month, when the Chinese leadership staged their brutal crackdown, the newly elected Congress of People's Deputies of the Soviet Union issued the initial Soviet response, asserting that the events in China were an internal affair. Finally, ten days after the bloody repression in the Chinese capital, Gorbachev expressed his regret at the violent culmination of the student protests. He said: "I believe we are all worried, we are all concerned not to break the process of reforms in this enormous state."[52] Subsequently, Gorbachev noted that he preferred political dialogue as a means of resolving social problems, but emphasized that this was his own opinion and that it was up to the Chinese to make their own decisions.[53] He was quick to stress the Soviet Union's continued interest in building on the results of the summit.[54]

As his translator recalled, both Gorbachev and Shevardnadze were in a quandary over the crackdown. Although memories of the violent repression of street demonstrations in Tbilisi just one month before remained fresh in their minds, they wanted to avoid undermining the long-awaited normalization of Sino-Soviet relations, or sanctioning any activities that could lead to instability and chaos in China.[55]

While Gorbachev's reaction expressed caution, some newly formed social groups in the USSR spoke out against the brutal crackdown. For example, the radical opposition in the Congress of People's Deputies issued a separate statement, read by Andrei Sakharov in the closing minutes, condemning the Beijing massacre and advocating the immediate recall of the Soviet ambassador to China.[56] The Memorial Society, an organization that pressed for the exposure of Stalinist abuses, and a new independent organization of academics passed resolutions condemning the Chinese actions. Moscovites protested against the crackdown in front of the Chinese embassy and in Luzhniki Park.

The Soviet response to the events in China seemed to reflect concern with the potential impact on the Soviet Union of problems similar to those encountered in the Chinese reform effort. Soviet officials and journalists saw the events in China in May and June 1989 not as unbiased observers, but as fellow participants in the reform struggle. As a result, they responded with a damage limitation strategy addressed to their fears about the course of the reform process in the Soviet Union, rather than exclusively to the events in China.

Gorbachev did not express outrage about the crackdown on the democracy movement in Beijing primarily because he was unwilling to sacrifice one of his few policy successes to attain the moral high ground.[57] The nature of the reform process also had an impact on the Gorbachev leadership's reaction. Mounting difficulties at home led some Soviet commentators to speak more about the possibility of backsliding during reform rather than about its irreversibility, although they continued to emphasize that reform was the only possible path for socialist countries.[58] Furthermore, the events in China dramatized a problem that the Soviets were then confronting to a lesser degree: economic change, and the uncertainty brought on by pressures for democracy, created a threat of instability.

The Beijing massacre fueled discussion in the USSR, both on the role of human rights in Soviet foreign policy,[59] and, perhaps more importantly, on the relationship between political and economic reform. Despite Gorbachev's commitment to a democratization process, critics claimed that by releasing control over society in the political sphere, the government would not be able to maintain control of the economy and guide it through radical reform.[60] The most extreme version of this argument justified the crackdown as necessary to restore social stability.[61]

In his memoirs, Gorbachev later commented that he "was not convinced by the opinions of some of our politicians that we should have followed the Chinese path—that is, to implement economic reforms first and only later take up political reforms—and that we could thus have avoided upheavals and instability." Gorbachev called such views naive because of the tendency of political structures in the Soviet Union to stifle reform efforts.[62]

Supporters of democratization rejected the view that the lesson of Tiananmen was that economic and political reform are incompatible. According to one Soviet journalist, the transformation of Chinese society as a result of economic reform engendered demands for change in the political sphere.[63] Supporters of democratization argued that guarantees were necessary and that for reform to be successful, economic and political changes had to proceed in step.[64]

CONCLUSIONS

The normalization of Sino-Soviet relations in May 1989 was one of many indications of the fundamental change that had swept through Moscow in the late

1980s. Indeed, the new basis for relations with China coincided with many of the new Gorbachev leadership's goals—refocusing resources on economic reform rather than on costly international conflicts, resolving remaining regional conflicts (such as Afghanistan and Cambodia) through peaceful means, and developing a new type of socialist community, founded on principles of equality and based on the common pursuit of reform.

After eliminating the "anti-China" coalition from the corridors of power in the Central Committee and the Foreign Ministry and installing a new team that viewed China's reform policies in a distinctly positive light, Gorbachev was able to achieve the breakthrough in Sino-Soviet relations that had eluded his predecessors. The new Sino-Soviet relationship was immediately put to the test, however, first by the June 1989 events on Tiananmen Square and then by the collapse of the Soviet Union itself.

Relations between China and a democratizing and decentralizing Russia would prove at least as complicated to manage as the Sino-Soviet relationship. As the following chapters reveal, in the 1990s China policy has been no less controversial in Moscow or in the Russian border regions than it was decades ago. To the contrary, Russia's differentiated political spectrum and diffuse division of power between center and peripheries have made its relations with China even more complex and challenging to manage.

7 / The Gorbachev Revolution and China Policy

Gorbachev's reevaluation of Stalinist ideology in foreign affairs, relations with other socialist states, and domestic politics led to fundamental changes in Soviet foreign policy in the mid-1980s.[1] To achieve the peaceful international environment necessary for economic reform, the Soviet Union had to reduce tensions with its capitalist opponents, particularly the United States, and to promote international relations based on mutual security.

CHANGING VIEWS IN THE MOSCOW POLICY COMMUNITY ABOUT WORLD POLITICS

In the mid-1980s, a consensus emerged in the Soviet foreign policy elite that capitalism was not inherently aggressive and militaristic, making cooperation possible. Stalinist dogma regarding the immutable enmity of capitalist states had fueled a costly arms race and competition with the West in the Third World, which the Gorbachev leadership gradually scaled down. Alignments in international politics were no longer seen as affecting the correlation of forces, which was the Soviet conception of the balance of military, ideological, political, and economic power between socialism and capitalism.[2]

The greater flexibility in the determination of Soviet foreign policy meant that Sino-American relations could be interpreted in terms of their substance, not their implications for the correlation of forces. Similarly, Soviet-Chinese problems could be analyzed as differences between two powerful neighbors—and more easily resolved.[3]

In the late 1980s, when changes in Sino-American and Soviet-American relations led to the formation of a relatively equidistant strategic triangle, Soviet officials reinterpreted Chinese foreign policy aims. Most analysts gave credit to the Chinese for recognizing that equidistance in the triangle would serve their foreign policy interests best in an increasingly multipolar and interdependent world.[4] According to many Soviet academics, the Chinese leadership recognized that cooperation with both the Soviet Union and the United States was required to achieve stability, peace, and economic development.[5]

Soviet analysts were quick to assert that the improvement in Soviet-Chinese relations would restore the balance in the triangle and would not lead to a return of a 1950s-style alliance.[6] Some observers admitted that the Chinese had sought to improve relations in the early 1980s because they perceived the USSR as isolated, facing intractable foreign and domestic problems, and consequently no longer as aggressive as before.[7] Later in the decade, as Zbigniew Brzezinski explained, the Chinese realized that the removal of the three obstacles (the Soviet Union's intervention in Afghanistan, support for the Vietnamese occupation of Cambodia, and military presence in Mongolia and along the Sino-Soviet border), which had symbolized the Soviet threat for a decade, was "a part of a process of the general weakening of the Soviet Union."[8]

On the positive side, Soviet analysts noted that American policymakers no longer spoke of the parallel strategic interests uniting the United States and China. In fact, Chinese dissatisfaction with relations with the United States contributed to the PRC's shift towards equidistance. Taiwan, restrictions on technology transfers, and human rights continued to cause problems in Sino-American relations. Fearing that excessively close ties with the United States would have a negative impact on China's relations with developing countries, other socialist states, and the international communist movement, Chinese leaders also consciously tried to distance themselves from Washington.[9]

Was the United States distressed at Chinese interest in a more balanced triangle and an improvement in Soviet-Chinese relations? Some Soviet scholars seemed to think so. Boris Zanegin argued that the United States wanted to maintain stable relations with China, including in the strategic sphere, to be able to count on the PRC as a "geopolitical reserve" in the future.[10] Other academics such as Aleksandr Larin argued, however, that the "China factor" was no longer as significant in American foreign policy since the United States had regained military strength. Moreover, Larin claimed that U.S. opposition to Soviet-Chinese relations would only boomerang against Sino-American relations.[11]

By the late 1980s, most Soviet officials and scholars had stopped highlighting the Chinese military threat and no longer expressed concern about Sino-American military cooperation. Reflecting the change in the official line, military commentators writing in *Voennaia Mysl'* refrained from discussion of China altogether, although in the 1970s the journal had been an important forum for articles about the Chinese threat. Soviet academics noted the significant cuts in the Chinese armed forces in 1985 and 1986 (one million men, or one-quarter of total personnel) that accompanied the PRC's new emphasis on peace and development.[12]

Even after the United States began selling China military equipment in the mid-1980s, a step the Soviet Union had tried to forestall for years, Soviet commentary was much less concerned with the Chinese military threat than at any other time in the past thirty years. Although the Chinese were authorized to purchase defensive weapons from the United States as of 1984, the first sale took place in the fall of 1985.[13] In general, there was little mention of Chinese military modernization in Soviet analysis, even though some qualitative improvements were made during this period. Since China's overall posture was no longer seen as threatening, incremental improvements in the Chinese military did not perturb the Soviets unduly.

By the mid-1980s, military cooperation between the United States and China had begun to develop in a variety of spheres. Exchanges of American and Chinese military personnel started taking place to discuss training, military doctrine, and logistics. In 1986, the U.S. Navy paid its first port call to the PRC since 1949.[14] Also in 1987, the Chinese allowed the United States to monitor Soviet nuclear tests from their territory.[15] The prevailing view in the Gorbachev leadership held that there was no reason to react with alarm to Sino-American military cooperation because these relations were limited and not directed against the Soviet Union. Officials who retained the orthodox ideological framework, however, continued to overestimate the Chinese military threat because of their distrust of the motives for the Sino-American relationship.[16]

THE INTERRELATIONSHIP BETWEEN PERESTROIKA AND THE CHINESE REFORMS

From 1986 through 1989, most Soviet policymakers and academics emphasized the common points in the Soviet and Chinese reform programs, although a minority noted that differences in conditions in the two countries and reform priorities remained.[17] There was a sense in the Soviet discussion that despite the historical, socioeconomic, and cultural differences between the USSR and the PRC, the congruence in the two reform efforts contributed significantly to the development of trust and cooperation between the two countries. While these parallels were made to explain the rapid pace of normalization in the late 1980s, already in 1987 a number of Soviet official commentators noted the similarity in Soviet and Chinese positions on many foreign and domestic problems. For example, Mikhail Titarenko, the director of the Institute of the Far East, stated in September 1987 that "the sphere of coincident approaches by the USSR and the CPR [PRC] to cardinal theoretical problems of the construction of socialism and international development is gradually expanding. It will be no exaggeration to say that, on a number of these problems, the degree of proximity that has now been reached is the greatest in the past 25 or even 30 years."[18]

Oleg Bogomolov, director of the Institute for International and Political Studies, admitted that different conditions were present in the various reforming socialist states, but saw certain basic similarities present in each one.[19] Other prominent academics emphasized that while socialist countries developed under diverse conditions, they faced common practical and theoretical reform tasks.[20] The implication here is that a new ideology of reform helped forge bonds among socialist states. At this time, for example, official observers wrote favorably about Chinese relations with other socialist states.[21] In Evgenii Bazhanov's view, "at long last the CPSU and the CPC [CCP] were able to see eye to eye on the principles and character of relations among socialist states and communist parties. Moscow agreed with Beijing that each country has the right to develop its own model of building socialism, that no one is the custodian of the ultimate truth and no one has the right to dictate to others."[22]

Although Soviet officials and academics stated that noninterference was a fundamental principle of the new Sino-Soviet relationship, the fate of the reform process in one country exerted considerable influence on the other. The Tiananmen Square protests showed that Gorbachev's political reform inspired the Chinese students to press for similar changes, while the crackdown in Beijing stimulated a debate in the Soviet Union about the relationship between democracy and economic reform.

Beginning in 1986, scholarly interest in the Chinese reforms increased tremendously. Articles on the Chinese experience appeared regularly in the Soviet press, and the main journal on Asian politics, *Problemy Dal'nego Vostoka*, boasted a section devoted entirely to the discussion of Chinese reforms, often including articles by Chinese scholars.[23] Once the Gorbachev leadership made a serious commitment to reform in 1986, Soviet observers began to comment favorably on the Chinese experience. Not only were their appraisals of current reforms highly positive, but they also traced the reforms to the Third Plenum in 1978 and gave a laudatory history of the entire decade of reform efforts.[24] Scholars directed a considerable amount of attention to a comprehensive economic analysis of specific issues of reform, such as public ownership and the problem of reforming Stalinist institutions.[25]

A few Soviet specialists even rebutted some of the earlier Soviet criticism. Lev Deliusin, for example, then the head of the China Department in Moscow's Institute of Oriental Studies, noted that the problems encountered during the reforms may not have been a consequence of the reform measures but may have been caused by policies that preceded them, such as the Cultural Revolution.[26] Although discussion of various aspects of the Chinese reforms was largely positive, academic analysts continued to express concern about side effects such as inflation and unemployment.[27] Deliusin was one of the few to point out before the Tiananmen events that future economic progress would depend on the fate of political reform in China.[28]

Criticism of the Chinese reforms during this period often took the form of discussion of more abstract concepts, such as the role of planning in a socialist society.[29] While under *glasnost'* the need to disguise discussion of Soviet reforms by commenting on Chinese reforms may have seemed superfluous, one striking incident in 1988 demonstrated the continued relevance of this tactic. In the same issue of *Pravda* that published the official rebuttal to the Nina Andreeva article in *Sovetskaia Rossiia* arguing against Gorbachev's reform agenda, the deputy director of the Institute of the Far East wrote a lengthy article on the Chinese reforms in which he argued that the problems that had arisen in the PRC (such as inflation) attested to the importance of not forcing the pace of reform and of proceeding with caution in a step-by-step manner.[30] Although discussion of China was used in this case to advocate a position opposed to reform, in other instances supporters of *perestroika* in the USSR discussed leftist criticism of the Four Modernizations policy in China (Deng's reform of agriculture, industry, science and technology, and defense). For example, commentators noted that some Chinese critics equated socialism with poverty and were upset with the reforms for introducing material incentives and ending wage leveling.[31]

The attempt at the Thirteenth CCP Congress in the fall of 1987 to situate the Four Modernizations within the context of socialist development in China (by claiming that China was at the "initial stage" of socialism) broadened the discussion in the Soviet Union of China's attempt to build socialism with Chinese characteristics. According to Vilia Gel'bras, then of the Institute of the International Workers' Movement, the *kto kogo* question was resolved in favor of socialism in China.[32] By the mid-1980s most scholars accepted that China's mixed economy was compatible with socialism.[33]

THE SOCIALIST COMMUNITY: A NEW ATTITUDE TOWARD DIVERSITY

Gorbachev began his rule with a new approach to the communist movement, an issue with important implications for Soviet-Chinese relations. At the Twenty-seventh Congress of the CPSU in February 1986, the Soviet leader emphasized the diversity of experience among the socialist states, adding that they had a lot to learn from one another.[34] As Vadim Medvedev, the top ideology official, noted two years later: "The time when such diversity was viewed with dogmatic, sectarian suspicion and considered a departure from Marxism-

Leninism and socialist internationalism is now past."[35] According to Gorbachev, states were free to choose their approach to socialist development, and others should respect their choice. By removing ideological considerations from international relations, greater cooperation—what he termed "unity in diversity"—could be achieved more readily.[36] That Gorbachev was truly committed to this principle was amply demonstrated by his restraint during the remarkable autumn of 1989 when the East European states one by one relinquished their commitment to the socialist path.

Gorbachev had no intention of prompting the demise of the socialist community through his new approach to relations among socialist states. What he had in mind was an end to the hierarchical structure of the communist movement and to Soviet leadership of it.[37] According to Deputy Foreign Minister Anatolii Adamishin, the attempt to impose one's views on others constituted an act of ideological aggression which served to fuel interstate conflicts. He stated:

> Why is injecting ideology into foreign policy so dangerous? The answer is that this is the direct path to foisting one's views, scale of values and ideals. Hence intolerance of the opinions of others. Hence one step to the imposition of one's convictions by force. Few like this, as a rule. Therefore, the reaction is enmity, conflicts and war, which often boomerangs against the adherents of messianisms. Acts of ideological aggression do not remove ideological contradictions; they instigate tensions in international relations and create explosive situations.[38]

Adamishin and others close to Gorbachev advocated replacing the Stalinist concepts that had shaped Soviet foreign policy for decades—what he called ideology—with new thinking, an ideological framework that better served Soviet foreign policy goals.

These principles were quickly put to the test when the Soviet general secretary paid a visit to Yugoslavia. Given that Yugoslavia's departure from the socialist community was considered for decades an act of apostasy, Gorbachev's praise for Yugoslavia's independent foreign policy, particularly its role in the nonaligned movement, was especially significant and indicative of the change in Soviet ideological concepts concerning socialist states.[39] The new principles of relations governing relations between socialist states were included in the Soviet-Yugoslav joint statement, and Gorbachev's visit paved the way for the first discussion of the causes of the break in Soviet-Yugoslav relations in 1948.[40] According to Oleg Troianovskii, Gorbachev's statement in Yugoslavia that the Soviet Union did not pretend to know the final truth about socialist development had an important impact on Sino-Soviet relations.[41]

These same principles figured prominently in the Sino-Soviet *Communiqué*, signed at the 1989 summit in Beijing. Reflecting on the history of Sino-Soviet relations, Gorbachev stated:

> The first conclusion, in my opinion, is that it is unfortunately far easier to sour or destroy relations between countries than to build and consolidate those relations and make them fruitful. A few erroneous decisions taken without regard for a partner's interests, attempts to impose one's own views, and the escalation of mutual grievances, possibly to a political level, as well as elevating ideological disputes and disagreements to the point of confrontation between states may result in dividing former friends with a wall of suspicion and animosity.[42]

The ideological dispute was repaired step by step throughout the 1980s, beginning with the admission by each side that the other was socialist. Subsequently, the perceived parallels in the Soviet and Chinese reforms, and Gorbachev's commitment to noninterference in the affairs of other socialist states, helped eliminate any lingering remnants of the previous two decades of acrimony in the ideological sphere. As a result of the normalization process, the Soviets and the Chinese began a mutually beneficial exchange of information about economic reform.[43]

IMPACT OF POLITICAL CHANGE IN EASTERN EUROPE AND THE SOVIET UNION ON SINO-SOVIET RELATIONS, 1989–91

Once the dust settled after the June 1989 crackdown, the Chinese leaders hoped to continue to develop their newly normalized relations with the Soviet Union and the East European countries. Instead, the Soviets instituted multi-candidate elections and the communist regimes in Eastern Europe collapsed one after the other like a house of cards. Beijing was faced with an even greater challenge than "spiritual pollution" from the West, in that the Chinese leadership feared that developments in the Soviet Union would reignite prodemocracy sentiment at home and challenge its legitimacy.[44]

Nicolae Ceauşescu's fall from power in Romania was the last straw for Chinese leaders. In late December 1989, a secret Central Committee document which criticized the Soviet Union for unleashing the turmoil in Eastern Europe was leaked to the press.[45] In early 1990, the Chinese leadership began publicly criticizing Soviet policies. Deputy Foreign Minister Rogachev traveled to Beijing in mid-January to try to preserve the relationship, and in the end the Chinese leaders agreed that it was important to maintain stable relations with the Soviet Union, even if socialism was being abandoned there.

Prime Minister Li Peng visited the Soviet Union, as planned, in April 1990. He was heckled by prodemocracy protestors in Moscow, however, and was later declared persona non grata by the Moscow City Council. Li Peng, for his part, stressed that the Soviet model of reform did not apply to China.[46] When President Jiang Zemin paid a visit to Moscow the following summer, he found an even more polarized Soviet political spectrum. Conservatives, who favored a limited reform of socialism, hailed his visit and advocated closer ties with China, while democrats, focused on relations with the West, had no interest in meeting him.[47]

Despite these ideological differences, relations between the USSR and the PRC expanded in 1990 and 1991. During Li Peng's 1990 visit to Moscow, the Soviet Union and China signed an agreement on guiding principles of mutual and balanced force reductions and confidence-building measures.[48] There have been several rounds of talks since then which covered issues such as the extent of the demilitarization of the border and the future location of disbanded units. Military contacts resumed in 1991, including high-level exchanges and arms sales, such as Beijing's agreement to purchase a squadron of Soviet SU-27 combat aircraft.[49]

As a consequence of the war in the Persian Gulf, the Soviet Union and China renewed cooperation in the foreign policy sphere. The two sides conferred four times about the Gulf War and shared similar concerns about the demonstration of American military might in the region. Sino-Soviet dialogue about the Middle East marked a departure from the pattern of the previous decade, when China and the United States emphasized their common foreign policy interests, which usually opposed Soviet positions. The narrowing of Soviet and Chinese differences on Cambodia by the beginning of the 1990s greatly facilitated their cooperation in other areas of foreign policy.

THE BORDER REGIONS AND
SINO-SOVIET NORMALIZATION

Following the 1989 summit, the Soviet Union and China also made real progress on border issues. During Jiang Zemin's May 1991 visit to Moscow, the two sides signed an agreement on the eastern portion of the border, involving the transfer of some riverine islands.[50] Under the terms of the accord, China received Damanskii/Zhenbao Island, the site of the bloody border clashes between the Soviet Union and the PRC in 1969. The fate of Bolshoi Ussuriiskii/ Heixiazi Island and Tarabarov/Yinlong Island, strategically located across from Khabarovsk, remained undecided, however, and these two islands were omitted from the May 1991 agreement.

Sino-Soviet bilateral trade never matched expectations, however, due to shortages of exportable goods in the USSR and China and inadequate transport.[51] Trade was further complicated in 1991 when the USSR and PRC switched to hard currency in their trade dealings. Coming at a time of considerable instability in the Soviet Union, the volume of Sino-Soviet trade dropped from $5.2 billion in 1990 to $3.8 billion in 1991.[52]

Border trade developed steadily in the late 1980s and early 1990s despite downturns in bilateral trade.[53] Given the difficulties involved in converting bilateral trade to a hard currency basis, border trade, conducted through barter, helped stabilize Sino-Russian trade relations in the short term. To promote barter trade, tough Soviet export controls imposed in 1989 and 1990 were removed.[54]

During the Gorbachev era, the growth of Sino-Russian regional relations continued to be regulated from Moscow. Just as in Brezhnev's day, when the CPSU administered the containment strategy pursued in the border regions, in the late 1980s central party officials fostered the restoration of regional political, economic, and cultural ties. It was the Moscow-based CPSU that had to sanction the resumption of the activities of the regional Sino-Soviet Friendship Societies and regional government exchanges.[55] As we will see in Chapter Nine, however, the rapid expansion of Sino-Russian regional relations, and especially the boom in border trade, would have to await the further decentralization of foreign economic relations in Russia, which occurred in the aftermath of the disintegration of the USSR.

CONCLUSIONS

By 1991, after three decades of hostility, the Soviet Union and China had succeeded in finding a stable basis for bilateral relations that was impervious to domestic upheaval in Beijing, the increasingly raucous debate about reform in Moscow, and even the demise of the communist system in the USSR. Although Soviet officials and academics continued to comment on the parallels between Soviet and Chinese reforms—even when they clearly diverged on the issue of political change in June 1989, Sino-Soviet bilateral relations remained on track and regional economic ties continued to flourish. The greatest challenges to the new relationship between Moscow and Beijing would come two years later, with the collapse of the USSR and the consequent rise in centrifugal pressures in the new Russia.

PART III
TOWARD SINO-RUSSIAN PARTNERSHIP

8 / Sino-Russian Relations in the Yeltsin Era

The end of communism in the USSR and its disintegration as a state had an immediate impact on relations between Moscow and Beijing. For decades the two neighbors had been divided over interpretation of a common ideology, but initially in 1991 and 1992 its absence caused some unease in Sino-Russian relations. Victorious Russian democrats balked at close cooperation with the Chinese leaders responsible for the Tiananmen Square massacre, while the communist leaders in Beijing wondered how to cope with a pro-Western government in Moscow.

Political winds shifted quickly in the Russian capital, however, bringing a cooling of Russia's enthusiasm about the West, new interest in relations with states in Asia, and a more nationalist political orientation. Soon Russian and Chinese leaders had forged a new common bond—opposition to a world order based on what they perceived as U.S. domination. Although Russia and China see their global role in different terms and often have divergent interests, they found sufficient common purpose in the creation of a more inclusive world order to enable them to forge a "constructive partnership" in 1994 and a "strategic partnership" by 1996. Despite anemic economic ties and periodic tensions in Sino-Russian regional relations, this partnership has grown closer, as grievances in Beijing and Moscow over U.S. policies toward Iraq, theater missile defense in Asia, and Kosovo, in particular, have mounted.

THE DAWN OF A NEW WORLD ORDER
AND MOSCOW'S CHINA POLICY

Just after Gorbachev and his advisors finally succeeded in breaking the hold of the dominant coalition favoring containment of China, the new foreign policy team that came to power in Yeltsin's Russia found new reasons to be wary of close ties with Beijing and greater cause for rapprochement with the West. Led by Foreign Minister Andrei Kozyrev, the democrats who set the tone for the new Russia's foreign policy advocated cooperation with the West so as to succeed in market-oriented economic reforms and democratic change at home.[1] Reflecting the primacy of this approach to foreign policy, Yeltsin told the UN Security Council in February 1992 that "Russia considers the United States and the West not as mere partners but as allies. It is a prerequisite for, I would say, a revolution in peaceful cooperation among civilized nations."[2]

Progress in political relations between Moscow and Beijing began to slow in the aftermath of the failed coup against Gorbachev in August 1991, an event that exacerbated the ideological differences that emerged after the collapse of communism in Eastern Europe. A Chinese Communist Party report criticizing the Soviet Union for restoring capitalism was leaked to the press. The Chinese leaders who circulated the report among senior Communist Party officials faulted the Soviet Communist Party for selecting Gorbachev as general secretary in 1985—a warning for greater discrimination when the succession process would take place in China.[3]

The Chinese leaders had even less sympathy for Boris Yeltsin, whom they accused of dismantling the socialist system in the Soviet Union. In fact, the Chinese government had been supportive of the coup plotters, thereby incurring the wrath of the victorious democrats and damaging Russian-Chinese relations for the next year. The Chinese leadership feared that political unrest in Russia would incite prodemocracy activists in China, but soon came to realize that the economic chaos in Russia might actually provide an important warning to Chinese dissidents regarding the potential consequences of their actions for their country's stability and economic welfare.[4]

Moreover, the devolution of power in the Soviet Union in the aftermath of the failed coup unleashed fears in Beijing of consequent turmoil in the Central Asian republics bordering on China.[5] Thus, despite their initial unease about the turn of political events in Moscow, the Chinese leadership soon recognized the importance of maintaining good-neighborly relations with their Russian counterparts.[6] The Chinese also initiated direct contacts with their new Central Asian neighbors: Kazakhstan, Kyrgyzstan, and Tajikistan.

The increased instability on the periphery of the former Soviet Union has given China, Russia, and the Central Asian states a greater incentive to come to agreement about their common boundaries. In February 1992, the Chinese and Russian parliaments ratified the eastern border agreement, which had been signed on May 16, 1991, during Jiang Zemin's visit to Moscow. The agreement marked the first time that both countries legally established their eastern border. Apart from this early breakthrough, political relations between Russia and China were strained in the first year after the collapse of the USSR. When Foreign Minister Kozyrev paid his first visit to Beijing in March 1992, the issues of contention were reminiscent of the problems on the Sino-American agenda—Taiwan and human rights. Despite these differences, Kozyrev emphasized that the two countries had a pragmatic interest in maintaining a stable relationship. To show that they had put their border conflict behind them, during his visit Russian and Chinese leaders exchanged the instruments of ratification for the eastern border agreement. The Chinese leadership also formally invited Yeltsin to visit the PRC.[7]

In November 1992, Kazakhstan, Kyrgyzstan, and Tajikistan joined Russia for the first time in a single delegation to the border talks in Beijing. The parties agreed to complete an agreement regarding confidence-building measures within 100 km from the border and large cuts in the number of offensive weapons in the zone.[8]

CHINA AND MOSCOW'S SEARCH
FOR A BALANCED FOREIGN POLICY

Despite the strains in relations between Moscow and Beijing since 1989, Yeltsin's visit turned out to be a success for two reasons.[9] First, by the end of 1992, the political center in Moscow had moved away from pro-West and pro-market positions. During that year, pressure had been mounting within the Yeltsin camp—by figures such as State Counselor Sergei Stankevich and Vladimir Lukin, then Russia's ambassador to Washington—to formulate a "Eurasian" alternative to Kozyrev's "Atlanticist" foreign policy.[10] Nationalist critics of the Yeltsin administration such as Ruslan Khasbulatov and ultra-right opponents like Vladimir Zhirinovskii were even more vocal in their criticism of Moscow's early pro-Western foreign policy.[11]

In response to the growing criticism of his foreign policy in 1992, Yeltsin used his China trip to demonstrate to critics at home that his policy was not overly biased towards the West. As Yeltsin stated at a press briefing on December 18, 1992: "We want balanced relations in Europe and Asia alike."[12] Similarly, the Chinese were feeling increasingly isolated in the world as tensions grew with Great Britain over Hong Kong, and the United States and France concluded arms deals with Taiwan. For this reason, the Chinese leaders shelved their political differences with the Yeltsin government and welcomed the opportunity to enhance cooperation with Russia.

In a public address in Beijing, Yeltsin, sounding very much like his predecessor, Mikhail Gorbachev, spoke of the parallel interests of Russia and China. Although he acknowledged that the two countries differed on certain questions, he noted that "ideological barriers have been removed."[13] During his visit Yeltsin appeared greatly impressed with the results achieved by the Chinese through their reliance on a more gradual approach to economic reform. The Chinese, who had repressed attempts at political reform for the sake of stability, could not have been more pleased when Yeltsin praised their strategy of avoiding haste, revolution, and shocks.[14]

The two countries successfully concluded a number of mutually beneficial agreements. These agreements provided for: (1) the acceleration of work on border force reduction and confidence-building measures, with the aim of signing a document within two years that would reduce troops in the border zone to a minimum by the year 2000;[15] (2) Russian assistance with the construction of two nuclear plants in China; (3) renovation of Chinese arms industries built by the Soviet Union in the 1950s; and (4) Chinese credits for the delivery of 10 million tons of corn to Russia over a two-year period.[16] Russia also agreed to provide the PRC with uranium-enrichment technology for its nuclear program.

The crowning achievement of the summit, however, was the signing of a joint declaration establishing a framework for Russian-Chinese relations. According to the declaration, Russia and China "regard each other as friends." They agreed not to enter into any alliances against each other and to refrain from hegemony in the Asian-Pacific region and elsewhere in the world. In response to Chinese concerns about the expansion of economic ties with Taiwan, Russia stated it would not officially recognize the Taipei government. Pledging to respect each other's model of development and to prevent ideological differences from impeding their bilateral relations, Russia and China outlined their goals for cooperation in a wide range of spheres.[17] Although the summit proved successful, Yeltsin cut it short by a day to deal with political concerns back in Moscow, dramatizing that Yeltsin's focus was neither on the West nor on Asia, but on his fragile hold on power.

Beginning in mid-1992, disappointment with the trickle of Western aid and disenchantment with Western-style economic reforms led Russian policymakers all along the political spectrum to question Russia's pro-West policy and to look at China with new eyes. While Yeltsin's supporters emphasized the mutual benefits to be gained from relations with China, his critics in Parliament contrasted China's economic successes with the disruptions brought about by the reforms of Prime Minister Yegor Gaidar.[18]

Despite their wariness about the dramatic changes taking place in Russia, the Chinese leaders focused on the positive aspects of their relations with their northern neighbor—mutually beneficial trade and a counterweight to pressures from the United States and Japan. According to Mikhail Titarenko, director of the Institute of the Far East, Russia and China understood that neither threatened the other and could provide each other with welcome support.[19]

Economic cooperation between Russia and China was expanding in several areas in the early 1990s. The volume of Sino-Russian trade reached $5.8 billion in 1991 and then jumped more than 30 percent from $5.86 billion in

TABLE 8.1   Volume of Sino-Russian Bilateral Trade, 1992–99

Year	Volume of Trade (million U.S. dollars)
1992	5.86
1993	7.68
1994	5.07
1995	5.00
1996	6.84
1997	6.12
1998	5.48
1999	5.70

SOURCE: Interfax, ITAR-TASS, *RFE/RL Newsline*, Xinhua

1992 to $7.68 billion in 1993, making China Russia's second largest trading part-
ner after Germany, while Russia ranked fifth among China's trading partners
(see Table 8.1).[20] Early on, Russia and China targeted energy as a promising
area for economic cooperation. In April 1993, ten Russian nuclear scientists
were dispatched to China to spend the next two-and-a-half years working with
their Chinese counterparts on the development of nuclear reactor technology.[21]
As stipulated by the 1991 Sino-Soviet agreement on the demarcation of the eastern border, Russian and Chinese experts also opened border demarcation talks
in June 1993 and began a five-year project that involved drawing the frontier
lines and addressing border control issues.[22]

Nonetheless, new irritants began surfacing in Russian-Chinese relations. In
the spring of 1993 a series of incidents took place in the East China Sea in which
Chinese vessels seized Russian ships because of alleged smuggling activities.[23]
Furthermore, renewed political instability in the Russian capital during the
conflict between Yeltsin and the Parliament in September–October 1993 put
the Russian-Chinese relationship to a new test. Unlike its response to the failed
coup in 1991, this time the Chinese leadership remained neutral. In the early
days of the conflict between the Yeltsin government and the Parliament, Prime
Minister Li Peng told a Mexican newspaper that "no matter what happens in
Russia, China is ready to maintain relations of good-neighborliness, friendship,
and mutually advantageous cooperation with it."[24] The Chinese government's
official statement on the bloodshed in Moscow simply expressed concern and
the hope that an appropriate settlement to the conflict would be found.[25]

For Yeltsin, the policy of expanding cooperation with China turned out to
be one of the few issues on which he could achieve agreement under conditions of increasing political fragmentation.[26] Yeltsin's emphasis on improving

relations with China appealed to all but those on the democratic and ultra-nationalist fringes of the political spectrum in Moscow. At least until early 1993, Yeltsin's China policy also served as a point of agreement between Moscow and Russia's increasingly fractious border regions.

Thus Sino-Russian relations continued to flourish, and in May 1994 Prime Minister Viktor Chernomyrdin traveled to Beijing to discuss a wide range of issues with President Jiang Zemin, especially the growing importance of border and interregional economic cooperation.[27] One key issue on the agenda was the precipitous drop in bilateral trade—50 percent in the first four months of 1994.[28] Although the rate of the decline in Russian-Chinese trade slowed by the end of 1994, trade between China and Russia amounted to only $5.07 billion in 1994, a 34 percent drop overall from 1993 levels.[29] From 1993 to 1994, China's share of the Russian market declined from second to fifth place among Russia's trading partners.[30] After Chernomyrdin's visit, Xinhua issued a statement attributing the fall in trade to new Russian visa rules and to Russian customs duties on imports. Observers in Moscow also cited the retraction of credit in China (which led to a diminished demand for resources for the construction industry, a traditional Russian export) as a reason for the decreased trade volume.[31]

Jiang Zemin's trip to Moscow in September 1994 marked the first time since 1957 that a Chinese president had visited the Russian capital. During his visit, Jiang agreed to Yeltsin's proposal to upgrade Sino-Russian relations to a "constructive partnership." Although China had committed to an independent foreign policy since 1982, concern about growing American unilateralism inclined the Chinese leadership to favor a closer relationship with Moscow.[32] Beijing agreed to this new formulation because the partnership relationship would be sufficiently limited to preserve China's freedom to maneuver.

At the summit meeting, Yeltsin and Jiang signed an agreement on the demarcation of the western part of the border. They agreed not to target each other with nuclear weapons and to non-first-use of nuclear weapons against each other. The two leaders addressed remaining bilateral problems relatively openly. In his remarks, Yeltsin acknowledged that relations between Moscow and Beijing had their ups and downs, but argued that there was "a need to build these relations on the basis of the national interests of the two countries, to resolve complex questions, and to find the opportunity to combine two great world civilizations—western and eastern."[33] Jiang emphasized that geography and complementary economies enhanced the potential for Sino-Russian cooperation. In response to mounting fears in the Russian border regions of an unstoppable flow of Chinese illegal immigrants to Russia, the Chinese leader defended China's policies in the border regions and stated that he hoped that Russia "would protect the legitimate rights and interests of Chinese citizens who are engaged in normal trade and other activities."[34] He stated that China was opposed to illegal immigration and attributed the problems with border trade to inadequate preparation in both countries to deal with the rapid opening of the border.

Jiang noted that Yeltsin and he had agreed to continue to develop cooperation between their two countries despite these problems, "rather than giving up eating for fear of choking, as the Chinese saying goes."[35] According to a Chinese scholar, the Chinese government had become concerned about negative public opinion in the Russian Far East concerning trade with China and conducted a public opinion survey in the region prior to Jiang Zemin's visit. The survey reportedly concluded that while some people in the region were dissatisfied with low-quality goods from China and considered the illegal immigration of Chinese people to be a problem, many others wanted cooperation with China to continue.[36]

Despite the difficulties that arose in economic cooperation between states, which were both in the process of major economic transformation, Russian and Chinese leaders continually emphasized the importance of cooperation. Officials in Moscow tended to remain upbeat about Russian-Chinese trade relations. Evgenii Afanasiev, a Russian Foreign Ministry official, complained that much of the criticism of trade with China in the Russian media was unfair.[37] Another official explained that the problems in relations needed to be balanced with the common interests the two countries had in trade: "Yes it is advantageous for us at the moment to cooperate with China. Let us be honest—we have to feed Russia now. Can China help in this? It can. We have to dress Russia. Can China help? Certainly."[38]

In 1995, despite continued controversy on border trade and growing opposition in the border regions to any territorial concessions to Beijing as a part of the border demarcation process, high-level meetings between Russia and China addressed many issues. Kozyrev's trip to Beijing in March laid the groundwork for the year's bilateral contacts, including Li Peng's upcoming trip to Moscow, the participation by high-ranking Chinese officials in ceremonies in Moscow marking the fiftieth anniversary of the end of World War II, and the third Sino-Russian summit to be held in Beijing later in the year. Although the Russian foreign minister hailed the achievement of stable and friendly Sino-Russian political relations, he noted that the main challenge for the two countries was to boost their sluggish trade balance "to a level worthy of the present status of bilateral relations. . . ."[39] To this end a meeting of the intergovernmental committee on economic, trade, and technical cooperation was scheduled for later in the spring.

In another sign of the continuing progress in Sino-Russian bilateral relations, President Jiang Zemin represented China at the May 1995 ceremonies in Moscow marking the fiftieth anniversary of the victory against Nazi

Germany. Some differences between the two countries persisted, as demonstrated by China's decision to hold a nuclear test during Defense Minister Grachev's visit to Beijing in mid-May. Although the Chinese reassured their visitor that they were prepared to call a halt to future tests,[40] the Russian Foreign Ministry responded that the blast would not "promote a favorable atmosphere" for upcoming multilateral talks on a comprehensive test ban and expressed "regret" about the Chinese move.[41]

During his visit, Grachev continued discussions about the reduction of forces in the border regions within 100 km of the boundary. Progress had been stalled due to differences over the number of weapons that would be allowed within the 100 km zone. Although China wanted to clear the zone of weapons, Grachev noted that moving Russian arms north by 100 km would be untenable due to the difficult terrain and harsh climate in that area.[42]

One month later, Premier Li Peng arrived in Moscow for a state visit, during which the Chinese and Russian leaders outlined their "constructive partnership for the twenty-first century." Noting that the views of the two countries on key international issues coincided, Li and Chernomyrdin affirmed that mutual support and cooperation in regional and global affairs was an important factor in stability and security in Asia and elsewhere in the world.[43] The picture of Sino-Russian harmony provided a sharp contrast to the deterioration in Sino-American relations over Taiwanese President Lee Tenghui's June 1995 visit to the United States. Indeed, Russia supported the PRC's position on the Taiwan issue and, in return, not a critical word was heard from Li Peng on Russia's military intervention in Chechnya, considered to be a Russian internal matter.[44]

In September 1995, Chinese Foreign Minister Qian Qichen arrived in Moscow to make final arrangements for Yeltsin's visit to China, scheduled for November 1995. Russian and Chinese officials prepared a package of documents for signing, including a treaty on confidence-building measures in the border region, which would include China's Central Asian neighbors as well as Russia. Once again the growing political cooperation between Russia and China was the highlight of the visit. As before, the two countries called attention to their identity of views on international questions, but this time they stressed their agreement on a common vision of a multipolar world order and advocated a stronger role for an independent and balanced United Nations.[45]

A STRATEGIC PARTNERSHIP
FOR THE TWENTY-FIRST CENTURY

Due to Yeltsin's hospitalization for a heart ailment on October 26, his visit to Beijing had to be postponed for several months. The third Sino-Russian summit eventually was held April 24–26, 1996, just weeks before the first round of the Russian presidential elections. Once again, Yeltsin could point to the development of Sino-Russian bilateral relations as a success of Russian foreign policy. This time the Russian and Chinese leaders hailed their relations as a "strategic partnership."

Building on earlier statements about their common foreign policy goals, Yeltsin and Jiang affirmed in their third summit meeting that the two countries "were entering into a new stage of partnership, based on equality and trust, and directed toward strategic interaction in the 21st century."[46] By cooperating in matters of strategy, Russia and China would better be able to work toward the difficult transition from a bipolar to a multipolar world, especially given continued attempts by certain unnamed states to apply pressure and engage in bloc politics.[47] During this summit meeting, it became apparent that Russia and China saw their bilateral relationship as a way of relieving perceived pressures from the West. Thus the Chinese side expressed its understanding for the Russian position on NATO expansion, while Yeltsin affirmed Russia's support for the PRC's position on Taiwan.[48]

Apart from expressions of mutual political support and reaffirmations of previous bilateral treaties, the two leaders negotiated many new substantive accords during the summit, including two of importance for the international community as a whole. Yeltsin gained China's agreement to accede to the Comprehensive Nuclear Test Ban Treaty, which would enable the treaty's signing at an upcoming G-8 meeting in September. A five-way treaty on border confidence-building measures that included China's Central Asian neighbors (Kazakhstan, Kyrgyzstan, and Tajikistan) was signed on the last day of the summit. According to this agreement, each party would inform the others about troop movements, military personnel, weapons, and armor within a 100 km zone. No more than 40,000 personnel could be involved in exercises on the eastern border and 4,000 personnel and 50 pieces of armor on the western part. The parties agreed to inform each other in the event that exercises using more than 25,000 personnel were contemplated and to invite observers if more than 35,000 would be involved. Naval forces were allowed to temporarily enter the 100 km zone to cope with natural disasters and to transit the zone for repairs.[49]

Russia and China also pledged to increase their overall trade turnover to $20 billion by the start of the twenty-first century.[50] This would prove to be an unattainable goal—although Sino-Russian trade regained some of its earlier momentum, attaining a level of $5.5 billion in 1995, it has yet to reach its 1993 record high. For the dramatic increase forecast by the Russian and Chinese leaders to be possible, trade turnover would have to include major cooperative projects in the energy sector, most of which have not yet found financial backing. Nonetheless, joint projects to build pipelines from Irkutsk and Yakutsk to China continue to be discussed at high-level meetings.[51]

In language hearkening back to the days of Sino-Soviet friendship in the 1950s, both the Russian and Chinese leaders spoke effusively about the results of their third summit meeting. Jiang Zemin called the meeting a "complete success," while Yeltsin noted appreciatively that there were "no problems" in Sino-Russian relations.[52] For Yeltsin, the bright results of the summit provided a boost for his electoral campaign. During a visit to Shanghai, for example, the Russian president hailed the city's impressive economic performance. He attributed the success of the Chinese reforms to the pragmatism of the leaders, rather than to the communist model, as his main opponent, Gennadii Ziuganov, had tried to argue.[53]

Just as much of the world became focused on Yeltsin's medical and political prospects in 1996, a crucial presidential election year for Russia, so did China become concerned about the potential impact of leadership change in Moscow on the future development of Sino-Russian relations. The Chinese leadership had no official position on the Russian elections, considered to be a Russian internal affair, and expressed the hope that Sino-Russian relations would continue to develop no matter who was elected president. According to high-ranking Chinese scholars, however, many in the leadership secretly hoped that Yeltsin would win. During the first round of the elections, there was some concern that Zhirinovskii's ultra-nationalists would earn a place on the second ballot, but even when the choice was between Yeltsin and Communist Party General Secretary Ziuganov, many Chinese leaders preferred a Yeltsin victory. The Russian leader was, after all, a known quantity who had proven his ability to develop relations with China on a favorable footing. In the view of many Chinese leaders, this was more important than ideological compatibility.

Moreover, there was a sense among some scholars that nationalism could be an important force in a Ziuganov leadership and could further inflame the political climate in the Russian Far East about the Sino-Russian border demarcation and Chinese illegal immigration.[54] An internal Chinese Foreign Ministry report cited in a Hong Kong newspaper noted that a Yeltsin victory would ensure greater political stability and prospects for economic growth in Russia, factors of importance for China.[55] Consequently, China's leaders greeted Yeltsin's reelection with considerable relief.

Russian and Chinese officials continued their bilateral meetings in 1996 in an effort to expand their economic cooperation. Sino-Russian trade revived somewhat, reaching $6.84 billion in 1996, but still falling short of the record high of $7.68 billion in 1993 and well below the desired volume of $20 billion. In early December 1996, Russia and China agreed to begin construction on a two-million-kilowatt nuclear power plant in Lianyungang, Jiangsu Province. The two countries originally had agreed in December 1992 to build the plant in Liaoning Province, but the Chinese side requested the change due to an energy crisis in Jiangsu.[56]

Deputy Prime Minister Aleksei Bolshakov of Russia traveled to Beijing on December 12, 1996, to meet with Deputy Prime Minister Li Lanqing at a session of the intergovernmental commission on commercial, economic, scientific, and technical cooperation. Noting that problems remained in Sino-Russian trade, Bolshakov stated that this was an issue to be addressed in the regular meetings of the premiers of the two countries.[57] The Russian deputy prime minister emphasized the prospects for Sino-Russian cooperation in the power sector, such as Russia's providing generators and turbines for the Three Gorges dam project. However, the bid for the project made by a consortium of Russian companies proved uncompetitive.[58]

When Li Peng traveled to Moscow later in December to meet with Viktor Chernomyrdin, the two leaders decided to commit themselves to biannual meetings and established subcommittees in key areas, such as economic relations and trade, energy resources, and transportation. Li and Chernomyrdin also signed an agreement on cooperation between the Bank of China and the Russian Federal Central Bank, and Russia agreed to help China train astronauts, build a controllable spaceship, and launch a carrier rocket.

Political relations turned out to be the most promising area of cooperation. In exchange for Russia's reaffirmation of its one-China policy, China expressed its support for Russian membership in the Asia-Pacific Economic Cooperation (APEC) forum.[59] During the April 1997 Sino-Russian summit in Moscow, the two countries again pledged to work toward the creation of a multipolar world, a timely task given what they perceived as attempts by "certain forces" to create a unipolar world order, a not very veiled critique of American foreign policy.[60] Indeed, perceived pressure from the United States brought Russia and China closer together. The dramatic progress in Sino-Russian political relations paralleled the development of NATO expansion, to which most Russian policymakers remain opposed despite the separate NATO-Russia agreement. Similarly, China has looked to Russia for support against what is viewed by many Chinese officials as an American attempt to prevent the PRC from assuming its rightful role in world affairs. Just as Russian officials saw NATO expansion as a way of containing Russian power, Chinese officials viewed the U.S. role in the 1996 Taiwan crisis and stiff conditions for China's entry into the World Trade Organization (WTO) as a means of countering its growing clout.

Apart from rhetorical calls for partnership, the main achievement of the 1997 summit was the signing of a five-party agreement on the reduction of forces along the entire 4,700 km border. This issue had been a stumbling block to the normalization of Sino-Soviet relations since the border clashes, and its resolution marked a watershed in Sino-Russian relations. According to the agreement, China, Russia, Kazakhstan, Kyrgyzstan, and Tajikistan agreed to numerical limits on their forces stationed in the border region—130,400 Chinese troops and an equal number divided among Russia and the Central Asian states.[61] The agreement only covered ground troops, forward air force units, air defense units, and certain classes of equipment.[62] Border troops, strategic missile forces, the navy, long-range aviation, and missile air defense units were excluded from numerical limits.[63] Also, Vladivostok and Khabarovsk, cities within the 100 km zone where there are major military bases, were exempted from these caps.[64]

According to Ambassador Genrykh Kireev, the head of the Russian delegation to the border demarcation talks, the agreement did not involve any redeployment of troops away from the border,[65] a point which China had demanded consistently since 1969. Moscow has resisted such a move because it would affect the disposition of its forces, originally located closer to the border due to adverse climatic and geographical conditions farther afield. Chinese forces, on the other hand, were never located so close to the border and would not have been affected by a redeployment provision.

THE SINO-RUSSIAN PARTNERSHIP
IN AN EVOLVING STRATEGIC CONTEXT

Since Chernomyrdin's April 1997 visit to Beijing, Russian and Chinese leaders have struggled to elaborate on their conception of a strategic partnership. This has been a difficult process because of the numerous changes in the international environment from 1997 to 1999. In 1997 and 1998, as U.S.-China relations improved and Russia signed a separate understanding with NATO, the Sino-Russian partnership appeared to represent both a plea for greater multilateral cooperation in world affairs and a vision of a more inclusive world order.[66] But from late 1998 to 1999, a series of developments took place (U.S. military strikes against Iraq, plans for the creation of U.S.-Japanese theater missile defense capabilities, NATO expansion and bombing of Yugoslavia) that led Russian and Chinese leaders to focus their efforts on opposing the current world order. Much as China joined forces with the United States in the 1970s and 1980s against Soviet hegemony, today Russian and Chinese leaders are attempting to coordinate their responses to what they view as U.S. unilateralism in world affairs.

Just as the Sino-American relationship in the 1970s and 1980s had to overcome the numerous differences between the two countries, so too have Russia and China had to cope with differing interests in their effort to implement their strategic partnership for the twenty-first century. In general terms, these differences stem from the changing roles played by Russia and China in international affairs. Russia, a declining great power, aims to recover its lost status, while China, a rising power, resists efforts to constrain its emerging global role.

For Russia, a great power position means sitting at the same table as the Western states—through cooperation with NATO, membership in the G-8, and efforts to play a meaningful role in Korean security and the Kosovo crisis. China, however, has endeavored to make the international community aware of its unique position in world affairs. Perceiving a growing threat to its interests from the West, China has relied on Russian technology to strengthen its military might. Chinese leaders have sought Russian cooperation on Taiwan and supported Russia's entry into APEC, but they have resisted Russian participation in the Korean security talks primarily to maintain their own role as power brokers. Strategic partnership has provided a framework for cooperation between Russia and China, especially at a time of tensions with the West, but in the long term may not be able to compensate for the widening gap between the international positions of the two partners.

ECONOMIC COOPERATION

Sino-Russian economic relations have been lagging far behind political relations, leading Chinese scholars to question whether the uneven development of economic and political cooperation bodes ill for their developing partnership.[67] Apart from the benefits of Sino-Russian economic relations for the development of the Russian Far East, most Russian analysts emphasize the political importance of the strategic partnership and attribute lagging economic ties to economic problems on both sides rather than to any fundamental problem in the overall relationship.[68]

Despite pledges at the last Sino-Russian summit meeting in April 1997 to achieve $20 billion in trade by the year 2000, the volume of bilateral trade for the first eight months of 1997 actually fell by 20 percent, and exports of machinery, one of the key products Russia was trying to promote, were hard hit.[69] In 1997, Sino-Russian trade only reached $6.12 billion, short of the 1996 level.[70]

Russian leaders have focused on the energy sector as one which held the promise for significantly expanding economic relations. China became an oil importer in 1993 and its dependency on imports is expected to grow to 40 percent by 2010.[71] Some energy experts argue that oil and gas have replaced Marx and Lenin as the basis for contemporary Russian-Chinese relations.[72]

Indeed, progress in this area would suit the interests of increasingly important economic interests in Russia, such as Gazprom, the gas monopoly where
former Prime Minister Chernomyrdin built his career, as well as oil companies and major banks.[73] Oil and gas interests have been playing an increasingly
important role in Russia's policy toward the former Soviet states and are beginning to show their clout in other areas of foreign policy as well.[74] Russian and
Chinese officials point to the Kovyktinskoe gas field near Irkutsk as one of the
more promising areas for cooperation. According to a June 27, 1997, agreement
between Sidanko, the Russian oil company that is the majority shareholder in
the Kovyktinskoe field, and the China National Petroleum Corporation, 30–35
billion cubic meters of gas would be exported per year over the next thirty-six
years, of which 20 billion cubic meters would go to China and other Asian states
once the pipeline is built in ten years.[75] The pipeline would address China's
growing energy needs and might also involve exports to Japan and South Korea.
The rest of the gas would go to consumers in Russia.

The project requires $12 billion in investment. Originally, the South Korean
East Asian Gas Company was to participate, but the company was a subsidiary
of Hanbo Steel, a large conglomerate which went bankrupt in January 1997.
However, in October 1999, Kogas, a South Korean state-owned company, joined
the project. Kogas plans to cooperate with Russia and China in building a
pipeline.[76] The Japanese Eximbank and Japan National Oil Corporation also
expressed interest in Kovyktinskoe, and a team formed in the fall of 1997 to
study it further.

To provide a boost to economic cooperation, Yeltsin brought Arkadii
Volskii, a leading Russian industrialist, to Beijing during the November 1997
summit meeting. In Volskii's view, Sino-Russian economic relations appeared
"frozen."[77] Boris Nemtsov, who had taken charge of Sino-Russian economic
cooperation as a part of his duties as first deputy prime minister, arrived in
Beijing a day early to address concerns over Chinese tariffs on other important Russian exports, such as chemical fertilizer and metals.[78]

Competition from the United States for a share of the Chinese market has
become a problem for Russia. After the November 1997 Sino-American summit, for example, the two countries announced that China would purchase
Boeing aircraft and would discuss U.S. sales of civilian nuclear technology, both
areas in which Russia has hoped to compete.[79] As of late 1997, just 5 percent
of Russia's exports went to China and only 2.5 percent of China's exports went
to Russia.[80]

Russia's uncompetitive and unsuccessful bid for the production of turbines
for the Three Gorges Project was an early indication that the rapid development of cooperation in the energy area would not be easily achieved. Despite

China's great interest in improving economic relations with Russia, when it comes time to make economic decisions the Chinese look at the bottom line first, a tendency that irks Russia's staunchest proponents of partnership with China.

At the November 1997 Beijing summit, Nemtsov and Chinese Vice Premier Li Lanqing tried to move forward with other energy projects and signed a technical memorandum regarding the construction of the Kovyktinskoe gas pipeline. They also signed an accord about the joint development of projects in diamond processing and discussed the possibility of Russia's construction of two nuclear plants in China, in addition to the one to be built in Lianyungang.[81]

In 1998 Sino-Russian trade continued to fall to $5.48 billion, a 10.5 percent drop from 1997, and reflective of the impact of economic crisis in Russia and Asia.[82] Throughout the year, Russian and Chinese leaders continued to seek ways to boost bilateral economic cooperation. In a series of high-level meetings, they explored additional projects, especially in the energy sector, and tried to involve large firms in new ventures. For example, Gazprom developed a $15 billion plan to build a pipeline to ship gas from deposits in Krasnoiarsk Krai and the Yamal-Nenets Autonomous Region to Shanghai over a 30–year period beginning in 2004.[83]

Some progress has been achieved already. In the summer of 1998, Russia and China began negotiating a project valued at several billion dollars to build an electrical grid for transmitting power from Irkutsk to Beijing.[84] In 1997, the Russian firm Yukos signed three agreements with China National Petroleum Corporation to sell 1.5 million tons of oil to China in 1999, the maximum capacity for rail shipments. To boost oil sales, Russia and China are discussing the construction of a pipeline from the Yukos oilfields in Tomsk to China.[85]

To overcome the poor reputation of Chinese goods, Beijing opened two major department stores and a trade center in Moscow.[86] The quality of Russian technology also proved to be an obstacle to economic cooperation, as China postponed participation in a joint project for the design and production of Tupolev-330 transport aircraft due to the Russian failure to meet Chinese safety standards.[87]

The Chinese prime minister's February 1999 visit to Moscow was the capstone of Russian and Chinese efforts to revitalize their economic ties. Both sides viewed the meeting as a success because many important agreements were signed for cooperation in energy, timber, regional economic relations, and joint ventures in electronics.[88] Prime Minister Zhu Rongji, known for his focus on expanding China's economic relations with the West, surprised his Russian hosts with his interest in moving ahead with Sino-Russian cooperation. The Chinese leader also proved able to find common language with then-Prime

Minister Evgenii Primakov, whose views of economic reform were much closer to the Chinese model than those of his predecessors.[89]

The fate of major energy projects will hinge on the future of the energy market as well as on the resolution of the economic crises facing Asia and Russia. Indeed, the main Russian partner for Kovyktinskoe, Sidanko, declared bankruptcy in May 1999. The fate of the Kovyktinskoe project soon became entangled in Russia's high-stakes oil politics. Although British Petroleum had a 10 percent share and had invested $571 million into Sidanko, in November 1999 the Tiumen oil company (TNK) managed to gain control over Sidanko's most lucrative asset, the Chernogorneft subsidiary, in what western analysts claim were rigged bankruptcy proceedings. BP Amoco countered by lobbying hard against TNK's request for a $500 million loan from the United States Export-Import Bank to finance other projects.[90] Meanwhile, another Sidanko shareholder, Sputnik Fund, representing high-profile investors such as George Soros, filed suit against TNK in Moscow and New York. In December 1999, the Russian court ruled that Chernogorneft would be returned to Sidanko.[91]

Although BP and its partners in RUSIA-Petroleum have title to the Kovyktinskoe gas field, the Ministry for Fuel and Energy plans to put the license to the field to tender, in what some observers say may be an effort to find a large Russian firm to buy a 51 percent share. Communist deputies, still the largest group in the State Duma, have stated that they would not approve a production sharing agreement for the project unless a Russian company had a majority share. The Duma also declared Kovyktinskoe to be a strategic gas field, thereby ensuring that deputies would have to approve the details of all future agreements.[92]

The outlook for multilateral cooperation in the energy sector also will depend on the configuration of domestic forces within Russia, China, and Japan. Progress in bilateral relations will be decisive for energy-sector developments, especially the ability of Russia and Japan and Japan and China to resolve outstanding problems in their relations.

CENTRAL ASIA

The border with China is no longer the exclusive purview of Russian policymakers. After the disintegration of the USSR, China acquired three new neighbors: Kazakhstan, Kyrgyzstan, and Tajikistan. China's ties with these countries have deep historical roots. Apart from brief periods of closure in the twentieth century, the border region has served as an important trade route and a gateway linking West and East. The region's most famous trade route is the Silk Road, which for 2,000 years connected the West to China through Central Asia and what is now the PRC's Xinjiang Uighur Autonomous Region.

More than fifty years ago, the explorer Peter Fleming called Xinjiang "the last home of romance in international politics" due to its dramatic landscape and reputation for intrigue and conflict among the numerous ethnic and commercial interests intermingled there.[93] Romantic to an explorer's eye perhaps, but to contemporary inhabitants of the region the openness of the border between the Central Asian states and Xinjiang has brought cooperation and new cause for concern. Since 1988, Xinjiang has conducted direct trade relations with its neighbors in Central Asia.[94] The volume of trade has expanded dramatically in recent years, from $100 million in 1992 to $695 million in 1995,[95] and reaching $869 million in 1998—approximately 57 percent of Xinjiang's total trade.[96]

The Central Asian states and China have been working to expand their economic links and facilitate transportation by rail and road. Under a March 1995 agreement, for example, China, Pakistan, Kazakhstan, and Kyrgyzstan agreed to open the Karakoram highway, a new 3,500 km transit route running from Almaty to Bishkek to Kashi in China, and then to the port of Karachi in Pakistan.[97] The first highway, from Tajikistan to China, completed in 1998, also connected Dushanbe to this route.[98] In 1996, a new Turkey-Iran-Turkmenistan-Uzbekistan-Kazakhstan-China (Istanbul-Druzhba-Beijing) rail line became operational.[99] A $450 million loan from Japan is being used to overhaul the Druzhba-Alanshankou rail line connecting Kazakhstan and China.[100] As in the case of the Russian Far East and the Chinese Northeast, inadequate transportation links and border infrastructure have limited the expansion of economic cooperation between Central Asia and China.

During a February 1997 summit meeting between Kazakhstan's President Nursultan Nazarbaev and Chinese President Jiang Zemin, the two leaders discussed further improving rail and air connections. Japan already had extended a $74 million credit to Kazakhstan to develop storage facilities and carriage capacity at the border rail station at Druzhba. The Kazakhstani president credited the improvements with the increase in rail tonnage from 1.2 million tons of freight in 1995 to 2.5 million in 1996 and called attention to the corresponding increase in Sino-Kazakhstani trade from $391 million in 1995 to $459 million in 1996 and $527 million in 1997.[101]

During the summit, Nazarbaev and Jiang also discussed the expansion of cooperation in the energy sector. At that time, the Chinese leaders expressed their support for Nazarbaev's proposal to lay a gas pipeline, and possibly an oil pipeline as well, from western Kazakhstan to western China. The Chinese and Kazakhstani leaders agreed to raise the level of their permanent contacts through a joint economic commission, which henceforth would be headed by deputy prime ministers.[102]

Kyrgyzstan enjoyed a similar expansion in economic linkages with China, as trade peaked at $230 million in 1995. During a visit by Jiang Zemin in July 1996, Kyrgyzstan and China agreed to strengthen their cooperation in transportation, communications, mining, energy, light industry, food processing, agriculture, and construction.[103] The Andijan-Osh-Kashgar highway, connecting Uzbekistan, Kyrgyzstan, and China, opened in July of 1997.[104] Trade with China decreased to $106 million in 1997, however.[105] Currently China, Kyrgyzstan, and Uzbekistan are discussing a new rail link that would run from Fergana in Uzbekistan through southern Kyrgyzstan to Kashgar in China. China reportedly is especially interested in developing trade routes in Central Asia that would bypass Kazakhstan, where Russia has greater influence.[106]

Trade between Central Asia and China has been plagued with many of the same problems afflicting Sino-Russian regional trade.[107] Like the Russian Far East, Kazakhstan and Kyrgyzstan have complained about unscrupulous Chinese traders and illegal immigrants streaming across their borders.[108] In Kyrgyzstan, for example, there was an outcry when a Chinese-speaking Kyrgyz discovered that the characters on a sign above a new Chinese restaurant in Bishkek referred to the "Northern Province" restaurant. To allay local concerns about possible Chinese territorial claims against Kyrgyzstan, the Chinese owner quickly renamed his restaurant something less provocative—"Silvery Moon."[109] Once visas were required again for business travel between Russia and China in 1994, similar regulations were instituted in Kazakhstan.

There is some indication that the controversy over alleged Chinese illegal immigration to Central Asia has led to a backlash against Chinese traders in the region. While Beijing has handled similar complaints from the Russian border regions more quietly, the Chinese embassy in Almaty actually issued a statement complaining about the treatment of Chinese citizens in Kazakhstan. The embassy alleged that Kazakhstani militia and border guards had been participating in attacks against Chinese traders in the market in Almaty, but Kazakhstani officials denied the allegations.[110]

Problems concerning the quality of goods and investment risks led to a downturn in trade between China and Kazakhstan, from $434 million in 1993 to $335 million in 1994. Sino-Kazakhstani trade has recovered more quickly than Sino-Russian trade, however, as 1996 trade surpassed the 1993 level.

Apart from problems with trade, other border issues have irritated relations between Central Asia and China. The governments of Kazakhstan and Kyrgyzstan, for example, were vocal in their protests against Chinese nuclear testing, which took place near their borders at Lop Nor in China's Xinjiang province.[111] In May 1996 Xinjiang complained that Kazakhstan had shipped radioactive scrap metal to the region.[112]

Like Russia, Kazakhstan and Kyrgyzstan had to resolve their outstanding border disputes with China. Historically, the border between Central Asia and China played a role in the Sino-Soviet conflict. In the summer of 1969, for example, when military clashes broke out sporadically on the Sino-Russian border, there also was a serious incident on August 13, 1969, on the Xinjiang border which culminated in fighting. Kazakhstan and China reached an agreement on the demarcation of most of their 1718 km border in 1994, while Kyrgyzstan and China signed a border treaty delimiting much of their 1000 km boundary in 1996. China settled remaining border issues with Kyrgyzstan in August 1999 at the five-state summit in Bishkek.[113] When Jiang Zemin and Kazakhstan's President Nazarbaev met in November 1999, they signed a border agreement resolving all outstanding questions between their countries.[114] However, border demarcation talks still continue between China and Tajikistan.

The border between China and its neighbors in Central Asia may be open now, but feelings of insecurity and distrust persist.[115] According to Kazakhstan's Prime Minister Akezhan Kazheldin, Kazakhstan today is "bottled up in a semistable space between Russia and China."[116] To remedy this precarious position, the government has agreed to increase military cooperation with Russia, including the creation of a joint command for patrols along the border with China.[117] This dovetails with one of the four newly created collective security zones in the Commonwealth of Independent States (CIS)—the eastern zone, which includes Kazakhstan, Russia, and part of Kyrgyzstan.[118] The February 1995 agreement between Russia and Kazakhstan on joint guarding of Kazakhstan's border with China represents a step towards a more coordinated China policy.[119] Kyrgyzstan came to a similar agreement with Moscow in March 1997 and Russian border troops now guard its border with China.[120] Russia also has intervened in Tajikistan to counter an insurgency by opposition forces operating from bases within Afghanistan. Russia's view of the southern borders of the Central Asian states as its southern security perimeter has coincided with the desire by these governments to enlist Russian assistance with border security.[121] Yet Kazakhstan and Kyrgyzstan also have engaged in dialogue with their Chinese neighbors, as well as with NATO, about military ties and exchanges.

In 1994, Kazakhstan and Kyrgyzstan were among four Central Asian states to join NATO's Partnership for Peace program, and beginning in 1997 a series of military exercises has taken place in Kazakhstan. Chinese analysts have paid close attention to growing military ties between Central Asians states and NATO, especially in the aftermath of the Kosovo crisis in the spring of 1999.[122] At a time when China and Russia were united in their condemnation of NATO's use of force to intervene in the domestic affairs of a country outside the alliance, none of the five Central Asian states agreed to Russia's proposal for a joint statement of the Commonwealth of Independent States condemning the NATO intervention. Moreover, Central Asian leaders chose to attend NATO's fiftieth anniversary celebrations.

Due to their history of relations with Moscow and their geographic position at the crossroads of Europe, Asia, and the Middle East, the Central Asian states have tried to maximize their freedom to maneuver. Nazarbaev has called "the preservation of independence" the most important aim for Kazakhstan,[123] while President Akaev of Kyrgyzstan has outlined a "Silk Road diplomacy," fostering relations with East and West alike.[124] As these leaders develop their own approaches to foreign policy, differing from perspectives in both Beijing and Moscow, Russia and China face an increasingly complex strategic environment in Central Asia.

One of the most serious potential flashpoints in relations between China and Central Asia, however, concerns ethnic relations. Central Asia and Xinjiang are linked by overlapping ethnic populations—more than one million Kazakhs and 375,000 Kyrgyz live in Xinjiang, while 262,000 Uighurs live in Kazakhstan and Kyrgyzstan.[125] China has always had a tenuous hold over Xinjiang, and since the collapse of the USSR, the Chinese government has feared the development of a cross-border Uighur self-determination movement.[126] While the collapse of the Soviet Union proved advantageous for China in some respects—diminishing the threat to its borders and opening new vistas for economic cooperation—these positive changes have been counter-balanced by new threats, especially potential for the spread of pan-Turkist and Islamicist sentiments into Xinjiang.[127]

China's determination to maintain control over this border region has been strengthened with the discovery of a major oil field in the Tarim Basin in Xinjiang.[128] Like the Russian Far East, however, Xinjiang has found new room for maneuver with Beijing due its mineral wealth and the possibility that it could market these resources internationally.[129] As a consequence, the Chinese leaders have been put in a difficult position—they have endeavored to subsidize some of Xinjiang's development needs, while responding harshly to any signs of political unrest.

Ethnic issues have complicated China's relations with Kazakhstan in particular. President Nazarbaev has pressed China to allow more Kazakhs to emigrate from Xinjiang.[130] So far, Kazakhstan's security concerns have won out over ethnic solidarity. In exchange for a Chinese pledge not to be the first to use nuclear weapons against Kazakhstan, President Nazarbayev agreed not to allow Uighur independence activists to operate in Kazakhstan.[131]

With unrest in Xinjiang on the increase from the mid-1990s, China has undertaken harsh measures within the region and pushed for agreements with its Central Asian neighbors to oppose ethnic separatism.[132] During Jiang Zemin's visits to Kyrgyzstan and Kazakhstan in July 1996 and Nazarbayev's February 1997 trip to China, the Central Asian leaders affirmed their opposition to separatism. While seeking to expand economic cooperation with neighboring Xinjiang, they have taken measures to contain Uighur activism in their own countries. In April 1996, for example, the Kyrgyz Justice Ministry issued a three-month suspension of a Uighur organization's right to publicize its activities in the media and to hold public meetings.[133] Nonetheless, despite efforts to contain their public protests, Uighurs living in Kazakhstan and Kyrgyzstan condemned the Chinese crackdown against separatist riots in Xinjiang in February 1997, and some 300 Uighurs picketed the Chinese embassy in Bishkek.[134] The Chinese government protested to Kyrgyzstan that the demonstration constituted interference in its internal affairs.[135] However, in response to Chinese executions of Uighur separatists, small demonstrations have continued to take place in Kazakhstan, during which some Uighurs protested in front of the Chinese embassy in Almaty.[136] Moreover, despite Kazakhstan's condemnation of ethnic separatism, the secretary of the Kazakhstani Security Council, Beksultan Barsekov, expressed his government's concern about the Chinese government's harsh crackdown in Xinjiang.[137]

Another potential source of friction concerns the possibility of Sino-Russian rivalry for influence in Central Asia. Already, there is some evidence that the expansion of economic relations between Kazakhstan and China occasionally occurred at Russia's expense. For example, in 1995 Nazarbaev signed an accord with China granting Kazakhstan the right to use China's Pacific port at Lianyungang in Jiangsu Province. The agreement improved Kazakhstan's access to trading partners in the Pacific rim by shortening the distance to the Pacific—it is only 3,500 km from Kazakhstan to Lianyungang, less than half the distance needed to reach Russian Far East ports.[138]

According to the director of Kazakhstan's Strategic Institute, Russia has been pursuing two incompatible roles—distancing itself economically from the Central Asian states it considered a burden, while trying to maintain its military-strategic presence there.[139] Indeed, it was only after other countries, especially Turkey and Iran, but also Japan and China, began to pursue their economic interests in the region actively that Russia began to play a more assertive role.[140]

China has been very careful in dealing with the Central Asian states, especially Kazakhstan, to avoid the appearance of competing with Russia in the economic sphere. At times, however, the Central Asian states have sought greater cooperation from China as a means of decreasing their dependence on Russia. Not surprisingly, Russia has viewed these ventures with suspicion, fearing that developments such as the new rail line linking Kazakhstan and China would be detrimental to its interests by competing for business with the Trans-Siberian railroad.[141]

Similarly, building oil pipelines from Kazakhstan through China would lessen Russian control over that strategic resource. On September 24, 1997, Li Peng traveled to Kazakhstan to sign a $9.5 billion deal to develop the Uzen and Aktiubinsk oil fields and build two oil pipelines, one running for 3000 km to western China, and another, 250 km in length, going through Turkmenistan to the Iranian border.[142] Despite Chinese caution regarding competition with Russia and Central Asia, China National Petroleum Corporation succeeded in beating Amoco's bid for the license to develop the Uzen oil field.[143]

A first shipment of 1,700 tons of oil from Kazakhstan was sent by rail to Xinjiang in October 1997. In recent years, shipments have increased substantially— China received 360,000 tons of crude in 1998 and is expected to purchase 500,000 tons by 2000. China and Kazakhstan have begun joint development of the Uzen oil field and the Aktiubinsk oil and gas fields.[144] During their November 1999 summit meeting, Jiang Zemin and Nazarbaev reaffirmed their 1997 commitment to building the pipeline, expected to pump at least 20 million tons of crude per year.

ASIAN SECURITY

If China was the cornerstone of Yeltsin's post-1992 attempt to achieve greater balance between East and West in Russian foreign policy, this was in part due to a lack of other options, especially vis-à-vis Japan. Russian-Japanese relations had been frozen for years due to their territorial dispute over the Kurile Islands. For a brief period in the first half of 1992, there was some hope that Yeltsin might be able to make progress toward resolving the issue during a scheduled visit to Japan. However, during the summer of that year, high-ranking members of the military increasingly spoke against negotiating the return of islands, citing strategic reasons and concern for the inviolability of Russia's borders.[145] Pressures to avoid compromise on the issue became so great and widespread that Yeltsin abruptly canceled his trip to Japan in mid-September. The hardening of the Russian position on the return of two islands, as well as Japan's insistence on linking political and economic issues in Russian-Japanese relations, ensured that little progress would be made in bilateral relations for quite some time. Thus for Russia to play a meaningful role in Asia, it had to count on China for support.

The Japanese government gradually has been moving away from its previous insistence on linking economic and political relations with Russia. It withdrew its objections to Russia's joining the G-7 and welcomed Russia's partic-ipation in APEC. Former Prime Minister Ryutaro Hashimoto's July 24, 1997, speech outlining a new "Eurasian policy" called for an improvement in Japanese-Russian relations and represented an important step forward.

Greater political will in Japan and Russia to ameliorate the strain in their relations was apparent at the November 1997 summit meeting between Yeltsin and Hashimoto in Krasnoiarsk—dubbed the "summit without ties" in recog-nition of its informal and cordial ambiance. While no breakthroughs on the Kuriles were achieved, the two leaders pledged at the meeting to sign a peace treaty by the year 2000.[146]

Just days before the Russian-Japanese summit in November 1997, Jiang Zemin and President Clinton met in the United States. Unlike the Russian-Japanese "meeting without ties," the Chinese leadership insisted on observing all the formalities of a state visit. Jiang, who faced the need to consolidate his rule in the aftermath of Deng's death, wanted to make sure that he was treated with the same respect as the former Chinese leader, who visited the United States nearly a decade earlier. As in the case of the Russian-Japanese summit, the con-tent of the Sino-American summit was less important than its symbolic value—to confirm the full restoration of Sino-American relations, curtailed after the Tiananmen massacre. Just days later, Yeltsin went on his third trip to Beijing to meet with Jiang Zemin. Fearing that the formality of the Russian leader's state visit compared unfavorably with the Yeltsin-Hashimoto "meet-ing without ties," Jiang pledged to spend his next vacation in Russia and par-ticipate in a "meeting without coats."[147]

Despite the warming trend in Russian-Japanese relations in 1997, political and economic crises in both Japan and Russia in 1998 made their pledge to sign a peace treaty seem wildly optimistic and provided new obstacles to eco-nomic cooperation, especially on projects requiring major Japanese investments, such as the Kovyktinskoe pipeline. Plans for a U.S.-Japanese theater missile defense system (discussed below), unveiled at the end of 1998, foiled earlier hopes for multilateral cooperation in Northeast Asia by bringing Russia closer to China's more suspicious position regarding American and Japanese inten-tions in the region.

The Asian financial crisis put similar obstacles in the way of Russian-South Korean economic relations. Russia and South Korea remain at an impasse over the $1.8 billion Soviet debt to Seoul, which the Russian government cannot repay. Instead, Russia has offset a part of the debt by supplying South Korea with $450 million in weapons, including T80U tanks, Ka-32 helicopters, and antitank and antiaircraft systems.[148] After downgrading Russia's relations with North Korea in 1992, the Yeltsin government has found itself marginalized on issues concerning the security of the Korean Peninsula: Beijing, Moscow's strategic partner, has chosen to maintain its leverage rather than support an expansion of the four-party talks to include Russia.[149] However, Prime Minister Kim Chong-pil of South Korea has expressed support for including Russia and Japan in meetings about the security of the Peninsula.[150]

While China did support Russia's membership in APEC in 1998, it only did so on the condition that Russia achieve the support of others countries, such as South Korea. Russia, on the other hand, has given China consistent support on the Taiwan issue. All in all, Russia and China have not demonstrated unified purpose in their policies toward key Asian security questions. To the contrary, the two countries appear to have very different interests. Russia has been trying to gain entrée into the region via China, while the latter has been amenable only if its own interests were not at stake and only if a major security threat required support.

MILITARY COOPERATION

The expansion of military cooperation between Moscow and Beijing is the most dramatic evidence of the improved political relations between the two countries. China emerged as Russia's most promising arms client in the 1990s. In fact, from 1992 to 1994 China purchased 97 percent of its weapons from Russia.[151] Chinese purchases have proved so important to the cash-starved defense industries, especially in the Russian Far East, that officials representing these sectors have managed to override concerns within the military regarding the possibility of a long-term threat from a resurgent China.[152]

Chinese military purchases increased steadily in the 1990s. In 1992, China spent $1.8 billion on Russian weapons, including 26 Sukhoi SU-27 fighter aircraft. The SU-27s were supposed to be the first installment of a total purchase of 72 planes, but a dispute over the terms of payment stalled the deal until 1996. China paid for part of the first installment of planes in bartered goods, mostly consumer items, which Russians later complained were of poor quality and not worth the price of the aircraft.[153]

China also purchased missile-guidance and rocket technology, rocket engines, and surface-to-air missiles (including up to 100 of the S300 air-defense missile system, similar to the Patriot). Given Russia's economic crisis, Yeltsin referred to Russian arms sales as one of its few economic successes.

The United States, however, has been concerned with the potential for Chinese re-export of their newly acquired technology to countries such as Iran.[154] According to one report, the United States pressed Russia to pledge not to sell power-projection systems to China.[155] The blossoming Sino-Russian military relationship also prompted Washington to resume its own high-level military contacts with Beijing in 1993.[156]

Unlike the cautious resumption of U.S.-China military relations, Russian-Chinese military contacts expanded quickly. During Defense Minister Pavel Grachev's visit to China in November, the two countries called for a five-year renewable military cooperation agreement. The agreement called for drawing annual bilateral military cooperation plans in the areas of logistics, communications, and land surveying, and involved joint military exercises and increased exchanges of military personnel.[157]

More than a thousand Russian defense specialists have traveled to China since 1991 on official military-industrial exchanges. Approximately 300 Russian scientists work on defense projects in China and a similar number of Chinese specialists participate in aerospace research in Russia.[158] According to some accounts, unsanctioned Russian-Chinese military contacts have been growing since the collapse of the USSR. Many Russian military scientists reportedly prolonged their work for Chinese military industries after the conclusion of their official exchange duties.[159]

Russian-Chinese relations in the military sphere continued to expand in the aftermath of the visit to Moscow by Defense Minister Chi Haotian in August 1994. Russia announced that it would provide training for Chinese military personnel who will be using newly purchased Russian equipment, particularly the Su-27 fighter-planes and the S-300 ground-to-air missile complexes.[160]

Defense Minister Grachev traveled to China in mid-May 1995 to further develop military relations. China had been steadily purchasing Russian weapons in 1995, including six Kilo-class diesel submarines and rocket motors for possible use in Chinese cruise missiles.[161] In December 1995, Russia and China signed an agreement expanding military-technical cooperation.[162] At this time, the two countries resolved their impasse over payment for the SU-27s sold to China in 1992, and Russia agreed to sell China a license to manufacture the planes.[163] It has been alleged that the Sukhoi design bureau sold the production rights to China without Moscow's permission, but it is more likely that the highly controversial decision was approved by Moscow once China agreed to purchase a certain number as a part of the deal for the production rights.[164] In 1996, China bought another twenty-two SU-27s and is permitted to produce 200 more of the aircraft in a Shenyang factory.[165]

The expanding Sino-Russian military relationship has continued to elicit American objections. The U.S. government opposed Russia's sale of rocket motors to China because they could be used in cruise missiles. While the Clinton administration claimed that the Russian sale would violate the Missile Technology Control Regime, the Russian government rejected the U.S. argument, since the American authorities had authorized a similar purchase by China of gas turbine engines.[166]

The showdown between China and the U.S. Seventh fleet in the Taiwan Strait in March 1996 demonstrated to the Chinese the importance of modernizing their seapower. According to military analysts, this was the motivation behind China's purchase of two Sovremennyi-class destroyers equipped with advanced missiles, including Sunburn ship-to-ship missiles, SA-N-17 surface-to-air missiles, and SSN-22 cruise missiles.[167] In addition, China has contracted for four advanced Kilo-class submarines.[168] To improve rapid reaction capabilities, the PRC has purchased 14 Il-47 transport aircraft.[169] Air defense appears to be another Chinese priority. A Russian-Israeli joint project is believed to have produced a detection device for the Chinese Air Force, and the Chinese have been contemplating additional purchases of Russian air defense systems such as the S-300 and Tor-M1.[170] In August 1999, Russia agreed to sell China forty to sixty of the SU-30MKK fighters for $2 billion. Chinese officials had expressed interest in this top of the line aircraft ever since India purchased similar planes (the SU-30MKI) in 1997. In 2000, Russia also will provide the Chinese with several dozen SU-27UBK fighters at a price tag of $1 billion, in partial repayment of the Soviet debt to China.[171]

In light of the economic crisis afflicting most of the Southeast Asian nations, at one time Russia's most promising new customers for military hardware, Russian Defense Ministry officials are focusing more and more attention on the Chinese market. The PRC remains Russia's number two weapons customer after India, accounting for more than one quarter of total foreign orders of $8.4 billion in 1998.[172]

GLOBAL POLITICS

The development of the Sino-Russian partnership paralleled the debate over NATO expansion in the West and was viewed in Moscow as a counterweight to the extension of a U.S.-dominated alliance system on Russia's western borders. By May 1997, however, the strategic context underlying the Sino-Russian partnership began to change appreciably. Once NATO made the final decision to extend membership to three former Soviet allies, the Czech Republic, Hungary, and Poland, Russia adjusted to the fact of NATO expansion by signing a separate agreement on relations with the organization.

At the same time that alliance relations were shifting in Europe, so was the basis for U.S.–Japanese strategic cooperation—a development with equally profound implications for Sino-Russian relations. The new U.S.–Japan Joint Declaration addresses "the importance of peaceful resolution of problems in the region" and implies that the PRC represents a key source of potential instability. The new U.S.–Japan security guidelines raise alarm bells in Beijing about the development of Japanese-American cooperation on an anti-Chinese basis, especially in the event of a future conflict in the Taiwan Strait.[173]

Despite repeated statements of support for China's position on the Taiwan issue and numerous Sino-Russian declarations about their common strategic perspectives, Russia initially took a surprisingly sanguine approach to the revised U.S.–Japan alliance guidelines—then-Defense Minister Igor Rodionov went so far as to welcome them as a positive development for Asia.[174] Moscow's response to the new guidelines reflected a reassessment of the importance of Japanese-American cooperation for stability in Asia, especially their joint efforts to ensure the peaceful evolution of relations between the two Koreas.[175]

By the fall of 1998, a less cooperative environment had taken shape. In the aftermath of the economic crisis in Russia, Evgenii Primakov was asked to form a new government. As anti-Western sentiment accompanied the growing disenchantment with market-oriented reforms, Primakov formulated foreign and domestic policies more likely to resonate with a deeply disappointed, increasingly weary, and nationalistic society. Meanwhile, in China the government began clamping down on dissent. U.S.-China relations worsened as scandals regarding security breaches in sales of U.S. satellite technology and alleged spying by China to acquire advanced nuclear technology dominated American news coverage of China.

Jiang Zemin's November 1998 visit to Russia took place within this changed context. Yeltsin was in poor health at the time, and Jiang had to visit the Russian leader in the hospital, where he was recovering from pneumonia. While the two leaders reaffirmed their strategic partnership and planned future exchanges of visits, little concrete progress was achieved.[176] In fact, the Russian side found itself somewhat on the defensive on the Taiwan issue. Although Moscow has maintained a one-China policy, Vladimir Zhirinovskii's October 1998 visit to the island prompted a reaffirmation of the official Russian government position.[177]

Even as Sino-Russian economic relations limped along, the strategic rationale for the Sino-Russian partnership strengthened as Russia increasingly felt marginalized in international affairs. Claiming that Russia was not consulted prior to U.S. air strikes against Iraq in December 1998, Russian and Chinese leaders joined forces in the United Nations to criticize the American action.

Primakov, a supporter of a more active foreign policy in Asia and the Middle East, then proposed an alliance with China and India—Russia's long-standing Asian partner, but China's rival. Despite its sympathy with Russia on the Iraq question, China quickly rejected Primakov's proposal. As Jiang explained, China was opposed to entering into an alliance with any country.[178]

U.S.–Russian and U.S.–Chinese relations deteriorated further over U.S. plans to move forward with a national missile defense (NMD) system and joint Japanese-American efforts to develop an antimissile defense system for Northeast Asia (theater missile defense, or TMD). Although the two countries' renewed interest in TMD arose after North Korea launched a test of a missile over Japan, China dismissed this rationale and argued that any Japanese-American TMD could be used to shelter Taiwan and prove an additional obstacle to reunification.

Russian analysts view the U.S. plan to develop TMD and NMD as yet another instance of U.S. disregard for Russian security concerns. Despite the fact that the Russian Duma had not yet ratified the START II treaty, which would sharply curtail U.S. and Russian nuclear arsenals, U.S. Secretary of Defense William Cohen proposed that the United States withdraw from the ABM treaty in the event that the Russian side objected to the Japanese-American theater missile defense plan.[179] Such a plan, if it excluded Russia, would prompt Russian leaders to increase the number of warheads on missiles, rather than to reduce them as stipulated by START II. In February 1999, Russian officials criticized U.S. efforts to revise the ABM treaty to accommodate such a system and spoke more critically about U.S.–Japanese military cooperation in general.[180] A few months later, on April 16, Russia and China issued a communiqué outlining future consultation on the ABM treaty and restating their opposition to any efforts to alter it.[181]

Sino-Russian strategic cooperation culminated in the increasingly close coordination of their responses to the NATO attacks against Yugoslavia in the spring of 1999, which the Western alliance argued was necessary to prevent a refugee crisis in Kosovo resulting from President Milosovic's ethnic cleansing policies in the region. In protest against the air strikes, Primakov, who had been on his way to Washington on March 25, the day the bombing began, ordered his plane to turn back to Moscow. From the very beginning, Russian and Chinese leaders had similar objections to the NATO bombing campaign. Rejecting NATO's rationale for the air strikes, and concerned about the precedent of a NATO-led attack against a sovereign state to aid an oppressed ethnic group, Russian and Chinese leaders condemned the air strikes as aggression.

Initially, Chinese leaders appeared more willing than their Russian counterparts to separate the overall Sino-American relationship from China's opposition to U.S. policy toward Yugoslavia. Unlike Primakov, Chinese Prime Minister Zhu Rongji went ahead with a planned visit to the United States in early April. However, after NATO mistakenly bombed the Chinese embassy in Belgrade on May 7, 1999, resulting in three deaths and numerous injuries, Chinese critics of cooperation with the West turned the Yugoslav conflict into a potent symbol of American disregard for Chinese interests.

The attack on the Chinese embassy brought Russia and China even closer together. China joined Russia in cutting off military contacts with the West. In Beijing and other cities, anti-Western demonstrators took to the streets and attacked the U.S. and British embassies, in scenes reminiscent of the Cultural Revolution. China also blocked any further action in the UN on a political settlement to the Kosovo crisis until a suitable apology was made.[182]

Viktor Chernomyrdin, designated in April 1999 as Yeltsin's special envoy for the Balkan crisis, traveled to Beijing for urgent consultations with Chinese leaders. Chinese and Russian leaders called for an immediate end to the bombing and for negotiations for a political solution which would respect Yugoslavia's sovereignty.[183] After being placed on the diplomatic sidelines in recent months, Russia suddenly found itself in the diplomatic limelight thanks to Chernomyrdin's shuttle diplomacy. The former Prime Minister, who is well respected in the West and enjoys good relations with Vice President Al Gore, succeeded in toning down the vitriol in Russian condemnations of NATO actions in Kosovo. Due to the Sino-Russian partnership, Russian leaders were then in a position to mediate between an irate China and the West to achieve consensus within the UN Security Council on a political solution to the Balkan crisis.

Great power relations soon shifted again. Once hostilities ceased in Kosovo, Sino-American relations slowly began to mend. After compensating the bombing victims, Washington agreed to pay Beijing $28 million for the destruction of the Chinese embassy in Belgrade. The Chinese government also pledged to reimburse the United States for damage to American diplomatic property in China that occurred during anti-American protests. Talks about China's entry into the World Trade Organization resumed and culminated in a landmark agreement on November 15, 1999.

As Sino-American relations registered some improvement, U.S.-Russian ties deteriorated over the conflict in Chechnya. U.S. policymakers were critical of Russian disregard for the plight of civilians in the republic, where Russian troops were at war again with Chechen fighters, whom Moscow held responsible for terrorist attacks in Russian cities. During his last summit meeting in Beijing, on December 9–10, 1999, Yeltsin lashed out at Clinton for pressuring Russia and forgetting that Russia is a nuclear power.[184] In their joint communiqué, the Russian and Chinese leaders called attention to "the negative momentum in international relations" caused by American unilateralism, efforts to develop an ABM system, and inability to ratify the Comprehensive Nuclear Test Ban Treaty.[185] At the summit, Yeltsin and Jiang exchanged protocols describing the demarcation work completed on the eastern and western sections of their common border. They also signed an agreement for the joint development of certain river islands.[186]

This would be Yeltsin's last visit to China as Russian President. Just three weeks later, on December 31, 1999, Yeltsin resigned and his newly appointed prime minister, Vladimir Putin, took over as interim president until elections could be held in March 2000. Although a decade earlier Chinese leaders had viewed Yeltsin with considerable suspicion and even alarm, by the time the Russian president retired they were praising him for his substantial efforts to establish the Sino-Russian strategic partnership and to create a firm basis for the future development of bilateral relations.[187]

CONCLUSIONS

After a rocky start in the immediate post-coup period, Yeltsin's China policy was able to achieve the impossible—to unite both the winners of economic reforms, such as the oil and gas lobby, and the losers, such as the defense industry.[188] Even regional interests originally supported expanding ties with China, although by mid-1993 center-regional differences over China policy would prove to be a growing source of tension, as detailed in chapter nine.

In the first half of the 1990s, the improvement of relations with China gave substance to Yeltsin's attempt to reorient Russia's foreign policy away from a pro-Western focus and appealed to all but the fringe elements of the Russian political spectrum. Moreover, Russian hostility to NATO expansion gave new impetus to rhetoric supporting a Sino-Russian partnership as a counter-balance. Despite changes in the strategic environment leading to closer cooperation between Russia and China in the short term, lagging Sino-Russian economic relations, the growing potential for Sino-Russian competition in Central Asia, and continuing distrust of China in the Russian border regions all set the scene for a more fluid Sino-Russian relationship in the new millennium. As we will see in the next chapter, Sino-Russian relations remain at the center of the debate in Moscow and the Russian Far East on Russia's role in Asia and on foreign policy priorities in general.

9 / Moscow and the Border Regions
Debate Russia's China Policy

Although Russian policymakers are seeking to achieve greater balance in Russia's foreign relations with European and Asian states, many Russians remain ambivalent about their country's engagement in Asia, especially the rapidly developing Sino-Russian partnership. Much hailed by Russian and Chinese national leaders, the increasing salience of China in Russian foreign policy has led to a debate in the Moscow policy community and to periodic bouts of intense criticism in some of the Russian border regions.

Most policymakers on all sides of the political spectrum in Moscow supported the Yeltsin government's effort to improve relations with its largest neighbor, but they have begun to discuss the long-term implications of China's impressive growth. While some in Moscow also question China's intentions vis-à-vis Russia, such concerns are more common in the Russian border regions, where adverse economic and demographic changes fuel insecurities regarding the regional balance of power with China.

Mounting opposition to U.S. unilateralism in international relations in 1998–99 has marginalized voices in Moscow pointing to a potential threat from China. However, discussion about the role of China in Russia's foreign policy has continued, albeit in a less ideological manner, focusing more and more on the identification of areas of strategic convergence and sources of divergent interests.

In the border regions, the economic woes brought about by the August 1998 financial crisis temporarily boosted China's profile as the source of the most reasonably priced food products and consumer goods. Stricter immigration and customs controls also have allayed some concerns about the possibility of unchecked Chinese demographic and economic expansion, but underlying suspicions about Chinese intentions persist in many circles.

DEBATES IN MOSCOW ON RUSSIA'S CHINA POLICY

Despite the rapid improvement of Sino-Russian political ties in the 1990s, the relationship has not been without its share of controversy. The debates in

Moscow on Russia's China policy reflect the emerging differentiation of the Russian political spectrum.[1] At issue is not just the future of Sino-Russian relations but of Russia as a great power.

There is considerable continuity in terms of the participants in these debates—many of the same China-watchers who have contributed to policy-making since the late 1960s remain key players. What is striking is that they have changed sides. The reformers of yesteryear (and radical democrats in today's Russia), who sought to normalize Sino-Soviet relations and praised Chinese reforms in the late 1980s, now are more critical of China's authoritarianism, concerned about a Chinese threat, and receptive of Western-style market-oriented reforms. Their main opponents in the debate on China are many of the same individuals who were the fiercest critics of Maoist hegemony in the 1970s. Mostly affiliated with the new Russian incarnation of the Soviet Communist Party, the KPRF (Communist Party of the Russian Federation), these analysts are motivated both by their desire to oppose U.S. policies and to lobby for the relevance of the Chinese model of reforms for Russia.[2]

Unlike earlier periods, the debate is less polarized because of the existence of a large number of centrists who advocate cooperation with both China and the West. While the centrists have been able to reach out to communists and democrats to achieve consensus on individual issues in China relations, the ultra-nationalists stand alone in their perception of a dual threat from West and East.

However, Russians on all sides of the political spectrum are united in their dissatisfaction with the present state of Russia's relations with the West.[3] Where they part company is in determining the role of China policy in Russia's overall foreign policy strategy and in ascertaining the long-term prospects for Sino-Russian conflict and cooperation.

The Yeltsin government stressed that both countries share a vital interest in the continued improvement of relations. As Evgenii Afanasiev and Grigorii Logvinov, Russian Foreign Ministry officials in charge of Asia policy, explained: "Russia certainly has a stake in having for a neighbor a strong, politically stable, fast-growing, and prospering friendly China. China appears to have the same feelings about Russia."[4]

Centrists have noted that it is in Russia's interest to maintain friendly relations with the United States and Europe, as well as with Asian states, but analysts associated with the KPRF go further than this, arguing that Russia has a unique international role to play due to its geographic position between East and West.[5] According to the proponents of the "civilizational approach," Russia is not a buffer between two continents but "a beneficial staging ground for inter-civilizational contacts, during which the peoples of both continents experience mutual spiritual enrichment."[6]

Beginning in 1992, when critical voices in the Russian foreign policy establishment called for a reexamination of the Yeltsin government's pro-West foreign policy, some began proposing Eurasianism as an alternative.[7] They advocated a foreign policy that would take into account Russia's unique position in the "Eurasian space," the area between Europe and Asia.

An emigré movement first developed the concept of Eurasianism in 1921 in an effort to find new solutions to the problems Russia was experiencing. The Eurasianists of the 1920s were reacting against "Westernizers" who saw Russia as a backwater of Europe and "Slavophiles" whose tendency to look to the past made them unable to solve current problems.[8] Modern-day Eurasianists are faced with the additional task of achieving greater balance in Russian foreign policy toward Europe and Asia.

For centrists, a balanced foreign policy is one based on Russia's interests in good relations with both the West and the East.[9] In terms of China policy, this involves improving relations with Beijing in a manner that does not harm Russia's other foreign policy priorities, such as constructive relations with the West.[10] As Lev Deliusin explained, the absence of the idea of a common enemy in the concept of the Sino-Russian partnership is the primary difference between the new relationship and the alliance of the 1950s.[11]

The platforms of parties such as *Yabloko* and *Nash Dom–Rossiia* (NDR) incorporated the idea of a balanced foreign policy.[12] Former Prime Minister Primakov also agreed with this approach, but towards the end of his tenure put greater emphasis on Russia's eastern and southern orientation. His proposal for a Russia-China-India alliance resonated with both ultra-nationalists from the Liberal Democratic Party (LDPR) and communist colleagues with similar geopolitical strategies for opposing the West through alliances with the East and South.[13]

Procommunist analysts, however, envisage a strong socialist China cooperating with Russia to redress the "intersystemic balance of power" between capitalism and socialism in Asia.[14] This is why, in their view, the United States fears the burgeoning Sino-Russian partnership.[15] Although for these analysts Russia's main opponent remains a West intent on marginalizing Moscow in world affairs, for centrists the enemy is less clear.

Centrists tend to view the main challenge to Russia as internal—will the Russian Federation remain united and prosper economically? In their view, discussion of the potential demographic threat from China and the rise of China as an economic power serves to highlight the importance of a sound regional policy within Russia.

The rise of China as an economic power has been the subject of much debate in Russia, just as it has in the West. Communist analysts have pointed to the successes of socialism with Chinese characteristics, while moderates and centrists have focused on the changing balance of economic power between Russia and China.

The disparity in population growth between Russia and China increasingly has attracted public notice in Russia. While there are more than 100 million people in the Chinese Northeast, the population in the neighboring Russian Far East has declined from a peak of 8 million in 1991 to approximately 7.5 million in 1996.[16] In 1993, the media in Moscow and in the border regions began raising the issue of Chinese illegal immigration to the Russian Far East. Since then, many alarmist articles have been published that cite widely varying and largely unverifiable estimates of the number of Chinese living and working illegally in Russia—from several thousand to 5 million.

Some Russian observers have warned of an alleged plot by the Chinese government to "quietly expand" in the Russian Far East and retake, through illegal immigration, the borderlands lost to the Russian Empire during the Qing Dynasty. Even some communist supporters of the Sino-Russian strategic partnership are concerned about China's long-term intentions in the Russian Far East.[17]

The difficult border demarcation process also has fueled these doubts. Vladimir Miasnikov, a leading scholar of the Sino-Russian border at the Institute of the Far East and consistent critic of Chinese policies on border issues, has warned that unchecked migration of Chinese citizens to Russian territory could exacerbate tensions between the two countries.[18]

Sober voices within the Russian government have rejected these allegations, and the Chinese authorities consistently have denied any such intentions.[19] Igor' Rogachev, Russia's ambassador to China, stated succinctly that "the problem of the illegal penetration of Russia by Chinese does not exist." Nevertheless, the ambassador admitted that there have been widespread violations of Russian passport rules by Chinese citizens.[20]

Some members of the Yeltsin government were more alarmist. In 1994, Sergei Stepashin, then head of Russia's Federal Counterintelligence Service, alleged that Chinese intelligence services had increased their activities in the Russian Far East.[21] In a similar vein, an October 1995 Russian Security Council meeting concluded that illegal immigration from China, Vietnam, Africa, and the Middle East was undermining Russia's national security,[22] and former Defense Minister Rodionov publicly stated in December 1996 that China should be viewed as one of Russia's potential enemies.[23] In May 1997, the Russian National Security Council outlined a conception of national security highlighting the importance of safeguarding the integrity of the state.[24] By late 1998, the Security Council's committee on border policy concluded that earlier measures to simplify border controls had made Russia more attractive to illegal immigrants from Asia, Africa, and the Middle East who often engaged in criminal activities.[25]

While some Foreign Ministry officials recognized that Chinese illegal immigration presented a serious problem, they argued that it was up to the regions themselves to regulate foreign workers and handle economic relations with China.[26] This may be too much for the regions to handle. According to Dmitrii Trenin, a scholar at the Moscow Carnegie Center, the main threat to the Russian Far East is not from China, but from the power vacuum which has been developing in the region.[27] The Yeltsin government only paid lip service to the development of this strategic area, increasingly cut off from the rest of Russia due to high transportation costs. During his 1996 presidential campaign, Yeltsin pledged $34 billion in federal funds for a new regional development plan for the Russian Far East and Trans-Baikal. By 1999, only 4.2 percent of these funds had been disbursed.[28]

According to Trenin, the presence of Chinese contract laborers and China's interest in investment opportunities in an economically and demographically declining Russian Far East may lead spontaneously to greater Chinese influence over the region and have the same effect as annexation.[29] For this reason, centrists highlight the importance of the economic development of the Russian Far East.

Former Deputy Prime Minister Sergei Shakhrai called for greater coordination in China policy among the regions of the Russian Far East, Moscow, and the Central Asian states. According to Shakhrai, this policy should include a development policy for the Russian Far East, an effort to limit Chinese immigration to the region, steps to improve the living conditions for Russian troops stationed there, a role for the Cossacks living in the border regions, stricter border controls, and a foreign economic policy based on real market levers.[30]

The more moderate members of the centrist group expressed greater concern about the long-term consequences of China's rise as a great power and its intentions vis-à-vis neighboring states. Highly placed academics such as Sergei Kortunov advocated greater caution in military cooperation with China to avoid harming other Russian foreign policy interests.[31] Other leading scholars, such as Sergei Rogov and Aleksei Arbatov, urged caution in Russia's long-term approach to China due to the uncertain direction of that country's development in the post-Deng era.[32]

Some moderates challenged the notion of equidistance between East and West in Russian foreign policy. Aleksei Bogaturov called such an approach illusory, claiming that for China improving relations with the West remains a priority. Moreover, in his view, China is likely to be Russia's main challenger in the future due to demographic and economic pressures.[33]

While most officials and scholars in Moscow favor the further development of the Sino-Russian partnership in the short term, Yeltsin's opponents on both sides of the political spectrum saw immediate negative consequences. Ever since the Chinese leadership's crackdown on the student protesters in Tiananmen Square, radical democrats have argued against an unduly close association with Beijing and in favor of expanding Moscow's relations with the West to ensure the success of Russia's development as a democratic state with a market economy. Former Prime Minister Yegor Gaidar, for example, contended that the main threat to Russia was not the strengthening of NATO, but the possibility of China's expansionism in the Russian Far East.[34]

Ultra-nationalists sharply criticize Chinese intentions in improving relations with Russia, especially in the border regions. Vladimir Zhirinovskii, whose Liberal Democratic Party received considerable electoral support in the Russian Far East in the 1993 Duma elections, has been vocal in condemning Chinese illegal immigration to Russia. During a 1994 tour of the Russian Far East, for example, Zhirinovskii called for strict limitations on the use of Chinese labor and a strengthening of border and visa controls. In Zhirinovskii's view, the Chinese "can do the manual labor that the Russians don't want to do. But no leased land, no property rights, no banks, no participation in privatization! The watch method: you can come here, do your work, then get out!"[35]

Ultra-nationalists view the border issue as yet another instance of Russian leaders caving in to the demands of foreign governments. Mikhail Khatsankov, writing in the right-wing newspaper *Den'* as well as in *Nezavisimaia Gazeta*, accused the Chinese of harboring territorial pretensions against Russia. Concerned that critics such as Khatsankov were distorting Russia's foreign policy record and exacerbating tensions in the border regions, Georgii Kunadze, then Deputy Foreign Minister, issued a point by point reply to his article, and representatives of the border forces published another article explaining the history of the border negotiations.[36]

For officials on the noncommunist nationalist fringe, China's economic success foreshadowed a shift in the balance of power in the region to Russia's detriment. Viktor Alksnis, for example, asserted that "only within the framework of a strong state" can Russia defend itself against China.[37] Colonel General Andrei Nikolaev, commander of the Border Guard troops, argued, however, that more restrictive border policies would not be in the best interests of the border regions. He observed that "some people want to create their own personal 'Iron Curtain' so to speak at *oblast'* level. . . . That is not the solution. The solution resides in a system that lays down on the basis of the laws the procedure for foreign citizens to stay in our country, for them to be granted rights of residence, an opportunity to work, and so on. Russia must not fence itself off from the world, but integrate into it."[38]

A POST-KOSOVO REALIGNMENT?

A consensus on the need for a foreign policy balanced between partners in the West, Asia, and the Middle East had formed by 1998 and appeared to be a long-term orientation—until the Kosovo crisis broke out in the spring of 1999.[39] The NATO bombing campaign against Yugoslavia reinforced the views of KPRF critics of the Yeltsin administration's foreign policy who had argued that NATO expansion ran counter to Russian interests and that Russia should form countervailing alliances. In effect, Russia had two foreign policy lines in the spring of 1999.[40] Despite its anti-Western rhetoric and decision to halt cooperation with NATO, the Yeltsin administration remained committed to cooperation with the West, as well as with China and other countries. At the same time, Prime Minister Primakov was proposing that Russia enter into a tripartite partnership with China and India.[41] However, once Chernomyrdin was appointed special envoy to the Balkans in April and the loyal Stepashin replaced Primakov in May, some semblance of consistency returned, reinforcing the Yeltsin administration's foreign policy line.

Anger at the marginalization of Russia's interests in the Kosovo conflict and concern over NATO's disregard for state sovereignty in its decision to intervene had an impact on the debate in Moscow about China. NATO's assertiveness overshadowed long-term concerns about China as a potential threat and such views were pushed further to the fringes of the discussion.[42]

Supporters of a closer partnership with China remained disappointed. According to Boris Zanegin of the Institute of the USA and Canada, Russia's policy was too ambiguous and sided with NATO in the end.[43] Indeed, Chernomyrdin's shuttle diplomacy also involved placating Beijing after NATO's mistaken attack against the Chinese embassy so as to facilitate a Security Council resolution on the Kosovo crisis. Although Russia and China were both opposed to the NATO bombing of Yugoslavia, many observers noted that the Sino-Russian relationship changed little as a result, either in terms of policy coordination or military cooperation.[44]

By the summer of 1999, Primakov had fallen out of favor, and in August Vladimir Putin replaced him as prime minister. Although the new Yeltsin government and the Chinese leadership still remained committed to the Sino-Russian partnership and continued to see eye to eye on issues such as their right to preserve territorial integrity, whether in Chechnya or Taiwan, Putin's more explicitly nationalistic positions have raised new questions about the direction of Russia's political development and its consequences for Moscow's partners.

CONTROVERSY OVER CHINA POLICY IN THE RUSSIAN FAR EAST

While policymakers and scholars in Moscow have been debating the foreign policy implications of Russia's unique status as a Eurasian state, officials and academics in the Russian Far East have been working out the dynamics of the region's engagement in Asia. Eurasianism has not been a topic for debate in the Russian Far East, where, despite the presence of native minorities with Manchu and Mongolian origins, most residents view themselves as cosmopolitans, living in a European outpost on the Asian-Pacific rim.[45] Indeed, prominent scholars in Vladivostok such as Viktor Larin, director of the Institute of History, point to vast cultural differences between Russia and China, which complicate mutual understanding in the border regions.[46]

For residents of the Russian border regions, China policy is an issue with immediate social and economic consequences rather than a question of strategy, as it is viewed in Moscow. The combination of the sudden opening of the border to trade and other exchanges, rapid economic decline and resulting population outflows, and the collapse of economic links between the Russian Far East and European Russia, make the perception of the shift in the geo-economic balance of power between Russia and China all the more acute in the Russian border regions. Instead of the philosophical discussions heard in Moscow, scholars and officials in Primor'e, Khabarovskii Krai, and Amurskaia Oblast have been trying to find practical solutions to their economic plight, especially through engagement in Asia.

Four issues in Sino-Russian regional relations highlight some current difficulties in the Russian Far East that bear on the region's relations with its Asian neighbors, especially China. First, although rapid expansion of Sino-Russian border trade in the early 1990s symbolized the dramatic progress in relations, it soon led to economic and social problems. A second issue, very much in the public eye, has been that of Chinese illegal immigration to the Russian Far East. Fears in the border regions about being overrun by Chinese have been exaggerated for local political ends, but nonetheless reveal serious concerns about the role of the economically declining Russian Far East in a more dynamic Asian economy.

A third issue, dissatisfaction over the Sino-Russian border demarcation, shows the continuing distrust of Chinese intentions in the region and the enduring legacy of the border conflict in Sino-Russian regional relations. Lastly, the Russian border regions have been slow to participate in multilateral economic arrangements. Although this may be changing, the difficulties encountered thus far—for example, in the Tumen River development project—highlight some enduring discomfort in the region over Russia's engagement in an open trading regime in Northeast Asia.

SINO-RUSSIAN BORDER TRADE

Initially trade, particularly in the border regions, appeared to be the most important barometer of progress in relations between Moscow and Beijing. The volume of border trade increased steadily from 1986 to 1993, paralleling the swift improvement in political relations between the two capitals. Border trade expanded more than tenfold from $50 million out of an overall Sino-Soviet trade volume of $3.25 billion in 1986 to $5.7 billion out of a total bilateral trade balance of $7.68 billion in 1993.[47]

Border trade began to grow exponentially in 1992 once Russia and China started to calculate bilateral trade in hard currency. This switch caused bilateral trade to diminish, while border trade—often accomplished on a barter basis—expanded tremendously. From 1991 to 1993, the share of border trade increased dramatically, amounting to more than two-thirds of total Sino-Russian trade.[48]

Liberalization of the rules governing border trade proceeded more swiftly in the PRC than in the Soviet Union in the late 1980s and early 1990s. While China gradually removed many export controls, the Soviet Union maintained them on a variety of goods needed by China, such as timber, steel, cement, mineral fertilizers, crude oil, coal, building materials, and food.[49] Despite the Soviet restrictions, Heilongjiang Province's border trade with the USSR boomed in the late 1980s. Raw materials and primary products made up 50 percent of Soviet and Chinese exports, with the remainder consisting of light industrial and textile products, machinery, and electronics.[50] Heilongjiang, for example, exchanged agricultural products, textiles, electronics, industrial products, building materials, and medical equipment for Soviet fertilizer, production materials, and aquatic products.[51]

The Chinese border regions, especially Heilongjiang Province, were very enthusiastic about the mutually beneficial development of Sino-Russian border trade. According to the "link with the south, open to the north" strategy devised in the mid-1980s, Heilongjiang opened its borders to trade with Russia, its northern neighbor, while also fostering transportation and trade links with the southern coastal areas. Expanding economic connections with the south have been crucial for the province's trade strategy; according to an official in the Heilongjiang provincial government, only some 20 percent of goods exported to Russia are produced in the province. Typically Heilongjiang imports unfinished goods, such as clothing, toys, and electronic goods, from southern provinces, which are then finished and packed in the border regions for export to Russia.[52]

The collapse of the USSR and development of economic reform in Russia presented new opportunities for Sino-Russian border trade. In 1991 and 1992, border trade became a necessity in the Russian Far East. Economic links with other areas of the former USSR were disrupted and the Russian Far East experienced particularly severe shortages of food products and consumer goods. The regions had concentrated on the production of defense technology and depended on imports of food and consumer goods from other areas of the Soviet Union. After the USSR collapsed, transportation costs skyrocketed and the Russian Far East turned to its closest neighbor, China, to meet many of its consumer needs. Central investment funds were cut off and the regional governments were unable to raise sufficient tax revenues to compensate. Even promised central funds did not come—in 1991, for example, the Russian Far East received only 30 percent of promised subsidies from Moscow.[53]

The rapid devolution of economic responsibility to the regions did not achieve the desired end—self-supporting regions—because this strategy assumed that they would maintain economic stability.[54] However, inflation drove up the cost of primary inputs and production in the Russian Far East. Production in the region's defense, machine-building, and resource industries plummeted, and more sharply than in other areas of Russia. In 1994, for example, when the free-fall in industrial production began to level out in Russia as a whole at approximately 17 percent, industrial production in the Russian Far East declined by 21 percent.

In the early 1990s, as the economic situation deteriorated, separatist trends began to develop in the Russian Far East.[55] Some radical political leaders proposed the creation of an independent Far Eastern Republic. Most political leaders, however, favored compensating for the central government's neglect with increased economic autonomy. They developed the slogan: "there's no money, give us freedom" (*net deneg, daite svobodu*).[56] If Moscow was unable or unwilling to provide sufficient revenue for the regions, then the regional leaders sought the freedom to seek funds elsewhere, as they saw fit.

During this period of economic disruption, however, policymakers in Moscow continued to vacillate in their approach to border trade. While some rules were tightened, others were relaxed. New regulations passed in July 1991 allowed certain state-run enterprises to trade directly with China, loosened restrictions on the creation of joint ventures, and allowed for barter trade in agricultural goods and basic necessities to help alleviate shortages.[57] In June 1992, Yeltsin signed a decree further regulating exports of strategic raw materials. The decree stipulated that only enterprises registered by the Russian Ministry of Foreign Economic Relations would be allowed to export raw materials.[58]

At the same time, the Chinese government continued to pass measures to expand border trade with its northern neighbors. Four border cities (Heihe, Suifenhe, Hunchun, Manzhouli) were granted the right to establish economic cooperation zones, with some of the preferential policies adopted at Shenzen on the southern coast of China. These northeastern cities were allowed to stimulate foreign investment and develop technology exchanges and labor exports. They were also encouraged to improve their processing and service industries.[59]

In 1992 and 1993, Sino-Russian border trade began to expand rapidly and relieved many of the shortages in consumer goods and food products in the Russian border regions (see Table 9.1). In 1992, the Russian government removed some of the restrictions on border trade. Under the new regulations, Russian firms could export up to 30 percent of their natural resources (timber, coal, and industrial products) without export licenses.[60] Export licenses were retained because of continued discrepancies between Russian prices for raw materials and world prices. Moreover, the collapse of the centralized Soviet economic system led to concerns about inadequate controls over sales of Russia's natural resources. As a result, the Ministry of Foreign Economic Relations decided in August 1993 to reduce sharply the number of authorized raw materials exporters.[61]

In 1993, China continued to liberalize border trade and removed export controls on all but three commodities—maize, soybeans, and tungsten ore. New rules permitted all foreign trade companies to conduct border trade and tariffs on imports were reduced by 50 percent—except for imported household electrical appliances, motorcycles, cosmetics, soft drinks, cigarettes, and liquor.[62] Import licenses were removed as well on goods from the CIS imported through barter trade.[63] Heilongjiang Province also continued to promote border trade in 1993 by opening new cities to border trade, granting twelve of them the right to manage their own foreign trade, and allowing more than 200 enterprises to engage in foreign trade directly.[64]

In Russia, as domestic prices began to match world prices, export controls began to be reduced. In 1993, the number of commodities subject to export duties declined from 54 to 29. A July 1994 Russian government decree repealed

TABLE 9.1 Sino-Russian Regional Trade

Million US dollars
percent of total exports

	1992	1993	1994	1995	1996	1997	1998
			Exports to China				
Amurskaia Oblast	201.5	202.6	53.4	32.4	35.4	34.1	31.1
	84.8%	86.9%	58.4%	50.7%	67.8%	65.9%	69.2%
Khabarovskii Krai	80.6	161.4	31.0	64.4	501.0	82.5	637.0
	21.7%	31.2%	0.08%	0.09%	50.4%	11.8%	57.4%
Primorskii Krai	106.8	187.0	101.0	88.4	111.0	185.0	159.0
	30%	42%	23%	19%	18%	16%	17%
			Imports from China				
Amurskaia Oblast	181.1	171.8	30.6	22.1	29.4	33.1	20.6
	95%	98.5%	31.0%	28.9%	56.0%	50.0%	40.0%
Khabarovskii Krai	33.7	230.0	22.4	46.6	49.6	67.2	52.8
	26.0%	64.0%	18.0%	15.7%	19.0%	23.0%	27.0%
Primorskii Krai	320.0	115.2	85.0	67.0	91.6	129.0	91.0
	55.0%	48.0%	6.3%	11.8%	12.8%	6.75%	16.8%

SOURCE: Association for the Russian Far East and the Transbaikal, "Mezhdunarodnaia i vneshneekonomicheskaia deiatel'nost' regionov Dal'nego Vostoka i Zabaikal'ia v 1998," Khabarovsk, 1999.

export duties on 16 types of goods (including sugar, certain metals and alloys, some petroleum products, and timber materials) and reduced duties on fertilizers, cellulose, and unprocessed aluminum.[65] Consequently, Russia's overall export levels increased by 10 percent from $44.3 billion in 1993 to $48 billion in 1994.[66]

The boom in border trade in the early 1990s not only reinvigorated the economies in the border areas, but also began to have a significant impact on the overall Sino-Russian trade balance. In 1993, for example, Heilongjiang Province's border trade with Russia accounted for one-third of the overall Sino-Russian trade balance of $7.68 billion.[67]

Nonetheless, although Russia's overall exports increased in 1994, Sino-Russian trade decreased dramatically to $5.1 billion, a 34 percent drop overall. Since the precipitous fall in border trade, Russian and Chinese economists and officials have been trying to understand the causes of its rapid development and decline. All agree that the boom in border trade was unsustainable because it was sparked by a very specific set of circumstances—the acute need in the

Russian border regions for consumer goods and food products produced in Heilongjiang and the other Chinese border regions due to the collapse of the Soviet economic system in 1990 and 1991.

THE LIMITATIONS OF BORDER TRADE

By 1993, the structure of exports and imports in the Russian border regions began to change. While in the early 1990s the Russian border regions exported machinery and equipment, in 1993 and 1994 raw materials accounted for the bulk of exports to China. In the early 1990s, much of the machinery and equipment exports from the Russian border regions were re-exports from elsewhere in Russia. In 1993 and 1994, tariffs on rail transportation increased at the same time as industrial production continued to fall in the Russian Far East, which led to a diminished supply of machinery and equipment in the border regions for export.[68]

By 1993, the consumer goods market in the Russian Far East had become saturated with low-cost, and often low-quality, Chinese goods. Higher-priced Korean and Japanese goods became more attractive to the increasingly discerning consumers in the border regions. Consequently, demand for Chinese consumer goods fell. This trend coincided with complaints in the Russian border regions that their raw materials exports were underpriced in barter trade. The shift to hard currency dealings in border trade occurred at the same time that the PRC was carrying out currency reform, causing additional dislocations.

Moreover, in 1993 and 1994, the Chinese government implemented tighter controls on the economy, resulting in decreased investment and reduced capital construction. Since construction materials were an important component of Chinese imports from the Russian border regions, the change in Chinese economic policy also adversely affected Sino-Russian border trade.[69] The Chinese government reimposed quotas on other key Chinese imports from the Russian Far East, such as vehicles, chemical fertilizer, and steel.[70] According to one Chinese specialist, these economic measures not only made border trade less attractive, but also made it difficult for firms to fulfill existing contracts.[71]

Chinese observers in Beijing and the border regions optimistically refer to the current stage in Sino-Russian border trade as one of transition (*guodu*) and adjustment (*tiaozheng*).[72] Analysts in the Russian Far East, on the other hand, considered the dramatic increase in trade with China in 1992 and 1993 to be unsustainable. In their view, the surge in Sino-Russian border trade in the early 1990s stemmed from short-term factors in Russia such as the rapid liberalization of foreign trade and the effort to compensate for the collapse of production and the disruption of domestic economic links by reorienting the economies of the Russian border regions to foreign markets, especially to China. When circumstances in Russia changed, Sino-Russian trade was affected. Rising transportation costs and customs duties increased the cost of industrial goods, previously shipped from European Russia via the Russian Far East to China. At the same time as demand for these industrial goods decreased, the prices of some key resource exports from the Russian Far East fell, leading in addition to a decline in the value of resource exports from these regions.[73] Russian scholars agreed with their Chinese counterparts that the barter transactions, used to jumpstart Sino-Russian border trade in the early 1990s, had outlived their utility and that the two sides needed to look for a more solid basis for the development of their economic relations.[74]

Fall-Out from Unregulated Border Trade

Rising concern in Russia and China about the economic, social, and political consequences of insufficiently unregulated border trade provided additional incentive to place Sino-Russian regional economic relations on firmer footing. While Chinese officials were more concerned about complaints about the quality of their exports to Russia and with inadequate administration of border trade in China's Northeast, Russian officials saw a new threat from illegal immigration of Chinese traders to the Russian Far East.

Chinese Criticism of the Management of Border Trade

Complaints about the quality of Chinese goods sold in border trade were the issue of greatest concern to both Heilongjiang provincial officials and policymakers in Beijing. China's Ministry of Foreign Trade, in particular, contended that the low-quality goods traded in the Russian Far East and brought into Moscow and other Russian cities by shuttle traders undermined the reputation of Chinese goods in general as well as China's stature as a trading partner.[75] In fact, officials in Beijing echoed many of the complaints heard in the Russian Far East about the inadequate sanitary standards for Chinese foodstuffs as well as their contamination by pesticides and other pollutants, and about the poor quality of Chinese exports of clothing and children's toys.[76]

While there was widespread agreement in the Chinese border regions and in Beijing about the need to improve quality controls and inspections, observers in Heilongjiang note that the problem was not just on the Chinese side. They admitted that Chinese merchants may have been guilty of producing and selling shoddy and counterfeit goods, but argued that Russian shuttle traders at times sought out the cheapest goods for resale in Russia. Policing the border for shipments of low-quality goods would require efforts by both countries. Some analysts in Heilongjiang argued that it was the Russian side that should have been faulted for its lack of thoroughness in customs and quality control inspections, usually done by hand, while Chinese border controls used x-ray equipment.[77]

Although the production of low-quality goods in Northeast China may have reflected deep-seated causes, some of the financial problems with border trade were truly transitional and reflect a lag between institutional development and the expansion of foreign trade.[78] In June 1995, at the regular meeting of the Sino-Russian Committee on Economic and Scientific-Technical Cooperation, Russia and China decided that bilateral trade should be transacted in hard currency rather than by barter.[79] The share of barter trade began to diminish—while it accounted for almost 60 percent of overall Sino-Russian trade in 1993, barter transactions dropped to 49 percent of the trade volume in 1994 and to just 28 percent in 1995.[80]

Apart from undermining the reputation of Chinese goods, border trade has been criticized equally sharply, especially in Beijing, for creating chaos on the PRC's borders. Throughout the 1980s, the liberalization of foreign trade was a controlled process, but in the early 1990s in Heilongjiang and other border provinces it turned into a mad rush to the Russian border. Established trading companies found themselves competing with small-scale, often inexperienced (and sometimes shady) businesspeople who undercut their prices. These small companies often had difficulty meeting the terms of contracts and sometimes sold counterfeit or poor quality goods.

Officials and scholars in Beijing and Harbin have described the situation on their northern border in the early 1990s as chaotic (*hunluan*) and anarchistic (*wuzhengfu*). Many Chinese specialists on Sino-Russian trade have noted that the authorities became concerned about a loss of government control in the border regions. Moreover, Chinese officials, fearing that these small-scale traders were harming the reputation of Chinese goods, reportedly criticized the border provinces for inadequately administering border trade.[81] China's Foreign Ministry has criticized Heilongjiang Province, in particular, for indiscriminately handing out thousands of passports allocated to the province for use in foreign trade.[82]

Much to the frustration of people in Heilongjiang, the province's border trade with Russia has come under particular scrutiny from Beijing, although Inner Mongolia and Jilin Province have been involved as well and experienced similar problems. According to a *Heilongjiang Ribao* journalist's account of border trade at Suifenhe in Jilin Province, the problem of shuttle trade has been perceived unfairly as a "Heilongjiang phenomenon," since more than 80 percent of the traders at the market there were from areas outside Heilongjiang.[83]

RUSSIAN CONCERN ABOUT THE THREAT OF CHINESE
ILLEGAL IMMIGRATION TO THE RUSSIAN FAR EAST

By 1993, illegal immigration of Chinese citizens to the Russian Far East had become a cause célèbre in the regional press. Considering that the border had been a closed military zone for thirty years, it was to be expected that the rapid expansion of border contacts in the late 1980s and early 1990s would create new problems and require some adjustment. For example, in 1998 Amurskaia Oblast reported only 6,233 border crossings, but by 1992 there were 287,215.[84] Moreover, the increase in Chinese visitors to the region coincided with the exodus of Russians from the Far East due to the high cost of living and layoffs at defense factories.[85] From 1993 to 1998, the population of the Russian Far East decreased annually by 4.3 percent.[86]

Although observers in the border regions recognized that the opening of the border to economic activity was a positive development, they argued that insufficient attention was being paid to the consequences of opening the door to a neighbor like China—with its large population, unemployment problem, and historical claims to Russian territory.[87] Some analysts recognized that problems could be attributed in part to the lack of experience of Russian regional officials, who rushed to trade with China to overcome shortages of goods.[88]

Nonetheless, local observers contended that Chinese provincial leaders were urging their citizens to establish "Chinatowns" in the Russian border regions.[89] Although this was an exaggeration, Chinese markets sprouted in all of the major cities. In Vladivostok and Khabarovsk, residents soon complained that the open-air markets where the Chinese traders sold their wares had become magnets for all sorts of criminal activity and were a threat to public health due to primitive sanitary amenities. In response to such complaints, these markets were obliged to move to the outskirts of town.[90] Chinese illegal immigrants also have been accused of a variety of other crimes, such as wildlife poaching in the border regions, and robbing passengers on the Trans-Siberian railroad.[91]

The lack of accurate data about Chinese immigration reinforced the perception that the Russian border regions were under siege. Despite wild claims of millions of Chinese living in Russia, during the peak period of Sino-Russian border trade, at most 50,000 to 80,000 Chinese worked in the Russian Far East, according to reliable data from the Institute of Economic Research in Khabarovsk. These figures included 10,000 to 15,000 contract workers and 10,000 to 15,000 students on long-term exchanges. Police data revealed that some 5,000 to 6,000 Chinese were in Khabarovskii Krai and Primorskii Krai illegally.[92]

Conspiracy theories have developed about the activities of the Chinese in the region. Local observers have alleged that many of the immigrants travel to the Russian Far East as investors in fictitious joint ventures, as temporary workers in the agricultural and construction sectors, as tourists en route to destinations in Central Asia, and especially as "shuttle traders," i.e., small-scale traders who travel back and forth between Russia and China to sell the bags of consumer goods they have brought with them.[93] In an article first appearing in a Khabarovsk newspaper, and then reprinted in a Primorskii Krai academic newsletter, one Khabarovsk scientist outlined five paths Chinese took in their alleged attempt to overrun the region peacefully: (1) trade; (2) purchase of land and property; (3) marriage to Russian citizens; (4) establishment of joint ventures; and (5) employment in Russian firms and farms.[94]

Despite the ominous tone of the article, all of the activities outlined above are perfectly legitimate, though they may appear to some Russians to be a pretext for illegal immigration. Many Chinese businesspeople are involved in joint ventures in the Russian border regions, and the People's Republic of China actually leads all other countries in terms of the number of joint ventures with these regions. Russian firms also contract to hire Chinese laborers for work in construction and on vegetable farms.

By and large, press coverage of Chinese economic activity in the Russian Far East has been most negative in Primorskii Krai.[95] This region has the largest number of Chinese contract workers, most of whom work in construction in the major cities. More than 6,000 of the 8,000 Chinese workers hired for projects in the Russian Far East in 1992, for example, went to Primorskii Krai.[96]

By contrast, in Khabarovsk, where the Chinese workers hired are mostly agricultural workers who live in out-of-the way settlements, the press coverage has been much more positive. In June 1995, for example, a Khabarovsk newspaper reported that a group of seventy Chinese harvested twice as many vegetables on the twenty acres of land they were leased than the Russians were able to do on 400 acres.[97] Considering the problems with food supply in the Russian Far East, the Chinese farmers' work is seen as mutually beneficial— they earn ten times more than they would at home, while Russians can buy locally produced fresh vegetables instead of more expensive imports.

Khabarovsk enterprises also have contracted to hire Chinese workers for jobs in the agricultural and construction sectors. Unemployment has been growing in the region, but farms and firms contend that local Russian workers are either unwilling or not sufficiently trained to do these jobs. Despite some dissatisfaction with the hiring of Chinese labor at a time of social tension, the Khabarovsk press generally has portrayed their contribution to the regional economy favorably.[98] Nonetheless, the regional press continued to cover problems with Chinese poachers, who allegedly were fishing illegally in Russian waters.[99]

TABLE 9.2   Chinese Contract Workers in Primorskii Krai

	1995	1996	1997	1998
Number of Chinese workers	8,349	8,292	6,968	7,179
Total number of foreign workers	12,848	13,535	11,306	10,333
Chinese workers as % of total	65.0%	61.3%	61.6%	69.5%

SOURCE: Primorskii Krai Committee of State Statistics, *Staticheskii ezhegodnik v 1998* (Vladivostok: 1999).

Public opinion data shows that residents of the Russian border regions remain cautious about hiring Chinese workers and fearful about their intentions in coming to Russia. In a 1994 joint Sino-Russian public opinion poll of 900 people in Khabarovsk and Blagoveshchensk, more than 50 percent of the respondents supported the contracting of Chinese workers only for certain specialized tasks, such as agricultural work. This contrasts with the 5 percent who unequivocally supported the presence of Chinese citizens in Russia and the 33 percent who expressed negative attitudes regarding Chinese in general.[100] Of those questioned about the intention of Chinese citizens to remain in Russia indefinitely, 40 percent stated that such a situation would be intolerable, 38 percent advocated maximum caution, and just 16 percent considered this to be a normal development.[101]

Despite the perception in the regional press that the central authorities were turning a blind eye to the threat of Chinese expansion in the Russian Far East, in 1993 border issues became a subject for discussion in the central press as well as among officials in Moscow.[102] In December 1993, President Yeltsin signed an edict requiring the authorization of the Federal Migration Service in order to hire foreign labor.[103] The new rules on foreign labor have had both positive and negative consequences. Although many people in Primorskii Krai were unhappy with the presence of Chinese workers in their cities, now that it is more difficult to hire them, the construction industry has had difficulty finding qualified workers.[104] The number of Chinese hired as contract laborers has been declining. In Primorskii Krai, for example, in 1993 there were 8,291 Chinese working in 100 firms.[105] By 1997, fewer than 7,000 were employed in the region (see Table 9.2).[106]

Beginning in 1993, the Russian border regions also took some measures of their own to address the problem of Chinese illegal immigration. The Khabarovskii Krai administration approved a series of measures to regulate the hiring and registration of foreign workers.[107] Primorskii Krai also attempted to address the problem in several ways. An April 1994 edict limited the number of hotels that could house foreign tourists and placed greater controls on tour groups from China.[108] According to new regulations, travel agencies are responsible for ensuring that Chinese tourists travel to their specified destinations and stay only for the time period specified, and agencies tolerating violations may face fines or the suspension of their licenses.[109] Although the Primorskii Krai administration mostly was concerned about Chinese immigrants, Governor Nazdratenko imposed new registration procedures and fees on temporary residents from other former Soviet states as well.[110]

Because of allegations of massive numbers of Chinese staying in Russia illegally, since the mid-1990s the Russian border regions have cracked down on markets and tour companies through police sweeps, called "Operation Foreigner" (*operatsiia inostranets*). These measures have not revealed evidence of massive violations of Russian visa rules. According to data from the Primorskii Krai Migration Service, for example, 2,870 Chinese were asked to leave the region in 1997 for violations of visa rules, primarily for engaging in trade while traveling on tourist visas.[111] In the same year, 125 Chinese were found guilty of similar visa violations in Khabarovskii Krai, and just 100 in 1998.[112] Anyone who visits the markets outside of Khabarovsk or Vladivostok can see that these figures understate the number of Chinese residing in these cities. Since legitimate Chinese businesspeople complain of difficulties in obtaining visas, frequent document checks, and police harassment, it is likely that the Chinese traders at the market, who work there for several years at a time, find some means of acquiring the necessary legal documentation to live and work in Russia. Although regional officials blame the Chinese government for encouraging illegal immigration to the Russian Far East, corruption in Russia makes it possible for Chinese economic migrants to remain there.

If caught, illegal immigrants are required to return home. The Primorskii Krai regional authorities have claimed that the police effort has not been directed against the Chinese specifically, but almost 80 percent of those apprehended in the first few days of one such operation were from the PRC.[113] As further evidence of the import given to securing the border from poachers and illegal immigrants, in the first four months of 1994, regional governments provided the troops of the Pacific Border district with assistance worth 8.5 billion rubles. Primorskii Krai allocated more than 2 billion rubles, for example, to build apartments for the troops.[114] Despite all these measures, many in the region believed that the problem of illegal immigration could only be tackled at the federal level and required new federal legislation.[115]

As in Vladivostok, Khabarovsk also implemented a campaign against illegal immigrants, mostly directed against Chinese citizens.[116] According to the head of the Khabarovsk office of the Federal Security Service, Vitalii Pirozhniak, the problems associated with the open border region ebbed due to counter-measures taken in the region to regulate Chinese employment.[117] The commander of the naval forces of the Far Eastern Military district, Viktor Nachaev, further noted that the Chinese border forces were cooperating with the Russian border troops and had no interest in permitting Chinese illegal immigration to Russia.[118]

NEW VISA RULES
AND THEIR CONSEQUENCES FOR TRADE

As a result of complaints by Russian regional leaders about Chinese illegal immigrants, in January 1994 the Russian and Chinese governments instituted new laws requiring visas for business travel. The Chinese government rebutted claims by some Russians that there was an official policy to support illegal immigration by Chinese citizens to the Russian Far East.[119] To the contrary, as noted, the authorities in Beijing became alarmed about Chinese trading practices and reportedly called provincial leaders to task for failing to administer border trade properly.[120]

China too faces problems with illegal immigration and criminal activity by Russians and has taken steps to address them, including a well-publicized campaign against illegal border crossings.[121] Nevertheless, the Chinese government has expressed some concern about the periodic police sweeps for illegal immigrants in the Russian border regions. In the wake of a December 1994 police action in Primorskii Krai, the press department of the Chinese Foreign Ministry issued a statement noting that although China understood Russia's efforts "to expel Chinese citizens who did not abide by Russian laws, China hopes . . . that Russia will comply with international procedures, and will not do harm to lawful rights, interests, and dignity of Chinese citizens. . . ."[122]

Although it is unclear what impact such rules will have on the perception in the Russian border regions of an illegal immigration problem, one unwelcome consequence became apparent right away—Sino-Russian trade fell sharply in 1994. The decline affected the regions unevenly. Amurskaia Oblast, which oriented its foreign trade almost exclusively to the Chinese market, saw its overall trade volume plummet from $407.6 million in 1993 to $189.5 million in 1994. Although trade with China also fell sharply in Primorskii Krai in 1994, the region's overall volume increased from $679.3 million to $965 million due to increased trade with countries such as Japan, South Korea, and the United States. While Primorskii Krai and Khabarovskii Krai supported measures to secure the border from Chinese illegal immigrants and unscrupulous shuttle traders, Amurskaia Oblast, more dependent on border trade with China, criticized aspects of the visa policy. According to Viktor Larin, director of the Institute of History, a golden mean had yet to be found in Russia's foreign economic relations with China.[123]

Thus, when Foreign Minister Andrei Kozyrev attended a conference of regional heads of administration from the Far East in Blagoveshchensk en route to Beijing in early 1994, he was greeted with complaints about the economic impact of the free fall in border trade. To remedy the situation, some representatives suggested that either Moscow provide credits, presumably to compensate the regions for their lost revenue, or establish free economic zones along the border.[124]

In recognition of the growing significance of the border regions in Russian-Chinese relations, Kozyrev also traveled to Heihe in the Chinese province of Heilongjiang, bordering on Amurskaia Oblast. He met with similar complaints from Chinese provincial leaders.[125] During his visit, Kozyrev and Chinese foreign minister Qian Qichen signed an agreement regulating the border crossing points between their two countries.[126]

In a March 1995 interview with an *Izvestiia* correspondent, Governor D'ianenko of Amurskaia Oblast, the region most affected by the new regulations, denied there was ever any real reason to fear Chinese colonization of the border regions.[127] Indeed, the local press in Amurskaia Oblast criticized the new visa measures imposed to regulate Chinese illegal immigration for further complicating trade with China, already impeded by tariff and transportation issues.[128] Although the neighboring regions preferred to expand economic cooperation with the United States, Japan, and South Korea, according to Governor D'ianenko the agreement to build a bridge from Blagoveshchensk to Heihe would be a boost for his oblast's status and have a major impact on the growth of regional economic relations.[129]

According to Pavel Minakir, director of the Institute of Economic Research in Khabarovsk, by the end of 1994 the border regions realized that they had overdone their criticism of trade with China. Said Minakir, "For the Far East, China is the only stable export market. . . . If we are going to set up barriers to Chinese imports and goods, nothing good will come of it."[130] According to Minakir, Khabarovskii Krai lost $1 billion in trade revenue as a result of the sharp drop in trade with China in 1994.[131]

In regions such as Primorskii Krai and Khabarovskii Krai that have the opportunity to trade with a variety of Asian states, the barter-based border trade with China was perceived as a transition phase—its chaotic nature has mirrored the difficulties in shifting to forms of trade that are not regulated by central planners in Moscow. According to the Primorskii Krai administration, the next step required the redirection of Sino-Russian economic relations from barter trade to more substantial forms of cooperation involving the export of capital.[132]

Regional authorities supported efforts to shift Russian-Chinese relations from small-scale barter deals to more substantial cooperation involving larger, more established firms. According to a Primorskii Krai official, although China established the largest number of joint ventures in the region, many of them existed on paper only and were not functioning. Those that were in business had a low level of foreign investment compared to Russian joint ventures with the United States and Japan.[133] At the height of Sino-Russian regional cooperation, 40 percent of all joint ventures in the Russian Far East involved Chinese capital, but firms with Japanese, South Korean, and American investment accounted for 70 percent of the capital invested in all joint ventures in the region.[134]

The Primorskii Krai administration argued that Moscow's intervention was necessary to draft additional legislation regulating illegal immigration and foreign workers, to reduce customs and export duties which have had a dampening effect on regional trade, and to develop free economic zones in the Russian Far East.[135] This view was not always shared by central government officials, some of whom have made the opposite claim—that it is up to the regions to enact the legislative basis necessary to regulate border trade.[136]

The Russian border regions pressed the central authorities to do something about these issues, however, and in 1994 some steps were taken to resolve the trade problems caused by low-quality goods, payment issues, transportation bottlenecks, and crime. The Russian-Chinese intergovernmental commission on economic and technical cooperation met in Beijing in May 1994 to address ways of moving beyond border trade. Many areas of potential cooperation were discussed: energy, space, aviation, metallurgy, machine-building, light industry, advanced technology, and transportation.[137] Representatives from the Russian and Chinese border guards signed an agreement for joint measures to prevent the trade in weapons, drugs, hard currency, and other contraband across the Russian-Chinese border.[138] Experts from Russia and China put forth suggestions regarding cooperation in the construction of new railroads, roads, and bridges in the border regions.[139] During Jiang Zemin's visit, Russia and China signed an agreement obliging Chinese firms to pay hard currency for a part of the Russian goods they purchased.[140]

In an effort to deal with complaints concerning the quality of merchandise traded, a law was passed requiring the Russian State Standards Bureau to certify that certain goods (foodstuffs, drinks, electronics, machinery, medical instruments, etc.) imported into Russia meet a set of minimum standards.[141] Although these laws address specific problems in trade with China, additional legislative measures dealing with taxation and foreign investment are necessary. Moreover, there was a sense in both the Russian border regions and in Moscow that many difficulties in economic relations with the Chinese border regions stemmed from Russia's lack of a regional strategy.[142]

READJUSTMENT IN SINO-RUSSIAN REGIONAL ECONOMIC RELATIONS

Sino-Russian bilateral trade stopped declining in 1995 and achieved a modest increase in 1996, although trade did not yet reach 1993 levels. The recovery in 1996 was due to a large extent to a resurgence in border trade—Heilongjiang's border trade with its Russian neighbors reached $350 million in 1996, twice its 1995 figure,[143] while Jilin reported $400 million in trade through just one of its crossing points, at Suifenhe. Nonetheless, the recovery in border trade could do nothing to address the more fundamental problems in bilateral trade, and the overall trade balance fell again by 20 percent in 1997 to $6.12 billion and then dropped further to $5.48 billion in 1998.

Although the switch to hard currency resolved some Russian complaints about the undervaluing of their resources in barter trade, a range of new problems soon emerged. The dearth of interbank agreements on credit between the Russian Far East and the Chinese Northeast meant that trading companies either would have to send representatives with large amounts of cash to complete transactions and risk becoming crime victims, or would have to resort to cumbersome methods, such as using banks in third countries, to complete transactions. So far, few interbank agreements have been signed. Among the first were agreements between the Nongye Bank in Heihe and the Amur Commercial Bank in Blagoveshchensk and between the Harbin branch of the China Investment Bank and Regiobank in Khabarovsk. The Russian banks involved are very small, however, and many Chinese businesspeople prefer to go to more established banks in third countries.[144] Two larger Russian banks, Rossiiskii Kredit and Inkombank, opened branches in China to improve the conditions for mutual payment, but they went bankrupt after the August 1998 financial crisis. In December, however, a Primorskii Krai bank, Dalrybank, opened a ruble-based correspondent account with China Investment Bank in Harbin to facilitate trade.

Inadequate arbitration mechanisms complicate the resolution of claims from both the Russian and Chinese sides about nonfulfillment of contracts and nonpayment. With no legal recourse available, Chinese and Russian businesspeople at times have resorted to criminal means, such as hiring the Russian mafia to enforce contracts, or Chinese criminals to kidnap Russian traders who refuse to pay their Chinese partners. In July 1996, China's Committee for the Promotion of International Trade and Russia's Industry and Trade Committee signed an arbitration agreement, but according to a senior Chinese specialist, it lacks the enforcement power that a higher-level bilateral agreement would have.[145]

Concerned by the criticism of Sino-Russian regional relations within the border regions and its potential adverse impact on the evolving strategic partnership, authorities in Moscow and Beijing have continued to take steps to address regional problems. In both Russia and China, however, these measures have only served to exacerbate center-regional tensions and to highlight the lack of regional strategy in both countries. Fearing strong support in the Russian Far East for his political opponents, Yeltsin unveiled the previously mentioned $34 billion federal program for the region during an April 24, 1996, presidential campaign stop in Khabarovsk. Since the election, however, the plan has languished unfunded in Moscow.[146]

As of 1996, the Chinese State Council instituted new measures to prevent disreputable and inexperienced firms from participating in border trade.[147] At the provincial level, efforts were taken to make sure that passports for foreign travel are distributed to reliable business people. These rules were applied so strictly that businesspeople in Heilongjiang Province complain that it is very difficult for them to travel at all.

Similarly in Russia, new rules effective on August 1, 1996, raised customs duties on shuttle trade. As a consequence, items typically sold in Russia, such as fruits and vegetables from China, as well as electronics from South Korea and Japan, became much more expensive. Hoping to raise tax revenues by collecting additional customs duties, Moscow's new policies targeted items that were in demand by residents of the border regions and gave unscrupulous traders greater incentive to bribe customs officials.[148]

Regional officials also have been taking more active steps to regulate the presence of Chinese citizens in their territories. For example, in May 1998 the Primorskii Krai Duma established quotas limiting the number of tourist agencies allowed to bring in Chinese tourists.[149] In Khabarovskii Krai, the police have been making spot checks in the markets to make sure that Chinese with tourist visas are not engaging in trade.

With all of the measures taken in the mid-1990s by Russian and Chinese officials on the national and regional levels to prevent illegal immigration from China, Russian residents of the border regions have become more tolerant of the presence of Chinese in Russia, as long as it is temporary and related to certain occupations. In a 1997 poll of 611 Russian residents of six cities in Khabarovskii Krai, Amurskaia Oblast, and Primorskii Krai, 43 percent approved of the temporary presence of Chinese in construction and agriculture and 35 percent supported their temporary involvement in trade, while 25 percent disapproved due to the potential for competition.[150] However, attitudes hardened when the discussion turned to a more permanent place for Chinese in society. For example, when asked how they would react to one of their relatives marrying a Chinese citizen, 50 percent of the Russians polled reacted negatively.[151] A similar poll undertaken from October 1996 to May 1997 with a larger sample (1,182 students, 1,086 residents, 100 experts from Khabarovskii Krai, Primorskii Krai, Amurskaia Oblast, Irkutskaia Oblast, and Chitinskaia Oblast) showed that while 49 percent of students would be opposed to the marriage between a close relative and a Chinese citizen, 80 percent of residents would view this negatively.[152] How real is the likelihood of Russian-Chinese intermarriage on a mass scale? This same poll also interviewed 244 Chinese and found that although 67 percent of those surveyed viewed marriage between a Russian and one of their relatives positively, 45 percent would be unwilling to enter into such a marriage.[153]

If public opinion in the Russian border regions continues to reflect considerable ambivalence about Russia's opening to China, this is in no small part due to the politicization of problems in Sino-Russian regional relations. According to Larin, regional leaders, especially in Primorskii Krai, have taken advantage of a compliant press and used the struggle against the "yellow peril" in their political battles with Moscow.[154]

IMPACT OF THE 1998 RUSSIAN FINANCIAL CRISIS

Economic crisis has created a countervailing trend, however. With a much weakened ruble in the aftermath of the August 1998 crisis, some of the Russian border regions have become more dependent on trade with China, which increased as a percentage of their overall trade. No longer able to afford many imports of food and consumer goods from preferred partners such as Japan, the United States, and to a lesser extent South Korea, regions such as Primorskii Krai and Khabarovskii Krai compensated by increasing purchases from China. Even before the onset of the crisis, Sino-Russian border trade had been adjusting to the new rules and stabilizing—climbing from $701 million in 1996 to $1 billion in 1997, about half of its 1993 peak figure.[155] Although the volume of Chinese imports to the Russian Far East in 1998 declined considerably relative to 1997, China replaced the United States as Primorskii Krai's second highest source of imports.[156] Khabarovsk's trade with China surged in 1998 (see Table 9.1), but this occurred only because the Chinese government purchased a large order of Sukhoi fighter planes, produced in Komsomolsk-na-Amure. Machinery exports, including these aircraft, accounted for 92 percent of the region's exports to China. China's investment in the Russian Far East continues to be very low, however: just $200,000 in the first nine months of 1998 compared to $133.7 million for the United States, the leading investor in the region.[157] In Primorskii Krai, for example, China invested just $15,000 in 1998, compared to $17 million for South Korea, $12.6 million for Japan, and $1.9 million for the United States.[158]

Russian and Chinese policymakers have made efforts to improve relations on the regional level. In 1997, the two countries came to an agreement outlining a legal framework on regional economic cooperation, and since then six sets of bilateral regional agreements have been signed—between Inner Mongolia and Chitinskaia Oblast, Tianjin and Novosibirsk, Primorskii Krai and Jilin Province, Liaoning Province and the Republic of Bashkortostan, Shanghai and Amurskaia Oblast, and Altai Krai and Xinjiang Province.[159]

A Working Group on Interregional and Border Cooperation was created in 1997 to participate in the work of the Sino-Russian intergovernmental commission on economic cooperation. When this proved ineffective, a new coordinating council was formed in 1998 to actively seek regional perspectives by involving the Association of the Russian Far East and the Trans-Baikal and representatives from China's northeastern provinces.[160]

BORDER DEMARCATION

The increased instability on the periphery of the former Soviet Union in the 1990s has given all the bordering states a greater incentive to come to agreement about their common boundaries. The Chinese and Russian parliaments ratified the 1991 eastern border agreement in February 1992, but once the Russian-Chinese border demarcation talks resumed in June 1993, leaders in the Russian border regions became concerned that some of their territory would be handed over to China. Primorskii Krai governor Nazdratenko, for example, discussed border issues with the central government for the first time during Prime Minister Chernomyrdin's visit to Vladivostok in August 1993.[161] One month later Khabarovskii Krai governor Viktor Ishaev complained to Chernomyrdin about the uncontrolled entry of Chinese citizens into the region as well as about Chinese military vessels navigating freely on the Amur River across from Khabarovsk. He urged the prime minister to make sure that no territorial concessions to China were made without the region's consent.[162]

The Primorskii Krai administration then requested that the Russian Supreme Court make an inquiry into the eastern border agreement, according to which the Krai would hand over 1500 hectares of its territory to the

Chinese.[163] In further instances of protest, Governor Nazdratenko refused to travel to China as part of a high-level delegation, and the Primorskii Krai parliament recalled its permanent representative from the border demarcation commission.[164]

The Foreign Ministry in Moscow quickly realized that poor public relations on its part had contributed to opposition in the Russian Far East to the border demarcation process.[165] The head of the Russian delegation to the border demarcation commission, Genrykh Kireev, published an article in a Vladivostok newspaper in which he asserted that there was no alternative to the demarcation of the border and reminded readers that the previous lack of clarity had led to armed conflict on Damanskii/Zhen Bao Island in 1969. Kireev noted that regional leaders were represented at a special informational seminar on the border demarcation talks in February 1993.[166] Since that meeting, however, there had been changes in the local leadership in Russia and the new leaders were more inclined to protest any transfer of territory to China.[167] In another attempt to placate the public in Primorskii Krai, a foreign ministry official explained that the border demarcation commission was conducting topographical studies to determine where the border was in three districts of Primorskii Krai and that no decisions would be made for another five years.[168] Nonetheless, the Ussuri Cossacks reportedly announced that they would defend the Russian-Chinese border and would not tolerate any changes.[169]

The political struggle in Moscow in 1993 between Yeltsin and the Duma exacerbated center-regional tensions in Russia, as regional leaders took sides. Even after Yeltsin prevailed, local leaders continued to confront Moscow on key issues. For example, at a May 1994 press conference, Governor Ishaev denounced the 1991 Russian-Chinese border agreement. He noted that both Khabarovskii Krai and Primorskii Krai were slated to lose valuable territory and objected to granting foreign ships (including military vessels) the right to navigate from the Ussuri to the Amur Rivers, right past Khabarovsk.[170] In reply, the Russian Foreign Ministry defended the fairness of the 1991 agreement and reiterated Russia's commitment to it, but acknowledged that the lack of rules governing border river navigation remained a problem and was the subject of ongoing negotiations.[171]

During Chinese Foreign Minister Qian Qichen's visit to Moscow in late June 1994, mostly dedicated to planning the upcoming summit meeting between Yeltsin and Jiang Zemin, the two countries initialed the agreement on the western section of the border, which runs from Mongolia west to Kazakhstan.[172] Border issues also topped the agenda during the subsequent visit of Chinese Defense Minister Chi Haotian. An agreement was signed to prevent incidents between the armies of the two countries, such as the unintended crossing of the border by military aircraft or vessels.[173]

In early 1995, however, Governor Nazdratenko rejected an offer from the Russian Foreign Ministry to participate in the Russian government's plan for joint use of border territories. In fact, Nazdratenko urged the renunciation of the 1991 border demarcation treaty. Primorskii Krai authorities claimed that the area to be returned to China was too valuable to give away because it included a graveyard, farmland, a pine forest, and land strategically located adjacent to the Tumen River in the Khasan district.[174] According to the Primorskii Krai administration, the transfer of this territory would enable China to construct a new port on the Tumen River, which would compete with Russian ports in the region.[175] Much to the dismay of the Russian Foreign Ministry, a Federation Council fact-finding mission to Vladivostok supported Nazdratenko's position on the Khasan district.[176]

Deputy Foreign Minister Aleksandr Panov warned that the governor's statement could cause serious damage to relations between Russia and China. In an effort to forestall any worsening in the relationship with Beijing, Foreign Minister Kozyrev asserted that the 1991 border demarcation agreement would be implemented no matter what.[177] Supporters of the agreement argued that, given the history of Chinese claims on Russian territory, reopening the border issue could cause more harm than good.[178]

The fact remains that the border demarcation agreement covering the eastern portion of the Russian-Chinese border had been ratified already by the parliaments of both countries. Speaking at a session of the newly elected Primorskii Krai Duma, Major General Rozov, the military adviser for Russia's delegation to the Border Demarcation Commission, stated that renunciation of an international agreement was only permissible during a state of war. In light of his comments, the Duma rephrased the issue as the "impermissibility of violating the territorial integrity of the Russian Federation in Maritime [Primorskii] Krai during the demarcation of the Russian and Chinese border."[179]

Initially, Chinese officials confined to diplomatic channels their critical reactions to Nazdratenko's comments. In late February 1995, however, China issued its first official statement on the issue. According to a Chinese spokesman, "a small number of people in Russia recently, taking advantage of the fact that some specific issues have arisen during bilateral trips by citizens, have made extremely irresponsible statements about the border between the two countries and have created confusion among the population of Russia's border regions." The spokesman warned that such statements would have a negative influence on Russian-Chinese relations.[180] During subsequent State Duma hearings on the subject, Primorskii Krai representatives backtracked somewhat, stating that only certain practical aspects of the agreement needed to be revised, not the whole document.[181]

In early March 1995, representatives from the Russian Government and Primorskii Krai met in Vladivostok to discuss border demarcation. Vladimir Lukin, chairman of the Duma's International Policy Committee, stated categorically that there was no question of repudiating the border demarcation agreement. While Governor Nazdratenko concurred, he reaffirmed that his administration would insist on amending it.[182] To reconcile the differences between the positions of the federal government and the regional authorities, Lukin proposed a meeting with regional officials and declared that parliamentarians were prepared to assist as observers and advisers.[183]

During his scheduled trip to China in mid-March, Kozyrev reaffirmed Russia's commitment to the 1991 demarcation agreement. According to Kozyrev, "in spite of some statements by individual Russian spokesmen with regard to a revision of the legal documents concerning the eastern sector of the border, decisions in the Russian Federation are taken and implemented by the State."[184] Kozyrev's Chinese hosts appeared satisfied with his comments. After her meeting with the Russian Foreign Minister, Deng Xiaoping's daughter, Deng Rong, noted that the Chinese leadership attached much significance to Kozyrev's affirmation of Russia's continued adherence to the 1991 demarcation agreement.[185] In a subsequent interview with ITAR-TASS, Chinese Foreign Minister Qian Qichen stated that some regional leaders chose to make "pronouncements that are incompatible with the Sino-Russian border agreement" and criticized the Russian press for its "irresponsible articles," but he declared that the Chinese government was satisfied overall with the development of relations with Russia.[186]

Despite continued center-regional sparring over the border issues, by the second half of 1994 anti-Chinese rhetoric had significantly diminished in the local press in Vladivostok. By 1995, various cooperative projects between Primorskii Krai and China increasingly were in the news and portrayed more positively.[187] In part, the change in rhetoric may have been political. At the time, Governor Nazdratenko, previously an outspoken opponent of Russia's border demarcation policy, was campaigning for reelection as a candidate from the government's party, *Nash Dom—Rossiia*, and may have felt some compunction, if not to support the government's positions, then at least not to work actively to undermine them.

Other activities such as poaching also have been periodic sources of conflict, at times leading to exchanges of fire along the border. In April 1995, for example, an officer in the Russian border guards was killed trying to capture a Chinese poacher. The Russian officer's death elicited considerable concern in the border regions regarding the prospects for cooperation and security in the area.[188] Moreover, environmental issues have become a source of Sino-Russian regional tensions. Russians claim, for example, that Chinese poachers come to the Russian side of the river to fish illegally or cross over into Russian territory to gather protected plant species such as Siberian ginseng and shoot rare animals for use in traditional Chinese medicines.

Also in the spring of 1995, the prediction of a Russian psychic, Tamara Globa, that there would be war between Russia and China in 1996 inflamed public opinion in the region once again. Vitalii Sedykh, head of the Pacific Border Forces, addressed these concerns in an interview in *Vladivostok* in July 1995. He told the Primorskii Krai paper that the Chinese had fully cooperated with the Russian authorities and that the parties responsible for the Russian officer's death had been arrested. He noted that the psychic's prediction had an unfortunate impact on public opinion, and stated that in his view the situation on the border was stable. Although he agreed that the border demarcation should take place in accordance with international and Russian laws, he expressed his personal view opposing any transfer of Russian territory.[189]

Even as the final work was taking place on the demarcation of the eastern border in 1995, the border issue remained a sore point for all the regions. *Amurskaia Pravda* wrote about the potential economic losses involved in returning any of the border islands to China.[190] A Khabarovsk scholar published historical evidence supporting the region's claim to the disputed Bolshoi Ussuriiskii and Tarabarov Islands.[191] Cossack forces protested to regional authorities in the Jewish Autonomous Oblast and began patrolling the border region—which led Chinese border forces to move closer to the boundary area in response.[192] A well-publicized expedition of scholars, journalists, and Cossacks from Primorskii Krai traveled to the Ussuri River border area to "demonstrate the historical roots of the settlement of Primor'e by Russians."[193]

Despite opposition in the region, the agreement on the eastern portion of the Sino-Russian border went into effect on October 17, 1995, and ITAR-TASS reported that the survey of the demarcation of the final segment of the Russian-Chinese border was completed by November 30, 1995. Yet Governor Nazdratenko denied that the demarcation had ended and that Primorskii Krai would transfer 1,500 hectares of territory to China—apparently signaling another about-face in his views on relations with China.[194] Moreover, after he was reelected in December 1995, Nazdratenko resumed his criticism of the border demarcation. In March 1996, Nazdratenko once again questioned the legality of the 1991 Sino-Soviet border demarcation agreement and asked the Constitutional Court to consider the issue. He claimed that the agreement violated Russia's national interests and should not have been carried out without a referendum.[195]

In April 1996, Nazdratenko's position received a boost when Major-General Valerii Rozov, formerly a specialist on border issues for the Russian Federation, left his position in protest against the decision to hand over Russian territory to China and began working as a consultant for the governor. Rozov called attention to alleged errors that led the Russian government to agree to give up Primorskii Krai territory.[196]

By June 1997, Russian and Chinese negotiators reached a compromise over the demarcation of the border between Primorskii Krai and Jilin Province. The two sides agreed that the Tumen River would remain the boundary line. Although Governor Nazdratenko ultimately signed off on an agreement he had denounced earlier, the compromise reestablished that the left bank of the Tumen River belonged to China, involved measures for the protection of the delicate ecology of Lake Khanka in Primorskii Krai, and enabled that region to retain control over the site of a Russian cemetery.[197]

Interestingly, despite years of loud protests from Primorskii Krai regarding the consequences of the border demarcation process, it was Khabarovskii Krai that received a reprieve after quietly but firmly informing Moscow that the region considered it intolerable to hand over the two islands located across from Khabarovsk (Bolshoi Ussuriiskii/Heixiazi and Tarabarov/Yinlong) and turn the city into a border post. Unlike his colleague in Primorskii Krai, Khabarovsk's Governor Ishaev has taken a less overtly confrontational approach in his discussions with the Moscow authorities regarding the border question. Ishaev's strategy paid off when Yeltsin gave a speech in Khabarovsk en route to a summit meeting in Beijing in April 1996. The president assured local residents that the border islands claimed by China in Khabarovskii Krai would never be returned.[198] Indeed these two islands, as well as Bolshoi Island in the Argun River, were the only issues that were not resolved by the time the agreement on the demarcation of the eastern border was signed at the November 1997 Sino-Russian summit meeting in Beijing.

Because no agreement has been reached regarding the islands across from Khabarovsk, Governor Ishaev continues to refer to the border issue as "far from resolved,"[199] unlike his colleagues in Moscow who have hailed the completion of demarcation work. In Khabarovsk, officials have rejected proposals for the joint use of the disputed islands and accused China of "cartographic aggression"—a phrase that hearkened back to the Sino-Soviet polemics over border issues in the 1960s—for portraying the islands as Chinese territory on their maps.[200] Some even have claimed that China has been trying to alter the river boundary physically to its advantage, pouring sand into the Kazakevich Channel south of Bolshoi Ussuriiskii/Heixiazi Island, and compounding the natural decrease in water levels so that ships could sail only in the channels on the Russian side of the border.[201] In case Khabarovsk's claim to Bolshoi Ussuriiskii Island were not clear enough, in October 1999 a new Russian Orthodox church was built there. In his comments at the church's opening, Governor Ishaev stated "this was, is, and always will be Russian land."[202]

MULTILATERAL COOPERATION
IN THE SINO-RUSSIAN BORDER REGION

Since the late 1980s, policymakers in Moscow have raised hopes about the creation of special economic zones in the Russian Far East. One of the most discussed projects involves the creation of a free economic zone in Nakhodka, Primorskii Krai. Plagued by corruption and derailed by the economic crisis in South Korea (the main foreign partner), the zone finally is being implemented, albeit on a smaller scale than originally planned. The first Sino-Russian project for special economic zones on either side of a proposed bridge connecting Blagoveshchensk, Amurskaia Oblast to Heihe, Heilongjiang Province has been stalled for more than five years due to lack of funds on the Russian side for bridge construction. Grandiose plans for the establishment of a special economic zone in the Tumen River area, where the borders of Primorskii Krai, Jilin Province, and North Korea meet, have not been fulfilled.

One of the biggest obstacles to the creation of special economic zones in the Russian Far East and elsewhere in Russia has been the absence of federal legislation, which was not passed until December 1998. Moreover, Moscow and the regions often have been at odds over the costs and benefits of multilateral cooperation.

The differing reactions in Moscow and in Primorskii Krai to the United Nations Development Program plan for international cooperation in the Tumen River Economic Development Area (TREDA), for example, are further evidence of the divergent views of Russia's role in Asia at the center and at the periphery. The $30 billion project was originally conceived in 1991 to develop transportation and telecommunications infrastructure necessary for establishing free trade zones in the area where the borders of Russia, North Korea, and China meet. Premised on infusions of technology and investment from Japan and South Korea, the development area was to have played a role in processing resources from Northeast China, Mongolia, and the Russian border regions for export to other countries in the Pacific Rim. The grand vision of the Tumen project has not been realized, however, largely due to the conflicting interests of participating states.[203]

While Moscow has been supportive of the plan as another means of deepening cooperation with China—the linchpin of Russia's Asia policy—officials in Primorskii Krai, who increasingly have focused their efforts on expanding economic cooperation with Japan, South Korea, and the United States, have seen the Tumen project as a threat to the Krai's interests in the region.

Primorskii Krai's reaction to the Tumen development project is indicative of the region's attitude towards economic integration in the Asia-Pacific region, especially with Northeast China. In regions such as Primorskii Krai with a variety of Pacific Rim trading partners, Northeast China is viewed both as a competitor and as a potential partner. Primorskii Krai and China's northeastern provinces all see themselves as future transportation hubs for cargo going from Asia to Europe.

For this reason, Governor Nazdratenko opposed the PRC's proposal to develop new ports on the Tumen River and refused to return the 330 hectares of territory initially mandated by the demarcation agreement to facilitate this.[204] Although any new ports would be built on territory that now belongs to China, the transfer of these 330 hectares would have enabled the Chinese to build roads and rail connections from these ports to Russian territory. The Primorskii Krai governor also objected to the provision of the border demarcation agreement of 1991 that would have given China the right of navigation on the lower portion of the Tumen River, which flows into the Sea of Japan.[205]

Nazdratenko has argued that if China were to build new ports in the region, they would detract from the viability of nearby Primorskii Krai ports and siphon investment from the region's main ports: Nakhodka, Vladivostok, Pos'et, and Zarubino. There was also considerable criticism of the Tumen project on ecological grounds, due to its potential adverse impact on nearby marshlands and a marine park.[206]

Despite continuing vocal opposition to the Tumen development program among officials and scholars in Primorskii Krai,[207] from the very beginning UNDP project planners called attention to the impracticality of Tumen River port construction projects due to river conditions. The Tumen River is difficult to navigate and is frozen for several months each year. Even if the river were dredged, it would still not be deep enough to become a worldwide shipping lane and could only accommodate barge traffic. Despite the claims by some Russian critics of the Tumen development plan that the Chinese hope to create a new major port with potential military uses, any new port facilities only could be used for transshipment by barge.[208]

Instead of building new ports in China as initially planned, the Tumen River Economic Development Area will facilitate regional trade by enhancing infrastructure.[209] TREDA supports the renovation of existing ports in Primorskii Krai, such as Zarubino, Nakhodka, and Vostochnii, as well as the improvement of the region's rail lines to promote border trade. Railroads and highways connecting border crossing points between China and North Korea are to be modernized. A new rail line was built that links the Sino-Russian border via Hunchun and Kraskino to the Russian port of Zarubino. The Chinese city of Hunchun in the Tumen trade zone has been attracting investment in light industry and the telecommunications sector, while some foreign capital has been pledged for infrastructure projects in North Korea's Rajin-Sonbong Trade Zone.[210]

The unrealized hopes of the Tumen development project have shown that while on the map the Russian Far East appears to be in a favorable position for integration into the Northeast Asian economy, geographic proximity alone is not enough to achieve this.[211] Although Chinese officials and scholars like to emphasize the natural economic complementarities between the resource-rich Russian border regions and China's abundant labor supply in its Northeast, such talk is anathema in the Russia Far East, where policymakers hope to avoid becoming a "Third World resource supplier" and fear an uncontrollable influx of Chinese workers.

While in Moscow China is viewed as Russia's strategic partner, a bulwark against pressure from the United States on a variety of foreign policy issues, in Vladivostok China is seen as a competitor. Indeed, the ailing defense industries in China's Northeast and the Russian Far East share many problems, which neither side will be able to resolve without major new investment. Since it is unlikely that such investment would issue from either Moscow or Beijing, both the Russian and Chinese border regions have had to turn to foreign sources. Thus, while Primorskii and Khabarovskii Krais have resisted development plans centering on cooperation with China, they have begun to court investment from the wealthier states in the Pacific Rim, especially Japan, South Korea, and the United States.[212] To this end, Governor Ishaev of Khabarovskii Krai, who serves as the head of the association of the regions of the Russian Far East and Trans-Baikal, called for greater coordination among the members to attract foreign investors from these countries.[213]

However, the succession of financial crises, first hitting Russia's partners in Northeast Asia, and then Moscow in August 1998, lowered regional expectations about the ease of diversifying foreign economic relations and refocused attention on finding workable options for expanding cooperation with China. Transit trade may be a promising area because it would involve combinations of foreign partners, including China, Japan, South Korea, and the United States. There also are plans for a shipping route connecting Pusan with Hunchun and Pos'et in Primorskii Krai.[214]

In June 1999, officials from Heilongjiang Province, Jilin Province, Primorskii Krai, and Washington State signed a protocol to create a trade corridor connecting Harbin and Changchun by rail to ports in Primorskii Krai and then to Seattle and Tacoma. If implemented, this corridor could stimulate trade between the Northwest United States and Northeast China and enhance transportation links between Heilongjiang Province and Primorskii Krai.

CONCLUSIONS

The rapid and steady improvement of Sino-Russian relations has been one of the most visible successes of Russia's foreign policy. Yet some scholars and officials in Moscow have begun to eye China's rise as a great power and Russia's coincident economic difficulties with some consternation. For all but those on the edges of the political spectrum—the radical democrats and the ultranationalists who question Chinese short-term intentions—the problem is the long-term balance between Russian and Chinese capabilities. In the short term, however, concern by most policymakers and scholars in Moscow about Russia's role in a unipolar world order have overshadowed these considerations. For the majority in the Moscow policy community, partnership with China is viewed as providing leverage necessary in a world with a largely unfavorable balance of power.

In the Russian Far East, however, geo-economic pressures from China are felt much more immediately. Many officials and scholars in the Russian border regions complain of being simultaneously cut off from European Russia and squeezed by an economically and demographically expanding China. While analysts in Moscow have become increasingly sensitive to the plight of the Russian Far East, the central authorities have done little more than pay lip service to regional complaints.[215] A group of prominent scholars from the Institute of the Far East in Moscow issued a report warning of the possibility of the further "sovereignization" of the Russian border regions and urging greater efforts by the central authorities to integrate the area into their overall strategy for Asia.[216]

In an odd twist of fate, since 1994 the tensest negotiations on Russian-Chinese relations have been taking place between the Russian government and its regional representatives, not between leaders in Moscow and Beijing. Although initially the central authorities tried to downplay the problems in regional relations, today these issues are on the top of the bilateral agenda. Chinese observers have even begun warning that "due to the long period of hostilities between the two nations in the past, any imprudent speech or activity will harm bilateral relations and hurt the mutual trust of both Russians and Chinese."[217] It remains to be seen whether relations along the lengthy Sino-Russian border will play a greater role in fostering new forms of regional cooperation or in introducing new tensions in the bilateral relations.

Certainly some regional leaders, such as Primorskii Krai governor Nazdr-atenko, have attempted to hold Russia's China policy hostage to center-regional bargaining. Nevertheless, given the apparent inability of the authorities in Moscow to implement a viable policy for the Russian Far East, there is a growing consensus in the region of the importance of engagement with a wide range of partners in the Asia-Pacific region.

Conclusions

Moscow's China policy since 1969 is a tangled tale, involving threats, conflict, bitter recrimination, cautious diplomacy, and pledges of cooperation. This study has endeavored to unravel the strands in the Sino-Russian relationship to shed light on the sources of its evolution from conflict along the Ussuri River in the 1960s to strategic partnership in the 1990s.

There were three stories behind Moscow's China policy—narratives carefully developed to meet the concerns during the Soviet era of three very different audiences: the international communist movement, the Moscow policy community, and the Russian border regions. Over the years, the coalition of top leaders in charge of China policy sought to develop an approach that simultaneously would maintain unity in the communist movement, meet domestic needs, and inspire confidence in Russia's regions on the front lines of the Sino-Soviet conflict.

At times the policy best suited to the interests of one audience conflicted with those of the others. Moreover, what Soviet leaders failed to appreciate was that each of these audiences was changing irreparably. The communist movement became increasingly fractious as demands for autonomy from "Moscow center" accelerated in the 1970s and reached a breaking point in the 1980s. Although regional leaders in the Russian Far East were required to show support for Moscow's China policy, from the very beginning it was clear that regional interests diverged from the center's. While in the Soviet period regional leaders kept an eye out for opportunities to press their case for resuming border trade with China, by the 1990s, politicians in the Russian Far East had developed alternative views of Russia's role in Asia.

Even in Moscow, the policy community was never united on China policy. Although reformers were a minority until the early 1980s, they used their connections to Andropov to lobby for an improvement in relations with China, as well as for domestic reform. By the mid-1980s, the conservatives who had dominated key party and state positions were scrambling for new jobs or reinventing themselves as "friends of China." Since Gorbachev's day, China policy has become a lightning rod for those dissatisfied with aspects of Russia's domestic reforms and role in the world.

FROM IDEOLOGICAL OPPONENT TO STRATEGIC ALLY

From the early days of the ideological split with China until the onset of the normalization process in the mid-1980s, the combination of China's ideological challenge and growing military capabilities caused serious concern for Soviet military planners and policymakers. Today the situation is much changed. Once Moscow's most worrisome ideological opponent, China now has become a valued strategic partner.

Russia and China have succeeded in resolving most of their differences over border demarcation and navigation. To be sure, the demarcation process has been the source of considerable controversy, aggravating tensions between Moscow and the border regions. Present-day border issues involve many more participants—Kazakhstan, Kyrgyzstan, and Tajikistan, as well as the Russian border regions. Despite the greater complexity of negotiating in the post-Soviet period, Moscow and Beijing have made notable progress since the Brezhnev era when border talks represented exchanges of invective.

Although some vestiges of the Sino-Soviet conflict persist—Russian and Chinese troops continue to be deployed in the border regions[1]—Sino-Russian military relations have taken on a fundamentally different character. Russian arms sales to China have been expanding, some say beyond the control of the Russian Defense Ministry, as ailing defense industries seek sources of hard currency.[2] Although a few dissident voices in Russia have warned against facilitating a Chinese military buildup,[3] on the whole cooperative Russian-Chinese military relations are perceived as one of the main achievements of normalization. While in the late 1970s and early 1980s policymakers in Moscow anxiously watched the burgeoning military relationship between the United States and the PRC, today the West is concerned by the pace and character of Russian arms sales to China.

It is one of the great ironies of history that just as Moscow was able to achieve a significant improvement in relations with China, the issues in the relationship suddenly changed. From the very beginning, the newly established Sino-Russian partnership had to address new challenges stemming from divergent paths to economic and political development, the growing influence of regions on foreign policy, the lagging bilateral economic relationship, legacies of mistrust, and changing domestic and international environments. All of these factors will shape the Sino-Russian relationship in years to come and introduce elements of uncertainty into the fledgling partnership.

DIVERGENT PATHS TO POLITICAL
AND ECONOMIC REFORM

Moscow and Beijing have never been able to view each other dispassionately. When Mao Zedong opted for a model of political and economic development which deviated from the Soviet standard, Soviet policymakers saw a threat to the USSR's leadership of the communist movement and sought to compensate through appeals for communist unity. Later, when Deng Xiaoping began his ambitious reform program at a time of continued Soviet economic and political stagnation, Soviet leaders saw a new challenge and criticized Chinese policies again.

It was only once Gorbachev embraced many of the same reform ideas and accepted the principle that socialist states could forge their own path to socialist renewal that China and the Soviet Union began making real progress toward normalization. Nonetheless, when opponents of Gorbachev's policies staged a coup in August 1991, initially Chinese officials welcomed it. They quickly reversed themselves once Yeltsin proved victorious and a democratizing Russia succeeded the Soviet Union. Yet Yeltsin and his colleagues remembered the Chinese reaction, and when democratic voices in the new administration called for a pro-Western foreign policy, ties with Beijing at first were placed on the back burner.

Nevertheless, within a year the political center had shifted in Russia. After a year of disenchantment with Western assistance and exhortations, more and more prominent voices called for a foreign policy balanced between East and West. China policy would soon become a key component of this strategic reassessment. As the early hopes for a new type of Russian-American relationship evolved into sober reflections on different interests, Russians began to look toward China as their preferred strategic partner for the twenty-first century.

THE GROWING INFLUENCE
OF REGIONS ON FOREIGN POLICY

Even in the days of the Sino-Soviet border clashes, the Russian border regions had a distinctive outlook on regional relations between Russia and China. Initially more fearful about the 1969 clashes and dissatisfied with Moscow's glib reassurances, the regions later became the first to demand a reopening of border trade, a key source of regional revenue.

In the post-Soviet period, as Russia's regions became more engaged in foreign policy issues, center-regional tensions within the Russian Federation played out in the context of the Sino-Russian relationship. The Russian border regions insisted on their right to play a role in Russia's China policy, leading some Russian analysts to go so far as to say that the center of gravity in Sino-Russian relations had shifted to the regional level.[4] Indeed, the regions made their dissatisfaction with the border demarcation process amply clear and even threatened to derail it. Regional leaders lobbied Moscow for changes in visa rules and trade policy in response to difficulties in regional economic cooperation.

Regional leaders, along with policymakers in Moscow and Central Asia, have been reassessing their geopolitical positions and are less than sanguine about the current outlook. Previously, the leadership in Moscow focused on the ideological and military aspects of the balance of power with Beijing. Today, Russian leaders on all sides of the political spectrum are concerned, above all, with economic and demographic issues. The results of Russia's own reform efforts compare unfavorably with China's impressive economic growth, and some Russian observers note that Russian technology shipments in recent years have only served to contribute to Chinese economic strength.[5] Russian officials feel pressure from China in another area as well. At the same time that the Russian population is leaving the Russian Far East due to the high cost of living and the economic downturn in the region, Chinese citizens have been migrating there, often illegally. The influx of Chinese traders and workers inflamed the already high social tensions in the region, causing what former Foreign Minister Kozyrev termed an "inescapable" problem for local inhabitants and authorities.[6]

Russia is not alone in facing problems with increasingly independent-minded regional leaders. In China, development has not proceeded evenly and has led to vast disparities in wealth between the coastal and interior provinces. Efforts by the Chinese border regions to redress these disparities through an enthusiastic commitment to border trade with Russia have at times led to unintended consequences—a rapid expansion of trade without the necessary infrastructure to regulate it.

By comparison with Russia, China's economic progress seems staggering, but fundamental problems remain that have broader implications for China's neighbors. Flagging state industries in China have exacerbated unemployment problems and spurred the migration of job-seekers, some of whom end up as shuttle traders in the Russian Far East. Although the influx of Chinese citizens is coming at a time when Russians increasingly are seeking to leave the area for an easier life in other regions of Russia, it is not a new problem for the Russian Far East. Chinese settlers periodically have come north to seek better opportunities, much to the consternation of their Russian neighbors. In an 1895 journal of his travels in the Russian Far East, for example, Lieutenant Colonel

Krasnov noted that one of the goals of his trip was to find out to whom the region belonged or would belong—to the Russians or to the Chinese.[7]

Russia's changed geopolitical situation, however, has reinforced regional concerns. While in the past Sino-Soviet tensions were viewed globally (i.e., in terms of their impact on the U.S.–Soviet relationship), today problems in Russian-Chinese relations are felt most acutely in the Russian Far East. Regional leaders look more critically at problems in bilateral relations with China because of the economic and demographic imbalance between the Russian and Chinese border regions.

The Russian foreign policy elite has struggled to keep pace with the dramatic changes in Russia's global position and to redefine its role in international relations. The perception that Russia finds itself in an unfavorable position relative to other great powers may have negative consequences for relations with China, particularly in the Russian border regions.

Regional issues—the long border between the two countries and the history of the interaction of their peoples—always have set the scene for relations between Moscow and Beijing. Today the momentum of the Russian-Chinese relationship has shifted east. How it will unfold in coming years will have important implications for regional security, economic development, environmental protection, and social stability in Northeast Asia.

LAGGING BILATERAL ECONOMIC COOPERATION

Despite the problems in regulating regional economic cooperation, border trade spurred the improvement in the overall trade balance, especially from 1991 to 1993. Still, progress in Sino-Russian political relations far exceeds the results achieved in bilateral economic cooperation. The pledge by Boris Yeltsin and Jiang Zemin to reach $20 billion in trade by 2000 remains a distant dream, impeded by constant changes in trade rules, a lack of infrastructure, and rapidly evolving markets. Arms sales have proceeded consistently, but not without controversy due to opposition to early agreements that allowed China to barter consumer goods for weapons. Despite Russia's unsuccessful bid to provide turbines for the Three Gorges project, energy cooperation may be one area where substantial bilateral, and even multilateral, cooperation (including Japan and South Korea) may be achieved.

LEGACIES OF MISTRUST

When Mikhail Gorbachev and Deng Xiaoping agreed at their May 1989 summit meeting to "close the past and open the future," the two leaders opted to put aside old disagreements in order to focus on facilitating the development of a constructive bilateral relationship. As the Sino-Russian partnership flourished in the 1990s, Russian and Chinese officials came to view the period of confrontation in Sino-Soviet relations as an aberration from the traditional friendship between the two neighbors.[8]

Sweeping aside more than a century of border disputes and the more recent history of tensions in communist party relations, however, served only to reinforce underlying suspicions in both countries. This was clear even as Deng made his historic pronouncement in 1989. After suggesting letting bygones be bygones, in the next breath the Chinese leader noted that it would be impossible to avoid all discussion of the unequal treaties imposed by the Tsarist regime and post-1917 Soviet encroachments.[9]

While opposition to the Sino-Russian border demarcation process and fears in the Russian border regions regarding the possibility of an uncontrollable influx of Chinese settlers into these territories are in part a reflection of Moscow's inadequate regional strategy, wariness in these areas also stems from the unwillingness of political leaders in the two countries to confront the legacy of centuries of tension. Even in China, where a controlled press unrelentingly emphasizes the smooth development of present-day Sino-Russian relations, the controversial issue of Harbin's centennial led to a debate in 1994 in one of that city's newspapers, where critics raised a complaint common in the Sino-Soviet polemics in the 1960s about Russia's use of unequal treaties to occupy 1,500,000 square kilometers of historically Chinese territory.[10]

CHANGING DOMESTIC
AND INTERNATIONAL ENVIRONMENTS

How Russia and China will cope with underlying mutual suspicions, the consequences of center-regional tensions, and the shortcomings in their bilateral economic relations will depend to a large degree on the direction of domestic political change in both countries and on the international environment. Both Russian and Chinese leaders face great economic and political challenges in pressing ahead with their economic reform agendas.

Despite the emphasis placed on the complementarity of the Russian and Chinese economies, together Russia and China may only be able to solve a fraction of their economic difficulties. The two countries have many similar problems, especially in their border regions, and may have to look elsewhere in the Pacific Rim for necessary investment capital and technology.

Multilateral cooperation may provide a better alternative for both countries to meet their economic needs, as well as to deflect Russian concerns regarding the Sino-Russian geo-economic and demographic balance of power. Pressures for diversification of foreign economic relations in Asia have already become apparent in the Russian Far East, where regional leaders have taken the lead in counterbalancing what some perceive as the region's excessive dependence on China in the early 1990s with more active relations with Japan, the Koreas, and the United States. Disappointed by the level of Moscow's support for regional development, officials in the Russian Far East also have looked increasingly to Japan, South Korea, and the United States for investment funds. Although the Russian Far East remains dependent on federal support, largely due to the high cost of energy, policymakers in Moscow are concerned that pressures for economic autonomy in the regions and differing views of the regional balance of power may lead regional officials to pursue foreign economic relations in Asia that are at odds with Moscow's priorities. An economically autonomous Russian Far East integrated into the Pacific Rim would not be in Moscow's interest—such a turn of events would make it difficult for the federal government to maintain control over Asia policy and shift the balance in center-regional relations.[11] It remains to be seen whether or not Moscow is prepared to make the commitment necessary to a regional strategy that would both pave the way for a more multilateral approach to involvement in Asia and to more cooperative relations with Russia's easternmost regions.

SCENARIOS FOR THE FUTURE

This study has shown that Soviet and Russian China policy has been shaped both by an evolving international context and by changing domestic coalitions. The post–Cold War international environment has not simplified matters. With the collapse of the USSR and the end of the bipolar structure of international relations, United States–China–Russia relations within the strategic triangle have changed fundamentally. Russia's weakness, China's rise (despite weak points), and American domination are new features in the current world geometry.[12]

Unlike the triangle of the Cold War era, partnerships of various types now link each of the three countries with the other two. Instead of the old dynamic calling for two of the states to balance against the third, today it is more appropriate to speak of the lack of parallel development in the three sets of bilateral relations, between China and Russia, China and the United States, and Russia and the United States.[13]

As Russia and China struggle to achieve their desired positions in this new world order, their responses to domestic pressures and international imperatives will influence the dynamics of the triangle as well as the content of the Sino-Russian strategic partnership.[14] Several outcomes are possible, depending on the interplay of domestic and international forces. The degree of inclusiveness in domestic politics in Russia and China, not to mention in international relations as a whole, will be key factors. Will democratic or nationalistic forces prevail in Russia and China and in what combination? Will the two countries be brought together through economic integration, or will political and regional fragmentation further complicate their partnership? What will be the shape of the new world order and how will they participate in it? Although the answers to these questions will not become clear immediately, given the rapid pace of domestic and international change affecting Russian and Chinese development, some preliminary thoughts by way of conclusions are presented below.

Rising Nationalism or Democratic Transition?

Communist ideology has faded from the nomenclature of Sino-Russian relations and has been replaced by a new geopolitical vocabulary emphasizing the balance of power and interests between the two neighbors. This has caused discomfort in some circles, and, as Lev Deliusin has noted, the absence of an ideological foe has led to a search for new enemies.[15]

The policymakers forming a centrist consensus today in both Moscow and Beijing have wavered in their choice of partners and understanding of threats depending on the issue. Thus, while the Russian and Chinese governments opposed NATO intervention in Kosovo, they each continued to rely mostly on economic relations with the West rather than with each other.

The events of 1998 and 1999 have strained this centrist consensus repeatedly, and there are real questions as to its long-term viability. The virulence of the nationalistic reaction to the NATO bombing of the Chinese embassy in Belgrade came as a warning call about potentially dangerous undercurrents in Chinese society and weakened the position of reform-minded leaders such as Zhu Rongji, who favors cooperation with the West. A more nationalistic Chinese regime might prove to be a better ally for Russia in international affairs, but a more dangerous neighbor if such a government would reignite territorial disputes.

If in 1996 Chinese officials secretly hoped for a Yeltsin victory over his communist opponent, this was out of fear of the nationalism associated with the KPRF. Recent elections in 1999–2000, in the aftermath of a year of economic crisis, inspired similar concerns. Although the ultra-nationalists who openly talk of a threat from China remain on the fringes of political life, the deep-rooted problems exacerbated by economic reform, pervasive corruption, and anger at Russia's loss of international prestige have shifted the political spectrum toward more nationalistic positions.

Unilateralism or Multilateralism?

The degree of inclusiveness in the post–Cold War world order will influence the configuration of domestic forces in Beijing and Moscow. As the twentieth century drew to a close, there was a real danger of creating what John Garver called a new "Far Eastern Rappallo" by painting Russia and China as global outcasts and thereby causing them to form a closer partnership.[16] America's reflexive exclusionary impulses and lack of strategic thinking, especially about Asia, have reinforced voices in Russia and China calling for a more equitable multipolar order, and more recently for checks on what they view as American hegemony. This works both ways, of course. Russia's foreign policy fragmentation and China's ambivalence about its future global role have fueled concerns in the United States about their real interests and ability to play according to any rules of the game, even more inclusive ones. Avoiding vicious cycles of exclusion and confrontation will be one of the main challenges facing all three countries in the next century.

In the short term, as Russia is focused mostly on emerging from its economic difficulties, avoiding marginalization has been a primary aim. Strategists have urged Russian policymakers to make better use of Russia's geographic advantages: for example, highlighting their country's potential role as a Eurasian landbridge linking Europe and Asia.[17] This would require a balanced approach to partners in Europe and Asia, rather than attempts to play one region against the other. Other scholars have focused on redressing previous imbalances in Russian foreign policy by emphasizing the benefits of a greater orientation toward Asia and the Middle East.[18]

Integration or Disintegration?

Regional processes of economic integration may provide a vehicle for multilateral cooperation, as long as they proceed in a balanced fashion and are not accompanied by political disintegration. For instance, in the early 1990s enthusiasm for regional economic cooperation between the Russian Far East and the Chinese Northeast far outpaced administrative control, and the result was increased regional tensions. Yet, while oversight by central and regional authorities may regulate interaction, policymakers have little control over other demographic and economic factors.

In the Russian Far East, for example, continued population outflows raise many questions for the future. Should Chinese labor be welcomed in the region to alleviate shortages of workers in certain sectors, such as agriculture? Would a greater number of Chinese residents in the Russian Far East mean a more multicultural Russia or a more fragmented one? Although the economic benefits of regional integration are promising, considerable debate continues on the social and political consequences for the development of the Russian border regions and the integrity of the Russian state.[19]

Russian and Chinese leaders have hailed their strategic partnership as the culmination of efforts to move beyond decades of enmity and as the basis for the new configuration of their relations in the twenty-first century. Its durability and content will depend considerably on the ability of Russian and Chinese leaders to address domestic challenges and find their way in an evolving world order.

Notes

1 / INTRODUCTION

1. There are only two works that cover Sino-Soviet relations through the 1980s, Thomas G. Hart, *Sino-Soviet Relations: Reexamining the Prospects for Normalization* (Aldershot, England: Gower, 1987); and Lowell Dittmer, *Sino-Soviet Normalization and Its International Implications, 1945–1990* (Seattle: University of Washington Press, 1990).

2. Creative myth-making on both sides has helped to perpetuate these grievances. See S.C.M. Paine, *Imperial Rivals: Russia, China, and Their Disputed Frontier, 1858–1924* (Armonk, N.Y.: M. E. Sharpe, 1996), chapter 1.

3. For example, the 1997 publication in Khabarovsk of an edition of Vladimir Miasnikov's *Dogovornymi stat'iami utverdili,* about the history of the Sino-Russian border from the seventeenth to the twentieth centuries, turned out to be the centerpiece of a May 1998 conference in the city about contemporary Sino-Russian border relations.

4. According to Robert Putnam, "The politics of many international negotiations can usefully be conceived as a two-level game. At the national level, domestic groups pursue their interests by pressuring the government to adopt favorable policies, and politicians seek power by constructing coalitions among these groups. At the international level, national governments seek to maximize their own ability to satisfy domestic pressures, while minimizing the adverse consequences of foreign developments." Robert D. Putnam, "Diplomacy and Domestic Politics: The Logic of Two-Level Games," *International Organization,* Summer 1988, p. 434.

5. These divergent historical narratives resemble literary narratives "in which the event itself is less important than our perception of it. . . ." Tsvetan Todorov, *Genres in Discourse* (Cambridge: Cambridge University Press, 1990), p. 31. In *Rescuing History from the Nation* (Chicago: University of Chicago Press, 1995), Prasenjit Duara notes the differences between centralist and federalist narratives in republican Chinese history. See Duara, *Rescuing History from the Nation* (Chicago: University of Chicago Press, 1995), chapter 5.

6. James D. Fearon, "Domestic Political Audiences and the Escalation of International Disputes," *American Political Science Review,* September 1994, pp.

577–92. Putnam notes that the impact of domestic constituencies on the ratification of international agreements is not unique to democracies. See Putnam, "Diplomacy and Domestic Politics," p. 437.

7. Richard D. Anderson, Jr., states that leaders in the Politburo are dependent on maintaining approval of constituencies outside the ruling elite. See "Why Competitive Politics Inhibits Learning in Soviet Foreign Policy," in *Learning in US and Soviet Foreign Policy*, ed. George W. Breslauer and Philip E. Tetlock (Boulder: Westview Press, 1991), p. 104.

8. Border trade refers here to trade between entities within the border regions but does not include shuttle trade.

9. For example, see Banning N. Garrett and Bonnie S. Glaser, "From Nixon to Reagan: China's Role in American Strategy," in *Eagle Resurgent?* ed. Kenneth A. Oye and Robert J. Lieber (Boston: Little, Brown, and Company, 1987); Raymond Garthoff, *Détente and Confrontation* (Washington, D.C.: The Brookings Institution, 1985); Ilpyong J. Kim, ed., *The Strategic Triangle* (New York: Paragon House Publishers, 1987); and Gerald Segal, *The Great Power Triangle* (London: MacMillan Press, 1982).

10. Donald W. Treadgold, "Alternative Western Views of the Sino-Soviet Conflict," in *The Sino-Soviet Conflict,* ed. Herbert J. Ellison (Seattle: University of Washington Press, 1982), p. 351.

11. For example, see Stephen M. Walt, *Explaining the Origins of Alliances* (Ithaca, N.Y.: Cornell University Press, 1987), chapter 2.

12. Michel Tatu, *Le Triangle Washington-Moscou-Pékin et les deux Europe(s)* (Paris: Casterman, 1972), p. 26.

13. Peter Gourevitch argues that international relations and domestic politics are interpenetrated. He states: "However compelling external pressures may be, they are unlikely to be fully determining, save for the case of outright occupation." Peter Gourevitch, "The Second Image Reversed: The International Sources of Domestic Politics," *International Organization,* Autumn 1978, p. 911.

14. Beverly Crawford finds that domestic concerns outweigh international ones when the issue at stake is not exclusively national security and when a situation of uncertainty prevails. See Crawford, "Explaining Defection from International Cooperation: Germany's Unilateral Recognition of Croatia," *World Politics,* July 1996, p. 518.

15. See, for example, Robert Jervis, "Cooperation under the Security Dilemma," *World Politics,* January 1978, pp. 168–214.

16. X [George F. Kennan], "The Sources of Soviet Conduct," *Foreign Affairs,* July 1947, pp. 566–82.

17. China's departures from the Soviet model of socialism included Mao's emphasis on the peasantry as a primary revolutionary force, the belief that revolution could take place in a backward agrarian state, Mao's conception of the com-

munist party requiring the support of the masses (in contrast to Lenin's vanguard party), the view that people's views could be changed by reeducation campaigns, not just class struggle, and Mao's theory regarding the need for a permanent state of revolution to resolve contradictions in society. On this topic, see Maurice Meisner, *The Deng Xiaoping Era* (New York: Hill and Wang, 1996), Part I.

18. The classic works on the origin of the Sino-Soviet dispute are Donald Zagoria, *The Sino-Soviet Conflict, 1956–61* (Princeton, N.J.: Princeton University Press, 1962) and William E. Griffith, *The Sino-Soviet Rift* (Cambridge, Mass.: MIT Press, 1964).

19. The Brezhnev leadership's policy line favoring the normalization of relations with China was outlined at successive party congresses, beginning in 1971.

20. At a time when Mao perceived an acute threat by the West, the Soviet Union was engaged in efforts to expand dialogue with the West, even at the expense of commitments to world socialism. On the link between the development of the Chinese model of socialism and tensions in Sino-Soviet relations, see Chen Jian and Yang Kuisong, "Chinese Politics and the Collapse of the Sino-Soviet Alliance," in *The Rise and Fall of the Sino-Soviet Alliance, 1945–1963* (Stanford, Calif.: Stanford University Press, 1998), pp. 246–94.

21. Joseph Schull, "The Self-Destruction of Soviet Ideology," *The Harriman Institute Forum,* July 1991, p. 5.

22. Alain Besançon, *Origines intellectuelles du Léninisme* (Paris: Calmann-Lévy, 1977), pp. 292, 297; and R. Judson Mitchell, *Ideology of a Superpower* (Stanford: Hoover Institution Press, 1982), p. 8. The present study is concerned with official ideology, not the personal beliefs of leaders. While individuals may adhere to competing ideologies, where matters of state are concerned official ideology is paramount. On this distinction, see Vladimir Shlapentokh, *Soviet Ideologies in the Period of Glasnost* (New York: Praeger Publishers, 1988), p. XII.

23. Alex Pravda, "Ideology and the Policy Process," in *Ideology and Soviet Politics,* ed. Stephen White and Alex Pravda (New York: St. Martin's Press, 1988), pp. 225–47; Carl Linden, *The Soviet Party-State: The Politics of Ideocratic Despotism* (New York: Praeger Publishers, 1983).

24. Judith Goldstein and Robert Keohane note that "Insofar as ideas put blinders on people, reducing the number of conceivable alternatives, they serve as invisible switchmen, not only by turning action onto certain tracks rather than others . . . but also by obscuring the other tracks from the agent's view." See their chapter, "Ideas and Foreign Policy: An Analytical Framework," in *Ideas and Foreign Policy, Beliefs: Institutions, and Political Change,* ed. Judith Goldstein and Robert O. Keohane (Ithaca, N.Y.: Cornell University Press, 1993), p. 12.

25. Schull, "The Self-Destruction of Soviet Ideology," p. 2. While Gorbachev's ideological revisions questioned fundamental aspects of the Soviet system such as one-party rule, unleashing a process of disintegration, Deng Xiaoping's left the social-

ist infrastructure intact while permitting greater flexibility in policy areas. On ideo-
logical change in China, see Steven I. Levine, "Perception and Ideology in Chinese
Foreign Policy," in *Chinese Foreign Policy: Theory and Practice,* ed. Thomas W.
Robinson and David Shambaugh (Oxford: Clarendon Press, 1994), p. 39.

26. Ken Jowitt, *New World Disorder: The Leninist Extinction* (Berkeley: University
of California Press, 1992), p. 16.

27. Ibid., p. 45.

28. This is illustrated by Brezhnev's announcement at the Twenty-fourth CPSU
Congress that Soviet-Chinese relations would be based on peaceful coexistence, a
principle usually reserved for states belonging to different social systems. The Soviet
leader stressed that this was not the Soviet preference, but that the Chinese were unwilling to accept the standard principles of interaction between socialist states in relations with the USSR (i.e., proletarian internationalism).

29. Jowitt, *New World Disorder,* p. 193. For another analysis which posits that ideology provided perceptual categories for Soviet policymakers and may have constituted the source of threats, see Allen Lynch, "The Continuing Importance of Ideology
in Soviet Foreign Policy," *The Harriman Institute Forum,* vol. 3, no. 7 (July 1990), p.
2. In his study of American foreign policy, Michael Hunt makes a similar argument.
According to Hunt, American policymakers reacted negatively to revolutions which
differed fundamentally from the American model. See Michael Hunt, *Ideology and
US Foreign Policy* (New Haven, Conn.: Yale University Press, 1987), p. 171.

30. Jowitt, *New World Disorder,* p. 198.

31. William Riker defines a coalition as the outcome of the coming together of
individuals who agree to follow certain rules to achieve their various goals. On coalitions as end-products, see Riker, *The Theory of Coalitions* (Westport, Conn.:
Greenwood Press, 1984), p. 103. According to a key official in the Central Committee's
International Department, Karen Brutents, the Ministry of Foreign Affairs, the KGB,
and the Ministry of Defense were the principal institutions involved in policymaking, although MID relied on the foreign policy departments of the Central Committee
on many issues. See Brutents, *Tridsat' let na Staroi Ploshchadi* (Moscow: Mezhdunarodnye Otnosheniia, 1998), p. 164.

32. For an overview of the contributions of the memoir literature, see Michael
Ellman and Vladimir Kontorovich, "The Collapse of the Soviet System and the
Memoir Literature," *Europe-Asia Studies,* vol. 49, no. 2 (1997), pp. 259–79.

33. A. M. Aleksandrov-Agentov, *Ot Kollentai do Gorbacheva* (Moscow: Mezhdunarodnye otnshosheniia, 1994), p. 248.

34. Arbatov describes Brezhnev's skill in *apparat* infighting and notes that he had
the impression that Andropov, Suslov, and Gromyko feared him. Georgi Arbatov,
The System (New York: Random House, 1992), p. 246.

35. Alexandrov-Agentov, *Ot Kollentai do Gorbacheva,* p. 263. On Suslov's dog-

matism, see Fedor Burlatskii, *Vozhdi i sovetniki* (Moscow: Izd. Politicheskoi Literatury, 1990), p. 177.

36. Mikhail Kapitsa, *Na raznykh paralleliakh: zapiski diplomata* (Moscow: Kniga i biznes, 1996), p. 76.

37. Aleksandrov-Agentov, *Ot Kollentai do Gorbacheva*, p. 264. On Suslov's influence over the International Department of the Central Committee, see Mark Kramer, "The Role of the CPSU International Department in Soviet Foreign Relations and National Security Policy," in *Soviet Foreign Policy*, ed. Frederic J. Fleron, Jr., and Erik P. Hoffmann et al. (New York: Aldine de Fruyter, 1991), p. 445.

38. Viktor Louis, a journalist in the employ of the KGB, told diplomats that Suslov was extremely hostile to Maoism, to a degree not shared by other circles in Moscow. Telegram #5884, U.S. Embassy Moscow to U.S. Department of State, October 1969, State Department Central Files.

39. Arbatov, *The System*, p. 140. Arbatov said that this was true of policy toward Japan, too.

40. Anatoly Dobrynin, *In Confidence* (New York: Random House, 1995) p. 519.

41. On Ustinov's views on disarmament, see ibid., p. 199. On his confrontational approach to the United States, see p. 519.

42. On Czechoslovakia, see Dobrynin, *In Confidence*, p. 184. On Afghanistan, see Aleksandrov-Agentov, *Ot Kollentai do Gorbacheva*, p. 270.

43. Dobrynin, *In Confidence*, p. 581.

44. Ibid., p. 580; Aleksandrov-Agentov, *Ot Kollentai do Gorbacheva*, p. 77; Burlatskii, *Vozhdi i sovetniki*, p. 318.

45. Aleksandrov-Agentov, *Ot Kollentai do Gorbacheva*, p. 172.

46. Ibid., p. 264; Dobrynin, *In Confidence*, p. 519; Burlatskii, *Vozhdi i sovetniki*, p. 360.

47. Aleksandrov-Agentov, *Ot Kollentai do Gorbacheva*, p. 172.

48. Ibid., p. 168.

49. Jack Snyder, *Myths of Empire* (Ithaca, N.Y.: Cornell University Press, 1991), p. 17.

50. Snyder calls these concepts strategic myths. Ibid., p. 17.

51. Archie Brown, "Power and Policy in a Time of Leadership Transition, 1982–1988," in *Political Leadership in the Soviet Union,* ed. Archie Brown (Oxford: Macmillan, 1989), p. 164.

52. Valerie Bunce, "Domestic Reform and International Change: the Gorbachev Reforms in Historical Perspective," *International Organization,* vol. 47, no. 1 (Winter 1993), p. 109. Jeffrey Checkel makes a similar point in *Ideas and International Political Change* (New Haven: Yale University Press, 1997), p. 10.

53. Cynthia Roberts, review of Checkel, in *Europe-Asia Studies,* vol. 50, no. 1 (January 1998), pp. 165–66.

54. James G. Richter, *Khrushchev's Double Bind* (Baltimore: The Johns Hopkins University Press, 1994), p. 18.

55. For a study of the impact of Gorbachev's mobilization of reform-minded experts on Soviet foreign policy, focusing on the decision to withdraw from Afghanistan, see Sarah Mendelson, *Changing Course* (Princeton, N.J.: Princeton University Press, 1998), p. 4.

56. William de Berard Mills, "Sino-Soviet Interactions, May 1977–June 1980" (Ph.D. diss., University of Michigan, 1981); Robert Michael Gates, "Soviet Sinology: An Untapped Source for Kremlin's Views and Disputes Relating to Contemporary Events in China" (Ph.D. diss., Georgetown University, 1974); Gretchen Ann Sandles, "Soviet Images of and Policy toward China, 1955–1979" (Ph.D. diss., University of Michigan, 1981); and Chi Su, "Soviet Image of and Policy toward China, 1969–1979" (Ph.D. diss., Columbia University, 1984). For a related approach which looks at images in the Chinese context, see David L. Shambaugh, *Beautiful Imperialist: China Perceives America, 1972–1990* (Princeton, N.J.: Princeton University Press, 1991).

57. According to Griffiths, these are "stated beliefs that may or may not correspond accurately to subjective perceptions, and that are the product more of influence and power relationships than of a positivistic search for truth." Franklyn John Charles Griffiths, "Images, Politics, and Learning in Soviet Behavior toward the United States" (Ph.D. diss., Columbia University, 1972), p. 2.

58. For definitions of learning, see Joseph Nye, Jr., "Nuclear Learning and US-Soviet Security Regimes," *International Organization,* Summer 1987, p. 380; Philip E. Tetlock, "Learning in US and Soviet Foreign Policy: In Search of An Elusive Concept," in *Learning in US and Soviet Foreign Policy,* ed. Breslauer and Tetlock, pp. 20–61; and Ernst Haas, "Collective Learning: Some Theoretical Speculations," in Breslauer and Tetlock, pp. 62–99. For an application of the learning approach to a study of Soviet economic reforms, see George W. Breslauer, "Soviet Economic Reforms Since Stalin: Ideology, Politics, and Learning," *Soviet Economy,* vol. 6, no. 3 (1990), pp. 252–80.

59. For an excellent summary of the methodology used in Kremlinology, see Zagoria, *The Sino-Soviet Conflict,* pp. 24–35.

60. One important exception is the transcript of a 1983 Politburo meeting during which Andropov, Gromyko, and Ustinov expressed different views about China policy. "Zasedanie Politburo TsK KPSS," May 31, 1983, Tsentr Khraneniia Sovremennykh Dokumentov (TsKhSD), f. 89, per. 42, dok. 53, pp. 1–14. This document is discussed in detail in chapter three. Newly released American documents from the Cold War, for example, revealed substantial differences between the thinking of American leaders on communism and their stated positions. Banning Garrett summarizes some new studies of these documents in "The Strategic Basis of Learning

in US Policy toward China, 1949–1988," in *Learning in US and Soviet Foreign Policy,* ed. Breslauer and Tetlock, pp. 208–63.

61. Another problem with the learning approach is that it can imply a link between learning and greater realism. This is often a subjective judgment, measuring the degree to which Soviet policies shifted in a direction which matches Western preferences. Although Soviet policy towards China may have conflicted with the stated goal of the Soviet leadership of improving relations with China, it contributed to the achievement of other ideological aims. Tetlock raises this issue. See Tetlock, "Learning in US and Soviet Foreign Policy," p. 24.

62. Robert Legvold, "Soviet Learning in the 1980s," p. 707.

63. As Rozman has argued, in responding to Chinese challenges to Soviet interests, Soviet discussion of China often veiled a more far-reaching factional debate in the Soviet foreign policy elite about the Soviet Union's foreign and domestic policies. See Rozman's "Moscow's China-Watchers in the Post-Mao Era: The Response to a Changing China," *The China Quarterly,* June 1983, p. 218, and *Mirror for Socialism* (Princeton, N.J.: Princeton University Press, 1985), p. 5. Nikolai Riabchenko, a scholar from Vladivostok, makes a similar argument, although he stresses the importance of the different stages of economic development in Russia and China as a source of tensions. According to Riabchenko, "in the course of the conflict [with China], it was as if the USSR was confronted with its former self." N. P. Riabchenko, "Sovetsko-kitaiskie otnosheniia v period 50–kh-nachala 80–kh godov," Academy of Sciences of the USSR, Far Eastern Section, Institute of History, Archeology and Ethnography of the Peoples of the Far East, Vladivostok, 1991, p. 11.

64. In his speech to the Twelfth Congress of the Chinese Communist Party in September 1992, Deng Xiaoping stated that independence and self-reliance remained the cornerstones of Chinese foreign policy. Although Deng was committed to an economic reform strategy involving opening to the outside world, China would not enter into an alliance with any country. Deng Xiaoping, *Speeches and Writings* (Oxford: Pergamon Press, 1984), pp. 86–87.

65. In his study of Soviet scholarship on China in the late 1970s and early 1980s, Gilbert Rozman found evidence of different views among Soviet China-watchers regarding the prospects for change in China since Mao's death. Rozman distinguished between two groups of officials and scholars: the defenders of the status quo, who saw no signs of change in Chinese policies and supported continuing the Soviet containment policy towards China, and the voices for change, who detected encouraging trends in China and argued that better Sino-Soviet relations would exert a positive influence on Chinese policies. Rozman, "Moscow's China-watchers in the Post-Mao Era," pp. 240–41.

66. Charles Ziegler makes this point in *Foreign Policy and East Asia* (Cambridge: Cambridge University Press, 1993), p. 59.

67. Brutents described the nefarious impact of self-censorship on scholars in research institutes and members of the apparat. See Brutents, *Tridsat' let na Staroi Ploshchadi*, pp. 168, 235.

68. On the ability of dominant coalitions with overlapping interests to sell myths, see Snyder, *Myths of Empire*, p. 17. Richard D. Anderson, Jr., further notes that the political bargaining necessary to retain the support of key constituencies limits the responsiveness of members of the Politburo to changes in the international environment. See "Competitive Politics," pp. 110–11.

69. As James Clay Moltz has shown in his study of the politics of Soviet economic reform, rather than pointing to a pattern of learning it is more accurate to say that Soviet leaders borrow selectively from new information according to their needs and interests. James Clay Moltz, "Divergent Learning and Failed Politics of Soviet Economic Reform," *World Politics*, vol. 45 (January 1993), p. 325. Moltz contends that learning is more likely to occur in the area of foreign policy when a threat to state security is present (p. 304), but Moscow's China policy doesn't support this hypothesis.

70. Brutents, *Tridsat' let na Staroi Ploshchadi*, p. 179.

71. Allen S. Whiting, "Soviet Policy Toward China, 1969–1988," in *Learning in US and Soviet Foreign Policy*, ed. Breslauer and Tetlock, p. 536.

72. Mendelson comes to a similar conclusion about Soviet policy toward Afghanistan. See Mendelson, *Changing Course*, p. 66.

73. Jack Levy notes that if a leadership succession "brings to power a new individual or regime with a different set of shared beliefs, then any subsequent policy change would derive from turnover rather than learning." Jack S. Levy, "Learning and Foreign Policy: Sweeping a Conceptual Minefield," *International Organization*, Spring 1994, p. 299. In his analysis of Sino-Soviet normalization, Allen Whiting takes an intermediate position and attributes the major change in China policy in the mid-1980s to leadership change involving a reassessment of goals. See Whiting, "Soviet Policy Toward China," p. 545.

74. Checkel, *Ideas and International Political Change*, p. 10. Matthew Evangelista first developed the concept of policy entrepreneurs in "Sources of Moderation in Soviet Security Policy," in *Behavior, Society, and Nuclear War*, vol. 2, ed. Philip Tetlock et al. (New York: Oxford University Press, 1991). For an application of this view to Sino-Soviet relations, see Andrew Carrigan Kuchins, "Cognitive Change and Political Entrepreneurship: The Evolution of Soviet Policy Toward China from 1976–1989," (Ph.D. diss., Johns Hopkins University, School of Advanced International Studies, 1992). In Kuchins' account, Soviet leaders are responding to international and domestic pressures rather than to a crisis.

75. Jowitt, *New World Disorder*, p. 131. For a study of the role of patron-client relations in the promotion of leaders to key positions in the Soviet leadership, see John H. Miller, "Putting Clients in Place: the Role of Patronage in Cooption into

the Soviet Leadership," in *Political Leadership in the Soviet Union,* ed. Brown, pp. 54–95. On the historical roots of patronage ties in the Soviet Union, see Daniel T. Orlovsky, "Political Clientalism in Russia: The Historical Perspective," in *Leadership Selection and Patron-Client Relations in the USSR and Yugoslavia,* ed. T. H. Rigby and Bohdan Harasymiu (London: George Allen & Unwin, 1980); pp. 174–99. The importance of patronage networks in Chinese society (known as *guanxi*) has been the focus of more considerable study. See, for example, Mayfair Mei-hui Yang, *Gifts, Favors & Banquets: The Art of Social Relationships in China* (Ithaca, N.Y.: Cornell University Press, 1994).

76. Burlatskii, *Vozhdi i sovetniki,* p. 258. Burlatskii later became a well-known columnist for *Literaturnaia Gazeta.*

77. Because Andropov's group developed such a reputation for intellectualism, Brutents's boss at the international department, Boris Ponomarev, decided to form his own group. Brutents, *Tridsat' let na Staroi Ploshchadi,* p. 226.

78. See Arbatov's account of his relationship with Andropov, *The System,* pp. 256–57. Arbatov describes his role in proposing a change in China policy. See p. 277.

79. Burlatskii, *Vozhdi i sovetniki,* pp. 361–62.

80. Aleksandrov-Agentov, *Ot Kollentai do Gorbacheva,* p. 172.

81. Archie Brown, "Gorbachev: New Man in the Kremlin," *Problems of Communism,* May–June 1985, pp. 3–4.

82. Seweryn Bialer explains how each generation of elites sets the agenda for future generations, but notes that succession provided an opportunity to break the hold of the older generation. See Bialer, *Stalin's Successors* (Cambridge: Cambridge University Press, 1980), p. 101.

83. Archie Brown, *The Gorbachev Factor* (Oxford: Oxford University Press, 1996), p. 69.

84. Timothy Colton, *The Dilemma of Reform in the Soviet Union* (New York: Council on Foreign Relations, 1986), pp. 103–4.

85. Archie Brown makes a strong case for this in *The Gorbachev Factor,* chapter 2.

86. Jack Snyder, "The Gorbachev Revolution: A Waning of Soviet Expansionism?" *International Security,* Winter 1987/1988, pp. 94–95; and Cynthia Roberts and Elizabeth Wishnick, "Ideology Is Dead! Long Live Ideology?" *Problems of Communism,* November–December 1988, p. 61. For contrary views that express the importance of policy failures in motivating Gorbachev to change long-standing Soviet policies, see Robert Legvold, "The Revolution in Soviet Foreign Policy," *Foreign Affairs: America and the World, 1988–89,* p. 83; and David Holloway, "Gorbachev's New Thinking," *Foreign Affairs: America and the World, 1988–89,* p. 69.

87. New documentary evidence from the 1950s shows that well before the Sino-Soviet conflict became public in the 1960s, Mao was critical of China's unequal treatment by the Soviet Union, particularly during the Stalin period. In September 1956,

for example, Mao commented to a Yugoslav delegation: "Is [our relationship with Moscow] a father-and-son relationship or one between brothers? It was between father and son in the past; now it more or less resembles a brotherly relationship, but the shadow of the father-and-son relationship is not completely removed." Minutes of Mao's conversation with a Yugoslavian Communist Union Delegation, Beijing, September 1956, in "The Emerging Disputes between Beijing and Moscow: The Newly Available Chinese Documents, 1956–58," translated and annotated by Zhang Shu Guang and Chen Jian, *Cold War International History Project Bulletin,* Winter 1995/96, p. 151. The greater equality in the Sino-Soviet relationship in the 1980s would provide the Soviet and Chinese leaders with a more stable basis for cooperation in matters of domestic reform. See Dittmer, *Sino-Soviet Normalization,* p. 35.

88. All sources were read in the languages cited.

2 / THE SOVIET UNION'S CHINA STRATEGY, 1969–79

1. Thomas Lahusen, "A Place Called Harbin: Reflections on a Centennial," *The China Quarterly,* June 1998, p. 406.

2. V. S. Miasnikov, "Vzaimootnosheniia Rossiia s Kitaem: Tendentsii, dinamika, perspektivy," paper presented to the international conference, "Russian Far East-Chinese Northeast: Historical Experience of Interaction and Perspectives for Cooperation," Khabarovsk, June 1–3, 1998.

3. Interview with Sergei Goncharov, Institute of the Far East, June 26, 1991 (now in the Russian Foreign Ministry).

4. Tai Sung An, *The Sino-Soviet Territorial Dispute* (Philadelphia: The Westminster Press, 1973), pp. 25–46.

5. On the negotiation of the treaties of Aigun and Peking, see S.C.M. Paine, *Imperial Rivals: Russia, China, and Their Disputed Frontier, 1858–1924* (Armonk, N.Y.: M. E. Sharpe, 1996); and R. K. I. Quested, *The Expansion of Russia in East Asia, 1857–1860* (Kuala Lumpur: The University of Malaya Press, 1968).

6. Cited in Paine, *Imperial Rivals,* p. 320. Karakhan's missive, subsequently called the Karakhan declaration, specifically mentioned the 1896 agreement on the Chinese Eastern Railway, the protocol on the Boxer uprising, and agreements signed with Japan from 1907 through 1916 about spheres of influence in China, but did not refer to any of the treaties concerning the Sino-Russian border. The Karakhan declaration also announced that the Soviet government would return the Chinese Eastern Railway to China, as well as all other concessions seized by the tsars, without compensation.

7. The second Karakhan declaration at first sounded much like the earlier version, reiterating that the Bolshevik government declared "as void all the treaties concluded by the former Government of Russia with China, renounces all the annexations of Chinese territory, all the concessions in China, and returns to China free of charge,

and for ever, all that was ravenously taken from her by the Tsar's Government and by the Russian bourgeoisie." Jane Degras, ed., *Soviet Documents on Foreign Policy* (London: Oxford University Press, 1951), p. 214. According to Paine, "Bolshevik generosity toward the Chinese diminished in proportion to the Red Army's success against the White forces in Siberia." Paine, *Imperial Rivals*, p. 320.

8. Adam B. Ulam, *Expansion and Coexistence: Soviet Foreign Policy 1917–73* (New York: Praeger Publishers, 1974), p. 105. At the time, the Bolsheviks denied ever making the first offer and later changed the text of the first declaration to support their position. See Bruce Elleman, *Diplomacy and Deception: The Secret History of Sino-Soviet Diplomatic Relations, 1917–1927* (Armonk, N.Y.: M. E. Sharpe, 1997), chapter 1.

9. John Stephan, *The Russian Far East* (Stanford, Calif.: Stanford University Press, 1994), p. 232; Wen Yaobing, "ZhongE bianjie fenzheng shimo ji jiannan quzhe de tanpan licheng," *Eluosi Yanjiu*, no. 2 (1996), p. 73.

10. Stephan, *The Russian Far East*, pp. 232–33; Neville Maxwell, "Why the Russians Lifted the Blockade at Bear Island," *Foreign Affairs*, Fall 1978, p. 141; and Sow-theng Leong, *Sino-Soviet Diplomatic Relations, 1917–1926* (Honolulu: University of Hawaii Press, 1976), p. 69.

11. Elleman, *Diplomacy and Deception*, p. 100. This protocol was never made public.

12. Ibid., p. 101.

13. "The Government of the Union of Soviet Socialist Republics, in accordance with its policy and Declarations of 1919 and 1920, declares that all Treaties, Agreements, etc., concluded between the former Tsarist Government and any third party or parties affecting the sovereign rights or interests of China, are null and void." In H. G. W. Woodhead, ed. *The China Yearbook, 1924–5* (Tientsin, China: The Tientsin Press, Ltd., 1924), p. 1192. During the same year, the governments of Moscow and Beijing agreed to joint management of the railway. Also see Stephan, *The Russian Far East*, p. 182.

14. Elleman, *Diplomacy and Deception*, chapter 4.

15. In a recent evaluation of the history of the border dispute, a Chinese scholar claims that not only did the Soviet government remain uncompromising in its refusal to annul the border treaties from the 1920s through the 1940s, but it also unilaterally occupied 600 of 700 islands on the Chinese side of the main river channel in the Amur and Ussuri Rivers, amounting to 1000 square kilometers of land. Li Danhui, "1969 nian ZhongSu bianjie chongtu: yuanqi he jieguo," *Dangdai Zhongguo Yanjiu*, no. 3 (1996), pp. 40–41. For a concurring Russian view, see Genrikh Kireev, "Demarcation of the Border with China," *International Affairs* (Moscow), vol. 45, no. 2 (1999), p. 99.

16. R. K. I. Quested, *Sino-Russian Relations: A Short History* (Sydney: George Allen Unwin, 1984), pp. 98–99.

17. Protokol no. 149, zasedanie Politburo TsK VKP/b/ ot 15 noiabria 1933g, Punkty "Ob ostrovakh na Amure" (t. Sokol'nikov), in *Rossiiskii Tsentr Khranenii i*

Izucheniia Dokumentov Noveishei Istorii (*RtsKhIDNI*), f. 17, Politburo TsK VKP/b/, o. 162 (osobye papki), d. 15., l. 129; cited courtesy of Jonathan Bone, "Socialism in a Far Country: Development and Socioeconomic Change in the Soviet Far East, 1922–1939" (Ph.D. diss., in progress, University of Chicago).

18. Cited in "Diplomatiia naiznaku," in *Nekotorye problemy demarkatsii Rossiisko-Kitaiskoi granitsy. 1991–1997 god. Sbornik statei i dokumentov* (Moscow: Nezavisimaia Gazeta, 1997), p. 44.

19. Vladislav Zubok, "Stalin's Goals in the Far East from Yalta to the Sino-Soviet Treaty of 1950," unpublished paper prepared for the international conference "New Evidence on the Cold War in Asia," Hong Kong, January 1996, p. 4.

20. Sergei N. Goncharov, John W. Lewis, Xue Litai, et al., *Uncertain Partners: Stalin, Mao, and the Korean War* (Stanford, Calif.: Stanford University Press, 1992), p. 3.

21. Ibid., p. 5.

22. Historically, Mongolia had not always been a part of China, however. Inner Mongolia was not absorbed until the Ming Dynasty and it was not until the Qing Dynasty that Outer Mongolia was incorporated, but only as a frontier zone, still retaining substantial control over its domestic affairs. Beginning in the late nineteenth century, China, Russia, and Japan competed for control over Mongolia, which sought independence from all the great powers. Although the Bolshevik government appeared to recognize Chinese suzerainty over Mongolia, in reality the Bolsheviks secretly promoted an autonomous Outer Mongolia within the Soviet security sphere. On the history of Mongolia's struggle for independence, see Paine, *Imperial Rivals,* part IV.

23. Mikhail Kapitsa, *Na raznykh paralleliakh: zapiski diplomata* (Moscow: Kniga i biznes, 1996), p. 41.

24. Vladislav Zubok and Constantine Pleshakov, *Inside the Kremlin's Cold War: From Stalin to Khrushchev* (Cambridge, Mass.: Harvard University Press, 1996), pp. 58–59. Kapitsa fails to mention the continued controversy over Mongolia. According to his account of the Stalin-Mao talks, Stalin received Mao upon his arrival but substantive talks were delayed because the Chinese leader had not brought the necessary experts with him. In Kapitsa's recollection, detailed discussions began on January 20, 1950, when Zhou Enlai arrived in Moscow with additional colleagues. See Kapitsa, *Na raznykh paralleliakh,* pp. 49–51.

25. For an excellent discussion of these negotiations, see Goncharov, Lewis, et al., *Uncertain Partners,* pp. 110–21. Dairen was returned in 1955.

26. Ibid., pp. 121–27. On the surface, the protocol committed the Soviet Union to similar terms, for example by forbidding third parties from settling in Central Asia or the Soviet Far East, but in practice no such activity had been permitted since 1937 (p. 122). Moreover, other secret protocols required China to sell the Soviet Union a specific quota of the minerals found in Xinjiang and forbid their sale to third parties without Soviet permission (p. 125).

27. See, for example, "From the Journal of P. F. Yudin, April 5, 1956, no. 289, Record of Conversation with Comrade Mao Zedong," *Cold War International History Project Bulletin (CWIHPB)*, Winter 1995/96, p. 166.

28. Mao recounted that during the negotiation of the 1950 Treaty of Friendship and Alliance, he argued with Stalin for two months over various questions, including the issue of national boundaries and the status of Mongolia (which Mao had proposed "reuniting" with China). Eventually he acquiesced to Soviet positions "for the benefit of socialism." "A Talk in the Chengdu Conference, March 10, 1958," *Mao Zedong Sixiang Wansui*, 1969 edition, pp. 163–64, cited in Chi Su, "Soviet Image of and Policy toward China, 1969–1979" (Ph.D. diss., Columbia University, 1984), p. 54.

29. George Ginsburgs, "The End of the Sino-Russian Territorial Disputes?" *Journal of East Asian Affairs*, Winter/Spring 1993, pp. 281–82. For the text of the 1951 treaty on border river navigation, see Ministerstva Inostrannykh Del, *Sbornik deistvuiushchikh dogovorov, soglashenii i konventsii, zakliuchennykh SSSR s inostrannymi gosudarstvami*, Vypusk 14 (Moscow: Gosudarstvennoe izdatel'stvo politicheskoi literatury, 1957), pp. 333–45.

30. Actually, as far back as 1867, the Committee of Ministers of Russia had recognized the Talweg as the river boundary. Kireev, "Demarcation of the Border with China," p. 103. According to the Talweg principle, the internationally recognized principle for the establishment of river boundaries, the river boundary runs through the center of the main channel (the Talweg) for navigable rivers and through the center of the river bed for non-navigable rivers. Ukaz Presidiuma Verkhovnogo Soveta SSSR, "Ob utverzhdenii ob okhrane gosudarstvennoi granitsy Soiuza SSR," *Vedemosti Verkhovnogo Soveta SSSR*, no. 34 (1018), August 30, 1960, p. 748. This was later revised in 1982 in such a way that other international treaties to which the Soviet Union was a party could supercede the Talweg rule. This led the Soviets to claim that the Treaty of St. Petersburg of 1881, establishing the principles of border river navigation without clarifying issues of jurisdiction, superceded the 1960 law. See *Vedemosti Verkhovnogo Soveta SSSR*, no. 48 (2174), December 1, article 3, p. 873.

31. Zhou later stated that in his meeting with the Soviet leader he "requested that the USSR [make] proper arrangements for the territorial issues covering Japan, China, the Middle East, and the Eastern European countries, including Finland" but that he "could not get a satisfactory answer from him then." Cited in Su, "Soviet Image of and Policy toward China," pp. 54–55.

32. Su, "Soviet Image of and Policy toward China," p. 56; Intelligence Note, U.S. Department of State, "Confidential Soviet Document Reviews Relations with China," December 21, 1967, p. 1, State Department Central Files (SDCF).

33. "A Comment on the Statement of the Communist Party of the USA," *Renmin Ribao*, March 8, 1963, in *Peking Review*, vol. 6 (March 1963), p. 61.

34. See the discussion in Ginsburgs, "The End of the Sino-Russian Territorial Disputes?" pp. 270–74.

35. Vladimir Miasnikov, *Dogovornymi stat'iami utverdili* (Moscow and Khabarovsk: Russian Academy of Sciences and Priamurskoe Geograficheskoe Obshchestvo, 1997), p. 405. Miasnikov is a leading Russian scholar of the Sino-Russian border conflict. For details of the Chinese territory ceded to Tsarist Russia, see An Tai-Sung, *The Sino-Soviet Territorial Dispute* (New York: Westminster Press, 1973), pp. 31–48.

36. Miasnikov, *Dogovornymi stat'iami utverdili,* p. 419.

37. Interview with a scholar at the Chinese Foreign Ministry's research institute, Beijing, June 18, 1996.

38. Kireev, "Demarcation of the Border with China," p. 100; Miasnikov, *Dogovornymi stat'iami utverdili,* p. 423, 427.

39. Cited in Alan J. Day, ed., *China and the Soviet Union, 1949–84* (New York: Facts on File Publications, 1985), pp. 90–91. In a September 15, 1964, interview with a Japanese delegation, Khrushchev directly replied to Mao's charges by commenting that Xinjiang and Inner Mongolia were territories occupied by the Chinese emperors. "We support self-determination . . . ," said Khrushchev.

40. On this point see, for example, Li Huichuan, "ZhongSu bianjie tanpan de zhengjie hezai?" *Guoji Wenti Yanjiu,* no. 1 (1981), p. 11. Li Huichuan headed the Chinese delegation to the border talks in the 1970s. Also see Miasnikov, *Dogovornymi stat'iami utverdili,* p. 394.

41. Ginsburgs, "The End of the Sino-Russian Territorial Disputes?" p. 278. For a detailed examination of this controversy see George Ginsburgs and Carl F. Pinkele, *The Sino-Soviet Territorial Dispute, 1959–64* (New York: Praeger, 1978), pp. 95–103, 106–17.

42. Harry Gelman, *The Soviet Far East Buildup and Soviet Risk-Taking against China,* Rand R-2943-AF, August 1982, p. 17.

43. A. M. Aleksandrov-Agentov, *Ot Kollentai do Gorbacheva* (Moscow: Mezhdurnarodnye Otnosheniia, 1994), p. 168.

44. Ibid. Shelepin, an opponent of improving relations with the West, reportedly also sided with Kosygin. See Aleksandrov-Agentov, *Ot Kollentai do Gorbacheva,* p. 169.

45. Ibid., p. 169.

46. Ibid., pp. 169–70.

47. Gelman, *The Soviet Far East Buildup,* p. 16.

48. Commentary by Sergey Goncharov and Viktor Usov, on a memoir by A. Elizavetin, "Peregovory A.N. Kosygina i Zhou Enlai v pekinskom aeroportu," part 1, *Problemy Dal'nego Vostoka (PDV),* no. 5 (1992), p. 41. While Goncharov and Usov claim that the Chinese began a corresponding buildup of their forces along the Sino-Soviet border, data from the International Institute for Strategic Studies in London,

however, provides a different picture. The IISS reports that in 1967 no major changes in the strength or disposition of Chinese frontier units were observed. In the late 1960s and early 1970s the Soviet military also was looking for a rationale to refocus resources on conventional forces, which had been a target of Khrushchev's budget cuts. The Chinese threat fit the bill. Nonetheless, the increased Soviet military presence in the Far East should be seen as a part of the overall buildup in the Soviet armed forces that had been commissioned for the 1966–1970 five-year plan. Increases in manpower and equipment in the Far East did not mean a decrease in deployments elsewhere, as forces were increased in all regions. Gelman, *The Soviet Far East Buildup,* pp. 12–15, 18.

49. Office of Strategic Research, Directorate of Intelligence, Central Intelligence Agency, "Intelligence Memorandum: Soviet Defense Policy, 1962–72," White House Special Files (WHSF): Staff Member and Office Files (SMOF): Ronald Ziegler; Briefing Materials, Meetings with Heads of State, 1971–74 [Soviet Summit, May 1972], Soviet Viewpoint and Objectives; Box 37; Richard M. Nixon Presidential Materials Staff at College Park, Md.

50. International Institute for Strategic Studies (IISS), *Strategic Survey,* 1973, p. 66.

51. Office of Strategic Research, "Intelligence Memorandum."

52. During this time, the Chinese forces were increased from 33 to 45 divisions. Chinese divisions were somewhat larger than Soviet ones. Soviet mechanized divisions had 11,000 men and armored divisions had 9,000. Chinese mechanized divisions contained 12,000 to 14,000 men, while armored had 10,000. IISS, *Strategic Survey,* 1973, p. 67.

53. Goncharov and Usov, in "Peregovory A.N. Kosygina i Zhou Enlai," p. 42.

54. Gelman, *The Soviet Far East Buildup,* p. 43.

55. John Wilson Lewis and Hua Di, "China's Ballistic Missile Programs," *International Security,* Fall 1992, pp. 17–18.

56. Interview with Lev Petrovich Deliusin by a Novosti correspondent, *Soviet-Chinese Relations in a Changing World* (Moscow: Novosti Press, 1989), p. 62. Although Deliusin noted that no one could guarantee that war with China would not occur, he argued that China was unlikely to start a major confrontation given the devastation of the Chinese economy and the inferior state of its army (especially the rudimentary Chinese nuclear capability and the absence of a well-equipped conventional force). Shevchenko also affirmed that the Chinese nuclear force posed no real threat at the time. See Arkadii N. Shevchenko, *Breaking with Moscow* (New York: Alfred A. Knopf, 1985), p. 286. For another critical view of the Soviet military buildup against China and its high economic cost, see Roy Medvedev, *Lichnost' i epokha. Politicheskii portret L.I. Brezhneva* (Moscow: Novosti, 1991), p. 186.

57. Interview with Arlen Meliksetov, Director of the Institute of the countries of Asia and Africa at Moscow State University, Moscow, May 1991, and Aleksandr Bovin,

former political commentator for *Izvestiia,* Moscow, June 1991. Shevchenko also makes this point. Also see Shevchenko, *Breaking with Moscow,* pp. 164–65.

58. Su, "Soviet Image of and Policy toward China," pp. 262–84. Chinese harassment of Soviet embassy personnel in Beijing and anti-Soviet propaganda fueled speculation about the possibility of a break in Sino-Soviet diplomatic relations. See Telegram, U.S. Embassy Moscow to U.S. Department of State, January 30, 1967, SDCF.

59. Telegram, U.S. Embassy Warsaw to U.S. Department of State, April 1969, in SDCF.

60. Telegram, "Soviet Attitude toward China," U.S. Embassy Moscow to U.S. Department of State, June 1969, SDCF; and Telegram, "Question of Soviet Belligerent Moves against China," U.S. Embassy Moscow to U.S. Department of State, September 1969, SDCF.

61. Memorandum of Conversation, U.S. Department of State, April 1, 1969, SDCF. Kuznetsov would go on to head the Soviet delegation to the Sino-Soviet talks in October 1969.

62. Interviews with General Aleksei Bazhenov, May 28, 1991; General Anatolii Boliatko, May 28, 1993; and Sergei Tikhvinskii, former Foreign Ministry official, now at the Institute of History, June 13, 1991.

63. Interview with Colonel Nikolai Osipov, Khabarovsk, September 1995.

64. Barry Naughton, "The Third Front: Defence Industrialization in the Chinese Interior," *The China Quarterly,* September 1988, p. 371. Interviews with senior scholars (Beijing), June 6, 1996 and June 18, 1996.

65. Telegram, "Communist China: Preparations against War," U.S. Consulate Hong Kong to U.S. Department of State, July 1969, in SDCF.

66. Telegram, "French Diplomat on Conditions in Communist China," U.S. Consulate Hong Kong to U.S. Department of State, September 1969, in SDCF.

67. Interview, Beijing, June 6, 1996. See Richard Wich, *Sino-Soviet Crisis Politics* (Cambridge: Harvard University Press, 1980), pp. 4–5; and Telegram #1649, U.S. Consulate Hong Kong, March 1969, SDCF. Also see Mao's October 1, 1968, conversation with the Albanian defense minister, Beqir Balluku, translated by Chen Jian from the CCP Central Archives, in *CWIHPB,* Winter 1998, pp. 156–57.

68. Thomas M. Gottlieb, *Chinese Foreign Policy Factionalism and the Origins of the Strategic Triangle,* Rand R-1902-NA, November 1977, pp. 84–94.

69. Leonid Brezhnev, Speech at 5th Polish United Workers Party Congress, November 12, 1968, in *FBIS* (Eastern Europe), November 12, 1968, p. G22.

70. Mikhail Titarenko, now director of the Institute of the Far East, who at the time worked under Oleg Rakhmanin in the Central Committee, claimed that the "Prague scenario" would have been impossible in China. Titarenko added that China specialists convinced the Soviet leadership that China was not like Poland or Hungary, that it was a more serious partner. Interview, June 16, 1993.

71. Wich, *Sino-Soviet Crisis Politics,* p. 61.

72. Ibid., p. 58.

73. Commentator, "Total Bankruptcy of Soviet Modern Revisionism," *People's Daily,* August 23, 1968, in *FBIS* (Communist China), August 23, 1968, pp. A5–8. On this point, see Harold C. Hinton, *The Sino-Soviet Confrontation: Implications for the Future* (New York: Crane, Russak & Company, Inc., 1976), p. 14. In his political report to the Ninth CCP Congress, Lin Biao explained: "In order to justify its aggression and plunder, the Soviet revisionist clique trumpets the so-called theory of 'limited sovereignty,' the theory of 'international dictatorship,' and the theory of 'socialist community.' What does all this stuff mean? It means that your sovereignty is 'limited,' while his is unlimited. You won't obey him? He will exercise 'international dictatorship' over you—dictatorship over the people of other countries, in order to form the 'socialist community' ruled by the new tsars, that is, colonies of social-imperialism. . . ." Lin Biao, Political Report to Ninth Congress, April 27, 1969, Xinhua, in *FBIS* (Communist China), Supplement, April 29, 1969, p. 25.

74. Wich, *Sino-Soviet Crisis Politics,* p. 62.

75. Ibid., p. 68.

76. The publication of a 1945 pamphlet by Mao on the permissibility of negotiating with one's adversary was another indication that the scene was being set for a shift in Chinese policy towards the United States. Hinton, *The Sino-Soviet Confrontation,* p. 15.

77. Henry Kissinger speculated that the Chinese canceled the meeting in protest against the defection one week earlier of a Chinese diplomat in the Netherlands to the United States. Kissinger, *The White House Years* (Boston: Little, Brown, & Company, 1979), p. 169.

78. For a detailed analysis of the border clashes, see Wich, *Sino-Soviet Crisis Politics.* Also see Gelman, *The Soviet Far East Buildup,* pp. 31–34; and Thomas W. Robinson, *The Sino-Soviet Border Dispute: Background Development, and the March 1969 Clashes,* Rand RM-6171-PR, August 1970, and "China Confronts the Soviet Union: Warfare and Diplomacy on China's Inner Asia Frontiers," in *The Cambridge History of China* (Cambridge: Cambridge University Press, 1991), pp. 254–65.

79. See for example, Gelman, *The Soviet Far East Buildup,* p. 32; Hinton, *The Sino-Soviet Confrontation,* p. 17; Robinson, *The Sino-Soviet Border Dispute,* p. 37, and "China Confronts the Soviet Union," p. 257; Gerald Segal, *Defending China* (Oxford: Oxford University Press, 1985), p. 177, note 6, p. 194. According to Robinson, three hundred Chinese border guards and regular soldiers ambushed a Soviet unit on disputed territory. See Robinson, "China Confronts the Soviet Union," p. 257. No documents in the Soviet archives about the clashes have been opened to the public as of yet. However, a Soviet account of the border clashes to the East German party leadership has recently been made available by the East German Communist Party archives.

See "Soviet Report to GDR Leadership on 2 March 1969," in Christian F. Ostermann, "New Evidence on The Sino-Soviet Border Dispute, 1969–71," in *CWIHPB*, Winter 1995/96, pp. 189–90. Recent Chinese scholarship admits that China may have started the March 2 clash, but attributes this to Soviet provocation. For example, see Li Danhui, "1969 nian ZhongSu bianjie chongtu," p. 47. However, some Chinese sources continue to claim that the Soviet side launched a surprise attack against Chinese border guards on Damanskii/Zhen Bao Island. See, for example, Zhou Wenqi and Chu Liangru, eds., *Teshu er fuza de keti—gongchang guoji, Sulian he Zhongguo gonchangdang guanxi biannianshi* (Beijing: Hubei renmin chubanshe, 1993), p. 552. For a comparison of Soviet and Chinese views of the clashes, see Barbara Barouin and Yu Changgen, *Chinese Foreign Policy during the Cultural Revolution* (London: Kegan Paul International, 1998), pp. 86–91.

80. For an official statement of this view, see "Memorandum of Conversation," Boris Sedov, Second Secretary, USSR embassy, and Raymond Garthoff, Counselor, U.S. NATO Mission, U.S. Department of State, September 5, 1969, SDCF 1967–1968; Box 1917; U.S. National Archives.

81. Li Ke and Hao Shengzhang, *Wenhua da geming de renmin jiefang jun* (Beijing: Chinese Communist Party History Materials Press, 1989).

82. During the Cultural Revolution, the street in front of the Soviet embassy in Beijing was renamed "Struggle against Revisionism Street."

83. Gelman, *The Soviet Far East Buildup*, p. 26, 29.

84. Li Ke and Hao Shenghang, *Wenhua da geming de renmin jiefang jun*, pp. 317–18.

85. Ibid., p. 319.

86. Ibid., p. 313.

87. Maurice Meisner, *Mao's China and After* (New York: The Free Press, 1986), p. 348.

88. "Reports of the Danish Ambassador to Peking," April 11, 1969, SDCF.

89. On March 8, for example, 100,000 demonstrators protested in front of the Chinese embassy in Moscow. Day, *China and the Soviet Union*, p. 94.

90. The Chinese restated their view that in 1964 border talks the Soviet Union had recognized the Talweg principle, and thus argued that "the Soviet side itself could not but admit that these islands (Zhen Bao and other nearby islands) are Chinese territory. Information Department of the Chinese Foreign Ministry, "Chenpao Island Has Always Been Chinese Territory," *Peking Review*, no. 11 (March 14, 1969), pp. 14–15. This interpretation was accurate, since in the 1964 border talks the Soviet Union and China had agreed that Damanskii would be handed over to China. Aleksei Brezhnev, *Kitai: ternistyi put' k dobrososedstvu* (Moscow: Mezhdunarodnye Otnosheniia, 1998), p. 177. The author, a diplomat with extensive service in China, claims that the Chinese started the border clashes for political reasons which had nothing to do with the territorial issue.

91. For details of this clash, see Robinson, "China Confronts the Soviet Union," p. 260.

92. On May 24, the Chinese government reiterated its position that the treaties governing the border were unequal and should be annulled, but said that they could serve as a basis for negotiations. The statement also called for a return to the status quo on the border—an end to aggressive patrolling and a withdrawal of forces. For an account of the Chinese leadership's response to Soviet proposals to resume talks, see Wich, *Sino-Soviet Crisis Politics,* pp. 117–19.

93. The Soviet Union agreed to discuss disputed sections on the basis of existing treaties, as the Chinese proposed in their May 24 statement. Note of the USSR Ministry of Foreign Affairs to the CPR (PRC) Ministry of Foreign Affairs, *Pravda,* June 12, 1969, p. 6, in *Current Digest of the Soviet Press (CDSP),* vol. 21, no. 24, pp. 9–13.

94. Goncharov and Usov, "Peregovory A. N. Kosygina i Zhou Enlai," p. 49.

95. Ibid., p. 45.

96. Office of Strategic Research, "Intelligence Memorandum," p. 12.

97. See, for example, Memorandum from INR-Thomas L. Hughes to the Secretary of State, May 9, 1969, p. 3, in SDCF; U.S.-NATO telegram to the Department of State, August 25, 1969, p. 4, in SDCF.

98. Bruce G. Blair, *The Logic of Accidental Nuclear War* (Washington, D.C.: The Brookings Institution, 1993), p. 25.

99. Allen S. Whiting, "Sino-American Détente," *The China Quarterly,* no. 82 (June 1980), p. 336. See, for example, Memorandum from INR-Hughes to the Secretary of State, p. 3; U.S.–NATO telegram to the Department of State, August 25, 1969, p. 4, in SDCF.

100. Raymond Garthoff, *Détente and Confrontation* (Washington, D.C.: The Brookings Institution, 1985), p. 209.

101. This was the report of a detailed conversation on the subject on August 18, 1969, between Boris Davydov, second secretary of the Soviet embassy in Washington, D.C., and William Stearman, special assistant for Vietnam at the U.S. Department of State. "Memorandum for the President: The Possibility of a Soviet Strike against Chinese Nuclear Facilities," September 10, 1969, in SDCF; "Memorandum of Conversation between Boris N. Davydov and William L. Stearman," U.S. Department of State, August 18, 1969, SDCF; Telegram, U.S. Department of State, August 23, 1969, SDCF. For other reports of Soviet attempts to sound out American and foreign responses, see "Soviet Editor Warns of Use of 'New Weapons' against Chinese in Event of New Border Clashes," Telegram from U.S. Embassy Moscow to U.S. Department of State, September 1969, SDCF; "Soviet-Chicom Hostilities," Telegram from U.S. Embassy Teheran to U.S. Department of State, September 4, 1969, SDCF; Memorandum of Conversation with the Ambassador of Pakistan, U.S. Department of State, September 10, 1969, SDCF. Aleksandrov-Agentov explained the diplomatic

probings as an attempt to warn other countries of the seriousness of the situation. In his view, U.S. officials manipulated Soviet warnings to further aggravate the Sino-Soviet dispute. Aleksandrov-Agentov, *Ot Kollentai do Gorbacheva,* pp. 216–17.

102. Seymour M. Hersh, *The Price of Power* (New York: Summit Books, 1983), pp. 357–59. A National Intelligence estimate carried out in the summer of 1969 speculated that the Soviets might try to use their air superiority to knock out Chinese nuclear and missile installations. Cited in Telegram, U.S. Department of State, August 21, 1969, SDCF.

103. Kissinger, *The White House Years,* p. 184. Whiting, "Sino-American Détente," p. 336.

104. Director of Intelligence and Research, U.S. Department of State, Intelligence Note, "USSR-China: Renewed Border Fighting Evokes Soviet Threat," July 9, 1969, in SDCF.

105. Editorial, "Peking's Adventurist Course," *Pravda,* August 28, 1969, pp. 2–3, in *CDSP,* vol. 21, no. 35, p. 5. On the August 13 clash, see Wich, *Sino-Soviet Crisis Politics,* pp. 178–79.

106. Cited in Telegram from U.S. Embassy Moscow to the U.S. Department of State, September 1969, in SDCF. According to U.S. diplomats, the article was written to warn the Chinese against further provocations on the Sino-Soviet border.

107. Li Zhisui, *The Private Life of Chairman Mao* (London: Chatto and Windus, 1994), p. 514. For a U.S. assessment of Chinese war fears, see Intelligence Note, U.S. Department of State, June 3, 1969, SDCF.

108. Telegram #4895, U.S. Consulate Hong Kong to U.S. Department of State, September 1969, SDCF.

109. In his testament, published posthumously, the Vietnamese leader had appealed for unity among the communist parties. See Day, *China and the Soviet Union,* p. 143. According to a newly declassified CPSU Central Committee report to the East German leadership, it was the Soviet side that proposed a meeting between Kosygin and Zhou in Hanoi. "Information about A.N. Kosygin's Conversation with Zhou Enlai on 11 September 1969," in Ostermann, "New Evidence on the Sino-Soviet Border Dispute," p. 192. Romania, the Vietnamese government, and the Italian Communist Party all played a role in urging the Soviets to hold the meeting. Airgram, U.S. Mission to the UN to U.S. Department of State, October 2, 1969, SDCF. By the time the Chinese leadership agreed, however, Kosygin had already left Hanoi and was on his way back to the USSR. Since Kosygin's plane had already reached Central Asia, he decided to reroute his plane to Beijing to meet Zhou at the airport. Kapitsa, who traveled with Kosygin to Beijing, confirmed this version of events. See Kapitsa, *Na raznykh paralleliakh,* p. 81.

110. "Letter, Zhou Enlai to Alexei Kosygin, September 18, 1969," translation by Chen Jian of document from *Zhou Enlai waijiao wenxuan,* pp. 462–64, in *CWIHPB,* Winter 1998, pp. 172–73.

111. "Zhou Enlai's Talk at a Meeting of the Chinese Delegation Attending the Sino-Soviet Border Negotiation (Excerpt), October 7, 1969," translation by Chen Jian of document from *Zhonghua renmin gonheguo shilu*, vol. 3, part 1, pp. 523–24, in *CWIHPB*, Winter 1998, pp. 172–73; "Statement of the government of the People's Republic of China," October 7, 1969, Xinhua, in *FBIS* (Communist China), October 8, 1969, p. A1; Chai Chengwen, "Zhou Enlai lingdao women jinxing Zhong-Su bianjing tanpan," *Dandiwenxian*, no. 3 (1991), p. 47. Five years after the talks, Zhou Enlai revealed their contents in an interview with a French newspaper. See "L'entente' de septembre 1969 entre MM. Kossyguine et Chou Enlai," *Le Monde*, November 10–11, 1974, p. 2.

112. "Information about A.N. Kosygin's Conversation with Zhou Enlai on 11 September 1969," in *CWIHPB*, Winter 1995/1996, p. 192. In his analysis of the document, Christian Ostermann paraphrases the East German document in a way that would indicate Kosygin's acceptance of the Chinese language on "disengagement from disputed border areas," although the text of the document states otherwise. Christian F. Ostermann, "New Evidence on the Sino-Soviet Border Dispute, 1969–71," in *CWIHPB*, Winter 1995/96, p. 189. According to the document, Kosygin and Zhou agreed to a withdrawal of forces from "controversial sectors." "Document No. 1: Soviet Report to GDR Leadership on 2 March 1969 Sino-Soviet Border Clashes," in ibid., p. 192. This formulation is more ambiguous and may have led the Chinese to believe that the Soviets had recognized the existence of disputed areas, while the Soviet side may have thought they were referring only to the specific places where clashes had occurred.

113. For an account of Kosygin's views, see Kapitsa, *Na raznykh paralleliakh*, p. 88.

114. Nonetheless, the Chinese government contended that it "never demanded the return of the territory tsarist Russia had annexed by means of the unequal treaties. On the contrary, it is the Soviet Government that has persisted in occupying still more Chinese territory in violation of the stipulations of these treaties and, moreover, peremptorily demanded that the Chinese government recognized such occupation as legal." Chinese government statement, October 7, 1969.

115. A. Elizavetin, "Peregovory A. N. Kosygina i Zhou Enlai v pekinskom aero-protu, "Vstupitel'naia stat'ia i kommentarii k tekstu S. Goncharova i V. Usova," part 1, *PDV*, no. 5, 1992, p. 61; and ibid., part 2, *PDV*, no. 1, 1993, pp. 114–16. Zhou insisted that the use of the border islands by the residents of the two countries would have no impact on the issue of sovereignty by one or the other over these territories. Kapitsa, *Na raznykh paralleliakh*, p. 89.

116. At the time of the border clashes, American and British intelligence detected that the Soviet Air Force had gone on a low-level alert. This was cause for alarm since the Soviet Air Force alert included both conventional and nuclear weapons. In fact, the Soviet alert may have prompted the United States to raise the alert status of its own bombers in October 1969. Blair, *The Logic of Accidental Nuclear War*, p. 180.

Blair says that the alert could also have been a reaction to Soviet submarine patrolling along the Atlantic coast or the detection of a problem with the reliability of the Polaris submarine fleet. See Blair, note 15, p. 339.

117. Elizavetin, a counselor at the Soviet embassy in the PRC, took notes during the Zhou-Kosygin meeting for his own use. Elizavetin, "Peregovory A. N. Kosygina i Zhou Enlai," part 1, p. 60. He reiterates his point about the buildup of Soviet forces in the border region later on in his meeting with Kosygin. See Elizavetin, part 2, p. 113.

118. Ibid., p. 61.

119. Kapitsa, *Na raznykh paralleliakh*, p. 89.

120. According to Kapitsa, when Zhou proposed that border forces should not enter the disputed areas, Kosygin allegedly stated: "We will study this, but under conditions that our rights are not violated." Kapitsa, *Na raznykh paralleliakh*, p. 89.

121. Elizavetin, "Peregovory A.N. Kosygina i Zhou Enlai," part II, p. 113.

122. Ibid., p. 115.

123. Kapitsa, *Na raznykh paralleliakh*, p. 90. Western diplomatic reports of the Zhou-Kosygin meeting all contend that Kosygin raised three points: (1) measures to improve bilateral relations; (2) reopening border negotiations; and (3) means by which future border clashes could be avoided. See, for example, Telegram #7638, U.S. Embassy Tokyo to U.S. Department of State, September 1969, SDCF.

124. Kapitsa, *Na raznykh paralleliakh*, p. 91. Kapitsa subsequently was made head of the First Far Eastern department of the Ministry of Foreign Affairs.

125. Interview with a senior scholar, June 18, 1996 (Beijing).

126. "Zhou Enlai's talk at a meeting," p. 172.

127. While the Soviet side understood that Kosygin and Zhou had come up with talking points to be discussed during the border talks, the Chinese, on the other hand, interpreted these points as elements of an agreement. Since Zhou's agenda included the recognition of disputed areas and the withdrawal of forces from these areas, this explains why subsequently the Chinese kept raising the issue of the continued Soviet military presence along the border. C.L. Sulzberger asked Zhou about the 1969 agreement in an interview, "Chou Attacks Russians for Delaying Border Pact, *The New York Times (NYT)*, October 29, 1973, pp. 1, 8. For recent Chinese analyses, see Zhou Wenqi and Chu Liangru, *Teshu er fuza de keti*, p. 557; Chai Chongwen, "Zhou Enlai lingdao women jinxing Zhong-Su bianjing tanpan," p. 49; Wen Yaobing, "ZhongE bianjie fenzheng shimo ji jiannan quzhe de tanpan licheng," p. 73; Li Huichuan, "ZhongSu bianjie tanpan de zhengjie hezai?" p. 15; Li Danhui, "1969 nian ZhongSu bianjie chongtu," p. 50. Confirmation of the Chinese account would require access to Zhou's letter, probably contained in the Presidential Archives in Russia.

128. Kapitsa, *Na raznykh paralleliakh*, p. 89.

129. Ibid., p. 92.

130. Interview with senior scholars (Beijing), June 6, 1996. Aleksei Brezhnev, *Kitai*, p. 190. Brezhnev was a counselor at the Soviet delegation to the Sino-Soviet border talks in October 1969.

131. Elizavetin, "Peregovory A.N. Kosygina i Zhou Enlai," part 2, and Goncharov and Usov commentary, p. 111.

132. Aleksandrov-Agentov, *Ot Kollentai do Gorbacheva*, p. 258.

133. Goncharov and Usov commentary in Elizavetin, part 1, p. 57.

134. On Victor Louis's KGB connections, see Telegram, U.S. Embassy London to U.S. Department of State, September 17, 1969, in SDCF; and Anatoly Dobrynin, *In Confidence* (New York: Random House, 1995), p. 359.

135. "Controversial Soviet Newsman Hints Russians Might Launch Attack on China," *NYT*, September 18, 1969, p. 5.

136. Harrison Salsbury, "War of Nerves," *NYT*, September 18, 1969, p. 5; Sydney Schanberg, "China Said to Be Moving Nuclear Plant to Tibet," *NYT*, September 13, 1969, p. 2. U.S. diplomatic sources contended that the threat of Soviet attack led the Chinese leadership to the negotiating table. See Telegram #5255, U.S. Consulate Hong Kong, October 1969, SDCF. Boris Davydov, the Soviet official who first floated the idea of a Soviet attack against China, denied that the Chinese had been pressured in this way. U.S. Department of State, Memorandum of Conversation, November 10, 1969, SDCF.

137. Naughton, "The Third Front," p. 371.

138. Shevchenko, *Breaking with Moscow*, p. 165. There is no corroboration for this allegation. On this point see Goncharov and Usov, in Elizavetin, "Peregovory A.N. Kosygina i Zhou Enlai," part 1, p. 47.

139. Shevchenko, *Breaking with Moscow*, p. 166. Dobrynin didn't mention this in his memoirs. While the accuracy of a defector's memoir may be open to question, a document from the recently declassified SDCF shows the consistency of Shevchenko's views. In 1969, he told U.S. diplomats that the Chinese were banking on two mistaken assumptions: (1) that the USSR would compromise on the territorial dispute; and (2) that the Soviets would never use more than tactical nuclear weapons. Telegram from U.S. Mission to the United Nations to the U.S. Department of State, "Soviet-Chinese Relations," September 1969.

140. Shevchenko, *Breaking with Moscow*, p. 43.

141. On these reassessments, see Robert S. Ross, *Negotiating Cooperation: The United States and China, 1969–1989* (Palo Alto, Calif.: Stanford University Press, 1995), pp. 18–23.

142. Garthoff, *Détente and Confrontation*, p. 245.

143. Hersh, *The Price of Power*, p. 356; Li Zhisui, *The Private Life of Chairman Mao*, p. 515.

144. Hersh, *The Price of Power,* p. 359.

145. Handwritten journals and diaries of Harry Robbins Haldeman, White House Special Files: Staff Member and Office Files: Harry Haldeman, Box 1; Richard M. Nixon Presidential Materials Staff at College Park, Md. The conclusion of the first round of Sino-Soviet talks in December 1969 without results and the recall of Kuznetsov, the head of the Soviet delegation, to lead the SALT talks, heightened Chinese apprehensions regarding a threat of Soviet attack. See Telegram, U.S. Department of State, December 17, 1969, SDCF.

146. Xiong Xianghui, "Dakai Zhong-Mei guanxi de qianzou," *Liaowang,* August 31, 1992, pp. 23–31. Also, see the excerpts from the marshals' report in *CWIHPB,* Winter 1998, pp. 166–68, 170–71.

147. Ross, *Negotiating Cooperation,* pp. 30–31.

148. Naughton, "The Third Front," p. 362.

149. Today, moderate interpretations of Sino-Soviet relations consider this dynamic. Evgenii Bazhanov, a former Foreign Ministry and Central Committee official, supports this interpretation, for example. See Evgenii Bazhanov, *Kitai i vneshnii mir* (Moscow: Mezhdunarodnye Otnosheniia, 1990), p. 72.

150. Arbatov, *The System* (New York: Random House, 1992), p. 204.

151. Anatolii Gromyko, *Andrei Gromyko. V labirintakh Kremlia* (Moscow: IPO "Avtor", 1997), p. 175.

152. Su, "Soviet Image of and Policy toward China," pp. 17–19. At times, the Soviets raised these broader issues during the border talks. See Kenneth G. Lieberthal, *Sino-Soviet Conflict in the 1970s: Its Evolution and Implications for the Strategic Triangle,* Rand R-2342-NA, July 1978, p. 9.

153. Sergei Goncharov makes this point in his annotation of the second part of Elizavetin's account of the Zhou-Kosygin meeting. See Elizavetin, "Peregovory A.N. Kosygina i Zhou Enlai," part 2, p. 109.

154. Aleksei Brezhnev claims that the Soviet Union proposed a nonaggression treaty to offset Chinese attempts to portray themselves as victims. Aleksei Brezhnev, *Kitai,* p. 194. On Sino-Soviet diplomacy in the early 1970s, see Lieberthal, *Sino-Soviet Conflict in the 1970s,* pp. 8–24, 49–56, and 145–60; Su, "Soviet Image of and Policy toward China," chapter one; Day, *China and the Soviet Union,* pp. 97–110.

155. Their ambassadors had been recalled in 1967 due to tensions caused by the Cultural Revolution.

156. Lieberthal, *Sino-Soviet Conflict in the 1970s,* p. 55.

157. This speech carried a double message. While advocating peaceful coexistence on the one hand, Brezhnev also called for the establishment of a system of Asian collective security, a thinly disguised anti-Chinese alliance.

158. Su, "Soviet Image of and Policy toward China," p. 24; Lieberthal, *Sino-Soviet Conflict in the 1970s,* p. 13.

159. L. I. Brezhnev, "The Decisions of the 24 CPSU Congress Are a Militant Program of Activity for the Soviet Trade Unions," *Pravda* and *Izvestiia*, March 21, 1972, pp. 1–3, in *CDSP*, vol. 24, no. 12 (1972), p. 8.

160. Zhou Enlai's report to the Tenth CPC National Congress, August 31, 1973, Xinhua, in *FBIS* (PRC), August 31, 1973, p. B4. Mao had designated Lin Biao as his successor, but by 1970 the chairman began to fear that Lin was competing with him for the leadership of the party. After plotting an abortive coup against Mao, Lin fled, on September 13, 1971. His plane crashed in Mongolia, and this event led to suspicions that Lin had been headed for the Soviet Union and had been prepared to betray China. On the Lin Biao affair, see Roderick MacFarquhar, "The Succession to Mao and the End of Maoism, 1969–82," in MacFarquhar, ed., *The Politics of China*, (Cambridge: Cambridge University Press, 1997), pp. 265–75.

161. Ibid., p. B9.

162. Lieberthal, *Sino-Soviet Conflict in the 1970s*, p. 19. Border talks were in fact broken off when the Chinese rejected Moscow's June 1973 proposals. Ibid., p. 102.

163. Lieberthal sees a link between these incidents and the factional struggle in the Chinese leadership. Ibid., pp. 129–34.

164. *TANJUG*, January 7, 1974, in *FBIS* (PRC), January 9, 1974, p. A3.

165. NCNA, January 8, 1974, in *FBIS* (PRC), January 9, 1974, p. A1.

166. According to Lieberthal, the arrest of the Soviet diplomats may have been a set-up to dramatize the threat of Soviet subversion. See Lieberthal, *Sino-Soviet Conflict in the 1970s*, pp. 109–11.

167. Ibid., p. 112.

168. "Note of the USSR Ministry of Foreign Affairs to the Embassy of the Chinese People's Republic," *Pravda*, March 29, 1974, p. 4, in *CDSP*, vol. 26, no. 12, p. 4.

169. "In the USSR Ministry of Foreign Affairs," *Pravda*, May 3, 1974, p. 4, in *CDSP*, vol. 26, no. 18, p. 15.

170. Lieberthal, *Sino-Soviet Conflict in the 1970s*, pp. 113–16, 126–33. Kissinger later teased Gromyko about the helicopter. In a meeting in January 1976, Kissinger stated: "China will certainly be very angry if there is success in SALT. But they haven't given us any helicopters lately, so perhaps you should tell us what you are doing." Gromyko replied (laughing): "China gave us a helicopter because it is ours! Of course they recognized they made a mistake." In William Burr, ed., *The Kissinger Transcripts* (New York: The New Press, 1998), p. 468.

171. Lieberthal, *Sino-Soviet Conflict in the 1970s*, p. 113.

172. Neville Maxwell, "Why the Russians Lifted the Blockade at Bear Island," *Foreign Affairs*, Fall 1978, p. 142.

173. Wen Yaobing, "ZhongE bianjie fenzheng shimo ji jiannan quzhe de tanpan licheng," p. 73.

174. V. Goncharov, "V ugodu mezhdunarodnoi reaktsii," *Pravda,* October 22, 1975, in *Opasnyi Kurs (OK),* no. 7, p. 244.

175. "Text of 6 November greetings telegram from the Standing Committee of the PRC National People's Congress and the PRC State Council to the USSR Supreme Soviet Presidium and the USSR Council of Ministers on the occasion of the 57th anniversary of the October Revolution," Beijing Radio in Russian, November 6, 1974, in *FBIS* (PRC), p. A1.

176. TASS contended that "the presentation of all kinds of preliminary conditions is a repetition of the former position of the leadership of the PRC and, of course, does not furnish foundations for an understanding. If the government of the PRC displayed real interest in the reaching of an understanding and, for its part, also took real steps in this direction, it would be, in our opinion, not difficult to resume good neighborly relations between our countries." TASS, November 24, 1974, in *FBIS* (Soviet Union), November 26, 1974, p. C1.

177. "Changes in the PRC Constitution," *Pravda,* January 21, 1975, p. 5, in *CDSP,* vol. 27, no. 3 (1975), p. 19.

178. "To the Standing Committee of the National People's Congress and the State Council of the Chinese People's Republic," *Pravda,* October 1, 1975, p. 1, in *CDSP,* vol. 27, no. 39 , p. 14.

179. *Time,* March 22, 1976, p. 26, cited in Lieberthal, *Sino-Soviet Conflict in the 1970s,* p. 130.

180. M. S. Ukraintsev [Mikhail Kapitsa], "Pekin v soiuze s imperializmom, reaktsiei i rasizmom," *PDV,* no. 1 (1976), p. 39. Also see Morris Rothenberg's analysis of this article in *Whither China: The View from the Kremlin* (Miami: University of Miami, 1977), p. 65.

181. I. Aleksandrov, "Pekin i sovetsko-kitaiskie otnosheniia," *Pravda,* April 28, 1976, pp. 4–5.

182. Zhou Wenqi and Chu Liangru, *Teshu er fuza de keti,* p. 581.

183. Gelman, *The Soviet Far East Buildup,* p. 65. According to Gelman, the deceleration may have reflected the fulfillment of force goals set by the Brezhnev leadership in the mid-1960s and a perception of greater border stability, rather than a decline in the Chinese threat. See Gelman, *The Soviet Far East Buildup,* pp. 66–67. In 1975, the Chinese deployed two medium-range CSS-2 missiles in western China that were capable of hitting Moscow with nuclear warheads. See Richard F. Staar, ed., *Yearbook on International Communist Affairs,* 1975 (Stanford, Calif.: Hoover Institution Press, 1975), p. 274.

184. See IISS, *The Military Balance, 1974–75* (London: IISS, 1974), p. 9; IISS, *The Military Balance, 1976–77* (London: IISS, 1976–77), p. 9. While in the earlier period these troops were a mixture of category one and two, in the mid-1970s they consisted of an even mix of category two and three divisions. Category one divisions

are at 3/4 to full strength; category two divisions are at 1/2 to 3/4 strength and category three are at 1/3 strength.

185. Staar, *Yearbook on International Communist Affairs*, 1975, p. 274.

186. Ibid., p. 284.

187. Banning Garrett, "The China Card and Its Origins: US Bureaucratic Politics and the Strategic Triangle," (Ph.D. diss., Brandeis University, 1983), p. 126. When Brezhnev and Ustinov visited Khabarovsk, they observed a "combined arms tactical exercise." Gelman, *The Soviet Far East Buildup*, p. 75.

188. The Soviets expressed regret at the incident, in which Soviet troops attacked Chinese civilians. William de Berard Mills, "Sino-Soviet Interactions, May 1977–June 1980" (Ph.D. diss., University of Michigan, 1981), p. 128.

189. William C. Green and David S. Yost, "Soviet Military Options Regarding China," in *China, the Soviet Union, and the West*, ed. Douglas T. Stuart and William T. Tow (Boulder, Colo.: Westview Press, 1982), p. 137.

190. Gelman, *The Soviet Far East Buildup*, pp. 65–77. In the end of March, the Soviet Union also began to deploy SS-20s. See Garthoff, *Détente and Confrontation*, p. 698.

191. CIA, "Soviet Goals and Expectations in the Global Power Arena," National Intelligence Estimate, May 1978, p. 20. This document was provided courtesy of the National Security Archive, Washington, D.C.

192. Ibid., p. 21.

193. Gelman, *The Soviet Far East Buildup*, p. 76.

194. Evgenii Bazhanov, "End of 'Chinese Syndrome'," *New Times*, no. 19 (1990), p. 5. The BAM finally became operational recently after over 15 years of construction.

195. Aleksandrov-Agentov recalled what he considered to be an unnecessarily hysterical reaction in the Soviet Union to the signing of this treaty. According to his account, Andropov saw the treaty in a more sober light. See Aleksandrov-Agentov, *Ot Kollentai do Gorbacheva*, p. 276.

196. Ibid., pp. 100–101.

197. Segal, *Defending China*, p. 221.

198. Aleksandrov-Agentov, *Ot Kollentai do Gorbacheva*, p. 171. Anatolii Gromyko, *Andrei Gromyko*, p. 175.

199. Immediately after Mao died, for example, the Central Committee of the CPSU sent a message of condolence, but the Chinese rejected this gesture on the grounds that the Soviet Union and China had no party-to-party ties. Fox Butterfield, "Soviet Condolences Rebuffed by Peking," *NYT*, September 15, 1976, p. 7.

200. I. Aleksandrov, "Twenty-seven Years of the CPR [PRC]," *Pravda*, October 1, 1976, p. 4, in *CDSP*, vol. 27, no. 39, pp. 1–3, 24.

201. Victor Louis, "Moscou guette un geste de Pékin," *France-Soir*, October 14, 1976, p. 7.

202. Unidentified Chinese leader interviewed by Georges Biannic, AFP, November 2, 1976, in *FBIS* (PRC), November 3, 1976, pp. A5–6.

203. Leonid Brezhnev, "The 25th Congress of the CPSU: The Report to the CPSU Central Committee on the Party's Immediate Tasks in Domestic and Foreign Policy," *Pravda*, February 25, 1976, in *CDSP*, vol. 28, no. 8, p. 7. This message was followed on October 27 by a letter of congratulations to Hua Guofeng, newly appointed chairman of the CCP, but the Chinese rejected it. Day, *China and the Soviet Union*, p. 130. Nonetheless, the annual Chinese government message on the occasion of the anniversary of the October Revolution stated that "disputes on questions of principle between China and the Soviet Union must not interfere with normal state relations between the two countries. . . ." Peking in Russian to USSR, November 6, 1976, in *FBIS* (PRC), November 8, 1976, p. A2.

204. Mills, "Sino-Soviet Interactions," pp. 32–37. Chinese attacks on Soviet policies appeared periodically in the media in the year after Mao's death. See, for example, "NCNA correspondent's commentary: Dance atop volcanoes," *NCNA*, December 30, 1976, in *FBIS* (PRC), January 4, 1977, pp. A1-3; Xinhua, "An Unworthy Trick," January 16, 1977, in *FBIS* (PRC), January 17, 1977, pp. A5–6; and Hua Guofeng's political report to 11th National CCP Congress, August 22, 1977, in *FBIS* (PRC), August 22, 1977, pp. D28–29.

205. Huang Hua said that China would develop relations with other countries on the basis of peaceful coexistence. Huang Hua, speech to UN General Assembly, *Peking Review*, October 7, 1977, p. 35.

206. Aleksei Brezhnev, *Kitai*, p. 229.

207. Report by M. V. Zimianin at a ceremonial meeting in Moscow dedicated to the 107th Anniversary of V. I. Lenin's birth, "Leninism is the revolutionary banner of our epoch," *Pravda* and *Izvestiia*, April 23, 1977, pp. 1–3, in *CDSP* vol. 29, no. 16, p. 4. In his memoirs Georgi Arbatov describes Zimianin as a patron of conservatives in the leadership, who took part in an attempt to destroy IMEMO, a leading think tank. Arbatov, *The System*, p. 147.

208. I. Aleksandrov, "Twenty-eight Years of the CPR [PRC]," *Pravda*, October 1, 1977, p. 4, in *CDSP*, vol. 29, no. 39, pp. 11–12.

209. For a detailed examination of the border navigation issue, see Maxwell, "Why the Russians Lifted the Blockade at Bear Island," p. 144.

210. Mills, "Sino-Soviet Interactions," p. 74. The November issue of the *Peking Review* was devoted entirely to the three worlds theory. See Mills, p. 84.

211. AFP, November 7, 1977, in *FBIS* (PRC), November 7, 1977, pp. A12–13.

212. The Soviets claimed that no such agreement was made at the 1969 meeting. Mills, "Sino-Soviet Interactions," p. 89.

213. Zhou Wenqi and Chu Liangru, *Teshu er fuza de keti*, p. 595. Editorial, "On Soviet-Chinese Relations," *Pravda* and *Izvestiia*, March 21, 1978, p. 4, in *CDSP*, vol.

30, no. 17 (1978), pp. 5–6. For the text of the letter from the Presidium of the Supreme Soviet of the USSR to the Standing Committee of the Chinese NPC, see *Peking Review*, no. 13, p. 18. Also, see Kapitsa's account in *Na raznykh paralleliakh*, p. 101. A Soviet radio commentary publicized the Chinese reply to the Soviet proposal, noting that Chinese preconditions for resolving the border issues were unacceptable because they required the Soviet Union to make "unilateral concessions," i.e., "a complete revision of the Sino-Soviet boundary." Moscow in Mandarin to China, May 14, 1978, in *FBIS* (Soviet Union), May 17, 1978, pp. C1–2. The Chinese reply came in a *Renmin Ribao* editorial, which restated the PRC's position that the Soviet Union had violated the 1969 agreement between Zhou Enlai and Kosygin. "Renmin Ribao" Commentator, "Real Deeds, Yes; Hollow Statements, No!" *Peking Review*, vol. 21 (1978), pp. 14–16.

214. Xinhua, April 3, 1979, in *FBIS* (PRC), April 3, 1979, p. C1.

215. Moscow World Service in English, April 17, 1979, in *FBIS* (Soviet Union), April 18, 1979, p. B1.

216. AFP, May 9, 1979, in *FBIS* (PRC), May 10, 1979, p. C1; Zhou Wenqi and Chu Liangru, *Teshu er fuza de keti*, p. 607.

217. TANJUG, October 4, 1979, in *FBIS* (Soviet Union), October 9, 1979, p. B1; Xinhua, October 5, 1979, in *FBIS* (PRC), October 9, 1979, p. C1.

218. Beijing Domestic Service in Mandarin, October 13, 1979, in *FBIS* (PRC), October 15, 1979, p. C1.

219. Deputy Foreign Minister Leonid Il'ichev, who had led the Soviet delegation at the Sino-Soviet border talks since 1970, headed the Soviet delegation, while Wang Youping, newly appointed Deputy Foreign Minister, headed the Chinese delegation. Day, *China and the Soviet Union*, p. 139. Also see TANJUG, October 12, 1979, in *FBIS* (Soviet Union), October 15, 1979, p. B1. The Soviet Union tabled a draft declaration of the principles of Sino-Soviet relations. TASS, December 5, 1979, in *FBIS* (Soviet Union), p. B1. An editorial in *Pravda* (using the pseudonym for the Soviet leadership, I. Alexandrov) stated that "Normalization of interstate relations, as is clear to any sane person, requires a definite legal foundation of principles agreed upon and recorded in an appropriate document which both sides follow in solving the existing problems, and in adjusting and developing their relations in the future. This is why the Soviet side continues to note definitely that the working out of the principles of mutual relations between the two countries must now become central to the efforts aimed at the normalization of Soviet-Chinese relations." I. Alexandrov, "Contrary to Historical Truth," *Pravda*, December 7, 1979, in *FBIS* (Soviet Union), December 8, 1979, p. B1; TANJUG, December 1, 1979, in *FBIS* (PRC), December 3, 1979, p. B1.

220. Zhou Wenqi and Chu Liangru, *Teshu er fuza de keti*, p. 612.

221. Kyodo, October 18, 1979, in *FBIS* (PRC), October 18, 1979, p. C1. The Chinese

official was Tan Zhenlin, Vice-Chairman of the National People's Congress Standing Committee.

222. Kapitsa, *Na raznykh paralleliakh,* pp. 102–10.

3 / THE SINO-SOVIET CONFLICT IN PERSPECTIVE

1. William Zimmerman, *Soviet Perspectives on International Relations, 1956–67* (Princeton, N.J.: Princeton University Press, 1969), p. 282; and Allen Lynch, *The Soviet Study of International Relations* (Cambridge: Cambridge University Press, 1989), pp. 67–69.

2. As R. Judson Mitchell points out, China's resolve served to further question the legitimacy of Soviet elites, and the problem escalated "from one of cohesion to one concerning the basis of authority." R. Judson Mitchell, *Ideology of a Superpower* (Stanford, Calif.: Hoover Institution Press, 1982), p. 39. On the impact of China's challenge to the unity of the communist movement, see Karen Brutents, *Tridsat' let na Staroi Ploshchadi* (Moscow: Mezhdunarodnye Otnosheniia, 1998), p. 140.

3. These efforts coincided with the Sino-Soviet ideological conflict and actually predated the border clashes. See, for example, "Voprosy, priniatye resheniem Sekretariata TsK - 12.III.1968 g. - O koordinatsii s bratskimi partiiami propagandistskoi i nauchno-issledovatel'skoi deiatel'nosti po kitaiskomu voprosu," Tsentr Khraneniia Sovremennykh Dokumentov (TsKhSD), f. 4, d. 504, pp. 116–17.

4. In January 1969, for example, in preparation for an upcoming session, the Central Committee gave the following instructions to the Soviet delegation: "In case the delegations from the fraternal countries do not consider it possible to agree to the development of joint material, do not dwell on this and accept agreement on general ideas and evaluations concerning the principal questions of the theme under discussion." "O vstreche predstavitelei mezhdunarodnykh otdelov Tse-ntral'nykh Komitetov semi bratskikh partii po kitaiskomu voprosu," January 21, 1969, p. 107; TsKhSD, f.4, op. 19, d. 525. Indeed, Romania did not participate in the yearly meetings of the Central Committee International Departments of the fraternal parties on the China question. These meetings included Bulgaria, Czechoslovakia, East Germany, Hungary, Mongolia, and Poland. According to a Chinese diplomat, Romania in particular opposed Soviet efforts to draft a unified statement on China in 1969. British embassy First Secretary John Kerr's April 16, 1969, "Conversation with Chinese Communist Embassy Second Secretary Chang Take on the Sino-Soviet border clashes," Airgram from U.S. Embassy Moscow to U.S. Department of State, April 24, 1969, State Department Central Files (SDCF). The Chinese diplomat reportedly also stated that he had heard rumors that the Soviet Union was trying to obtain token detachments from all the Warsaw Pact countries to defend the USSR's

eastern border. The U.S. embassy could not confirm this rumor. Telegram from U.S. Embassy Moscow to U.S. Department of State, April 21, 1969, SDCF.

5. Interview with Andrei Denisov, June 4, 1991. Soviet propaganda on the China question went well beyond the socialist community. Within weeks of the first border clash on Damanskii/Zhen Bao Island, Soviet diplomats in such far-flung posts as Ouagadougou, Upper Volta, had begun circulating pamphlets about the confrontation. See Airgram, U.S. Embassy Ouagadougou to U.S. Department of State, March 21, 1969, SDCF.

6. Interview with Aleksander Grigor'ev, June 24, 1993.

7. Central Committee officials Oleg Rakhmanin and Boris Kulik said in *Kommunist* that China was claiming that conflict existed only with the Soviet Union, while in fact the Chinese leadership was hostile to the entire communist movement. O. Borisov and B. Koloskov, [pseudonyms for O. Rakhmanin and B. Kulik], "Antisovetskii kurs gruppy Mao Tze-Duna," *Kommunist,* no. 7 (1969), in *Opasnyi Kurs (OK)* no. 1, p. 257.

8. Giuseppe Boffa, "La Cina pesa, e lo si sente," *L'Unità,* April 9, 1969, p. 3. While only the Soviet rebuttal accusing Boffa of forgetting internationalism was published in *Pravda* on April 13, 1969, a translation of the *L'Unità* piece was included in *Politicheskii Dnevnik,* a samizdat publication, and consequently was read by a small circle of intellectuals, some whom wrote about China. *Politicheskii Dnevnik,* vol. 1, 1964–70 (Amsterdam: The Herzen Foundation, 1972).

9. "For Strengthening the Solidarity of Communists, for a New Upswing in the Anti-Imperialist Struggle," Speech by Comrade L.I. Brezhnev at the International Conference of Communist and Workers' Parties in Moscow on June 7, 1969, *Pravda* and *Izvestiia,* June 8, pp. 1–4, in *Current Digest of the Soviet Press (CDSP),* vol. 21, no. 23 (July 2, 1969), pp. 10, 12–13, 16.

10. Elizabeth Wishnick, "Soviet Asian Collective Security from Brezhnev to Gorbachev," *Journal of Northeast Asian Studies,* Fall 1988, pp. 3–28.

11. "Sino-Soviet Relations," Telegram from U.S. Consulate General, Hong Kong, to U.S. Department of State, June 21, 1969, in SDCF.

12. Lev Deliusin, "Nekotorye razmyshleniia o nachale sovestko-kitaiskogo konflikta," *Rossiia i Sovremennyi Mir,* no. 2 (1998), pp. 233–34. Deliusin asserts that ideological differences were not the real issue in the Soviet-Chinese conflict, although they were portrayed as such. The two states had the same ideology, but different interests.

13. "O vstreche predstavitelei mezhdunarodnykh otdelov Tsentral'nykh Komitetov semi bratskikh partii (KPSS, BKP, VSRP, SEPG, MNRP, PORP, and KPCh)," (Comrades Suslov, Kirilenko, Demichev, Rusakov, Rakhmanin), TsKhSD, f.4, op. 19, d. 605, pp. 2–3.

14. "Aktual'nye problemy Kitaia," Kruglyi Stol Zhurṇala, *Problemy Dal'nego Vostoka* (*PDV*), no. 2 (1975), p. 18.

15. At a meeting on trade issues with East European officials, the Soviet delegation was instructed, for example, to urge the fraternal countries to improve coordination on trade policy and other economic issues concerning China. "O direktivakh sovetskoi delegatsii na soveshchanie predstavitelei ministerstv vneshnei torgovli NRB (Bulgaria), VNR (Hungary), GDR, the Republic of Cuba, MNR (Mongolia), PNR (Poland), USSR, and ChSSSR (Czechoslovakia) po koordinatsii torgovoi i ekonomicheskoi politiki v otnoshenii KNR," October 7, 1975, TsKhSD, f. 4, op. 22, d. 1601, p. 3.

16. Trond Gilberg, "The Impact of the Sino-Soviet Dispute on Eastern Europe," in *The Sino-Soviet Conflict*, ed. Herbert J. Ellison (Seattle: University of Washington Press, 1982), p. 282. According to Ernst Kux, the Soviet need for the support of the East European states against China increased their leverage vis-à-vis Moscow, further accentuating pressures for greater autonomy within the socialist community. See Ernst Kux, "Growing Tensions in Eastern Europe," *Problems of Communism*, March-April 1980, p. 35.

17. "Ob ukazaniakh i sostave delegatsii KPSS na ocherednuiu vstrechu predstavitelei mezhdunarodnykh otdelov Tsentral'nykh Komitetov bratskikh partii po kitaiskomu voprosu," June 13, 1975, TsKhSD, f.4, op. 22, d. 242, p. 3. As Oleg Rakhmanin explained, a party's position on Maoism marked the dividing line between the friends and enemies of the Soviet Union. O. Vladimirov [Rakhmanin], "Sovremennyi etap ideologicheskoi bor'by protiv maoizma," *PDV*, no. 3 (1974), p. 124.

18. See the commentary from the press of various socialist states in "Bratskie kommunisticheskie i rabochie partii razoblachaiut," *PDV*, no. 3 (1974), pp. 231–34.

19. At the Twenty-fifth Congress of the CPSU, for example, many of the foreign guests made appropriate condemnatory remarks, although the Yugoslav and Romanian delegates emphasized the importance of autonomy within the communist movement.

20. Richard F. Staar, ed., *Yearbook on International Communist Affairs* (Stanford, Calif.: Hoover Institution Press, 1976), pp. 571–72 and 574–75.

21. Branko Bogunovic, "China: Continuity or Change?" *Review of International Affairs* (Belgrade), vol. 27, no. 625 (1977), pp. 20–22.

22. Nicolae Ceaușescu, Report to Eleventh Congress of the Romanian Communist Party: Section on Foreign Affairs, BBC World Broadcasts, EE/4766/C/5, November 27, 1974. Because of such statements, some Soviet commentators noted with dismay that China was not just a problem for the Soviet Union but for the socialist community as a whole, even if certain parties did not realize this yet. V. Lazarev, "Sotsial'nye istoki maoistskii rezhim," *Kommunist*, no. 12 (1976), p. 114.

23. "Ob ukazaniiakh poslam SSSR v sotsialisticheskikh stranakh po kitaiskomu voprosu," March 4, 1980, TsKhSD, f. 4, op. 24, d. 1200, pp. 2–4.

24. For Soviet coverage of Hua Guofeng's visit to Romania, see BBC World Broadcasts, Soviet Union, August 21, 1978, SU/5896/i; and August 22, 1978, SU/5897/i.

25. Vitaly Korionov, "Survey: International Week—Concerning a Certain Tour," *Pravda*, August 27, 1978, p. 4, in *CDSP*, vol. 30, no. 35, pp. 2–3.

26. Kevin Devlin, "The Challenge of the 'New Internationalism'," in *The Sino-Soviet Conflict*, ed. Herbert J. Ellison (Seattle: University of Washington Press, 1982), p. 166. The CPSU considered the PCI's Eurocommunist ideas to be bourgeois propaganda, and insisted that although different conditions were present in various countries, there could be no tactical departures from basic principles or features of socialist development. See, for example, the speech by Suslov to an international theoretical conference, "The Light of the Ideas of October," *Pravda*, November 11, 1977, pp. 1, 4, in *CDSP*, vol. 29, no. 45, p. 4.

27. Joan Barth Urban, *Moscow and the Italian Communist Party* (Ithaca, N.Y.: Cornell University Press, 1986), p. 307.

28. For a description of the normalization process, see Devlin, "The Challenge of the 'New Internationalism'," pp. 166–71. Also see Urban, *Moscow and the Italian Communist Party*, p. 310.

29. Urban, *Moscow and the Italian Communist Party*, p. 311.

30. "Vopros otdela KPSS" (Comrades Andropov, Ponomarev, Suslov), TsKhSD, f. 4, op. 17, d. 529.

31. During the Soviet era, this institute was one of the leading centers in Moscow for the study of current issues in Chinese politics. "Ob uluchshenii nauchno-issledovatel'skoi raboty po Kitaiu i rasshirenii podgotovki kitaevedov," TsKhSD, f.4, op. 19, d. 439, p. 4. On the development of Soviet sinology in the 1960s, see Chi Su, "Sovet China-Watchers' Influence on Soviet China Policy," *Journal of Northeast Asian Studies*, December 1993, pp. 25–49; and David Wolff, "On the Borders of the Sino-Soviet Conflict: New Approaches to the Cold War in Asia," unpublished paper presented to the international conference, "New Evidence on the Cold War in Asia," University of Hong Kong, January 1996, pp. 12–14.

32. "O propagandistskikh meropriiatiiakh po kitaiskomu voprosu," (Comrades Kirilenko, Rakhmanin, Kulakov, Solomentsev, Kapitonov, Ustinov), TsKhSD, f.4, op. 19, 490; "Postanovleniia Sekretariata TsK, Priniatye oprosom-July 29, 1970–O zakrytom izdanii Ocherkov istorii Kompartii Kitaia," TsKhSD, f.4, op. 19, d. 584, pp. 12, 53–54.

33. Other group members included Igor Rogachev, now Russia's Ambassador to China, N.T. Federenko, V.I. Lazarev, K.E. Ses'kin, and V.V. Sharapov. "O gruppe sovetnikov-ekspertov po kitaiskoi probleme," TsKhSD, f. 4, op. 22, d. 1004, pp. 1–2.

34. Gilbert Rozman, "Moscow's China-Watchers in the Post-Mao Era: The Response to a Changing China," *The China Quarterly*, no. 94 (June 1983) p. 219.

35. "O nepravil'nom osveshchenii v sovetskoi uchebnoi i nauchnoi literature i v kartografii ustanovleniia granitsy SSSR s Kitaem," (Comrades Andropov, Il'ichev, Ponomarev, Brezhnev), TsKhSD, f. 4, op. 17, d. 579, p.4.

36. Yuri Andropov, Andrei Gromyko, and Oleg Rakhmanin sent a proposal to the Central Committee about this problem, "O meropriiatiiakh, napravlennykh na pravil'noe osveshchenie istorii formirovaniia sovetsko-kitaiskoi granitsy v sovetskoi istoricheskoi literature i uchebnikakh," TsKhSD, f.4, op. 19, d. 555, pp. 23–17. "Zapiska t.t. Andropova, Yu.V., Gromyko, A.A., Rakhmanina, O.B. ot 8.IX.1969 g. no. 1714/gc to t.t. Kirilenko, Katushev, Ponomarev, Ustinov, Kapitonov, Demichev, Kulakov, Trapeznikov, September 24, 1969," TsKSD, f.4, op. 19, d. 555, pp. 2–3. Also see "O rasshirenii podgotovki kadrov kitaevedov i uluchshenii nauchno-issledovatel'skoy raboty po Kitaiu," April 28, 1969, TsKhSD, f.4, op. 19, d. 543, p. 2, 37–38. On the impact of Sino-Soviet ideological polemics on the work of the Institute of the Far East, see V. Glunin and A. Grogior'ev, "Izuchenie istorii Kitaia v IDV RAN," *PDV*, no. 5 (1996), p. 96.

37. The Chinese government bitterly denounced these decrees. See *NCNA*, March 6, 1973, in *FBIS* (PRC), March 7, 1973, p. A1–3.

38. M.S. Kapitsa, *Eskalatsiia verolomstva: Politika Pekina i Sovetsko-Kitaiskie otnosheniia* (Moscow: Znanie, 1970), p. 3.

39. "O merakh po razoblacheniiu kitaiskikh fal'sifikatsii istorii i otporu territorial'nym prityazeniiam Pekina k SSSR," TsKhSD, f. 4, op. 24, d. 684, p. 2–4.

40. Rumiantsev, as well as Gel'bras and Kiuzadjian (the latter from the Institute of Scientific Information in the Social Sciences), mentioned that the Chinese justified their policies in terms of building socialism with Chinese specifics, but then discounted this view in light of the extreme positions taken by the Maoist leadership. By alluding to the Chinese explanation, however, these scholars were unique in presenting an alternative explanation for Chinese behavior, even if this is one they disavowed in print. See A. Rumiantsev, "Maoizm i anti-marksistskaia sushchnost' ego 'filosofii'," *Kommunist*, no. 2 (January 1969), p. 96; V. Gel'bras and L. Kiuzadjian, "Uzel protivorechii sovremennogo Kitaia," review of A. Bovin and L. Deliusin, *Politicheskii krisis v Kitae, 1968*, in *MEiMO*, no. 2 (1969), p. 144.

41. Mikhail Sladkovskii noted that "In effect [the Chinese leaders] renounced the construction of socialism in China." M. Sladkovskii, "'Special Course' in a Blind Alley," *Izvestiia*, April 28, 1970, pp. 4–5, in *CDSP*, vol. 23, no. 17, p. 4.

42. N. Konstantinov, "Antisotsialisticheskaia sushchnost' ideologii Maoizma," *Kommunist Vooruzhennikh Sil*, no. 5 (1972), p. 22 (reprinted in *OK*, no. 3). Given that articles published in *Opasnyi Kurs* represent the official party line, Konstantinov's argument against China's excommunication from the communist movement indicated that the Soviet leaders were opposed to such an extreme step. The article was first published in the ideologically orthodox journal, *Kommunist Vooruzhennykh Sil*,

an arm of the Main Political Administration of the Soviet Armed Forces. Since political officers rely on materials from this journal for the political training of the Armed Forces, the position of the writer must have been accepted by the most ideologically orthodox circles.

43. "Zaiavlenie pravitel'stva SSSR," *Pravda*, June 14, 1969, *OK*, no. 1, p. 284.

44. A. Butenko, "Nekotorye teoreticheskie problemy razvitiia mirovoi sistemy sotsializma," *MEiMO*, no. 9 (1971), p. 101.

45. V. Gantman, "Tipy soderzhanie struktura i fazy razvitiia mezhdunarodnogo konflikta," in *Mezhdunarodnye konflikty*, ed. V. Zhurkin and E.V. Primakov (Moscow: Mezhdunarodnye Otnosheniia, 1972), p. 36.

46. According to Stephen Cohen, who edited a volume of translated excerpts from *Politicheskii Dnevnik*, the publication was a monthly bulletin, edited by Roy Medvedev, and circulated among a small group of prominent intellectuals and dissidents from the mid-1960s and early 1970s. Cohen emphasized that *Politicheskii Dnevnik* was unique because it was the only uncensored journal known to have been read by intellectuals with ties to the Communist Party. See Stephen F. Cohen, "Editor's Preface: Roy Medvedev and Political Diary," in *An End to Silence* (New York: W.W. Norton & Company, Inc., 1982), pp. 7–9.

47. A.R. [pseudonym], "Zametki po nekotorym problemam vneshnei politiki SSSR," in *Politicheskii Dnevnik*, vol. 1, pp. 670–71. Allen Lynch suggests that Roy Medvedev may have written this piece (Lynch, *The Soviet Study of International Relations*, p. 97, footnote 22).

48. A.R., "Zametki," p. 680.

49. "Informatsiia o sostoianii sovetsko-kitaiskikh otnoshenii," (Comrades Suslov, Kirilenko, Pel'she, Demichev, Ustinov, Ponomarev, Katushev, Solomentsev, Rusakov), TsKhSD, f. 4, op. 19, d. 605, pp. 6, 8.

50. Reinhard Rummel, "China's Fixation on Western Europe," *Aussenpolitik*, English edition, vol. 29, no. 3, p. 280.

51. See Brezhnev's comments on China's position on the EEC and NATO in his speech to a ceremonial session in Berlin, "A Quarter Century on the Path of Socialism," *Pravda*, October 7, 1974, pp. 1–3, in *CDSP*, vol. 26, no. 40, p. 2.

52. Joan Barth Urban, "The Impact of the Sino-Soviet Dispute on Western Europe," in *The Sino-Soviet Conflict*, ed. Herbert J. Ellison (Seattle: University of Washington Press, 1982), p. 309.

53. On the implications of the theory for the developing states, "Aktual'nye problemy sovremennogo Kitaia," Kruglyi stol zhurnala, *PDV*, no. 3 (1974), p. 29.

54. I. Alexeev and G. Apalin, "Peking's Ideological Subversion," *International Affairs (IA)*, no. 5 (1975), p. 45 (also in *OK* no. 7).

55. B. Kubarov, "Socialism in Peking's Policies, *IA*, no. 3, p. 66.

56. "Aktual'nye problemy Kitaia," p. 29.

57. V.T. Zubakova, *Osnovnye aspekty Kitaiskoi problemy, 1969–75* (Moscow: Politizdat, 1975), p. 245.

58. Triangular diplomacy has been discussed at length in many works. One of the most comprehensive treatments of the issue is by Raymond Garthoff, *Détente and Confrontation*, rev. ed. (Washington, D.C.: The Brookings Institution, 1994), part III. On the impact of the Sino-Soviet border clashes on Sino-American relations, see Robert S. Ross, *Negotiating Cooperation: The United States and China, 1969–1989* (Stanford, Calif.: Stanford University Press, 1995), chapter 2.

59. Anatoly Dobrynin, *In Confidence* (New York: Times Books, 1995), p. 207.

60. Ibid., p. 212.

61. Georgi Arbatov, *The System* (New York: Random House, 1992), p. 180.

62. Arbatov explained in his memoirs that he asked Politburo member Andrei Kirilenko for permission to write an article on the Kissinger trip, mostly to explain to the Soviet public that the Sino-American rapprochement represented the normal development of relations, not necessarily a new threat to the Soviet Union. Arbatov recounted: "I also drew the conclusion that our final evaluation of the Americans' motive would depend on the general political context in which the normalization of Sino-American relations took place. If similar shifts followed in regard to other socialist countries (I had in mind, above all, the USSR) . . . we would interpret the American initiative positively, part of an overall change in global policies. If not, we would entertain legitimate suspicions about American motives and possible harm to other countries (including the USSR)." Arbatov, *The System*, p. 182.

63. Viktor Maevskii, "Mir i bezopasnost' v Azii—delo vsekh narodov," *Pravda*, March 28, 1971, p. 4.

64. I. Alexandrov, "Concerning Peking's Contacts with Washington," *Pravda*, July 25, 1971, pp. 4–5, in *CDSP*, vol. 23, no. 30, p. 4 (reprinted in *OK*, no. 2).

65. G. Arbatov, "Questions Demanding Answers in Practice. On the Planned American-Chinese Summit Meeting," *Pravda*, August 10, 1971, pp. 4–5, in *CDSP*, vol. 23, no. 32, p. 1 (also in *OK*, no. 2).

66. Vladimir Lukin, "Kitaiskii faktor v politike SShA," in *SShA: Regional'nye problemy vneshnei politiki*, ed. Yu.P. Davydov and V.S. Rudnev (Moscow: Nauka, 1971). p. 112.

67. See for example, S.S. Sergeichuk [Ivan'ko], *SShA i Kitai, isdanie vtoroe, dopolnenoe i ispravlennoe* (Moscow: Mezhdunarodnye Otnosheniia, 1973), p. 224.

68. O. Borisov [Rakhmanin] and B. Koloskov [Kulik], "Vneshniaia politika Pekina posle X S'ezda KPK," *Mezhdunarodnaia Zhizn'*, no. 6 (1974), in *OK*, no. 6 (1974), p. 189. Also see Oleg Vladimirov [Rakhmanin], "Sovremennyi etap ideologicheskoi bor'by protiv maoizma," *PDV*, no. 3 (1974), p. 133. In this article, Rakhmanin accused the Chinese of "collusion" (*sgovor*) with the imperialist camp.

69. For an official view, see unsigned article, "Maoistskii rezhim na novom etape," *Kommunist*, no. 12 (August 1975), p. 114 (in *OK*, no. 7).

70. Oleg Vladimirov [Rakhmanin], "Velikoderzhavnyi kurs Pekina," *Izvestiia*, September 10, 1975, in *OK*, no. 7, p. 158.

71. N. Kapchenko, "Maoism's Foreign Policy Platform," *IA*, no. 2 (1972), p. 37.

72. K. Titov, "Inostrannaia pechat' o vooruzhennikh sil Kitaia," (The foreign press on China's armed forces) *Voennaia Mysl'* (*VM*), no. 7 (1972), p. 80; V. Akimov, A. Pamer, "Inostrannaia pechat' o voenno-ekonomicheskikh prigotovleniiakh KNR," *VM*, no. 9 (1973), p. 78.

73. V. Zubarev, "Antimarksistskii avantiuristicheskii kharakter voennikh kontseptsii maoistov," *VM*, no. 5 (1969), p. 63; M. Milshtein, "O kharaktere voenno-strategicheskikh kontseptsii maoizma," *VM*, no. 2 (1972), p. 68.

74. V.P. Lukin, "Amerikano-Kitaiskie otnosheniia: Kontseptsii i deistvitel'nosti," *SShA*, no. 2 (February 1973), p. 22.

75. Boris Zanegin, "Kitai i Soedinennye Shtaty: Motivy i kharakter sblizheniia," *PDV*, no. 4 (1974), p. 64. This would become a common theme in Soviet analysis of Sino-American relations in the early 1980s.

76. Briefing materials, "Soviet Objectives at the Summit," pp. 2–3, in White House Special Files: Staff Member and Office File: Ronald Ziegler; Briefing Materials, 1971–74; Box 37.

77. Dobrynin, *In Confidence*, p. 259. Briefing materials prepared for the U.S.-Soviet summit in 1972 note that Soviet officials had warned their American counterparts repeatedly about the frustrations awaiting anyone expecting reasonable behavior from Beijing.

78. Ibid., p. 287.

79. Burr, ed., *The Kissinger Transcripts*, p. 131. Kissinger related this to Chinese diplomats at a May 1973 meeting.

80. According to a Soviet official, the Sino-American rapprochement in the early 1970s came about in response to the Chinese leadership's shift "to positions inimical to the Soviet Union and other socialist countries. As the trend developed, Washington evinced a growing desire for better relations with Peking." B. Koloskov [Kulik], "The Sino-American Talks," *New Times*, no. 11 (March 1972), p. 5.

81. See Gromyko's comments to Kissinger in January 1976 in Burr, ed., *The Kissinger Transcripts*, p. 467.

82. Brezhnev, "Speech to Anniversary Meeting of Kazakhstan Communist Party Central Committee and Kazakhstan Supreme Soviet," August 29, 1970, *Pravda*, pp. 1–2, in *CDSP*, vol. 22, no. 35, p. 7. For an analysis of Brezhnev's view of détente, see Robert Legvold, "Containment without Confrontation," *Foreign Policy*, Fall 1980, p. 84.

83. Brezhnev, "Speech to Anniversary," p. 10.

84. I. Alexeev and G. Apalin, "Peking's Ideological Subversion," *IA*, no. 10 (1975) (in *OK*, no. 7), p. 53; and G. Apalin, "Peking and the Third World," *IA*, no. 3 (1976), p.89.

85. I. Aleksandrov, "Politika Pekina—ugroza miru," *Pravda*, June 13, 1978, in *OK*, no. 9, p. 69, and Aleksandrov, "Pekin: kursom nagnetaniia napriazhennosti," *Pravda*, May 26, 1980, in *OK*, no. 10, p. 90.

86. Unsigned article, "Chto stoit za maoistskoi 'teoriei trekh mirov'," *Kommunist*, no. 17 (1978), p. 81.

87. Unsigned, "Pekin: Vchera—reserv imperializma, segodnia ego soiuznik," *Kommunist*, no. 4 (1979), p. 74.

88. "Record of the Main Content of A.A. Gromyko's Conversation with U.S. President J. Carter, September 23, 1977, Washington [excerpts dealing with China], Russian Foreign Ministry Archives, document available in translation courtesy of the National Security Archive, Washington, D.C.

89. Ambassador Anatolii Dobrynin, "Soviet-American Relations in the Contemporary Era," Political letter sent to the USSR Ministry of Foreign Affairs, July 27, 1978, TsKhSD, f. 89, d. 28, pp. 3–4. Document translated by the National Security Archive, Washington, D.C.

90. Ibid., p. 5.

91. Yuri Andropov, "Svodka iz SShA na 15 fevralia, 1979 goda," iz informatsionnogo otdela no.63936–kopii soobshchenii po SShA, tom no. 40 arkh. no. 109919, p. 1; document available courtesy of the National Security Archive, Washington, D.C.

92. I. A. Alekseev, "SSha-Kitai: raschety, manevry, problemy," *SShA*, no. 2 (1978), p. 26.

93. For an academic discussion, see, for example, Georgy Kim, "Détente and Social Progress," in *Soviet Oriental Studies Today*, part 1 (Social Sciences Today, 1980), p. 120.

94. When Kissinger proposed in November 1973 that the United States and China should set up a hotline, Zhou Enlai deferred the matter for further study. In Burr, ed., *The Kissinger Transcripts*, p. 210. The hotline agreement was not signed until 1998!

95. In a November 1974 meeting, for example, Deng Xiaoping appeared to be less than convinced by Kissinger's assurances that the United States would never agree to any Soviet efforts to include anti-Chinese language in agreements. In Burr, ed., *The Kissinger Transcripts*, p. 302.

96. I. Alexandrov, "Pekin: Kursom nagnetaniia napriazhennosti," *Pravda*, May 26, 1980, in *OK*, no. 10, p. 93.

97. M. Galin [Titarenko], "30 let KNR: nekotorye itogi i uroki," *Novoe Vremia*, no. 40 (1979), in *OK* no. 10, p. 260.

98. Burlatskii, *Mao Tse-dun i ego nasledniki* (Moscow: Mezhdunarodnye Otnosheniia, 1979), pp. 332–34, 337; and unsigned article in *PDV*, "30 let KNR," no. 3 (1979), p. 23.

NOTES TO CHAPTER 3

99. General-Mayor D. A. Volkogonov, "Militaristicheskii kharakter ideologii i politiki Pekina," *VM*, no. 1 (1978), p. 76; A.K. Mirenko, B.N. Gorbachev, "Nekotorye aspekty voennoi doktriny pekinskogo rukovodstva," *VM*, no. 6 (1978), p. 68; Polkovnik Iu.N. Petrov, "Sotsial'no-politicheskaia rol' armii Kitaia," *VM*, no. 10 (1978), p. 85; and G. Apalin, "Novyi etap ekspansionistskoi politiki Pekina," *VM*, no. 6 (1979), p. 76.

100. Jonathan D. Pollack, "Chinese Global Strategy and Soviet Power," *Problems of Communism*, January–February 1981, p. 64.

101. John Wilson Lewis, "China's Military Doctrines and Force Posture," in *China's Quest for Independence: Policy Evolution in the 1970s*, ed. Thomas Fingar (Boulder, Colo.: Westview Press, 1980), p. 158. Also see Angus M. Fraser, "Military Modernization in China," *Problems of Communism*, September–December 1979, p. 45.

102. Fraser, "Military Modernization in China," p. 40.

103. Kenneth Hunt, "Sino-Soviet Force Comparisons," in *China, the Soviet Union, and the West*, ed. Douglas T. Stuart and William T. Tow (Boulder, Colo.: Westview Press, 1982), pp. 110–11.

104. IISS, *The Military Balance, 1979*, p. 60

105. Francis J. Romance, "Modernization of China's Armed Forces," *Asian Survey*, no. 3 (1980), p. 309.

106. Fraser, "Military Modernization in China," pp. 47–49.

107. Romance, "Modernization of China's Armed Forces," pp. 306–10.

108. Interviews with General Anatolii Boliatko, May 27, 1993; Lev Deliusin, former consultant to the Central Committee, February 8, 1991. Konstantin Pleshakov attributed this view to the Soviet Union's "besieged fortress mentality," common to all totalitarian regimes; interview, June 28, 1991. According to former National Security Advisor Zbigniew Brzezinski, China's dismal performance in its war against Vietnam should have demonstrated to the Soviet Union that there was no reason to be fearful. Interview, January 27, 1993. On the other hand, a recently declassified CIA report argued just the opposite: "At worst, on the other hand, a future military clash remains quite conceivable in Soviet eyes, and particularly so in view of the February-March 1979 Chinese attack on the Soviet Union's Vietnamese ally." National Intelligence Estimate, "Sino-Soviet Relations in the Early 1980s," NIE/11/13–80, June 5, 1980, p. 5. This document was provided courtesy of the National Security Archive, Washington, D.C.

109. Unsigned, "Chto stoit," p. 111. Burlatskii noted, for example, that the United States was surprisingly receptive to the Chinese proposal to create an anti-Soviet alliance. See "Nasledniki Mao," *Novyi Mir*, no. 9 (1978), p. 76.

110. G. Apalin, "Peking, the West and Detente," *IA*, no. 2 (1979), p. 57; and V. Petukhov, "Chto ishchet Pekin v Evrope?" *Aziia i Afrika Segodnia*, no. 11 (1980), p. 30. According to Mikhail Galin [Titarenko], influential people like Henry Kissinger were growing concerned about the consequences of the Munich-like policies of the

Carter Administration. Mikhail Galin [Titarenko], "Peking's Travelling Salesman," *New Times*, no. 47 (1979), p. 15.

111. For an official view, see M. Sladkovskii and T. Rakhimov, "Veliko-kitaiskii shovinizm v deistvii," *Pravda*, February 16, 1979, in *OK*, no. 9, p. 205.

112. Borisov and Koloskov, *K 30–letiiu KNR* (Moscow: Znanie, 1979), p. 67.

113. Unsigned article, "30 let KNR," *PDV*, no. 3 (1979), p. 23 (also in *OK*, no. 10).

114. N. Kapchenko, "Beijing Policy," p. 41.

115. Unsigned, "Pekin: vchera," p. 71.

116. Dobrynin, *In Confidence*, p. 423.

117. V. Goncharov, "V ugodu mezhdunarodnoi reaktsii," *Pravda*, October 22, 1975, in *OK*, no. 7, p. 246. For an opposing view, stating that there was no difference between the two lines, see Zubakova, *Osnovnye Aspekty*, p. 220. For an account of the development of these two lines throughout the PRC's history, see Oleg Borisov [Rakhmanin], *Sovetskii Soiuz i Man'zhurskaia revoliutsionnaia baza* (Moscow: Mysl', 1975), pp. 16–29.

118. V. G. Gel'bras, "Izvrashchenie maoistami voprosov sotsialisticheskogo stroitel'stvo," *Narody Azii i Afriki*, no. 3 (1975), p. 33. Fedor Burlatskii made a similar point in "Ideologiia i vlast' v KNR," *Rabochii Klass i Sovremennyi Mir*, May–June 1976, p. 111.

119. Larev, "Priroda i korni Maoistkogo antisovietizma," *Voprosy Istorii*, in *OK*, no. 7, pp. 91–92.

120. Fedor M. Burlatskii, "Ideologiya i vlast' v KNR," *Rabochii Klass i Sovremennyi Mir*, no. 3, 1976, p. 100.

121. For example, in the rather hard-line *Osnovnye aspekty Kitaiskoi problemy*, the authors state: "For the first time in history, a country that embarked on the socialist path turned away from this path for internal reasons, began to pursue a policy of hostility and injury to the unity of socialist states and the world socialist system as a whole, and its leaders openly assumed the positions of the reactionary representatives of imperialism. Moreover, it is the first time that the Marxist movement was confronted by an opposing force which originated within its confines and has at its disposal the resources and capabilities of one the most populous states in the world." Zubakova, *Osnovnye aspekty*, p. 270.

122. Ibid., p. 272. Another Soviet analyst, Nikolai Kapchenko, explained that the struggle against Maoism is an effort to help the Chinese people see a clear socialist perspective, not to excommunicate the Chinese communists as a group. See Nikolai Kapchenko, *Antikommunisticheskaia sushchnost' ideologii i politiki Maoizma* (Moscow: Znanie, 1976), p. 4.

123. "O nekotorykh aktual'nykh voprosakh marksistskogo kitaevedeniia," *PDV*, no. 4 (1975), pp. 8–10.

124. O. Borisov, "Ocherednoi raund bor'by za vlast' v Pekine," *Partiinaia Zhizn'*

no. 7 (1980), in *OK*, no. 10, p. 294; and Y. Semenov, "China: The Crisis Continues," *IA*, no. 7 (1980), p. 25.

125. V. Lazarev has written most extensively on this point. See his *Klassovaia bor'ba*, pp. 283–97, and "Antimaoistskie dvizhenie," p. 100.

126. For an authoritative view, O. Borisov, "Avantiuristicheskaia politika Pekinskogo rezhima," *Partiynaia Zhizn'*, no. 3 (1979), in *OK*, no. 9, p. 132. For an academic discussion, see V. I. Lazarev, *Klassovaia bor'ba*, p. 242.

127. For an official view, see Borisov, "Ocherednoi raund," p. 299.

128. Burlatskii, *Mao Tsze-dun i ego nasledniki*, p. 230.

129. On the continuation of Maoism without Mao, see Gretchen Ann Sandles, "Soviet Images of the PRC, 1955–1979" (Ph.D. diss., University of Michigan, 1981), pp. 199–201. An unsigned article in *Kommunist* commented, for example, that clear criteria existed for determining whether the Chinese leadership had abandoned Maoism. Among these criteria, the authors included the attitude of the Chinese leaders towards Marxism-Leninism, their renunciation of antisocialist policies, and resumption of cooperation with socialist states.

130. Editorial, "Mirovoi sotsializm—glavnaia revoliutsionnaia sila nashei epokhi. K 30–letiiu SEV," *PDV*, no. 1 (1979), p. 13.

131. Borisov and Koloskov, *K-30–letiiu KNR*, p. 67.

132. Burlatskii, *Mao Tsze-dun i ego nasledniki*, p. 337. For similar views by authoritative commentators, see V. A. Vasil'ev, "Antimarksistskaia sushchnost' voennoi teorii i praktiki Maoizma," review of *Maoizm: Voennaia teoriia i praktika* (Institute of Military History of Ministry of Defense, 1978), in *PDV*, no. 4 (1978), p. 173. Most of the academic commentary, however, stressed that the Chinese reform program was not realistic given the PRC's economic capabilities. See, for example, V. I. Akimov and V. I. Potapov, "Ekonomika KNR v 1979 godu," *PDV*, no. 1 (1980), p. 46.

133. Interview with Andrei Denisov, June 4, 1991. Denisov served in the Soviet embassy in Beijing during Hua's rule.

134. Obshchii otdel, Protokol no. 57, biuro Khabarovskogo Kraikoma KPSS, November 17, 1972, "Ob organizatsionnykh i ideologicheskikh meropriiatiiakh vytekaiushchikh iz sovetsko-kitaiskikh otnoshenii," Gosudarstvennyi arkhiv Khabarovskogo Kraia (GAKK), f.p.-35, op. 100, d. 67, p. 48.

135. Telegram #1422, U.S. Consulate Hong Kong to U.S. Department of State, March 1969, SDCF.

136. Stenogramma sobraniia kraevogo i Khabarovskogo gorodskogo partiinogo aktiva, September 22, 1969, GAKK, f.p.-35, op. 96, d. 234, pp. 1–12. For an English translation, see "Soviet Reactions to the Sino-Soviet Border Rift. Introduction and Translations by Elizabeth Wishnick," *The Cold War International History Project Bulletin*, Winter 1995/1996, pp. 194–97.

137. Khabarovskii Kraevoi Kommitet, "Informatsiia ob oznakomlenii vybornogo

aktiva Khabarovskogo partiinoi organizatsii s Informatsiei TsK KPSS o poezdke sovetskoi partiino-pravitel'stvennoi delegatsii v Hanoi i besede t. Kosygina A.N. s Zhou
Enlai September 11, 1969," sent to the TsK KPSS, Otdel Organizatsionno-partiinoy
raboty, September 22, 1969, GAKK, f.p. 35, op. 96, d. 374, pp.16–20. For an English
translation, see "Soviet Reactions," cited in note 136.

138. Stenogramma, September 22, 1969, p. 9.

139. Ibid., p. 3.

140. Ibid., pp. 9, 11.

141. "Informatsiia," September 22, 1969, p. 19.

142. Obshchii otdel, Protokol 57, Biuro Khabarovskogo Kraikoma KPSS, "Ob
organizationnykh i ideologicheskikh meropriiatiiakh vytekaiushchikh iz sovetsko-
kitaiskikh otnoshenii," p. 8.

143. "Spravka ot V. Sal'nikova, glav otdel agitatsii i propagandy khabarovskogo
kraikoma k A.K. Chernomu, ob osushchestvlenii postanovlenii 17–ogo noiabria ob
organizatsii ideologiskikh meropriatiia v sviazi sovetsko-kitaiskikh otnoshenii,"
GAKK, f.p.-35, op. 100, d. 101, p. 115.

144. "Informatsiia ob otklikakh trudiashchikhsia Khabarovskogo Kraia na notu
MID Ministerstvu inostrannykh del KNR ot 13 avgusta 1969 goda," Report to TsK
KPSS, "Otdel Organizatsionno-partiinoi raboty," August 18, 1969, GAKK, f.p. 35, op.
96, d. 374, pp. 41–42.

145. Secretary of the Khabarovskii Krai Party Committee M.F. Gaychman's
report to the TsK KPSS, "Otdel Organizatsionno-partiinoi raboti," February 1, 1972,
GAKK, f. p35, op. 100, d. 4, p. 12.

146. "Informatsiia ob oznakomlenii kommunistov Khabarovskogo Kraia s informatsiei TsK KPSS 'O sovetskikh-kitaiskikh otnosheniiakh," sent to TsK KPSS Otdel
Organizatsionno-partiinoi raboty, December 29, 1972, GAKK, f.p. 35, op. 100, d. 106,
p. 7.

4 / LEADERSHIP CHANGE IN THE USSR
AND SINO-SOVIET RELATIONS, 1980–85

1. Anatolii Dobrynin reported that after the Chinese invasion, Brezhnev and Carter
exchanged messages on the hot line, then he himself was sent to ascertain from the
American president that there had been no secret agreements between the United
States and China regarding Vietnam. Dobrynin, *In Confidence* (New York: Random
House, 1995), p. 423.

2. On the struggle between Deng and Hua, see Richard Baum, *Burying Mao*
(Princeton, N.J.: Princeton University Press, 1994), chapters 4 and 5, passim.

3. Laszlo Ladany, *The Communist Party of China and Marxism, 1921–1985: A Self-
Portrait,* (Stanford, Calif.: Hoover Institution Press, 1988), pp. 413–14.

4. "Summary of Proceedings of the Second National Seminar on Contemporary Literature," *Wenyi Baijia [Cultural Professional]* no. 2 (December 20, 1979), pp. 254, in *FBIS* (PRC), April 14, 1980, p. C1.

5. Interview with a senior scholar, Harbin, July 23, 1996.

6. Deng Xiaoping, "The Present Tasks and the Situation before Us," in *Selected Works of Deng Xiaoping (1975–1982)* (Beijing: Foreign Languages Press, 1984), a translation of the Chinese edition published by the People's Publishing House in July 1983, p. 235.

7. Maurice Meisner, *The Deng Xiaoping Era* (New York: Hill and Wang, 1996), p. 156.

8. Alan J. Day, ed.. *China and the Soviet Union, 1949–84* (New York: Facts on File Publications, 1985), p. 138.

9. Xinhua in English, January 20, 1980, in *FBIS* (PRC), January 21, 1980, p. C1.

10. In his memoir, Kapitsa recounts that when he traveled to Beijing in the fall of 1980 as the guest of the ambassador, Central Committee officials accused him of "selling out to the Chinese." Mikhail Kapitsa, *Na raznykh paralleliakh: zapiski diplomata* (Moscow: Kniga i biznes, 1996), p. 111. Aleksei Brezhnev, a counselor to the Soviet embassy in Beijing, has the opposite recollection—of Kapitsa maintaining a hard line on China despite Foreign Ministry's interest in finding a more pragmatic basis for relations. If Central Committee officials accused Kapitsa of selling out, this was because he used to share their views. See Aleksei Brezhnev, *Kitai: Ternistyi put' k dobrososedtsvu* (Moscow: Mezhdunarodnye Otnoshnenii, 1998), pp. 231–33.

11. [Evgeniy Bazhanov], "Policy by Fiat," *Far Eastern Economic Review (FEER)*, June 11, 1992, p. 16.

12. Andropov had begun making his bid for power in late 1981 when he launched his campaign against corruption by refusing to drop the investigation of a case of stolen diamonds which implicated Brezhnev's daughter, Galina. Serge Petroff, *The Red Eminence* (Clifton: The Kingston Press, Inc., 1988), p. 200; and Zhores Medvedev, *Andropov* (Oxford: Basil Blackwell, 1983), p. 165.

13. Dobrynin, *In Confidence*, p. 215.

14. A. M. Aleksandrov-Agentov, *Ot Kollentai do Gorbacheva*, (Moscow: Mezhdurnarodnie Otnosheniia, 1994), pp. 270–73; Dobrynin, *In Confidence*, p. 519.

15. Dobrynin, *In Confidence*, p. 519.

16. Jonathan Steele and Eric Abraham, *Andropov in Power* (Garden City: Anchor Press, 1984), p. 67. Cherniaev recalls that he was less optimistic than Bovin and Arbatov about Andropov, considering the leader's "dark side" (i.e., his oppression of dissidents and his efforts to perpetuate the arms race and spread propaganda about imperialist intrigues). See Cherniaev, *Moia zhizn' i moe vremia* (Moscow: Mezhdunarodnie Otnosheniia, 1995), p. 447.

17. Fedor Burlatskii, "Posle Stalina," *Novyi Mir*, no. 10 (1988), p. 185.

18. *Pravda*, April 23, 1964, cited in Steele and Abraham, *Andropov in Power*, pp. 78–79. This contrasted with the speech by Suslov, in which the ideology secretary envisioned a prolonged struggle with the Chinese. See Steele and Abraham, *Andropov in Power*, p. 78.

19. Conversation with Sergei Goncharov, then a scholar at the Institute of the Far East, August 24, 1989. According to Zhores Medvedev, Brezhnev suffered a stroke on the plane back which left him unconscious for a few days and unable to speak for several weeks. Medvedev, *Andropov*, p. 9. On Gromyko's position, see Aleksandrov-Agentov, *Ot Kollentai do Gorbacheva*, pp. 172–73. Material on Andopov's influence comes from interviews with the former Soviet Ambassador to China, Oleg Troianovskii, January 6, 1993; and with Lev Deliusin, February 8, 1991.

20. Leonid Brezhnev, "Brezhnev speech at ceremony," Moscow Television Service, in *FBIS* (Soviet Union), March 25, 1982, Moscow television service, p. R7.

21. Cited in Day, *China and the Soviet Union*, p. 176.

22. I. Aleksandrov, "On Soviet-Chinese Relations," *International Affairs (IA)*, July 1982, pp. 16–19.

23. "Qian on Deng's Decision on Sino-USSR Ties," Xinhua, February 20, 1998, from *Renmin Ribao*, February 20, 1998, in *FBIS* (PRC), February 23, 1998 (on-line at http://www.fedworld.gov).

24. "Leonid Brezhnev Speaks at Ceremony in Baku," *Pravda*, September 17, 1982, in *Current Digest of the Soviet Press (CDSP)*, vol. 34 (October 27, 1982), p. 4.

25. Interviews with Oleg Troianovskii, January 6, 1993, and with Lev Deliusin, February 8, 1991.

26. Huang Hua also met with Gromyko during his visit. "Qian on Deng's Decision," and Medvedev, *Andropov*, p. 161.

27. Kapitsa, *Na raznykh paralleliakh*, p. 112.

28. They included Lev Deliusin, a prominent China expert and long-time critic of the Soviet policy of containing China. For detailed descriptions of the consultants, see Fedor Burlatskii, *Vozhdi i sovetniki* (Moscow: Izd. politicheskoi literaturoi, 1990), pp. 250–54.

29. Georgi Arbatov, *The System* (New York: Random House, 1992), p. 277.

30. See Arbatov's account of his own falling out with Andropov in December 1982 in *The System*, p. 281.

31. For analysis of Andropov's China policy, see Harry Gelman, "Andropov's Policy toward Asia," *Journal of Northeast Asian Studies,*" June 2, 1983, p. 10.

32. Meeting of the Politburo, May 31, 1983, Tsentr Khraneniia Sovremennykh Dokumentov (TsKhSD), f. 89, per. 42, d. 53, p. 4.

33. Ibid., p. 7.

34. Ibid., p. 8.

35. Ibid., p. 10. Nikolai Tikhonov replaced Aleksei Kosygin as prime minister in October 1980.

36. Ibid., p. 11. Viktor Grishin was the Moscow party secretary. In Kapitsa's account, when the Politburo Commission on China, Gosplan, and the Ministry of Foreign Trade worked out the details of Arkhipov's trip, Gromyko opposed it because he was irritated that he wasn't going himself. See Kapitsa, *Na raznykh paralleliakh,* p. 115.

37. Cited in Day, *China and the Soviet Union,* p. 183. Andrei Denisov mentioned this in an interview, June 4, 1991.

38. Yuri Andropov, "Yu. V. Andropov's Answers to Pravda Questions," *Pravda,* August 27, 1983, p. 1, in *FBIS* (Soviet Union) August 29, 1983, p. CC3; "Progress of Soviet-PRC Talks Viewed," *FBIS,* October 24, 1983, p. B1 (from Tanjug, Belgrade).

39. Day, *China and the Soviet Union,* p. 182.

40. Lawrence Sherwin, "Significant Developments in Sino-Soviet Relations Following Brezhnev's Death," Radio Liberty, 82/82, November 22, 1982, p. 1.

41. This theater includes forces in Mongolia which increased from 1 tank division and 2 motorized rifle divisions in 1981 to 2 tank and 3 motorized rifle divisions in 1985. These figures for 1981–85 come from IISS, *The Strategic Balance.*

42. Harry Gelman, "The Siberian Military Buildup," in *Siberia and the Soviet Far East,* ed. Rodger Swearingen (Stanford, Calif.: Hoover Institution Press, 1987), p. 212. Some in the military displayed little sensitivity to the possible impact of the deployment of SS-20s on Chinese perceptions of the Soviet threat. According to General Anatolii Boliatko, for example, "the Chinese also had nuclear missiles—their relative quality was not important." Interview, May 28, 1993.

43. Arbatov, *The System,* p. 205.

44. Interview with Evgenii Bazhanov, in *USSR-China in the Changing World* (Moscow: Novosti, 1989), pp. 70–71.

45. Comrades Brezhnev, Kosygin, Andropov, Gromyko, Kirilenko, Suslov, Tikhonov, Ustinov, Ponomarev, Rusakov, Zamiatin, Smirtiukov, "O provedenii dopolnitel'noi raboty v tseliakh protivodeistviia amerikano-kitaiskomu voennomu sotrudnichestvu," October 2, 1980, TsKhSD, f.89, op. 34, d. 10, p. 1.

46. I. Aleksandrov (pseudonym for Soviet leadership), "Eskalatsiia Bezrassudstva: Po povodu, vizita A. Kheiga [Haig] v Pekine," *Pravda,* July 27, 1981, in *Opasnyi Kurs (OK),* no. 11, p. 59.

47. Banning Garrett and Bonnie Glaser, "From Nixon to Reagan: China's Changing Role in American Strategy," in *Eagle Resurgent?* ed. Kenneth A. Oye, Robert J. Lieber, and Donald Rothchild (Boston: Little, Brown, & Co.), p. 275. China's trade status was changed to that of a friendly but nonallied country. This enabled the Chinese to purchase dual-use technology and defensive weapons. See Raymond Garthoff, *Détente and Confrontation* (Washington, D.C.: The Brookings Institution, 1985), p. 1040.

48. Robert S. Ross, *Negotiating Cooperation: The United States and China, 1969–1989* (Stanford, Calif.: Stanford University Press), pp. 180–83. Haig's visit also coincided with a policy review in China, which would culminate the following year in the proclamation of a new independent foreign policy. The reassessment of Chinese foreign policy goals reflected a reevaluation of the U.S.-Soviet balance of power, as well as concern about the danger for China of excessive dependence on the West. See Carol Lee Hamrin, "Competing 'Policy Packages' in Post-Mao China," *Asian Survey,* May 1984, p. 508.

49. Boris Zanegin contended that the Reagan Administration was willing to sell the PRC weapons in exchange for support for Washington's anti-Soviet strategy. See Boris Zanegin, "Kitaiskaia politika administratsii Reigana," *MEiMO,* no. 12 (1983), pp. 46–47. Vladimir Lukin argued, on the other hand, that the United States was using arms sales to ease tensions with China. See Lukin, "Relations between the US and China in the 1980s," *Asian Survey,* vol. 24, no. 11 (November 1984), p. 1155.

50. Garrett and Glaser, "From Nixon to Reagan," p. 280.

51. Iu. Semenov, "Beijing's Hegemonism and International Security," *IA,* July 1982, p. 20.

52. V. Laptev, "'Kitaiskii faktor' v politike amerikanskogo imperializma," *MEiMO,* no. 1 (1982), p. 29.

53. S. Olesin, "Sino-American Relations as Seen by US Political Scientists," *FEA,* no. 2 (1985), p. 134.

54. Zanegin, "Kitaiskaia politika," p. 51; and V. Petukhov and G. Ragulin, "US-PRC: Ties in the Military Sphere," *FEA,* no. 1 (1985), p. 53.

55. Editorial, "The Institute of Far Eastern Studies and Its Research into Problems of China's Social and Economic Development," *PDV,* no. 3 (1981), p. 35; and V. Matiaiev and V. Fetov, "China: Some Aspects of Domestic Development," *FEA,* no. 3 (1982), p. 40.

56. Harry Harding, *China's Second Revolution* (Washington, D.C.: The Brookings Institution, 1987), pp. 215–18.

57. John Frankenstein, "Military Cuts in China," *Problems of Communism,* July–August 1985, p. 60.

58. Colonel O.A. Krasutskii and Lieutenant-Colonel V.B. Timofeev, "Operativnaia i boevaia podgotoka sukhoputnykh voisk Kitaia," *VM,* no. 7 (July 1981), pp. 73–75; Major-General M.M. Mikhailov, "O nekotorykh tendentsiiakh v stroitel'stve vooruzhenykh sil Kitaia," *VM,* no. 3 (March 1982), pp. 70–73.

59. Colonel V.P. Starostin, "Voenno-vozdushnye sily Kitaia," (po materialam zarubezhnoi pechati), *VM,* no. 2 (February 1981), pp. 72–73.

60. Ibid., pp. 73–4.

61. Captain N.V. Georgiev, "Voenno-morskie sily Kitaia," *VM,* no. 4 (April 1981), p.70.

62. Ibid., p.75.

63. Mikhailov, "O nekotorykh tendentsiiakh," p. 70.

64. See Timothy Colton, *The Dilemma of Reform in the Soviet Union* (New York: Council on Foreign Relations, 1986), pp. 75–77; Ed A. Hewett, *Reforming the Soviet Economy* (Washington, D.C.: The Brookings Institution, 1988), pp. 260–73.

65. *Pravda,* October 1, 1983.

66. Cherniaev, *Moia zhizn' i moe vremia*, p. 16.

67. Konstantin Chernenko, "Chernenko Speaks to Moscow Constituents," *Pravda,* March 3, 1984, pp. 1–2, in *CDSP,* vol. 36 (March 28, 1984), p. 6.

68. Nayan Chanda, "The Deep Freeze," *Far Eastern Economic Review,* June 14, 1984, p. 46.

69. They also agreed to move beyond previous annual trade agreements and negotiate a long-term trade agreement for 1986–90, laying the foundations for long-term economic cooperation. John F. Burns, "Soviets to Modernize Chinese Industries," *The New York Times,* December 12, 1984, p. A3. Also in 1984, Sergei Tikhvinskii, a former Foreign Ministry official, led two delegations of the Soviet-Chinese friendship society on visits to China.

70. Zheng Weizhi, "Independence Is a Basic Concern," *Beijing Review,* January 7, 1985, p. 18.

71. TASS statement, January 25, 1985, in *CDSP,* vol. 37, no. 4, p. 5.

5 / PRESSURES FOR CONTINUITY AND CHANGE
IN SOVIET CHINA POLICY IN THE EARLY 1980S

1. Alan J. Day, ed., *China and the Soviet Union, 1949–84* (New York: Facts on File Publications, 1985), p. 186.

2. "Spravka o sostoianii prigranichnikh sviazei s kitaiskimi provintsiiami po linii mestnykh organizatsii Khabarovskogo Kraia," Report prepared by the Otdel Torgovli i Bytovogo Obsluzhivaniia Khabarovskogo Kraikoma KPSS for the TsK KPSS, Gosudarstvennyi Arkhiv Khabarovskogo Kraia (GAKK), fp.35, op. 111, d. 196, page 29.

3. Interview with a former high-ranking Heilongjiang provincial official, July 1996.

4. Sergei Goncharov, "Ot soiuza cherez vrazhdebnost'—k dobrososedstvu," *Literaturnaia Gazeta,* October 4, 1989, p. 14. Andrei Denisov, a former Central Committee official, noted that at the time Soviet policymakers were only prepared to take small steps to improve relations with China. "We considered that our position was a constant, and that others were either closer to it or farther away," said Denisov. Interview, June 4, 1991.

5. Gilbert Rozman, "Moscow's China-Watchers in the Post-Mao Era: The Response to a Changing China," *The China Quarterly,* June 1983, p. 239.

6. M.S. Ukraintsev, "Sovetsko-Kitaiskie otnosheniia: Problemy i perspektivy,"

Problemy Dal'nego Vostoka (*PDV*), no. 2 (1982), pp. 23–24; O.B. Borisov [Rakhmanin], "Polozhenie v KNR i nekotorye zadachi Sovetskogo kitaevedeniia," *PDV*, no. 2 (1982), p. 3. On the differences of views between Rakhmanin and Kapitsa, see Rozman, "Moscow's China Watchers," p. 228; and Chi Su, "Soviet China-Watchers' Influence on Soviet China Policy," *Journal of Northeast Asian Studies*, December 1983, pp. 44–45.

7. For Kapitsa's litany of complaints about Chinese policies in the early 1980s, see Mikhail Kapitsa, *Na raznykh paralleliakh: zapiski diplomata* (Moscow: Kniga i biznes, 1996), p. 108.

8. Anatolii Cherniaev, *Moia zhizn' i moe vremia* (Moscow: Mezhdunarodnie Otnosheniia, 1995), p. 448.

9. Ibid.

10. Interview with Konstantin Pleshakov, Institute of the USA and Canada, June 28, 1991. Also see Georgi Arbatov's account in *The System* (New York: Random House, 1977), p. 277.

11. "Bovin, Beglov on USSR Relations with PRC," "People and the World Program," special correspondent Bohumil Hirak's interview with Aleksandr Bovin of *Izvestiia* and Spartak Beglov of *Novosti*, Prague domestic service in Czech, May 2, 1984, in *FBIS* (Soviet Union), March 4, 1984, p. CC12.

12. Raymond Garthoff, *Détente and Confrontation* (Washington, D.C.: The Brookings Institution, 1985), pp. 1038–41.

13. *FBIS* (PRC), June 17, 1981, cited in Robert Sutter, "Realities of International Power and China's Independence," *Journal of Northeast Asian Studies*, no. 3 (1984), pp. 9–12.

14. Harry Harding, "China's Changing Roles in the Contemporary World," in *China's Foreign Relations in the 1980s*, ed. Harry Harding (New Haven: Yale University Press, 1984), p. 197.

15. Interviews with Andrei Denisov, Central Committee, June 4, 1991; Evgenii Bazhanov, Diplomatic Academy, June 5, 1991; Henry Trofimenko, Institute of the USA and Canada, May 2, 1991; and Boris Zanegin, Institute of the USA and Canada, June 3, 1991.

16. Garthoff, *Détente and Confrontation*, pp. 1042–43.

17. Interview, January 27, 1993.

18. Allen S. Whiting, "Soviet Policy toward China," in *Learning in US and Soviet Foreign Policy*, ed. George W. Breslauer and Philip E. Tetlock (Boulder, Colo: Westview Press, 1991), p. 539.

19. Comrades Brezhnev, Kosygin, Andropov, Gromyko, Kirilenko, Suslov, Tikhonov, Ustinov, Ponomarev, Rusakov, Zamiatin, Smirtiukov, "O provedenii dopolnitel'noi raboty v tseliakh protivodeistviia amerikano-kitaiskomu voennomu sotrudnichestvu," October 2, 1980, Tsentr Khraneniia Sovremennykh Dokumentov (TsKhSD), f.89, op. 34, d. 10, pp. 1–2.

20. A. Kruchinin, "Partnerstvo imperializma i pekinskogo gegemonizma—novaia ugroza miru," *Voennaia Mysl'* (*VM*), no. 5 (1981), p. 53. Kruchinin saw a danger not only from what he viewed as the American aim of upsetting the strategic balance, but also from the increased foreign policy adventurism of the United States and the PRC, the former playing the "China card" and the latter using the "imperialist trump." Kruchinin, p. 52.

21. "O provedenii dopolnitel'noi raboty," pp. 1–2.

22. Borisov [Rakhmanin], "Polozhenie v KNR," p. 377.

23. Evgenii Primakov, "Osvobodivshiesia strany v mezhdunarodnykh otnosheniiakh," *MEiMO*, no. 5 (1982), p. 8.

24. Harding, "China's Changing Roles," pp. 242–43.

25. For an example of an official view, see M. Sladkovskii, "The Role of Proletarian Internationalism in the CPC's Formation and Activity," *Far Eastern Affairs* (*FEA*), no. 3 (1981), p. 121. Academic writers and journalists also wrote about the Maoist legacy in Chinese foreign policy in 1981–82. See, for example, R. Aslanov and B. Bolotin, "The CPC Leadership: New Tacks in World Communist Movement," *FEA*, no. 4 (1981), p. 119.

26. O. Vladimirov [Rakhmanin], *Sovetsko-Kitaiskie otnosheniia* (Moscow: Mezhdunarodnye Otnoshenie, 1984), p. 336. Some academics at the USA and Canada Institute detected some important shifts in Chinese policies. See S. Olesin [Sergei Trush], "Sino-American Relations as seen by US Political Scientists," *FEA*, no. 2 (1985), p. 123; and Vladimir Lukin, "Relations between the US and China in the 1980s," *Asian Survey*, vol. 24, no. 11 (1984), p. 1154.

27. See comments by Aleksandr Bovin in discussion by Aleksandr Bovin and Vladimir Lukin, "Uzhe ne bil'iard, no eshche ne shakhmaty," in ed. Aleksandr Bovin, *Nachalo vos'midesiatykh* (Moskva: Izvestiia, 1984), pp. 103, 107.

28. See, for example, Unsigned article, "Proimperialisticheskaia politika Pekina," *PDV*, no. 1 (1981), p.25.

29. Evgenii Bazhanov, *Dvizhushchie sily politiki SShA v otnoshenii Kitaia* (Moscow: Nauka, 1982), pp. 212–18.

30. V. Petukhov and G. Ragulin, "SSha-KNR: Sviazi v voennoi oblasti," *PDV*, no. 4 (1984), pp. 50–51.

31. See, for example, I. Aleksandrov, "Eskalatsiia bezrassudstva," *OK*, no. 11, p. 59. A few academics and journalists shared this view. See, for example, I. Alexeev and F. Nikolaev, "PRC State Council Premier Visits the USA," *IA*, no. 4 (1984), p. 51.

32. In the last year of Brezhnev's rule, while Soviet analysts recognized that China was trying to emerge from the crisis brought about by Mao's policies, particularly the Cultural Revolution, they sharply criticized the Chinese reform program—the "Four Modernizations"—as an attempt to create a "special path," a Chinese variant

on socialist development. I. Aleksandrov, "K 60–letiiu kompartii Kitaia," *OK*, no. 11, p. 189; and V. Lazarev, "Kompartiia Kitaia," *OK*, no. 11, p. 255.

33. O. B. Borisov [Rakhmanin], *Vnutrennaia i vneshniaia politika Kitaia v 70e gody* (Moscow: Izd. Politicheskoi Literatury, 1982), p. 357.

34. Lev Deliusin, "KNR: Vosdeistvie vnutrennei politiki na vneshnepoliticheskuiu deatel'nost'," unpublished paper presented at a 1990 conference in Wisconsin.

35. V. Matiaev and V. Fetov, "Fourth Session of the PRC National People's Congress," *FEA*, no. 2 (1982), p. 28 and 35; and L. Gudoshnikov, "Pekin: Poisk vykhod iz krizisa," *Azia i Afrika Segodnia*, no. 3 (1981), p. 22.

36. "The Triumph of the Leninist Policy of Internationalism," *FEA*, no. 1 (1983), p. 1.

37. Anatolii Butenko, "Once More about the Contradictions of Socialism," *Voprosii Filosofii*, no. 2 (1984), pp. 124–29.

38. L. I. Brezhnev, "Iz doklada general'nogo sekretaria TsK KPSS . . . 'otchet tsentral'nogo komiteta KPSS XXVI s'ezdu . . . ,'" in *OK*, no 11, p. 3.

39. Iu. Semenov, "Vnutripoliticheskie i sotsial'nye problemy Kitaia," *Mezhdunarodnye Otnoshenie*, no. 3 (1981), in *OK*, no. 11, p. 304.

40. See A. Bovin, "Vashington-Pekin," *SShA*, no. 8 (1984), p. 22.

41. Interviews with Vilia Gel'bras, Institute of the International Workers' Movement, May 6, 1991; Aleksandr Bovin, then a political commentator at *Izvestiia*, June 24, 1991; Konstantin Pleshakov, Institute of the USA and Canada, June 28, 1991; and Iakov Berger, Institut Nauchnoi Informatsii po Obshchestvennym Naukam (INION), May 23, 1991. For an analysis of this debate, see Rozman, "Moscow's China-Watchers," pp. 257–75.

42. Rozman, "Moscow's China Watchers," pp. 215–41.

43. In his memoir, Burlatskii later explained that he chose the term "mezhdutsarstvie" or "interregnum" because he saw the Soviet Union, as well as China, experiencing a protracted succession struggle before a new leader would emerge who could ensure political stability. See Burlatskii, *Vozhdy i Sovetniki* (Moscow: Izdatel'stvo Politicheskoi Literatury, 1990), p. 354.

44. Fedor Burlatskii, "Mezhdutsarstvie, ili khronika vremen den siaopin," *Novyi Mir*, no. 4 (1982), pp. 205–28.

45. Burlatskii, *Vozhdy i Sovetniki*, p. 356.

46. S. Manezhev and L. Novoselova, "The Role of External Factors in China's Economic Development," *FEA*, no. 2 (1983), p. 45.

47. Iu. Konovalov and S. Manezhev, "Social and Economic Contradictions in China," *FEA*, no. 2 (1981), p. 36.

48. V. Novzybkov, "An Important Event in the PRC's Political Life," *FEA*, no. 4 (1983), p. 53.

49. V. Kurbatov, "Kitai: Problemy sel'skogo khoziaistva," *Aziia i Afrika Segodnia*, no. 12 (1984), p. 41.

50. Marc D. Zlotnik, "Chernenko's Platform," *Problems of Communism*, November–December 1982, p. 73; and Konstantin Chernenko, "The Leninist Strategy of Leadership: On Certain Questions of the Party's Activity Under the Conditions of Developed Socialism," *Kommunist*, no. 13, pp. 6–22. Cited in Zlotnik, p. 72.

51. Marc Zlotnik, "Rethinking Soviet Socialism: The Politics of Ideological Change," unpublished paper presented to the national conference of AAASS, Chicago, November 1989, pp. 8–12.

52. "Modernization, Economic Reform in China Viewed," from *International Panorama* program of Moscow television, presented by *Literaturnaia Gazeta* political observer Burlatskii, in *FBIS* (Soviet Union), August 6, 1985, pp. B1–2.

53. Ibid.

54. Iu. Riakin, "What Do Certain Debates Conceal?" *FEA*, no. 4 (1985), p. 87.

55. A. Kruglov, "Small-Scale Industry," *FEA*, no. 1 (1985), p. 79.

56. S. Ratnikov and D. Radikovskii, "The PRC Discusses Its Way of Development," *FEA*, no. 1 (1985), p. 116.

57. Heinz Timmermann, *The Decline of the World Communist Movement* (Boulder, Colo.: Westview Press, 1987), p. 100. By the Twelfth CCP Party Congress in 1982, the Chinese had developed a new conception of a communist movement without a leader, which would be governed by principles of independence, mutual respect, and noninterference. See Timmermann, p. 101.

58. Ibid., p. 108.

59. The Secretariat of the Soviet Central Committee held these meetings yearly. Protocols of the CPSU Central Committee Secretariat (Twenty-fourth and Twenty-fifth sessions), TsKhSD. According to Aleksandr Grigor'ev, director of the Center for Modern China at the Institute of the Far East, from the late 1960s through the early 1980s institute directors from the Soviet Union and the East European countries also met regularly to coordinate their research on China. Interview, June 24, 1993.

60. Central Committee of the CPSU, "Ob ukazaniiakh i sostave delegatsii KPSS na ocherednuiu vstrechu bratskikh partii po kitaiskomu voprosu v Varshave," May 19, 1980, p. 3; TsKhSD, f. 4, op. 24, d. 1268.

61. Stalin developed the distinction between antagonistic and non-antagonistic contradictions in the 1930s. According to Stalin, antagonistic contradictions exist between groups whose interests are mutually exclusive, as between workers and capitalists. Non-antagonistic contradictions may appear in societies where the interests of social groups coincide, as in socialist societies. See Ernst Kux, "Contradictions in Soviet Socialism," *Problems of Communism*, November–December 1984, p. 14.

62. For anlysis of this debate, see Elizabeth Teague, *Solidarity and the Soviet Worker* (London: Croom Helm, Ltd., 1988), pp. 294–320; and Kux, "Contradictions in Soviet Socialism," pp. 20–23.

63. P. Fedoseev, "The communists' social optimism," *Pravda*, November 13, 1981,

pp. 2–3, in *CDSP*, vol. 33, no. 46, p. 20. Also see R. Kosolapov, "Socialism and Contradictions," *Pravda*, July 20, 1984, pp. 2–3, in *CDSP*, vol. 36, no. 29, p. 20.

64. Kosolapov, "Socialism and contradictions," p. 21.

65. Teague, *Solidarity and the Soviet Worker*, pp. 300–301.

66. Butenko, "Once More about the Contradictions of Socialism," pp. 6–7.

67. E. A. Ambartsumov, "Analiz V.I. Leninym prichin krizisa 1921 g. i putei vykhoda is nego," *Voprosy Istorii*, no. 4 (1984), pp. 15–29.

68. "K 60–letiiu obrazovanie kompartii Kitaia," *Kommunist*, no. 9 (1981), in *OK*, no. 11, p. 14.

69. O. Borisov [Rakhmanin], "Soiuz novogo typa," *Voprosy Istorii KPSS*, April 1984, p. 45.

70. Joan Barth Urban, *Moscow and the Italian Communist Party* (Ithaca, N.Y.: Cornell University Press, 1986), pp. 315–21. Unlike the PCI, however, the Chinese leadership did not support Solidarity, fearing the development of a workers' movement in China. Gilbert Rozman noted some evidence that Deng Xiaoping favored a neutral attitude toward Solidarity rather than a hostile approach. See Rozman, *The Chinese Debate about Soviet Socialism, 1979–85* (Princeton, N.J.: Princeton University Press, 1987), p. 359.

71. Urban, *Moscow and the Italian Communist Party*, p. 323.

72. Ibid., p. 338.

73. Cherniaev, *Moia zhizn' i moe vremia*, p. 20.

74. Bazhanov, *Kitai i vneshnii mir*, pp. 165–67.

6 / FROM RAPPROCHEMENT TO NORMALIZATION

1. Allen S. Whiting comes to a similar conclusion in "Soviet Policy toward China, 1969–1988," in *Learning in U.S. and Soviet Foreign Policy*, ed. George W. Breslauer and Philip E. Tetlock (Boulder, Colo.: Westview Press, 1991), p. 543.

2. I describe these changes in greater detail in "Soviet and Post-Soviet Approaches to World Order," in *Old Nations, New World*, ed. David Jacobsen (Boulder, Colo.: Westview Press, 1994), pp. 173–83.

3. These included the assumption of the inevitable hostility between socialist and capitalist states, the conception of a hierarchical communist movement, and rigid concepts of socialist development.

4. According to a French press report, Gorbachev joked during his meeting with Deng at the Beijing summit that the three obstacles to the normalization of Soviet-Chinese relations were eliminated at the rate of one per year since 1985, a remark that is not far from the truth. Agence France-Presse, May 16, 1989, in *FBIS* (PRC), May 16, 1989, p. 20.

5. Evgenii Bazhanov's remarks in *USSR-China in a Changing World* (Moscow: Novosti, 1989), p. 71.

6. Gorbachev, "Rech' Gorbacheva M.S. na torzhestvennom sobranii, posviashchennom vriucheniu Vladivostoka ordena Lenina" (Vladivostok speech), *Pravda*, July 29, 1986, pp. 1–3. Although Gorbachev did not provide specific figures for Mongolia in the Vladivostok speech, by the following spring the Soviets had removed one motorized rifle division, or 13,000 men, from the country. See Dan L. Strode, "Soviet China Policy in Flux," *Survival*, July/August 1988, p. 339. At the Beijing summit, Gorbachev announced that the Soviet Union would withdraw 75 percent of the remaining forces (approximately 50,000 men), and the last contingents were removed by the end of 1992.

7. The Chinese position was based on the Talweg principle.

8. Anatolii Cherniaev, *Shest' let s Gorbachevym* (Moscow: Progress Publishers, 1993), p. 36. Karen Brutents explains that the Politburo commissions were geared to responding to crises, and were not as effective in managing day-to-day foreign policy issues. Karen Brutents, *Tridsat' let na Staroi Ploshchadi* (Moscow: Mezhdunarodnye Otnosheniia, 1998), p. 172.

9. Archie Brown, *The Gorbachev Factor* (Oxford: Oxford University Press, 1996), p. 229. Sokolov was later replaced by Dmitrii Yazov, who at the time appeared loyal to Gorbachev, as did the new head of the KGB, Vladimir Kriuchkov. By 1991, however, both Yazov and Kriuchkov had turned against Gorbachev and proved instrumental in the August coup attempt.

10. The transfer of the former Soviet ambassador to the United States to this new position reportedly amazed President Reagan, who asked "Is he really a communist?" Anatoly Dobrynin, *In Confidence* (New York: Random House, 1995), p. 600.

11. Brutents, *Tridsat' let na Staroi Ploshchadi*, pp. 169–71. This led to competition between the International Department and the Ministry of Foreign Affairs.

12. The appointment of such an experienced diplomat, who traveled to China in the 1950s as a Foreign Ministry official and served subsequently as ambassador to Japan, signified the importance that the Soviet leadership attached to the improvement of relations with China.

13. [Evgenii Bazhanov], "Policy by Fiat. Inside Story: Kremlin Twisted Its Facts on China," *Far Eastern Economic Review* (*FEER*), June 11, 1992, p. 17.

14. Anatolii Cherniaev, *Moia zhizn' i moe vremia* (Moscow: Mezhdunarodnye Otnosheniia, 1995), p. 50.

15. Ibid., pp. 16–17. Cherniaev made similar allegations, claiming that Rakhmanin had been pursuing his "own" China policy contrary to the interests of the Central Committee and the Soviet state. See ibid., p. 51.

16. [Bazhanov], "Policy by Fiat," p. 17.

17. Ibid.

18. While Rakhmanin was still at the Liaison Department, Shakhnazarov had nothing to do with ideological questions concerning China. Conversation with Evgenii Bazhanov, June 11, 1993.

19. The Liaison Department was eventually abolished in mid-1988, and a China section was then incorporated into the Central Committee's International Department. According to Charles Gati, the abolition of the Liaison Department was an indication of the Gorbachev leadership's commitment to new thinking. See Gati, *The Bloc That Failed* (Bloomington: Indiana University Press, 1990), p. 164.

20. Igor' Rogachev played an active role in the Sino-Soviet reconciliation and the promotion of Soviet initiatives in Asia. Conversation with Evgenii Bazhanov, June 11, 1993. Rogachev is now the Russian ambassador to China.

21. Gilbert Rozman, "Moscow's China-Watchers in the Post-Mao Era: The Response to a Changing China," *The China Quarterly*, no. 94 (1983), pp. 215–41.

22. While Kapitsa claimed he supported an improvement of relations with China and played a role in drafting the Vladivostok speech, he often downplayed the significance of the three obstacles, much to the irritation of the Chinese side. In effect, Kapitsa supported the oft-stated Soviet position that normalization should be pursued first. According to this logic, an improvement in political relations would lead the three obstacles to fall away of their own accord. See Mikhail Kapitsa, *Na raznykh paralleliakh: Zapiski diplomata* (Moscow: Kniga i biznes, 1996), p. 113.

23. Moscow Television, "International Panorama," presented by Vladimir Shishlin; interview with Aleksandr Yakovlev by Novosti correspondent Stanislav Polizkov, May 21, 1989, in *FBIS* (Soviet Union), May 22, 1989, pp. 17–18.

24. Strode, "Soviet China Policy in Flux," p. 336.

25. Bill Keller, "Moscow Says Afghan Role Was Illegal and Immoral; Admits Breaking Arms Pact," *New York Times*, October 24, 1989, p. A1.

26. In a December 1988 speech to the United Nations, Gorbachev announced that the Soviet Armed Forces would be reduced by 200,000 men, more than half of whom were based in the Far East.

27. Mikhail Gorbachev, "Interview with Liaowang," *Far Eastern Affairs (FEA)*, no. 3 (1988), p. 5.

28. Subsequently the Soviets urged the Vietnamese to speed up their withdrawal, which actually was completed in September 1989. Nayan Chanda, "Summit in the Offing," *FEER*, October 13, 1988, pp. 17–18.

29. For trade figures, see *PlanEcon Report*, vol. 7, nos. 18–19 (1991), p. 9; and Robert Delfs, "Trade on Track," *FEER*, May 25, 1989, p. 14.

30. Sino-Soviet border trade reached approximately $800 million in 1988. Lowell Dittmer, *Sino-Soviet Normalization and Its International Implications, 1945–90* (Seattle: University of Washington Press, 1992), p. 86.

31. "Protokol No. 44, Zasedanie biuro Khabarovskogo Kraikoma KPSS," October 13, 1987, Gosudarstvennyi Arkhiv Khabarovskogo Kraia (GAKK), f.p. 35, op. 115, del. 41, p. 86.

32. Delfs, "Trade on Track," p. 14; and Sergei Tsyplakov, "Great Friends Again," *Business in the USSR*, July–August 1990, p. 48.

33. M.S. Gorbachev, "Inter'viu Kitaiskomu Televideniu," *Izvestiia*, May 18, 1989, p. 1; "Sino-Soviet Talks on 400 Cooperative Projects," *Zhongguo Tongxun She* (Hong Kong), May 15, 1989, in *FBIS* (PRC), May 17, 1989, p. 35.

34. Delfs, "Trade on Track," p. 15.

35. See Eduard Shevardnadze's comments on Sino-Soviet economic cooperation in "Panorama of International Life—USSR-PRC: Good Prospects," *Izvestiia*, May 16, 1990, p. 4, in *FBIS* (Soviet Union), May 16, 1990, p. 17.

36. "Excerpts from the 2 Presidents' Remarks at Opening Banquet," *The New York Times*, May 16, 1989, p. A12.

37. Jonathan Pollack, "Gorbachev in Peking," *FEER*, June 1, 1989, p. 22.

38. Wang Gangyi, "Deng-Gorbachev Meeting," *China Daily* (Beijing), May 17, 1989, in *FBIS* (PRC), May 17, 1989, p. 10.

39. Ibid.

40. TASS, "Beseda M.S. Gorbachev s Den Siaopinom," *Izvestiia*, May 16, 1989, p. 1.

41. Antonio Kamiya, "Deng, Gorbachev Fail to Agree on Cambodia," Kyodo (Tokyo), May 16, 1989, in *FBIS* (PRC), May 16, 1989, p. 21.

42. "In Meeting with Gorbachev, Zhao Ziyang Says that Relations with the Chinese and Soviet Parties Will Be Based on Four Principles," *Renmin Ribao* (Beijing), May 17, 1989, p. 1, in *FBIS* (PRC), May 17, 1989, p. 16; and TASS, "Beseda s Chzhao Tszyianom (Zhao Ziyang)," *Pravda*, May 17, 1989, p. 3.

43. "Sino-Soviet Joint Communiqué," in *Visit of Mikhail Gorbachev to China, May 15–18, 1989* (Moscow: Novosti, 1989), p. 61.

44. Captain First Rank V. Kuzar, "For the Good of All Mankind. Our Special Correspondent Reports from the PRC," *Krasnaia Zvezda*, May 19, 1989, p. 3, in *FBIS* (Soviet Union), May 19, 1989, p. 26.

45. Yurii Bandura, "Entering the third stage: Notes on the Sino-Soviet Summit," *Moscow News*, no. 22 (June 4, 1989), p. 5.

46. Gorbachev was so impressed by the warm welcome by the students that he concluded that he was right to go ahead with the summit, against the advice of some comrades who suggested its postponement due to the demonstrations. Mikhail Gorbachev, *Memoirs* (New York: Doubleday, 1995), p. 492. Kapitsa was one of those "comrades" calling for a postponement. See Kapitsa, *Na raznykh paralleliakh*, p. 118.

47. Pavel Palazchenko, *My Years with Gorbachev and Shevardnadze* (University Park: Pennsylvania State University Press, 1997), p. 135.

48. Cited in Robert Delfs, "One Stage, Two Plays," *FEER*, May 25, 1989, p. 12.

49. Agence France-Presse, May 17, 1989, in *FBIS* (Soviet Union), May 17, 1989, p. 30.

50. "Mikhail Gorbachev's Interview to China Central Television and to Radio Beijing," *Visit of Mikhail Gorbachev to China*, p. 27.

51. Palazchenko, *My Years with Gorbachev and Shevardnadze*, p. 136.

52. "Gorbachev Expresses Regret on China Strife," *The New York Times*, June 16, 1989, p. A9.

53. See Gorbachev's answers to questions after his speech at the Sorbonne, Moscow television, July 5, 1989, in *FBIS* (Soviet Union), July 7, 1989, p. 37.

54. "Vystuplenie M.S. Gorbacheva," (Gorbachev's speech to the Supreme Soviet), *Pravda*, August 2, 1989, pp. 1–2.

55. Palazchenko, *My Years with Gorbachev and Shevardnadze*, pp. 137–38.

56. Andrei Sakharov, "A Speech to the People's Congress," *The New York Review of Books*, August 17, 1989, p. 26.

57. "Vystuplenie M.S. Gorbacheva."

58. See, for example, Oleg Bogomolov, "Meniaiushchiisia oblik sotsializma," *Kommunist*, July 1989, p. 34. 59. Aleksei Iziumov and Andrey Kortunov, "Diplomacy and Morals in Perestroika," *Moscow News* no. 32 (1989), p. 6; and Vladimir Lukin, "On Diplomacy, Sermons, and Sense of Proportion," *Moscow News*, no. 33 (1989), p. 7.

60. See, for example, Igor Kliamkin, "What Lies Ahead?" *Moscow News*, no. 27 (1989), pp. 12–13.

61. Vsevolod Ovchinnikov, "Journalist's Notes: Turning a Tragic Page," *Pravda*, June 8, 1989, p. 5, in *FBIS* (Soviet Union), p. 8.

62. Gorbachev, *Memoirs*, p. 494.

63. Yurii Tavrovskii, "Kitai: Dukhovnye Korni Krizisa," *Literaturnaia Gazeta*, July 5, 1989, p. 14.

64. Sergei Goncharov, "After Tiananmen," *Moscow News*, no. 28 (1989), p. 6.

7 / THE GORBACHEV REVOLUTION AND CHINA POLICY

1. Eduard Shevardnadze, "Lecture," *Vestnik Ministerstva inostrannykh del SSSR*, August 15, 1988, p. 32.

2. For general discussion of these changes in Soviet foreign policy, see Robert Legvold, "The Revolution in Gorbachev's Foreign Policy," *Foreign Affairs: America and the World 1988/89*, pp. 82–98; Allen Lynch, "Gorbachev's International Outlook: Intellectual Origins and Political Consequences," Institute for East-West Security Studies, Occasional Paper No. 9, 1989; Cynthia Roberts and Elizabeth Wishnick, "Ideology Is Dead! Long Live Ideology?" *Problems of Communism*, November-

December 1989, pp. 57–69; and Stephen Shenfield, *The Nuclear Predicament* (New York: Methuen, 1987).

3. The change in the overall Soviet approach to international affairs affected analyses of Chinese foreign policy. See Vladimir Lukin and Aleksandr Nagornii, "Kontseptsiia 'treugol'nika' SSSR-SShA-KNR' i novye real'nosti mirovoi politiki," *SShA*, no. 6 (1988), p. 13.

4. See Evgenii Bazhanov, "Shifts of Emphases," *New Times* (*NT*), no. 17 (1988), p. 28; and Lukin and Nagornii, "Kontseptsiia 'treugol'nika,'" p. 7.

5. See, for example, A. G. Larin, "Kitaisko-amerikanskie otnoshenie v meniaiushchemsia mire," *Problemy Dal'nego Vostoka*, (*PDV*), no. 2 (1989), p. 50.

6. Editorial, "Moskva-Pekin: potentsial sotrudnichestva," *PDV*, no. 2 (1989), p. 5.

7. Bazhanov, "The Arduous Path of Socialism," *NT*, no. 40 (1989), p. 21.

8. Interview with Zbigniew Brzezinski, January 27, 1993.

9. Evgenii Bazhanov, "Novoe Myshlenie s kitaiskoi spetsifikoi," *Novoe Vremia. Kitai meniaiushchiisia na glazakh: Desiat' let po puti reform*, April (1989), p. 2–3.

10. B. Zanegin, "US Strategy in the Asian Pacific Region," *Far Eastern Affairs* (*FEA*), no. 6 (1988), pp. 19–20.

11. A. G. Larin, "Kitaisko-amerikanskie otnosheniia," p. 51.

12. Alexander Nagornii and Sergei Tsyplakov, "The PRC: The First Decade of the Policy of Reforms," *International Affairs* (*IA*), no. 1 (1989), p. 29.

13. This involved $100 million for equipment and technical help to modernize a large-caliber artillery plant. "US Reported Close to Arms Sale To China to Modernize Air Force," *The New York Times* (*NYT*), January 25, 1986. In the following year, the United States and China agreed on a major transaction, worth $500 million, to modernize the electronics systems on Chinese F-8 fighters. Other purchases in 1986 included the sale of four MK-46 torpedoes costing $8.5 million and four artillery-locating radar sets valued at $62.5 million. Bernard Weinraub, "President Spurns Other Sanctions," *NYT*, June 6, 1989, p. A15. Deliveries of these items had not been completed by June 4 (1989), when they were suspended in response to the Beijing massacre.

14. John H. Cushman, Jr., "Courting the Chinese with Military Flowers and Candy," *NYT*, November 2, 1986.

15. Richard Halloran, "Secret Is Out on Listing China as Hostile Country," *NYT*, January 25, 1988.

16. According to Evgenii Bazhanov, Oleg Rakhmanin and Vadim Medvedev, the new ideology secretary, were very concerned about Sino-American military cooperation during the latter half of the 1980s. Interview with Evgenii Bazhanov, June 5, 1991.

17. L.M. Gudoshnikov, "Politicheskie reformy v SSSR i KNR (opyt sravnitel'nogo analiza)," *PDV* no. 1 (1989), p. 77. Gel'bras argued that comparisons were not sufficiently analytical and that further research was necessary. See V. Gel'bras, "Impuls dlia razmyshlenii i nadezhd," *Aziia i Afrika Segodnia*, no. 9 (1988), p. 2.

18. M. Titarenko, "The USSR and China: For the Further Development of Cooperation," *Izvestiia*, September 26, 1987, p. 6, in *Current Digest of the Soviet Press (CDSP)*, vol 39, no. 39, p. 8. In an editorial in *Problemy Dal'nego Vostoka* in 1989, however, Sergei Goncharov outlined the official view—what mattered was that the Soviet Union and China had finally attained the same stage of domestic development: both were absorbed with the problems of economic reform and could help each other. In addition, the "synchronization" of their domestic processes made it easier for the two states to understand and predict each other's behavior. "Moskva-Pekin," p. 9. On the lack of synchronization of reform in the USSR and the PRC as a cause of previous conflicts, also see K. Pleshakov and D. Furman, "Obshchee i osobennoe v sotsial'no-politicheskom i ideologicheskom razvitii KNR i SSSR," *MEiMO*, December 1988, p. 35.

19. O. Bogomolov, "Meniaiushchiisia oblik sotsializma," *Kommunist*, July 1989, p. 36.

20. L. Deliusin, "Osobennosti stroitel'stva sotsializma v Kitae," *Aziia i Afrika Segodnia*, no. 12 (1988), p. 10; V.G. Gel'bras, "Khoziaistvennaia reforma v KNR i diskussiia po problemam sobstvennosti na sredstva proizvodstva," *Rabochii Klass i Sovremennyi Mir*, no. 2, March–April 1988, p. 58.

21. Vsevolod Ovchinnikov, "Commentator's Column: Positive Process," *Pravda*, June 20, 1987, p. 5, in *CDSP*, vol. 39, no. 25, pp. 15–16.

22. Bazhanov, "The Arduous Path," p. 22.

23. *Far Eastern Affairs (FEA)* is the English translation of this journal. See, for example, Wang Jiye, "On the PRC Economic Reforms," *FEA*, no. 3 (1986), pp. 70–72; Hu Seng, "Why China Cannot Turn Capitalist," *FEA*, no. 6 (1987), pp. 90–102; O. Artemeva, "The Chinese Press on the Socio-Political Aspect of Perestroika in the USSR," *FEA*, no. 2 (1988), pp. 61–71. Also see the interview with the *Renmin Ribao* editor, Tan Wenzhi, *Novoe Vremia*, no. 16 (April 14, 1989), p. 32.

24. See Aleksei Iziumov, "Kitai: Puti reformy," *Sel'skaia zhizn'*, September 4, 1987, p. 3; Aleksei Iziumov, "Kitaiskii variant," *Znamia*, no. 3 (March 1988), p. 202.

25. For example, L.S. Vasil'ev, "Izuchenie vostoka i problemy perestoiki," *Narody Azii i Afriki*, no. 3 (1989), pp. 49–66; Ia. Shishkov, "Public Ownership: Correcting a Historical Mistake," *FEA*, no. 5 (1989), pp. 105–11.

26. Lev Deliusin, "Osobennosti Stroitel'stva Sotsializma v Kitae," p. 14. For an account of the problems of superimposing old and new economic structures and methods, see the round-table discussion, "Opyt khoziaistvennykh preobrazovanii," *Rabochii Klass i Sovremennyi Mir*, no. 2 (March–April 1989), pp. 44–66 (includes V. Gel'bras, L.P. Deliusin, E.S. Kul'pin, Iu. S. Markhashev, G.A. Abramov). According to Iakov Berger, there were three impediments to reform: the feudal legacy, the fear of capitalist influence, and backwardness. Ia. M. Berger, *Sotsial'nye protsessy v sovremennoi kitaiskoi derevne* (Moskva: Nauka, 1989), p. 9.

27. Fedor Burlatskii, "Kitai na puti reform," *Kommunist*, December 1987, p. 117.

28. Lev Deliusin, "10 let po puti reform," *Argumenty i Fakty*, May 13–19, 1989, p. 2.

29. This was attributed to two factors: (1) Gorbachev's effort to promote many of the same reform measures that China had implemented and (2) the realization that the reform program in China presented a comprehensive theoretical challenge to existing beliefs about the nature of economic development in a socialist society. See V. Avremov, "Changes in the System of Planning in China," *FEA*, no. 4 (1986), pp. 57–61.

30. See *Pravda*, April 5, 1988. Nina Andreeva wrote an article criticizing Gorbachev's reform program and his departures from ideological orthodoxy.

31. Fedor Burlatskii, "Kakoi sotsializm narodu nuzhen," *Literaturnaia Gazeta*, April 20, 1988, p. 2.; L. Deliusin, "Osobennosti stroitel'stva sotsializma v Kitae," p. 13.

32. *Kto Kogo* literally means "who whom" and was often used by Soviets to ask who will come out on top. Lenin came up with the phrase as a way of asking whether capitalist or proletarian elements would emerge victorious in the struggle. V. Gel'bras, "Rol' kompartii Kitaia v reshenii problem obshchestvennogo razvitiia," *Aziia i Afrika Segodnia*, no. 5 (1988), p. 14. For a discussion of *kto kogo*, see Wolfgang Leonhard, *Three Faces of Marxism* (New York: Holt, Rinehart, and Winston, 1970), p. 72.

33. For example, Gel'bras, "Rol' kompartii," pp. 14–16.

34. M.S. Gorbachev, "Politicheskii doklad tsentral'nogo komiteta KPSS XXVII s'ezdu kommunisticheskogo partii sovetskogo soiuza," *Izbrannye rechi i stat'i*, tom 3, pp. 185, 253.

35. V. Medvedev, "K poznaniiu sotsializma," *Kommunist*, no. 17 (November 1988), p. 7.

36. M.S. Gorbachev, "Speech at the UN Organization," *Pravda*, December 8, 1988, pp. 1–2, in *FBIS* (Soviet Union), December 8, 1988, p. 13. Still, at least according to one highly placed Chinese academic observer, this did not mean that the Soviet Union would relinquish entirely its leading role in the socialist community. In Song Yimin's account, for example, Gorbachev persuaded the GDR leader, Erich Honecker, not to normalize relations before the Soviet Union had done so. Song Yimin, "Sino-Russian, Russian-US, Sino-US Relations and Interaction among the Three," unpublished paper, 1997, p. 15.

37. M.S. Gorbachev, "Politicheskii goklad," p. 255. Also see M.S. Gorbachev, "Rech' na mitinge chekhoslovatsko-sovetskoi druzhby," April 10, 1987, *Izbrannye rech'i*, tom 4, p. 479.

38. Anatolii Adamishin, "Humanity's Common Destiny," *IA*, February 1989, p. 7.

39. "Rech' M.S. Gorbacheva" (speech at official dinner hosted by the Yugoslav Presidium, March 15, 1988), *Vizit general'nogo sekretaria M.S. Gorbacheva v Sotsialisticheskuiu Federativnuiu Respubliku Iugoslaviiu*, p. 30.

40. V.P. Gagnon, Jr., "Gorbachev and Yugoslavia: A New Era of Socialist

Internationalism," unpublished paper presented to Trilateral Student Conference, May 5, 1990, pp. 12–18.

41. Interview with Oleg Troianovskii, January 6, 1993; interview with Evgenii Bazhanov, June 5, 1991.

42. "Sino-Soviet Joint Communiqué," in *Visit of Mikhail Gorbachev to China, May 15–18, 1989* (Moscow: Novosti, 1989), pp. 60–61.

43. "In Meeting with Gorbachev, Zhao Ziyang Says that Relations with the Chinese and Soviet Parties Will Be Based on Four Principles," *Renmin Ribao* (Beijing), May 17, 1989, p. 1, in *FBIS* (PRC), May 17, 1989, p. 16; and TASS, "Beseda s Chzao Tszyianom (Zhao Ziyang)," *Pravda*, May 17, 1989, p. 3.

44. Robert Sutter, "Changes in the Soviet Union and Eastern Europe: The Effects on China," *Journal of Northeast Asian Studies*, Summer 1990, p. 34.

45. Nicholas D. Kristof, "Diplomats Report China's Premier Will Visit Soviet Union in April," *NYT*, February 2, 1990, p. A8. According to a Hong Kong press report, Jiang Zemin accused Gorbachev of being "of the ilk of Karl Kautsky of the 2nd International, as he has betrayed the international communist movement and the communist party. He just cannot shirk responsibility for the current deteriorating situation in Eastern Europe." *Chen Ming* (Hong Kong), January 1, 1990, pp. 6–8, in *FBIS* (PRC), January 16, 1990, pp. 1–3.

46. Bill Keller, "Li Peng Says Soviet Ideas of Change Do Not Apply to China," *NYT*, April 26, 1990, p. A8.

47. Interviews with Boris Zanegin, June 3, 1991; Evgenii Bazhanov, June 5, 1991; Konstantin Pleshakov, June 28, 1991; Evgenii Bazhanov, June 10, 1993; and Nail Akhmetshin, Institute of State and Law, June 7, 1991.

48. Radio Moscow in Mandarin to Southeast Asia, April 27, 1990, in *FBIS* (Soviet Union), April 30, 1990, p. 12.

49. Tai Ming Cheung, "More Punch for the PLA," *Far Eastern Economic Review* (*FEER*), April 11, 1991, p. 18.

50. Interfax, June 28, 1991, in *FBIS* (Soviet Union), July 1, 1991, p. 5.

51. Yurii Starostenko, "Have We Missed the Caboose?" *NT*, no. 31 (1990), pp. 16–17.

52. ITAR-TASS, March 5, 1992, in *FBIS* (Central Eurasia), March 6, 1992, p. 15. ITAR-TASS, March 6 and March 9, 1992, in *FBIS* (Central Eurasia), March 10, 1992, pp. 13–14; Jeff Lilley, "Russian Handicap," in *FEER*, November 26, 1992, p. 24.

53. Xinhua, July 6, 1991 in *FBIS* (PRC), July 8, 1991, pp. 5–6.

54. For a discussion of other problems with barter trade, see Starostenko, "Have We Missed the Caboose?" p. 17.

55. See for example, "Protokol No. 33 zasedaniia sekretariata TsK KPSS, October 17, 1985," Gosudarstvennyi Arkhiv Khabarovskogo Kraia (GAKK), f. 35, op. 112, d. 105, pp. 133–34; "Protokol No. 44 zasedaniia TsK KPSS, October 13, 1987," GAKK, f. 35, op. 115, d.41, pp. 86–87.

8 / SINO-RUSSIAN RELATIONS IN THE YELTSIN ERA

1. For Andrei Kozyrev's views, see "Rossiia stremitsia na zapad," *Moskovskie Novosti*, September 29, 1991, p. 3; and the interview with him in *Nezavisimaia Gazeta*, April 1, 1992, p. 1.

2. Excerpts from "Speeches by Leaders of Permanent Members of the U.N. Council," *The New York Times (NYT)*, February 1, 1992, p. 5.

3. Sheryl WuDunn, "China Says Soviets Erred Earlier in Picking Leader," *NYT*, September 8, 1991, p. 13.

4. Interview with Evgenii Bazhanov, Moscow, June 10, 1993.

5. Lincoln Kaye, Tai Ming Cheung, and Julian Baum, "Bitter Medicine," *Far Eastern Economic Review (FEER)*, September 5, 1991, p. 10.

6. According to a Hong Kong publication, at a meeting of the Chinese Communist Party's Politburo held to discuss the failure of the August coup in Moscow, the Chinese leadership reportedly stated: "Even if Yeltsin is very reactionary, we can internally curse him and pray for his downfall, but we still have to maintain normal state-to-state relations with him and have to endeavor to maintain good-neighborly ties with the Soviet Union. This is for the sake of our country's peace, stability, and social development." *He Po Shih, Tangtai* (Hongkong), no. 10 (January 15, 1992), pp. 41–52; in *FBIS* (PRC), February 7, 1992, p. 7.

7. Maksim Yuzin, "Moscow-Beijing: Period of Trials," *Izvestiia*, March 24, 1992, p. 6, in *Current Digest of the Post-Soviet Press*, vol. 44, no. 12 (1992), p. 21.

8. *RFE/RL Daily Report*, December 3, 1992; Chen Hui, *ZhongE guanxi jishi* (Beijing: Chinese Academy of Social Sciences, Institute of East European, Russian, and Central Asian Studies, 1996), p. 55. China originally wanted a 300 km zone but this was problematic for Russia. Jing-dong Yuan, "Sino-Russian Confidence-Building Measures: A Preliminary Analysis," *Asian Perspective*, vol. 22, no. 1 (Spring 1998), p. 87.

9. For an overall appraisal of the visit, see Vasilii Kononenko and Vladimir Skokyrev, "Rossiisko-Kitaiskaia deklaratsiia, po sushchestvu, ravnosil'nyi pakt o nenapadenii," *Izvestiia*, December 21, 1992, p. 4.

10. Sergei Stankevich, "Derzhava v poiskakh sebia," *Nezavisimaia Gazeta*, March 28, 1992, p. 5; and Vladimir Lukin, "Our Security Predicament," *Foreign Policy*, Fall 1992, p. 58. Also see Alexander Rahr, "'Atlanticists' versus 'Eurasians' in Russian Foreign Policy," *RFE/RL Research Report*, May 29, 1992, pp. 17–22.

11. Ruslan Khasbulatov, "O vneshnei politike i diplomatii Rossii," *Rossiiskaia Gazeta*, March 6, 1992, p. 7; Interview by Alexander Ianov with Vladimir Zhirinovskii, "Milliard dollarov—i ia u vlasti. Kto ego dast?" *Rossiia*, June 1–7, 1992, p. 3.

12. Yeltsin's press briefing, December 18, 1992, Moscow Russian Television Network, in *FBIS* (Central Eurasia), December 21, 1992, p. 4.

13. Yeltsin's address to the Chinese public, ITAR-TASS, December 18, 1992, in *FBIS* (Central Eurasia), December 21, 1992, pp. 9–10.

14. Yeltsin's press briefing, December 18, 1992, p. 5.

15. "Memorandum of Mutual Understanding between the Russian and Chinese Governments on Questions of Mutual Reductions of Armed Forces and Strengthening of Trust in the Military Sphere in the Border Region," ITAR-TASS, December 18, 1992; in *FBIS* (Central Eurasia), December 21, 1992, pp. 11–12.

16. ITAR-TASS, December 18, 1992; in *FBIS* (Central Eurasia), December 18, 1992, p. 6; *RFE/RL Daily Report*, December 18, 1992; Yeltsin's press briefing, December 18, 1992.

17. Joint declaration, Xinhua, December 18, 1992, in *FBIS* (PRC), December 18, 1992, pp. 7–8.

18. Interview by Vladimir Fedoruk and Pavel Spirin with Yurii Voronin, deputy chairman of the Supreme Soviet of the Russian Federation, ITAR-TASS, January 13, 1993, in *FBIS* (Central Eurasia), January 15, 1993, pp. 13–14.

19. Interview with Mikhail Titarenko, Moscow, June 16, 1993.

20. Interfax (Moscow), December 10, 1992, in *FBIS* (Central Eurasia), December 11, 1992, pp. 13–14; Huang Huizhu, "Roundup: Sino-Russian Ties Progressing Steadily," Xinhua, August 29, 1994, in *FBIS* (PRC), September 1, 1994, p. 9. Japan and the United States were China's top trading partners. Sergei Feoktistov, Beijing correspondent, Radio Maiak (Moscow), August 15, 1993, in *FBIS* (Central Eurasia), p. 10.

21. *RFE/RL Daily Report*, April 20, 1993.

22. *RFE/RL Daily Report*, June 23, 1993.

23. For an analysis of these incidents, see Aleksandr Avdoshin's column, "Info-Rossiia," in *Rossiia*, no. 30 (July 21, 1993), p. 2.

24. Interview with China's Premier Li Peng in *Sol de Mexico*, September 10, 1993, in *FBIS* (PRC), September 10, 1993, p. 15.

25. ITAR-TASS, in *FBIS* (Central Eurasia), October 4, 1993, p. 85.

26. On political fragmentation in Russia in 1991–93, see John B. Dunlop, *The Rise of Russia and the Fall of the Soviet Empire* (Princeton, N.J.: Princeton University Press, 1993), pp. 285–301; Michael Urban et al., *The Rebirth of Politics in Russia* (Cambridge: Cambridge University Press, 1997), chapter 11.

27. "Information Communiqué on the Results of the Official Visit to the Chinese People's Republic of V.S. Chernomyrdin, Chairman of the Government of the Russian Federation," *Diplomaticheskii Vestnik*, no. 11–12 (June 1994), pp. 6–7, in *FBIS* (Central Eurasia), September 22, 1994, pp. 62–63.

28. Vladimir Soskyrev, "Pekin vozlagaet vinu za spad v torgovle na Moskvu," *Izvestiia*, May 26, 1994, p. 3.

29. ITAR-TASS, April 16, 1995, in *FBIS* (Central Eurasia), April 19, 1995, p. 34.

30. *Open Media Research Institute Daily Report*, vol. 1, no. 15, part 1.

31. Soskyrev, "Pekin voslagaet vinu," p. 3. Difficulties in Sino-Russian regional relations began to have an impact on border trade, an issue which will be discussed in detail in chapter nine.

32. Jennifer Anderson, "The Limits of Sino-Russian Strategic Partnership," *Adelphi Paper* no. 315 (London: IISS, 1996), pp. 18–20.

33. ITAR-TASS, September 3, 1994, in *FBIS* (Central Eurasia), September 6, 1994, p. 13.

34. Text of speech by PRC President Jiang Zemin at the Institute of International Relations of Russia, September 3, 1994, in *FBIS* (PRC), September 6, 1994, p. 18.

35. Ibid.

36. Interview, August 22, 1996.

37. Interview with Evgenii Afanasiev on Moscow Ostankino television, November 10, 1993, in *FBIS* (Central Eurasia), November 12, 1993, p. 18.

38. Interview with Lev Antoshchenkov, deputy chief of the Russian Ministry of Foreign Economic Relations, Administration for Economic Relations with Asian Countries, by Grigorii Koshkarov, *Kuranty*, February 24, 1993, p. 5, in *FBIS* (Central Eurasia), February 25, 1993, p. 12.

39. ITAR-TASS, March 2, 1995, in *FBIS* (Central Eurasia), March 3, 1995, p. 4.

40. INTERFAX, May 16, 1995, in *FBIS* (Central Eurasia), May 16, 1995, p. 8.

41. ITAR-TASS, May 15, 1995, *FBIS* (Central Eurasia), May 16, 1995, p. 12.

42. ITAR-TASS, May 16, 1995, in *FBIS* (Central Eurasia), May 16, 1995, p. 9.

43. "Rossiia-KNR, Vizit Li Pena [Li Peng] v Rossiiu, Sovmestnoe Rossiisko-Kitaiskoe kommiunike," *Diplomaticheskii Vestnik*, no. 7 (July 1995), pp. 4–5.

44. Georgii Kunegin, "Podarok Li Penu [Li Peng]," *Rossiiskie Vesti*, June 28, 1995, p. 3.

45. "Rossiia-KNR, Vizit Tsian Tsichenia [Qian Qichen] v Rossiiu," *Diplomaticheskii Vestnik*, no. 10 (October 1995), p. 14.

46. "Rossiia-KNR, Visit B.N. Yeltsina v KNR," *Diplomaticheskii Vestnik*, no. 5 (May 1996), p. 16.

47. Ibid.

48. Ibid., pp. 16, 18.

49. Cecile Kung, "Treaty Boosts Border Friendship," *Hong Kong Standard*, April 27, 1996, p. 1.

50. Pavel Shinkarenko, "Partnership Geared to the 21st Century," *Rossiiskie Vesti*, April 26, 1996, p. 1, in *FBIS* (Central Eurasia), April 26, 1996, p. 20.

51. Vsevolod Ovchinnikov, "Velikii gazovoi put'. Fantastika? Net, nasushchaia neobkhodimost'," *Vek*, no. 2 (January 1997).

52. Yuliia Petrovskaia, "El'tsin za velikoi stenoi," *Nezavisimaia Gazeta*, April 26,

1996, p. 1; Tatiana Malkina, "Rossiia i Kitai vstaiut na puti 'gegemonizma'," *Segodnia*, April 26, 1996, p. 1; ITAR-TASS, April 25, 1996, in *FBIS* (Central Eurasia), April 25, 1996, p. 11.

53. "Yeltsin Leaves China, Liking It," *International Herald Tribune*, April 27–28, 1996, p. 4.

54. Interviews, Beijing, June 1996. Also see Lu Nanquan, "Eluosi zongtong dadiehou de ZhongE guanxi," *Guoji Jingji Pinglun*, July–August 1996, p. 7.

55. Jen Hui-wen, "Beijing Political Situation: Sino-Russian Relations as Viewed from Internal Report," *Hsin Pao* (Hong Kong Economic Journal), June 28, 1996, p. 18, in *FBIS* (PRC), July 3, 1996, p. 9.

56. Xinhua, December 5, 1996, in *FBIS* (PRC), December 5, 1996 (electronic).

57. ITAR-TASS, December 13, 1996, in *FBIS* (Central Eurasia), December 13, 1996 (electronic).

58. *OMRI Daily Digest*, part I, August 20, 1997. Russian power industries have had difficulties making competitive bids to provide equipment due to their inability to obtain sufficient bank credits to finance production. See "Mashinostroiteli nadeiutsia na gosudarstvennuiu podderzhku eksporta produktsii v Kitai," *Segodnia*, January 16, 1996.

59. Bai Hua, "Sino-Russian Partnership Has Entered a New Stage," *Wen Wei Po* (Hong Kong), December 28, 1996, p. A6.

60. Dmitrii Gornostaev and Aleksandr Reutov, "Moskva i Pekin v sovmestnoi deklaratsii vyskazalis' protiv postroeniia odnopoliarnogo mira," *Nezavisimaia Gazeta*, April 24, 1997, p. 1.

61. Nataliia Pulina and Aleksandr Reutov, "Vchera s KNR zakliucheno soglashe-nie, podgotovka kotorogo nachalas' eshche vo vremena SSSR," *Nezavisimaia Gazeta*, April 25, 1997, p. 1.

62. Covered equipment included battle tanks, armored vehicles, tactical missile launchers, and artillery systems with more than 122mm caliber. Leonid Moiseev, deputy director, First Asia Department, Russian Foreign Ministry, "Russian-Chinese Partnership: New Horizons," *Far Eastern Affairs (FEA)*, no. 3 (1997), p. 7.

63. Genrikh Kireev, "Strategic Partnership and a Stable Border," *FEA*, no. 4 (1997), p. 13.

64. Moiseev, "Russian-Chinese Partnership," p. 7.

65. Kireev, "Strategic Partnership," pp. 13–14.

66. Andrew C. Kuchins and Alexei V. Zagorskii outline this approach in "The Russian Federation and Asian Security: Marginalization or Integration?" Conference paper presented August 20–22, 1998, Asia/Pacific Research Center, Stanford University.

67. For Chinese views, see Tian Chunsheng, "Zhongguo jingji guanxi de zoushi ji qi yuanyin fenxi," *Taipingyang xuebao*, no. 1 (1999), pp. 85–89; and Lu Nanquan,

"Fazhan liangguo jingmao guanxi de duice jianyi," in *ZhongE JingMao Guanxi* (Beijing: Chinese Academy of Social Sciences, 1999), pp. 255–84.

68. Interviews in Moscow with Evgenii Bazhanov, Diplomatic Academy, April 12, 1999; and Aleksei Voskresenskii, Institute of the Far East, April 13, 1999.

69. Dmitrii Kosyrev and Stanislav Petrov, "Spasti torgovliu s Kitaem," *Nezavisimaia Gazeta*, November 10, 1997, pp. 1–2.

70. Xinhua, November 4, 1998, in *FBIS* (PRC), November 4, 1998 (electronic).

71. Anthony Davis, "The Big Oil Shock," *Asiaweek*, October 10, 1997, p. 18. China still depends on coal for 70 percent of its energy needs. Natural gas accounts for less than 2 percent of energy use.

72. Daniel Yergin, Dennis Ekloff, and Jefferson Edwards, "Fueling Asia's Recovery," *Foreign Affairs*, March/April 1998, p. 46.

73. On the impact of these interests on Russia's foreign policy, see Michael McFaul, "A Precarious Peace: Domestic Politics in the Making of Russian Foreign Policy," *International Security*, Winter 1997/98, p. 24.

74. Igor Khripunov and Mary M. Matthews, "Russia's Oil and Gas Interest Group and Its Foreign Policy Agenda," *Problems of Post-Communism*, May/June 1996, pp. 38–48; Peter Rutland, "Lost Opportunities: Energy and Politics in Russia," *NBR Analysis*, December 1997, pp. 25–26.

75. Matthew J. Sagers and Jennifer Nicoud, "Development of East Siberia Gas Field and Pipeline to China: A Research Communication," *Post-Soviet Geography and Economics*, vol. 38, no. 5 (1997), pp. 288–95.

76. East European Press Service, *CIS Oil and Gas Report*, October 11, 1999 (http://www.securities.com).

77. Kosyrev and Petrov, "Spasti torgovliu s Kitaem," p. 2.

78. Ibid., p. 1.

79. Aleksei Portanskii and Anatolii Sautin, "Visit El'tsina v Kitai podverdit vostochnye prioritety Kremlia," *Finansovye Izvestiia*, November 6, 1997, p. 1.

80. Li Jingjie, "The Progress of Chinese-Russian Relations: From Friendship to Strategic Partnership," *FEA*, no. 3 (1997), p. 46.

81. Konstantin Baskaev, "Rossiia skrepliaet druzhby s Kitaem s pomoshchiu gazo-provoda," *Finansovye Izvestiia*, November 13, 1997, p. 1.

82. *RFE/RL Newsline*, February 8, 1999. Russian imports of Chinese food and consumer products declined by 50 percent in the fourth quarter of 1998. The collapse of banks and Russian firms involved in Sino-Russian trade, as well as the shortage of foreign currency in Russia, further complicated an already difficult economic relationship.

83. Gazprom President Rem Viakhirev presented his project to the November 1998 APEC meeting in Kuala Lampur (Prime-TASS economic news agency, Novem-

ber 17, 1998). The pipeline could be extended to Japan and other countries in Northeast Asia.

84. Russia already supplies China with thermal power, in a $2 billion contract. He Chong, "Both China and Russia Expect to Step Up Economic and Trade Cooperation," *Zhongguo Tongxun She* (Hong Kong), July 13, 1998, in *FBIS* (PRC), July 13, 1998 (electronic). A senior economist at Moscow State University, Vilia Gel'bras, argues that the excessively low price China demanded has made it unprofitable for Russia. Interview, April 19, 1999.

85. Alexander Davydov, "Yukos Reaches Out for the Chinese Market," *Moscow News*, December 8, 1999 (http://www.securities.com).

86. ITAR-TASS, November 18, 1998, in *FBIS* (Central Eurasia), November 18, 1998 (electronic).

87. "China Postpones Participation in Aircraft Project," *Segodnia*, May 12, 1999, p. 4, in East European Press Service, May 14, 1999.

88. These included another feasibility study for the Kovyktinskoe project, an agreement for processing timber in the Russian Far East, and frameworks for regional cooperation between Jilin Province and Primorskii Krai, Xinjiang Province and Altai Krai, Liaoning Province and the Republic of Bashkortostan, and Shanghai and Amurskaia Oblast. Lu Nanquan, "Xiang xin de gaodu fazhan," *Guoji Shangbao*, March 10, 1999. In addition to Kovyktinskoe, several other major energy projects are under discussion, including a $30 billion East Siberian gas pipeline project involving Gazprom and a gas pipeline from Sakhalin to Khabarovsk and then to the Chinese Northeast.

89. Interviews with senior scholars at the Institute of the World Economy and Politics (Beijing), March 18, 1999, and the Institute of East European, Russian, and Central Asian Studies (Beijing), March 15 and March 23, 1999; and with Lev Deliusin, Institute of International Economy and Political Research (Moscow), April 20, 1999.

90. International Petroleum Finance, *Energy Intelligence Group*, January 1, 2000 (http://www.securities.com). The U.S. State Department vetoed the loan out of concern over Russian business practices.

91. Neela Banerjee, "Foreign Investors Win Court Order in Russian Oil Case," *The New York Times*, November 24, 1999, p. C4. BP Amoco retained its 10 percent equity and its voting rights were improved. International Petroleum Finance, *Energy Intelligence Group*, January 2000 (http://www.securities.com).

92. East European Press Service, *CIS Oil and Gas Report*, October 29, 1999 (http://www.securities.com).

93. Peter Fleming, *News from Tartary* (London: Jonathan Cape, 1936), p. 245.

94. Xinhua, March 3, 1995, in *FBIS* (PRC), March 3, 1995, p. 51.

95. Xinhua, April 17, 1996, in *FBIS* (PRC), April 17, 1996, p. 42; Dru C. Gladney,

"Ethnicity in the Xinjiang Region," *Analysis of Current Events*, vol. 9, no. 4 (April 1997), p. 7.

96. Xinhua, March 15, 1999.

97. Xinhua, March 9, 1995, *FBIS* (PRC), March 10, 1995, p. 5.

98. Ron Synovitz, "Kyrgyzstan/Tajikistan: Improved Transport Infrastructure Likely to Link to China" (http://www.rferl.org/nca/features/1998).

99. Aleksei Artemev, "Central Asia: Playing on the Road. Russia's Passiveness in the Period 1991–1994 Made for the Assertiveness of Other Forces in This Region," *Rossiiskaia Gazeta* (Ekonomicheskii Soiuz supplement), p. 11, in *FBIS* (Central Eurasia), January 18, 1997 (electronic).

100. Interfax, August 12, 1999, in *FBIS* (Central Eurasia), August 12, 1999 (electronic).

101. Qing Chang, "Zhongguo yu Zhongya wuguo de maoyi yu jingji keti hezuo," *Ouya shehui fazhan yanjiu*, July 1998, p. 80.

102. "Good Relations between the Peoples and Industry Will Lead to Confidence and Prosperity," *Kazakhstanskaia Pravda*, February 25, 1997, pp. 1–2, in *FBIS* (Central Eurasia), February 5, 1997 (electronic version).

103. Xinhua, July 4, 1996, in *FBIS* (PRC), July 5, 1996, p. 9.

104. *RFE/RL Newsline*, no. 78, part 1 (July 22, 1997).

105. Qing Chang, "Zhongguo yu Zhongya wuguo de maoyi yu jingji keti hezuo," p. 80.

106. Ron Synovitz, "Kyrgyzstan/Tajikistan: Improved Infrastructure Likely to Link to China," *RFE/RL Newsline*, June 29, 1998.

107. These problems include an excessive reliance on barter trade, the low level of economic cooperation, the difficult investment environment in Central Asia, the lack of experience in foreign trade in the border regions, and the resulting chaos in border trade. See Lui Qingjian, "Shiji zhi jiao de Zhongguo yu ZhongYa guojia de jingmao guanxi," *DongOu ZhongYa Yanjiu*, no. 6 (1995), pp. 50–51.

108. Yelbay Saghym, "Relations with China," *Aziia* (in Kazakh), no. 44 (October 1993), pp. 1,3, in *FBIS* (Central Eurasia), January 12, 1994, p. 58; Arkady Dubnov, "Kyrgyzstan: Whoever Is Afraid of the Chinese Will Not Eat Noodles," *New Times International*, no. 41 (October 1993), pp. 18–20, in *FBIS* (Central Eurasia), November 11, 1993, p. 106. Because the Kyrgyz-Chinese border is mountainous, the transit points are through Kazakhstan, which connects by rail with Urumqi in Xinjiang. Chinese traders were able to come into Kyrgyzstan from Kazakhstan without a visa.

109. Dubnov, "Kyrgyzstan."

110. *RFE/RL Newsline*, no. 190, part 1 (January 7, 1998), and no. 192, part 1 (January 9, 1998).

111. On the nuclear contamination issue, see David Nissman, "Nuclear Tests, Oil, and Justice in East Turkestan," *Analysis of Current Events*, vol. 9, no. 4, (April 1997), pp. 6, 8.

112. *OMRI Daily Digest*, May 24, 1996. The Kazakhstani embassy in Beijing denied the allegation.

113. Editorial, "Write a New Chapter of Good-Neighborly Relations and Friendly Cooperation," *Hong Kong Ta Kung Pao*, in *FBIS*, (PRC), August 24, 1999 (electronic).

114. *RFE/RL Newsline*, vol. 3, no. 230, part 1 (November 29, 1999).

115. Andrei V. Grozin and Valerii N. Khliupin, *Natsional'naia bezopasnost' Kazakhstana: problemy i perspektivy* (Moscow: Agent, 1998), p. 15. The authors are scholars based in Kazakhstan.

116. Cited in Viktor Verk, "Claims to Sovereignty: Or What is Happening Between Russia and China," *Karavan* (Almaty), no. 9 (March 3, 1995), p. 7, in *FBIS* (Central Eurasia), March 8, 1995, p. 69.

117. Agence France-Presse, January 24, 1994, in *FBIS* (Central Eurasia), January 27, 1995, p. 1.

118. Interfax, February 14, 1995, *FBIS* (Central Eurasia), February 15, 1995, p. 1.

119. ITAR-TASS, February 7, 1995, in *FBIS* (Central Eurasia), February 8, 1995.

120. ITAR-TASS, March 19, 1997, in *FBIS* (Central Eurasia), March 19, 1997 (electronic).

121. Herbert J. Ellison and Bruce A. Acker, "The New Russia and Asia: 1991–1995," *NBR Analysis,* vol. 6, no. 1 (June 1996), p. 30.

122. See, for example, Xu Tao, "Strategic Direction of Central Asia," *Hong Kong Ta Kung Pao*, August 4, 1999, p. D1, in *FBIS* (PRC), August 4, 1999 (electronic).

123. Interview with President Nazarbaev by Sultankhan Aqquly-Uly, *Vremia Po Grinvichu*, May 4, 1999 (http://www.securities.com).

124. President Askar Akaevich Akaev, "Diplomatiia shelkogo puti," *Nezavisimaia Gazeta*, March 10, 1999 (http://www.securities.com).

125. Keith Martin, "China and Central Asia: Between Seduction and Suspicion," *RFE/RL Research Report*, June 24, 1994, pp. 28–29.

126. China has always had trouble maintaining its hold over Xinjiang. See Lillian Craig Harris, "Xinjiang, Central Asia, and the Implications," *The China Quarterly*, March 1993, pp. 112–19.

127. On the impact of the independence of the Central Asian states for China, see Xing Guangcheng, "Zhongguo he ZhongYa geguo: Xin de guanxi," *DongOu ZhongYa Yanjiu*, no. 1 (1996), pp. 62–64.

128. Ibid.

129. Gaye Christoffersen, "Impact of Transnational Forces on Chinese Regional Economic Planning," *The China Quarterly*, March 1993, p. 150.

130. Martin, "China and Central Asia," p. 27. Kyrgyzstan has also protested Chinese nuclear testing. See, for example, the Kyrgyzstani Foreign Affairs Ministry statement

in *Slovo Kyrgyzstana* (Bishkek), October 21, 1994, p. 1, in *FBIS* (Central Eurasia), November 2, 1994, p. 43.

131. Teng Pi-yun, "Kazakhstan Reportedly Bans Xinjiang Independence Movement in Exchange for Beijing's Commitment not to Be the First to Use Nuclear Weapons," *Lien Ho Pao* (Hong Kong), February 27, 1995, p. 7, in *FBIS* (PRC), February 28, 1995, p. 7.

132. On the unrest in Xinjiang, see Patrick E. Tyler, "In China's Far West, Tensions with Ethnic Muslims Boil Over in Riots and Bombings," *NYT*, February 28, 1997, p. A8; and Gladney, "Ethnicity in Xinjiang Region."

133. *OMRI Daily Digest*, part 1, April 9, 1996.

134. *OMRI Daily Digest*, part 1, February 17, 1997.

135. *OMRI Daily Digest*, part 1, February 19, 1997.

136. *OMRI Daily Digest*, part 1, March 20, 1997; *OMRI Daily Digest*, part 1, April 19, 1997; *RFE/RL Newsline*, no. 86, part 1, August 1, 1997.

137. *OMRI Daily Digest*, part 1, March 26, 1997.

138. Xinhua, June 3, 1996, in *FBIS* (PRC), June 3, 1996 (electronic).

139. Umirserik Kasenov, director of Kazakhstan Strategic Research Institute of President of Kazakhstan Republic, "What Russia Wants in the Transcaucusus and Central Asia; Together or Apart," *Nezavisimaia Gazeta*, January 24, 1995, p. 3, in *FBIS* (Central Eurasia), February 3, 1995, p. 2.

140. Artemev, "Central Asia."

141. Interview with senior scholar, Beijing, June 1996.

142. See Gaye Christofferson, "Chinese Intentions for Russian and Central Asian Oil and Gas," *NBR Analysis*, vol. 9, no. 2 (March 1998).

143. In April 1997, China had pledged $4 billion to develop the Aktiubinsk oil field in Kazakhstan and committed another $1.3 billion to the Uzen field, in addition to future investment in the pipeline projects. Jeffrey C. Lumpkin, "Investing in Kazakhstan's Energy Sector: The Geopolitical Environment," *NBR Executive Insight*, February 1998, pp. 30–31.

144. Interfax, December 2, 1999, in *FBIS* (Central Eurasia), December 2, 1999 (eletronic).

145. Stephen Foye, "The Struggle over Russia's Kuril Islands Policy," *RFE/RL Research Report*, September 11, 1992, pp. 37–38.

146. Ekaterina Grigor'eva, "Moskva i Tokio postaraiutsia zakliuchit' mirnyi dogovor k 2000 godu," *Nezavisimaia Gazeta*, November 4, 1997, p. 1.

147. Andrei Smirnov, "Moskva-Pekin: Diplomatiia v domashnikh tapochkakh," *Segodnia*, November 11, 1997, p. 1.

148. Yekaterina Labetskaia and Alexander Timofeev, "Russia Sells Arms to Seoul," *Moscow News*, September 8, 1999 (http://www.securities.com).

149. Anderson, *The Limits of Sino-Russian Strategic Partnership*, p. 65.

150. BBC Worldwide Monitoring, BBC, September 2, 1999 (http://www.securities com).

151. Nigel Holloway and Charles Bickers, "Brothers in Arms," *FEER*, March 13, 1997, p. 20.

152. Stephen J. Blank, "Who's Minding the State? The Failure of Russian Security Policy," *Problems of Post-Communism*, March/April 1998, p. 8.

153. *Jamestown Monitor*, February 8, 1996.

154. Michael R. Gordon, "Moscow Is Selling Weapons to China, US Officials Say," *NYT*, October 18, 1992, p. 1, 6; Tai Ming Cheung, "Arm in Arm," *FEER*, November 12, 1992, p. 28. For discussion of the arms sales in the Russian media, see A. Kabannikov, "We Swap SU's for Sausages. Who Controls Russian Arms Deliveries to China?" *Komsomol'skaia Pravda*, December 11, 1992, p. 3, in *FBIS* (Central Eurasia), December 15, 1992, pp. 13–14; and Sergei Tikhomirov, "Neither Allies Nor Enemies— Simply Neighbors," *Rossiiskaia Gazeta*, December 22, 1992, p. 7, in *FBIS* (Central Eurasia), December 23, 1992, p. 11.

155. Patrick E. Tyler, "Russia and China Sign a Military Agreement," *NYT*, November 10, 1993, p. A15.

156. These were suspended in the aftermath of Tiananmen. Patrick Tyler, "US and China Agree to Expand Defense Links," *NYT*, November 3, 1993, p. A13.

157. Lincoln Kaye, "Courtship Dance," *FEER*, May 26, 1994, p. 24; *RFE/RL Daily Report*, November 10, 1993.

158. Tai Ming Cheung, "China's Buying Spree," *FEER*, July 8, 1993, p. 24.

159. Vladimir Soskyrev, "Aziia napugana," *Izvestiia*, November 9, 1993, p. 3. In February 1999, five Russians and two Chinese faced criminal charges for theft and resale to China of spare parts for SU-27 aircraft. ITAR-TASS, February 5, 1999.

160. ITAR-TASS, August 25, 1994, in *FBIS* (Central Eurasia), August 26, 1994, p. 7.

161. *Lien Ho Pao* (Hong Kong), May 16, 1995, p. 10, in *FBIS* (PRC), May 23, 1995, p. 8; Aleksandr Koretskii, "Pavel Grachev's Visit to China: Minister Greeted by Underground Nuclear Fireworks," *Kommersant-Daily*, May 16, 1995, p. 3, in *FBIS* (Central Eurasia), May 16, 1995, p. 11. On China's submarine purchase, see the *OMRI Daily Report*, part 1, February 13, 1995.

162. Reuters, December 7, 1995.

163. Reuters, February 4, 1996. China had been pressing Russia for several years to sell the licensing rights to the aircraft. The Chinese began assembling the aircraft in 1998 at a plant built in Shenyang with Russian assistance. ITAR-TASS, in *FBIS* (Central Eurasia), October 27, 1998 (electronic).

164. A Russian military source raised the issue of a quid pro quo in an interview with Interfax on March 10, 1995, in *FBIS* (Central Eurasia), March 13, 1995, p. 14.

165. Ilya Bulavinov, "The Chinese Air Force Will Soon Receive Replenishment

in Form of Another 60 Russian Fighters," *Kommersant-Daily*, August 6, 1999, p. 3, in European Press Service (http://www.securities.com). The factory in Shenyang will use ready-made Russian parts from the Sukhoi factory in Komsomolsk-na-Amure, and Russian specialists will help assemble the planes. ITAR-TASS, February 11, 1999.

166. Bill Gertz, "Russia Sells Rocket Motors to China," *The Washington Times*, February 13, 1995, p. A4.

167. Bates Gill, "China's Newest Warships," *FEER*, January 27, 2000, p. 30.

168. Holloway and Bickers, "Brothers in Arms," p. 20.

169. Loren Thompson, "China Continues to Rise to Regional Dominance," *Sea Power*, January 1999, p. 6.

170. Interfax, November 20, 1998, in *FBIS* (Central Eurasia), November 20, 1998 (electronic).

171. Mikhail Kozyrev, "China to Receive Russian-Made SU-27UBK Fighters as Form of Payment of Russia's Debt," *Vedemosti*, December 16, 1999, p. 1, in East European Press Service (http://www.securities.com).

172. Ibid.

173. Banning Garrett and Bonnie Glaser, "Chinese Apprehensions about Revitalization of the US-Japan Alliance," *Asian Survey*, vol. 37, no. 4 (April 1997), pp. 387–88.

174. *RFE/RL Newsline*, no. 33, part 1, May 19, 1997.

175. Tsuneo Akaha, "Russo-Japanese Relations at a Turning Point," unpublished paper prepared for the national meeting of AAASS, Seattle, November 15, 1997, p. 11. On Rodionov's position, see K.O. Sarkisov, "Rossiisko-iaponskie otnosheniia posle pereizbraniia El'tsina prezidentom Rossii (1996–97)," unpublished paper presented to a Princeton University conference on the history of Russian-Japanese relations, September 6–8, 1997, p. 6.

176. Beijing Central Television, November 23, 1998, in *FBIS* (PRC), November 23, 1998 (electronic). The highlight of the Yeltsin visit was the signing of a declaration on the completion of the demarcation of the eastern portion of the Sino-Russian border (with the exception of the two islands across from Khabarovsk and one in the Argun river).

177. Xinhua, November 24, 1998, in *FBIS* (PRC), November 24, 1998 (electronic).

178. Pavel Spirin, "China Learns the Lessons of the Iraqi Crisis," *Nezavisimaia Gazeta*, December 23, 1998, p. 6, in East European Press Service (http://www.securities.com). In subsequent discussions of Primakov's proposal in early May, Chinese officials explained that their country's traditional close relationship with Pakistan, India's main enemy, and recent nuclear tests by both countries were further grounds for rejecting a tripartite alliance including India. Russian News Agency (RIA), May 5, 1999.

179. Sergei Rogov, "The Ups and Downs of Strategic Partnership," *Vek*, no. 10 (March 1999), p. 3, in East European Press Service, March 16, 1999.

180. Foreign Ministry spokesman Vladimir Rakhmanin criticized the new U.S.-Japanese defense guidelines. *RFE/RL Newsline*, February 12, 1999. For a Defense Ministry reaction to the ABM issue, see *RFE/RL Newsline*, February 4, 1999.

181. Xinhua, April 16, 1999.

182. The apology by President Clinton on the day of the embassy bombing was not publicized in China until three days later. Once Clinton's apology was broadcast, the demonstrations were curtailed. See, Susan Lawrence and Shawn Crispin, "Double-Edged Fury," *FEER*, May 20, 1999, pp. 10–12.

183. Xinhua, May 11, 1999.

184. "Russian President Was Just Using Terms the West Can Understand," *Nezavisimaia Gazeta*, December 13, 1999, in East European Press Service (http://www.securities.com).

185. "PRC, Russian Leaders Issue Joint Statement," Xinhua, December 10, 1999, in *FBIS* (PRC), December 13, 1999 (electronic).

186. "Sovmestnoe informatsionnoe kommiunike o neformal'noi vstreche prezidenta rossiiskoi federatsii B.N. El'tsina i predsedatelia Kitaiskoi Narodnoi Respubliki Tsian Tseminia [Jiang Zemin]"(http:///www.mid.ru).

187. "Yeltsin's Contribution to development of Russian-Chinese relations praised," ITAR-TASS, January 1, 2000, BBC Worldwide Monitoring (http://www.securities.com).

188. On the winners and losers of reform, see McFaul, "A Precarious Peace," pp. 17–21.

9 / MOSCOW AND THE BORDER REGIONS DEBATE RUSSIA'S
CHINA POLICY

1. Alexander Lukin, "Russia's Image of China and Russian-Chinese Relations," *East Asia: An International Quarterly*, Brunswick, Spring 1999, pp. 1–16 (electronic); and Aleksei D. Voskresenskii, "The Perceptions of China by Russia's Foreign Policy Elite," *Issues and Studies* (Taipei), vol. 33, no. 3 (March 1997), pp. 1–20.

2. Interview with Aleksei Bogaturov, Moscow, April 15, 1999. Many supporters of greater cooperation with China are based at the Institute of the Far East, including the director, Mikhail Titarenko, and Boris Kulik, who used to work under Boris Rakhmanin in the Central Committee, the chief organizer of the anti-China coalition from the mid-1960s through the mid-1980s. On this point see Lukin, "Russia's Image of China."

3. Alexei Arbatov, "Vneshnepoliticheskii konsensus v Rossiii," *Nezavisimaia Gazeta*, March 14, 1997, p. 5; and Aleksei Bogaturov, "Pliuralisticheskaia odnopoliarnost' i interesy Rossii," *Svobodnaia Mysl'*, no. 2 (1996), p. 25.

4. Evgenii Afanasiev and Grigorii Logvinov, "Russia and China: Girding for the Third Millenium," *International Affairs* (Moscow), no. 11–12 (1996), p. 45.

5. For the centrist position, see Afanasiev and Logvinov, "Russia and China," p. 47. For the "civilizational" approach, see Mikhail Titarenko and Boris Kulik, "Vneshniaia politika Rossii: Dal'nevostochnii Vektor," *Problemy Dal'nego Vostoka* (*PDV*), no. 1 (1993), p. 19; M. Titarenko, "Za dobrososedstvo i sotrudnichestvo Rossii s dal'nevostochnymi stranami," *PDV*, no. 5 (1996), p. 6.

6. Titarenko and Kulik, "Vneshniaia politika Rossii," p. 19.

7. See, for example, Vladimir Lukin, "Our Security Predicament," *Foreign Policy*, Fall 1992, p. 58; Sergei Goncharov, "Osobye Interesy Rossii—v chem oni zakliuchaiutsia," *Izvestiia*, February 25, 1992, p. 6; Sergei Stankevich, "Derzhava v poiskakh sebia," *Nezavisimaia Gazeta*, March 28, 1992, p. 5. On these debates, see David Kerr, "The New Eurasianism: The Rise of Geopolitics in Russia's Foreign Policy," *Europe-Asia Studies*, vol. 47, no. 6 (1995), pp. 977–88.

8. Petr Savitskii, Petr Suvchinskii, Nikolai Trubetskoi, and Georgii Florovskii, *Iskhod k vostoku* (Sofia: Balkan', 1921), pp. iii–vii. For an analysis of Eurasianism, see Nicholas V. Riasanovsky, "The Emergence of Eurasianism," *California Slavic Studies*, volume 4 (Berkeley: University of California Press, 1967), pp. 39–72. On changing views of Russia's role in Asia, see Edward Allworth, "The Controversial Status of Soviet Asia," in *Soviet Asia: Bibliographies* (New York: Praeger, 1975), pp. xvi–iix.

9. Aleksei Voskresenskii, "Na razlome tysiacheletii," *Nezavisimaia Gazeta*, March 29, 1996, p. 4.

10. Evgenii Bazhanov, "Russkie narodnye skazki o sredinnoi imperii," *Segodnia*, April 7, 1997, p. 2.

11. Lev Deliusin, "Ne vragi i ne soiuzniki," *Aziia i Afrika Segodnia*, July 1998, p. 50.

12. Evgenii Bazhanov, "Evoliutsii Rossiiskoi vneshnei politiki," in *Mezhdunarodnye Otnosheniia*, (Moscow: MGIMO, 1998), pp. 17–18.

13. Lukin, "Russia's Image of China," p. 7. See KPRF leader Gennadyi Ziuganov, *Geografiia pobedy. Osnovyi Rossiiskoi geopolitiki* (AOA Saint-Petersburg Typography: Saint-Petersburg, 1997), p. 237; and Aleksei Mitrofanov (deputy to Vladimir Zhirinovskii and head of the Duma's Geopolitics Committee), *Shagi do novoi geopolitiki* (Moscow: Russkii Vestnik, 1997), p. 223.

14. Aleksandr Iakovlev, "Mezhdunarodno-politicheskaia stabil'nost' v aziatsko-tikhookeanskom regione i Kitai," *PDV*, no. 5 (1995), pp. 5, 8–9.

15. Boris Zanegin, "SShA i Kitai: Konfliktnyi potentsial," *SShA*, no 3–4 (1999), p. 46; and interview with Mikhail Titarenko by Boris Glukhov, "Reforms Should Be Such that Everyone Benefits from Them," *Moscow Pravda*, June 9, 1998, p. 4 (electronic).

16. Vladimir Portiakov, "Migratsionnaia politika na Dal'nem Vostoke Rossii," in *Migratsionnaia situatsiia na Dal'nem Vostoke i politika Rossii* (Moscow: Carnegie Moscow Center, 1996), p. 40.

17. Zanegin, "SShA i Kitai," p. 54.

18. Vladimir Miasnikov, *Dogovornymi stat'yami utverdili* (Moscow and Khabarovsk: Institute of the Far East and Priamurskoe Geographic Society, 1997), pp. 466.

19. For a summary of this discussion, see Vilia Gel'bras, "Samoe slaboe zveno v ekonomicheskoi politiki Rossii v Dal'nevostochnom regione," in *Migratsionnaia situatsiia*, pp. 111–12.

20. Igor' Rogachev, "Rossiia-Kitai: sotrudnichestvo, obrashchennoe v XXI vek," *PDV*, no. 4 (1996), p. 7.

21. Moscow Radio Rossii Network, September 18, 1994, in *FBIS* (Central Eurasia), September 19, 1994, p. 19.

22. *OMRI Daily Digest*, part 1, October 12, 1995.

23. Dmitrii Trenin, *Kitaiskaia problema Rossii* (Moscow: Carnegie Moscow Center, 1998), p. 34.

24. Ivan Rybkin, then secretary of the National Security Council of the Russian Federation, "O kontseptsii natsional'noi bezopasnosti Rossii," *Nezavisimaia Gazeta*, April 29, 1997, pp. 1–2.

25. "Illegal Immigration Threatens Russia's National Security," *Segodnia*, November 5, 1998, p. 2, in East European Press Service, November 9, 1992 (http://-www.securities.com).

26. Interview with a former first deputy foreign minister of the Russian Federation and leader of the Radical Democrats faction in parliament, Fedor Shelov-Kovediaiev, in "The China Factor," *Vostok Rossii* (Magadan), no. 33 (August 1993), p. 6, in *FBIS* (Central Eurasia), October 20, 1993, p. 37; interview with Andrei Iakimchuk, head of the Analytical Department at the Ministry of Foreign Affairs, in "Kitaiskii gambit v Primor'e," *Novosti*, October 12, 1993.

27. Dmitrii Trenin, "Rossiia-Kitai: Voennyi aspekt otnoshenii," report of lecture presented to the Carnegie Moscow Center, Carnegie Endowment for International Peace, March 19, 1997, p. 13.

28. "No Federal Funds: What's a Governor to Do?" *Russia and FSU Monitor*, vol. 3, no. 4 (July 1999), p. 2.

29. Trenin, "Rossia-Kitai," p. 8.

30. Sergei Shakhrai, "Neobkhodimaia strategiia otnoshenii s Kitaem," *Izvestiia*, May 20, 1994, p. 4. Scholars also urged the Yeltsin government to reinforce the frayed economic links between the Russian Far East and the rest of Russia. Aleksei Voskresenskii, "Grozit li Rossii 'Zheltaia opasnost'?" *Vremia*, November 23, 1998, p. 3.

31. Sergei Kortunov, "Rossiia ishchet soiuznikov," *Mezhdunarodnye Otnosheniia*, no. 5 (1996), p. 20. Kortunov was a consultant and assistant to the president on national security affairs. Also see Sergei Trush, "Prodazha Rossiiskogo Oruzhiia Pekinu: Rezony i Opaseniia," *Nezavisimaia Gazeta*, April 25, 1996, p. 6.

32. Aleksei Arbatov, "Russia: National Security in the 1990s," *Mirovaia Ekonomika i Mezhdunarodnye Otnosheniia*, July-September 1994, pp. 5–18, in *FBIS* (Central

Eurasia), November 29, 1994, p. 56.; Sergei Rogov, "The Results are Pitiful, but There Is a Way Out: Three Years of Trial and Error in Russian Foreign Policy," *Nezavisimaia Gazeta*, December 31, 1994, pp. 1, 4–5, in *FBIS* (Central Eurasia), January 26, 1995, p. 10.

33. Bogaturov, "Pliuralisticheskaia odnopoliarnost'," p. 34. On this point, also see Sergei Shakhrai, "'Netraditsionnaia meditsina kitaiskikh ekonomicheskikh mudretsov," *Nezavisimaia Gazeta*, April 22, 1997, p. 1. For a contrary view, see Vladimir Miasnikov, "Vtoroe khozhdenie prezident v Kitai," *Segodnia*, April 18, 1996, p. 5.

34. Yegor Gaidar, "Rossii XXI veka: ne mirovoi zhandarm, a forpost demokratii v Evrasii," *Izvestiia*, May 18, 1995, p. 4.

35. Grigorii Iunin, under the rubric "Leaders": "Not the Last Dash to the East and the North: Over the Taiga, the Ocean, and the Tundra, with the LDPR Leader," *Zavtra*, no. 33 (August 1994), p. 3, in *FBIS* (Central Eurasia), September 26, 1994, p. 11. Zhirinovskii also proposed expelling all Chinese and Japanese citizens from the Russian Far East. See *OMRI Daily Digest*, part 1, February 17, 1995.

36. "Letter to *Nezavisimaia Gazeta* by Georgii Kunadze, Russian Federation deputy minister of Foreign Affairs: 'Does Not Serve the Interests of Russia . . . ': The Russian Federation Deputy Minister of Foreign Affairs on the Article on the Russian-Chinese Border," *Nezavisimaia Gazeta*, September 24, 1993, p. 4, in *FBIS* (Central Eurasia), October 27, 1993, p. 96; also see Border Troops Lieutenant General Iurii Neshumov and Lieutenant Colonel Nikolai Golub, "Problem: 'There Is No Reason to Talk about Ceding Russian Lands': Assistant Chairman and a Member of the Russian Federation Government Delegation on the Border Talks with China," *Nezavisimaia Gazeta*, September 29, 1993, p. 4, in *FBIS* (Central Eurasia), October 27, 1993, p. 97.

37. Interview with Viktor Alksnis, *Vostok Rossii* (Magadan), no. 33 (August 1993), p. 6, in *FBIS* (Central Eurasia), October 20, 1993, p. 35.

38. Interview with Colonel General Andrei Nikolaev, in "Border Guards Becomes Zone of Cooperation," *Krasnaia Zvezda*, November 17, 1993, p. 3, in *FBIS* (Central Eurasia), November 18, 1993, p. 8.

39. Interview with Evgenii Bazhanov, Moscow, April 12, 1999.

40. Interview with Lev Deliusin, Senior Scholar, Institute of the International Economy and Political Research, Moscow, April 20, 1999.

41. Russian News Agency, May 5, 1999 (electronic). China rejected the idea because of its friendly relations with Pakistan and continuing difficulties with India.

42. Interviews in Moscow with Aleksei Voskresenskii, Institute of the Far East, April 13, 1999, and Dmitrii Trenin, Moscow Carnegie Center, April 20, 1999.

43. Interview with Boris Zanegin, Moscow, April 26, 1999.

44. Interviews with Vladimir Li, Diplomatic Academy, April 12, 1999; and Aleksei Bogaturov, April 15, 1999.

45. Gilbert Rozman, "Sino-Russian Border Relations: Turning Fortresses into Free

Trade Zones," paper presented to the Carnegie Endowment for International Peace workshop on Sino-Russian Regional Relations, May 1997, p. 13.

46. Viktor Larin, "Rossiia i Kitai na poroge tret'ego tysiacheletiia: kto zhe budet otstaivat' nashi natsional'nye interesy? Vzgliad s Rossiiskogo Dal'nego Vostoka," *PDV*, no. 1 (1997), p. 24.

47. "Vneshnetorgovaia statistika regionov Da'lnego Vostoka i materialy vyezdnoi sessii Soveta Federatsii RF (Khabarovsk, Dekabr' 1994g.)," in Mikhail Nosov, "Rossiiskii Dal'nii Vostok i Kitai," in *Migratsionnaia Situatsiia*, p. 14.

48. Vladimir Soskyrev's coverage of Prime Minister Chernomyrdin's meeting with Li Peng in Beijing, "Pekin vozlagaet vinu za spad v torgovle na Moskvu," *Izvestiia*, May 26, 1994, p. 3; and Igor Kazakov, "Enterprises in China and Russia Prefer to Trade Directly," *Moscow News*, no. 51 (December 1993), p. 9, in *FBIS* (Central Eurasia), February 9, 1994, p. 54.

49. *Guoji Shangbao*, April 6, 1991, p. 3, in *Soviet Union in the Pacific-Asian Region (SUPAR) Report*, no. 11 (July 1991), pp. 32–33.

50. *Beijing Review*, no. 32, (August 6–12, 1990), p. 22, in *SUPAR Report*, no. 10 (January 1991), p. 44.

51. Xinhua, July 6, 1991, in *SUPAR Report*, no. 12 (January 1992), p. 30.

52. Interviews with mid-level provincial government researchers, Harbin, July 26, 1996.

53. Pavel Minakir and Nadezhda Mikheeva, "Ekonomika Rossiiskogo Dal'nego Vostoka: Mezhdu tsentralizatsiei i regionalizatsiei," unpublished paper presented at an international conference, "Russia on the Pacific: Past and Present," Khabarovsk, August 1995, p. 5. Minakir, the former vice-governor of Khabarovskii Krai, is director of the Institute of Economic Research in Khabarovsk. Mikheeva is deputy director of the institute.

54. L. Vardomskii and E. Samburova, "Rossiia i Kitai: sravnitel'nii analiz regional'nikh protsesov," *PDV*, no. 3 (1994), p. 27.

55. Viktor Pavliatenko, "Rossiiskii Dal'nii Vostok v sisteme otnoshenii Rossii so stranami SVA," *PDV*, no. 4 (1995), p. 11.

56. Minakir and Mikheeva, "Ekonomika Rossiiskogo Dal'nego Vostoka," pp. 2–3, 5–6.

57. *Ching chi tao pao* (Hong Kong), no. 28 (July 15, 1991), p. 12, in *SUPAR Report*, no. 12 (January 1992), p. 113.

58. *Rossiiskaia Gazeta*, June 18, 1992, in *SUPAR Report*, no. 13 (July 1992), p. 112.

59. Xinhua, March 11, 1992, in *SUPAR Report*, no. 13 (July 1992), p. 38.

60. Radio Harbin, August 22, 1992, in *Russia in Asia (RA) Report*, no. 14 (January 1993), p. 108.

61. ITAR-TASS, August 18, 1993, in *RA Report*, no. 16 (January 1994), p. 86.

62. *Ching chi tao pao* (Hong Kong), no. 6 (February 15, 1993), in *RA Report*, no. 15 (July 1993), p. 53.

63. *Cheng chi tao pao* (Hong Kong), no. 31 (August 9, 1993), in *RA Report*, no. 16 (January 1994), p. 27.

64. Xinhua, August 29, 1993, in *RA Report*, no. 16 (January 1994), p. 24. As of June 1999, Heilongjiang Province had opened 25 border ports.

65. Igor' Ilingin, Deputy Chief of the Ministry of Foreign Economic Relations of the Russian Main Economic Administration, "Russian Export Will Grow Some More, But Only a Little," *Segodnia*, March 17, 1995, p. 9, in *FBIS* (Central Eurasia), April 7, 1995, p. 1.

66. These figures do not include Russia's trade with other former Soviet states.

67. Li Zhuanhai, "Bianmao, zheli keyi zai pai huai?" *Yuandong Jingmao Daobao Xinxi*, May 1996, p. 16.

68. For an account of the impact of these economic changes on border trade between Amurskaia Oblast and China, see Yurii Moṣkalenko, "Vneshneekono-micheskoe sotrudnichestvo Amurskoi oblasti so stranami Severo-Vostochnoi Azii," *PDV*, no. 1 (1996), p. 48. Moskalenko serves in Amurskaia Oblast's Department on Foreign Economic Relations.

69. Ma Weixian, "Sino-Russian Border Trade," unpublished paper presented at the international conference "Russia on the Pacific," August 1995, p. 8.

70. Interview with Wen Ke, Head of the Heilongjiang Planning Commission, in "Bian mao zou xiang chengshu 'jia kuai' shi zai bi xing," *Heilongjiang Jingji Ribao*, May 1, 1996, p. 1.

71. Ma Weixian, "Sino-Russian Border Trade."

72. See, for example, Lu Nanquan, "Dui muqian ZhongE jingmao guanxi ruoguan wenti de sikao," *Guoji Shangbao*, May 27, 1996, p. 2.

73. Viktor Ishaev and Pavel A. Minakir, *Dal'nii Vostok Rossii: Real'nosti i voz-mozhnosti ekonomicheskogo razvitiia* (Khabarovsk: DVO RAN, 1998), p. 63.

74. Andrei G. Admidin and Elena I. Devaeva, *Mezhdunarodnoe ekonomicheskoe sotrudnichestvo v Vostochnoi Azii* (Vladivostok: Dal'nauka, 1998), p. 77.

75. Interviews, Ministry of Foreign Trade Research Institute, Beijing, August 6, 1996.

76. See, for example, Sun Xiufeng, "Zhengdun ZhongE bianjing maoyi zhixu, tuidong liangguo piling diqu jingmao hezuo," *Guoji Maoyi Wenti* (Beijing), no. 12 (1995), p. 51. The author was a commercial attaché at the PRC's Moscow embassy.

77. Interviews with senior scholars, Harbin, July 2, 1996.

78. The Chinese Ministry of Foreign Trade became concerned about these finan-cial problems and is devoting attention to them. For example, the June 20, 1996, issue of the Ministry's newspaper, *International Trade News*, published a special section

on financial problems in Sino-Russian border trade, which included articles on the lack of an arbitration mechanism and adequate insurance, the problems caused by the switch to hard currency, and transportation bottlenecks. See p. 2.

79. Ma Weixian, "Sino-Russian Border Trade," p. 13.

80. Oleg Davydov, "Rossiia i Kitai-novy shag navstrechu drug druga," *Segodnia*, April 23, 1996, p. 10. Davydov was deputy premier and minister of foreign economic ties.

81. Interviews with senior scholars, Beijing, June 3, 1996, and June 10, 1996.

82. Interview with a senior scholar, Beijing, June 3, 1996.

83. Fang Peien, "'Dao bao' zhe de qishi," *Heilongjiang Ribao*, April 10, 1996, p. 2.

84. Galina Vitkovskaia and Zhanna Zaonchkovskaia, "Novaia Stolypinskaia politika na Dal'nem Vostoke Rossii," in *Perspektivy Dal'nevostochnogo regiona: Mezhstranye vzaimodeistviia*, ed. Galina Vitkovskaia and Demitrii Trenin, (Moscow: Carnegie Moscow Center, 1999), pp. 96–97.

85. Leonid Savitskii from Primorskii Krai on "Vesti," Ostankino Television, First Channel, August 5, 1993, in *FBIS* (Central Eurasia), August 10, 1993, p. 31.

86. Vitkovskaia and Zaonchkovskaia, "Novaia Stolypinskaia politika na Dal'nem Vostoke Rossii," p. 84.

87. Vladimir Soskyrev, "Kitaiskie derevni v Sibiri i na dal'nem vostoke. Chto prineset Rossii politika otkrytykh dverei," *Utro Rossii* (Vladivostok), June 1, 1993, p. 3.

88. Editorial, "Kitaitsy bezoruzheny, no ochen' opasny," *Novosti* (Vladivostok), November 26, 1993.

89. Andrei Kabannikov, "Developing Siberia to the 'Amur Waves' Waltz," *Komsomol'skaia Pravda*, June 17, 1993, p. 5, in *FBIS* (Central Eurasia), July 7, 1993, p. 62. According to Kabannikov, officials from Heilongjiang Province tried unsuccessfully to include provisions on the establishment of Chinese settlements in interregional documents signed with the Primorskii Krai and Khabarovskii Krai administrations. Also see Soskyrev, "Kitaiskie derevni," p. 3.

90. Svetlana Zhukova and Viacheslav Boiakin, "Velikaia kitaiskaia stena na Ulitse Kotel'nikova," *Vladivostok*, December 29, 1993, p. 3; O. Kul'gin, "V Ussuriiske— malen'kii Kitai," *Krasnaia Znamia* (Vladivostok), July 15, 1993, p. 2; Tat'iana Kurochkina, "Kitaitsy v 'ugol' ne khotiat, i 'kitaiskii vopros' po-prezhnomu ostaetsia otkrytym," *Krasnaia Znamia*, November 11, 1993, p. 1, 4; and Liudmilla Boldyreva, "Gde iskat' kitaiskii rynok," *Tikhookeanskaia Zvezda*, August 27, 1993, p. 1.

91. Vladimir Soskyrev, "Iz Pekina v Moskvu s finkoi i naganom," *Izvestiia*, October 22, 1993; Boris Reznik, "Sozdany osobye otriady po bor'be s kitaiskimi brakonerami," *Izvestiia*, September 14, 1993.

92. Vitkovskaia and Zaonchkovskaia, "Novaia Stolypinskaia politika na Dal'nem Vostoke Rossii," p. 84.

93. P. Ivashov, "Point of View: The China Syndrome in the Outlying Areas of Russia," *Tikhookeanskaia Zvezda*, September 16, 1993, p. 2, in *FBIS* (Central Eurasia),

October 27, 1993, pp. 65–66; and Vladimir Medvedev, "Pukhovik iz Pekina: miagko steletsia, da zhestko spat'," *Komsomol'skaia Pravda*, October 30, 1993.

94. Petr Ivashov, "Kitaiskii Sindrom na okraine Rossii," *Tikhookeanskaia Zvezda*, September 16, 1993, p. 2. This article was also reprinted in the magazine of the Far Eastern branch of the Academy of Sciences as "Ugrozhaet li rossiiskomu Dal'nemu Vostoku 'Kitaiskii sindrom'?" *Dal'nevostochnyi Uchenyi* (Vladivostok), no. 30 (1993), pp. 3–4.

95. In 1993–94, articles critical of regional relations with China appeared frequently in Primorskii Krai publications, especially the newspaper *Vladivostok*. While Chinese officials generally attribute criticism of Sino-Russian relations in the Russian media to irresponsible individuals taking advantage of a free press, investigators from an NGO, the Glasnost Defense Foundation, noted the absence of a free press in Primorskii Krai and criticized the Nazdratenko administration for seizing control of the media in the region. *OMRI Regional Report*, vol 1, no. 8, part 1 (October 16, 1996).

96. Won Bae Kim, "Sino-Russian Relations and Chinese Workers in the Russian Far East: A Porous Border," *Asian Survey*, December 1994, p. 1067.

97. Evgenii Tuzhulin, "Kitaitsam vygodno vyrashchivat' u nas ovoshchi," *Priamurskie Vedomosti* (Khabarovsk), June 23, 1995, p. 2.

98. See, for example, Raisa Eldashova, "Blagodarnost' kitaiskim stroiteliam," *Tikhookeanskaia Zvezda*, June 1, 1995, p. 1; Valerii Golovin, "Net problem? Chto by my delali bez Kitaia?" *Priamurskie Vedomosti*, March 29, 1995, p. 1.

99. Aleskei Shabanov, "Pogranichniki-narody: Ryt' okopy, zakupat' sol' i spichki ne nado," *Tikhookeanskaia Zvezda*, June 16, 1995, p. 1; and Aleksii Shabanov, "Kitaitsy prodolzhaiut narushat' zakony Rossii," *Tikhookeanskaia Zvezda*, November 18, 1994, p. 1.

100. Evgenii Plaksen, "Rossiia i Kitai v tikhookeanskom regione: Obshchestvennoe mnenie rasstavliaet aktsenty i vybiraet prioritety," unpublished paper presented at an international conference, "Russia on the Pacific," Khabarovsk, August 1995, p. 8.

101. Ibid., p. 9.

102. Among the articles in the central press on Russian-Chinese border problems, see Boris Filippin, "El Dorado for Chinese Businesses," *Delovoi Mir*, September 24, 1993, p. 7, in *FBIS* (Central Eurasia), October 20, 1993, pp. 79–80; Andrei Gavrilenko, "Russia Risks Becoming an Economic Adjunct of China. The Chinese Are Already Doing Everything Possible To Bring This About," *Krasnaia Zvezda*, September 28, 1993, p. 3, in *FBIS* (Central Eurasia), September 30, 1993, p. 14.

103. Yurii Orlovskii, deputy director of the Institute for Legislation and Comparative Law, *Pravo i Ekonomika*, June 15, 1994, p. 14, in *FBIS* (Central Eurasia), July 22, 1994, p. 30.

104. Interview with Viktor Larin, the director of the Institute of History, Archeology, and Ethnography of the Peoples of the Far East (Vladivostok), May 16, 1994.

105. Kim, "Sino-Russian Relations and Chinese Workers in the Russian Far East," p. 1067.

106. Iurii Avdeev, Sergei Pushkarev, and Valentina Ushakova, "Migratsionnaia situatsiia i rynki truda v Primorskom krae: problemy trudovoi immigratsii," in *Perspektivy Dal'nevostochnogo regiona: Naselenie, migratsiia, rynki truda, Rabochie materialy, Vypusk 2*, ed. Galina Vitkovskaia and Dmitrii Trenin (Moscow: Carnegie Moscow Center, 1999).

107. Raisa Eldashova, "V perevode na kitaiskom vse vykhodit ne zer gud," *Tikhookeanskaia Zvezda*, September 30, 1993, p. 1, and "Eshche raz ob inostrannykh rabochikh," *Tikhookeanskaia Zvezda*, March 19, 1994, p. 1.

108. Nikolai Nepsha, "Kitaiskie turisty stanoviatsia rossiiskimi prestupniki," *Vladivostok*, July 7, 1994, p. 2.

109. Natal'ia Ostrovskaia, "Kitaitsev-nelegalov pytaiutsia vydvorit' iz Primor'e," *Izvestiia*, June 7, 1994, p. 1.

110. ITAR-TASS, November 17, 1994, in *FBIS* (Central Eurasia), November 17, 1994, p. 34.

111. Avdeev et al., "Migratsionnaia situatsiia i rynki truda v Primorskom krae," p. 67.

112. Stanislav Khodakov, "Immigratsiia i immigratsionnaia politika v Khabarovskom krae," in *Rabochie materialy*, ed. Vitkovskaia and Trenin, p. 29.

113. Aleksandr Glezer and Valentin Trudnanenko, "Operatsiia 'Inostranets': tri chetverti 'gostei' prozhivaiut v Primor'e nezakonno," *Vladivostok*, May 19, 1994, p. 4. On "Operatsiia Inostranets" in Khabarovskii Krai, see Sergei Auslender, "Blagodaria nashim organam v Kitae stanet bol'she kitaitsev," *Tikhookeanskaia Zvezda*, January 28, 1995; V. Kniazov, "Kriminal: 'Inostranets' zakonchilsia. Inostrantsev v Khabarovske stalo men'she," *Tikhookeanskaia Zvezda*, February 7, 1995, p. 1; and Aleskei Shabanov, "I vse sniatsia nam kitaitsy, bezborody, no s ruzh'em," *Tikhookeanskaia Zvezda*, March 29, 1995, p. 1.

114. Vitalii Strugovets, "Border Is Secure When Rear Services Are Reliable: In Four Months the Maritime Krai and Sakhalin Oblast Administrations Have Given 8.5 Billion Rubles' Worth of Aid to the Pacific Border District," *Krasnaia Zvezda*, July 1, 1994, p. 3, in *FBIS* (Central Eurasia), July 5, 1995, p. 33.

115. Marina Iashina, "Raz kitaets, dva kitaets," *Vladivostok*, July 8, 1994, p. 5; "Press-sluzhba administratsii Primorskogo kraia: priostanovit' nekontroliruemu migratsiiu," *Vladivostok*, July 2, 1994, p. 2.

116. Aleksei Shabanov, "I vse sniatsia," p. 1; Sergei Auslander, "Blagodaria nashim organam."

117. In Tat'iana Komendant, "Nado boiat'sia kitaiskoi ekspansii?" *Priamurskie Vedomosti*, July 1, 1995, p. 2.

118. In Aleksei Shabanov, "Pogranichniki-narody," p. 1.

119. See, for example, Chinese Foreign Minister Qian Qichen's speech at Moscow University in June 1994, Xinhua, June 28, 1994, in *FBIS* (PRC), June 30, 1994, p. 8.

120. Interviews with senior scholars, Beijing and Harbin, June–August 1996.

121. Xinhua, January 14, 1995, in *FBIS* (PRC), January 23, 1995; Gai Jindong and Li Daijun, "Border Defense Guards Clamp Down on Illegal Border Crossing," *Renmin Ribao*, January 16, 1995, p. 4, in *FBIS* (PRC), January 24, 1995, p. 36.

122. ITAR-TASS, January 26, 1995, in *FBIS* (Central Eurasia), January 27, 1995, p. 10. In an anonymous letter to the editor of *Segodnia*, a Chinese citizen living in Russia complained that Operation Foreigner provided law enforcement authorities with a pretext for mistreating Chinese citizens and extorting money from them in exchange for passports. "Everyone Robs the Chinese Immigrants in Russia, One After Another," *Segodnia*, March 3, 1995, p. 6, in *FBIS* (Central Eurasia), March 23, 1995, p. 10.

123. Interview with Larin, May 16, 1994.

124. Konstantin Eggert, "Provintsial'nye chinovniki liubiat kitaiskie tovary. I ne liubiat chinovnikov iz Moskvy," *Izvestiia*, February 4, 1994, p. 3. The author suggested that the regions were criticizing the very policies they had requested because they were looking for yet another hand-out from Moscow.

125. *Heilongjiang Ribao*, January 27, 1994, p. 1, in *RA Report*, July 1994, p. 34.

126. ITAR-TASS, January 27, 1994, in *FBIS* (Central Eurasia), January 28, 1994, p. 4.

127. In Vladimir Soskyrev, "Grozit li nashemu Dal'nemu Vostoku kitaiskaia kolonizatsiia?" *Izvestiia*, March 16, 1995, p. 1.

128. Andrei Aksai, "Blizkii Kitai stanovitsia vse dal'she i dal'she," *Amurskaia Pravda*, June 27, 1995, p. 1.

129. Aleksandr Petrushev and Yurii Mostoslavskii, "Mostu cherez Amur—byt'," *Amurskaia Pravda*, June 28, 1995, p. 1.

130. Interview with Pavel Minakir, Khabarovsk, August 1995.

131. Ibid. At the time China accounted for 43 percent of Khabarovskii Krai's foreign trade. Khabarovskii Krai had sent some 15–20 percent of its exports to China, and received more than 60 percent of its imports from its southern neighbor. "Zainteresovany v sotrudnichestve s KNR," *Tikhookeanskaia Zvezda*, May 25, 1994, p. 1.

132. Committee on Foreign Economic Cooperation and Regional Relations, Primorskii Krai administration, "Rossiisko-kitaiskie otnosheniia," Vladivostok, May 1994, pp. 12–13.

133. Interview with Nadezhda Novikova, Committee on Foreign Economic and Regional Relations, Primorskii Krai Administration, May 24, 1994.

134. Admidin and Devaeva, *Mezhdunarodnoe ekonomicheskoe sotrudnichestvo v Vostochnoi Azii*, pp. 54–55.

135. Committee on Foreign Economic Cooperation and Regional Relations, Primorskii Krai administration, "Zakliuchenie: po itogam parlamentskikh slushanii 'O problemakh rossiisko-kitaiskikh otnoshenii i perspektivakh ikh resheniia'," *Vladivostok*, April 25, 1994.

136. Verchenko, "Rossiia i Kitai," p. 45.

137. Ibid., p. 42.

138. ITAR-TASS, February 11, 1995, in *FBIS* (Central Eurasia), February 13, 1995, p. 18.

139. Xinhua, September 9, 1994, in *FBIS* (PRC), September 9, 1994, p. 13; and Igor Kazakov, "Enterprises in China and Russia Prefer to Trade Directly," *Moscow News*, December 17, 1993, p. 9, in *FBIS* (Central Eurasia), p. 55.

140. ITAR-TASS, August 31, 1994, in *FBIS* (Central Eurasia), September 1, 1994, p. 5.

141. Xinhua, September 21, 1994, in *FBIS* (PRC), September 22, 1994, p. 5.

142. See Primorskii Krai Administration, "Zakliuchenie"; and Sergei Shakhrai, "Neobkhodimaia strategiia otnoshenii s Kitaem," *Izvestiia*, May 20, 1994, p. 4. Also see Verchenko, "Rossiia i Kitai," p. 44.

143. Xinhua, January 23, 1997, *FBIS* (PRC), January 23, 1999 (electronic).

144. Interviews, Ministry of Foreign Trade Research Institute, Beijing, August 6, 1996; Davydov, "Rossiia i Kitai."

145. Lu Nanquan, "ZhongE jingmao guangxi," unpublished paper, March 15, 1997, p. 9.

146. Gilbert Rozman, "The Crisis of the Russian Far East. Who Is to Blame?" *Problems of Post-Communism*, September–October 1997, p. 4.

147. On the new Chinese border trade rules, see "Guowuyuan guanyu bianjing maoyi you guan wenti de tongzhi," *Yuandong Jing Mao Xinxi* (Harbin), no. 5 (1996), pp. 3–9.

148. Rozman, "The Crisis of the Russian Far East," p. 6.

149. Tamara Troiakova, "Primor'e—provintsii KNR: Kachesto Otnoshenii," *Rossiia i ATR*, no. 3 (1998), p. 82.

150. Poll taken by Evgenii Plaksen, director, laboratory for the Study of Public Opinion, Institute of History, Vladivostok, July–August 1997.

151. Ibid.

152. Vitkovskaia and Zaonchkovskaia, "Novaia Stolypinskaia politika," pp. 112–15.

153. Ibid., p. 25.

154. Viktor Larin, *Kitai i Dal'nii Vostok Rossii* (Vladivostok: Dal'nauka, 1998), pp. 74, 200.

155. Li Jianmin, "Heilongjiang shen de duiE bianjing maoyi," in *ZhongE maoyi*

guanxi, ed. Lu Nanquan and Xue Jundu (Beijing: Chinese Academy of Social Sciences Press, 1999), p. 167.

156. South Korea remains Primorskii Krai's leading source of imports, and Japan still ranks number one in terms of the region's exports. Because sales to China of SU-27 aircraft, produced in Khabarovskii Krai, are counted as exports of machinery in regional trade statistics, this region reported $636.9 million in exports to China in 1998, compared to $67.2 in 1997. Elena Devaeva, "Vneshniaia Torgovlia Dal'nego Vostoka Rossii," unpublished paper prepared for a March 1999 Japan External Trade Organization (JETRO) conference in Khabarovsk, pp. 15, 19.

157. The United States accounted for 40 percent of all investment in the region during the same period. Anatolii Bouryi, "Interregional Association 'Far East and Transbaikal' and Perspectives for Integration," unpublished comments for an IREX Conference "The Russian Far East on the Road to Openness: Regional Development and Prospects for Integration with the Pacific Rim," Vladivostok, June 1999.

158. *Vneshneekonomicheskaia deiatel'nost' v Primorskom krae* (Vladivostok: Primorskii Kraevoi Komitet Gosudarstvennoi Statistiki , 1999), p. 22.

159. Interview with a senior scholar, Beijing, March 15, 1999.

160. Association of the Russian Far East and the Trans-Baikal et al., ed., *Investment Atlas, volume 1* (Khabarovsk: Far East Office for Initiation and Expertise of the Investment Projects, 1999), p. 65.

161. Report by Primorskii Krai Administration Committee on Foreign Economic and Regional Relations (early 1994); also cited in Vladislav Dorofeev and Anastasiia Romashkevich, "Survey of the Economy of the Regions of Russia, August–November 1993. The Chinese Factor in Russia," *Kommersant*, no. 46 (November 1993), pp. 26–27, in *FBIS* (Central Eurasia), December 22, 1993, p. 30.

162. Contents of a September 1993 letter cited in Rozman, "Sino-Russian Border Relations," p. 20.

163. Moscow Radio Rossii Network, September 17, 1993, in *FBIS* (Central Eurasia), September 20, 1993, p. 15.

164. Sergei Avdeev, "Chinese Diplomats Take Damanskii Without a Fight and Advance Swiftly Deep Into Russian Territory," *Komsomol'skaia Pravda*, August 6, 1993, p. 1, in *FBIS* (Central Eurasia), August 9, 1993, p. 20.

165. This was the result of years of secrecy about the border issue, according to Evgenii Afanas'ev, a member of the Russian delegation to the border demarcation talks. Afanas'ev warned, however, that some regional leaders also tried to play the "border card" for their own political purposes. Aleksandr Platkovskii, "Moskva i Pekin vyiasniaut komu prinadlezhit ostrova na Amure i Ussuri," *Izvestiia*, April 26, 1994, p. 3. Also see Aleksei Voskresenskii, "Zone of Cooperation or of Potential Conflict?" *Nezavisimaia Gazeta*, June 3, 1994, p. 5, in *FBIS* (Central Eurasia), June 30, 1994, p. 83.

166. G. Kireev, "Granitsa s Kitaem: emotsii i real'nost'," *Utro Rossii*, July 29, 1993, p. 2.

167. Avdeev, "Chinese Diplomats Take Damanskii without a Fight."

168. N. Solov'ev, "Na granitse s Kitaem spokoino," *Krasnoe Znamia*, October 10, 1993, p. 2.

169. Adveev, "Chinese Diplomats Take Damanskii without a Fight."

170. Boris Reznik, "Gubernator Khabaroskogo kraia trebuet denonsirovat' soglashenie s Kitaem o granitse," *Izvestiia*, May 17, 1994, p. 3. The demarcation of the border in the section of the Amur which flows past Khabarovsk is particularly contentious because the main river channel has been moving closer to the Russian side.

171. "MID ne soglasen," *Izvestiia*, May 17, 1994, p. 3; and "Rossiia vedet peregovory s Kitaem o vyrabotke pravil sudokhodstva v raone Khabarovska," *Vladivostok*, May 19, 1994, p. 11.

172. Moscow Radio in Mandarin, July 3, 1994, in *FBIS* (Central Eurasia), July 6, 1994, p. 19. The Russian-Chinese border is only 55 km long in the western section.

173. ITAR-TASS, July 12, 1994, in *FBIS* (Central Eurasia), July 12, 1994, p. 2.

174. Valeriia Sycheva, "Zreet konflikt iz-za zalivnykh luzhkov i kedrovykh kushch," *Kommersant-Daily*, February 7, 1995, p. 4.

175. V. Venevstev and D. Demkin, "Governor on the Warpath Against 'Chinazation' and the Russian Ministry of Foreign Affairs," *Kommersant-Daily*, January 17, 1995, p. 4, in *FBIS* (Central Eurasia), February 3, 1995, pp. 3–4.

176. Sycheva, "Zreet konflikt"; Oleg Kruchek, "Demarcation or Renunciation? Federation Council Members Dislike Russia-China Border," *Segodnia*, February 7, 1995, p. 3, in *FBIS* (Central Eurasia), February 7, 1995, pp. 3–4. For a Foreign Ministry reaction, see Interfax, February 7, 1995, in *FBIS* (Central Eurasia), February 8, 1995, p. 6.

177. Aleksandr Platkovksii, "Pogranichnii spor mozhet vzorvat nashi otnosheniia s Kitaem," *Izvestiia*, February 10, 1995, p. 3.

178. Vladimir Soskyrev, "In Order to Make Friends with China, It Is Necessary First to Fix the Border with It," *Izvestiia*, February 28, 1995, p. 3, in *FBIS* (Central Eurasia), February 28, 1995, p. 12.

179. Damir Gaunutdinov, "We Really Do Have a Lot of Land, but This Does Not Mean that It Is Unnecessary, and Especially that It Is Foreign," *Utro Rossii*, February 24, 1995, p. 1, in *FBIS* (Central Eurasia), March 1, 1995, p. 34.

180. ITAR-TASS, February 22, 1995, in *FBIS* (Central Eurasia), February 23, 1995, p. 14.

181. ITAR-TASS, March 3, 1995, in *FBIS* (Central Eurasia), March 8, 1995, p. 12.

182. ITAR-TASS, March 8, 1995, in *FBIS* (Central Eurasia), March 15, 1995, p. 16.

183. Interview with Vladimir Lukin, *Nezavisimaia Gazeta*, March 14, 1995, pp. 1–2, in *FBIS* (Central Eurasia), March 20, 1995, p. 7.

184. ITAR-TASS, March 1, 1995, in *FBIS* (Central Eurasia), March 6, 1995, p. 9.

185. Interfax, March 2, 1995, in *FBIS* (Central Eurasia), March 6, 1995, p. 9.

186. ITAR-TASS, March 10, 1995, in *FBIS* (Central Eurasia), March 10, 1995, p. 15.

187. Evgenii Nazdratenko, "Seichas politika dlia bol'shinstva liudei peremestilas' za dvertsu kholodil'nika," *Vladivostok*, August 24, 1995, p. 7.

188. ITAR-TASS, April 12, 1995, in *FBIS* (Central Eurasia), April 13, 1995, p. 7.

189. In Aleksandr Kartashov, Evgenii Kul'kov, and Valentin Trukhanenko, "O kitaiskoi 'voennoi ugroze,' 'territorial'nom voprose,' i drugikh problemakh granitsy Primor'e," *Vladivostok*, July 14, 1995, p. 5.

190. Andrei Aksai, "Ob etom govoriat: voiny s Kitaem ne budet: Sosedi i tak 'pribiraiut' nashi zemli," *Amurskaia Pravda* (Blagoveshchensk), July 12, 1995, p. 1.

191. Georgii Levkin, "Kitaitsy khochetsia plavat' pod oknami u khabarovchan ili 'k voprosu ob ust'e reki Ussuri," *Dal'nevostochnyi Uchenyi*, June 12, 1995, pp. 8–9.

192. V. Pasmanik, "Demarkatsiia: zakonodateli protiv ottorzheniia ostrovov," *Birobidzhanskaia Zvezda* (Birobidjan), June 14, 1995, p. 3. On the Chinese reaction see Shabanov, "Pogrannichniki—narody," p. 1.

193. Ivan Egortsev, "Tropoiu Arseneva—vdol' rubezhei Rossii," *Utro Rossii*, August 1, 1995, p. 1. The group placed a cross in the border area to mark the farthest point of Russian settlement. Ivan Egortsev, "Rubezhnye versty," *Utro Rossii*, August 22, 1995, p. 4. An article in *Izvestiia* criticized the historical basis for their mission. See Natal'ia Ostrovskaia, "Zhiteli Primor'e sprashivaiut u podgranichnikov kogda nachnetsia voina s Kitaem," *Izvestiia*, September 20, 1995, p. 3.

194. Interfax, December 7, 1995, in *OMRI Daily Digest*, part 1, December 8, 1995.

195. *Jamestown Monitor*, March 19, 1996.

196. Valerii Rozov, "Prezident neverno informirovali," *Trud*, January 15, 1997, p. 7.

197. Genrykh Kireev, "Demarcation of the Border with China," *International Affairs* (Moscow), vol. 45, no. 2 (1999), pp. 106–7. The 1860 Treaty of Beijing and other documents signed from 1860–66 had stated that the border was the Tumen watershed and that the left bank belonged to China. Over time, the left bank had eroded, however, and 500 meters of the border had shifted in such a way that the Chinese could not go from one part of their territory to another. The 1997 agreement reestablished the intent of the 1860–66 documents, but enough of a compromise was reached to enable Nazdratenko's supporters to call it a victory for Primorskii Krai. See Margarita Usova and Andrei Nikolaev, "Granitsa, Nazdratenko i pogranichnyi general," *Zolotoi Rog*, October 5, 1999, pp. 1, 28.

198. Tat'iana Malkina and Oleg Kriuchek, "Boris Yeltsin vidit sebia prodolzhatelem Petra I i Nikity Khrushcheva," *Segodnia*, April 25, 1996, p. 2.

199. Viktor Ishaev, preface to Miasnikov, "Dogovornymi statiami utverdili," p. 2.

200. Interview with Yurii Efimenko, head of the public committee to strengthen Khabarovskii Krai's jurisdiction over Bolshoi Ussuriiskii and Tabarov Islands, in *Prospekt*

Polius (Khabarovsk), no. 41 (1998), p. 11. An unidentified hand-drawn Chinese map indicating China's control over the islands accompanied the text of the interview.

201. Interview with Vladimir Simakhin, advisor to Russian-Chinese Demarcation Commission and Chief Inspector, Far Eastern Territorial Inspectorate of the State Geodesic Service (Khabarovsk), June 3, 1997.

202. Cited by Sergei Lebedev, "Kukola v Rossii kroiut chestym zolotom, chtoby chashche gospod' zamechal...," *Khabarovskie Izvestiia*, October 28, 1999, p. 1.

203. Amos A. Jordan and Jane Khanna, "Economic Interdependence and Challenges to the Nation-State: The Emergence of Natural Economic Territories in the Asia-Pacific," *Journal of International Affairs*, Winter 1995, pp. 448–49; Daniel Aldrich, "If You Build It They Will Come: A Cautionary Tale about the Tumen River Projects," *The Journal of East Asian Affairs*, Winter/Spring 1997, p. 314.

204. A compromise ultimately was reached and this part of the border has been demarcated. For the details, see Genrykh Kireev, "Demarcation of the Border with China," *International Affairs*, vol. 45, no. 2 (1999), pp. 106–7.

205. Evgenii Nazdratenko, "Radi nashikh potomkov, Dukhovnoe nasledie," December 1996, p. 5, reprinted in *Nekotorye problemy demarkatsii Rossiisko-Kitaiskoi granitsy. 1991–1997 god. Sbornik statei i dokumentov* (Moscow: Nezavisimaia Gazeta, 1997). Nazdratenko noted that while the Tumen River marked a portion of the Sino-Russian border 130 years ago, the river has changed its course since that time. It now delimits the border between Russia and North Korea.

206. See for example, Artem Pronkin, "Morskoi zapovednik: edinstvennyi i poslednii?" *Vladivostok*, November 7, 1996, pp. 1, 5.

207. See, for example, Larisa Zabrovskaia, Institute of History (Vladivostok), "Proekt 'Tumengan': Komu eto nuzhno," in *Nekotorye problemy demarkatsii*, pp. 53–58.

208. UNDP, "Tumen River Area Development," Mission Report, Pyongyang, October 16–18, 1991, p. 73.

209. Gaye Christoffersen, "Nesting the Sino-Russian Border and the Tumen Project in the Asia-Pacific: Heilongjiang's Regional Relations," *Asian Perspective*, vol. 2, no. 2 (Fall–Winter 1996), p. 291.

210. Aldrich, "If You Build it They Will Come," p. 319.

211. Jordon and Khanna, "Economic Interdependence and Challenges to the Nation-State," p. 449.

212. E. I. Devaeva and V. G. Norin, "Sovmestnaia predprinimatel'skaia deiatel'nost' na Dal'nem Vostoke Rossii," *PDV*, no. 6 (1966), p. 5. Even during the period of great expansion in Sino-Russian regional economic relations, public opinion data from Primorskii Krai revealed a preference for cooperation with Japan, the United States, and South Korea over China. See Vladimir Larin and Evgenii Plaksen, "Primor'e: perspektivy razvitiia cherez prizmu obshchestvennogo mneniia," *Rossiia i ATR* (Vladivostok), no. 1 (1993), p. 11.

213. Oleg Kriuchek, "Dal'nevostochnye territorii gotoviatsia k ekonomicheskii integratsii so stranami ATR," *Segodnia*, April 25, 1997, p. 6. Members of the association include the Republics of Sakha (Iakutiia); Buriatiia; Primorskii and Khabarovskii Krais; Amur, Chita, Kamchatka, Magadan, Sakhalin, and Jewish Autonomous Oblasts; and the Chukhotka and Koriak Autonomous Okrugs.

214. *Zolotoi Rog*, May 25, 1999 (electronic).

215. See, for example, Larin's critique of the Foreign Ministry's China policy, in "Rossiia i Kitai," pp. 16–17.

216. Institut Dal'nego Vostoka, "Interesy Rossii v Severo-Vostochnoi Azii i perspektivy ispol'zovaniia mnogostoronnego storudnichestva so stranami regiona dlia razvitiia rossiiskogo Dal'nego Vostoka" (Proekt Rossiiskogo Gumanitarnogo Nauchnogo Fonda no. 95–06–17574), Moscow, 1996, p. 152.

217. Jiang Yi, "Sino-Russian Ties: New Constructive Partnership," *Beijing Review*, November 13–19, 1995, p. 11. Jiang Yi is a scholar at the Institute of Russian and East European Studies, Chinese Academy of Social Sciences.

CONCLUSIONS

1. Tai Ming Cheung, "Quick Response," *Far Eastern Economic Review*, January 14, 1993, p. 20.

2. Andrew Bouchkin, "Russia's Far Eastern Policy in the 90's: Priorities and Prospects," unpublished paper presented at the Russian Littoral Project's conference, "Foreign Policy Priorities and Decision-Making," March 1994, p. 13.

3. Aleksei Iablokov, Chairman of the Interdepartmental Commission on Environmental Security, for example, stated that Russia should not have sold uranium enrichment technology to China because it could be used to develop nuclear weapons. Interfax, March 16, 1995, in *FBIS* (Central Eurasia), March 21, 1995, p. 14.

4. V. D. Andrianov, V.N. Pavliatenko, and E.V. Sprogis, "Napravlenie ekonomicheskogo vzaimodeistviia s SVA," *Rossiiskii Dal'nii Vostok i Severo-Vostochnaia Aziia* (Moscow: Editorial URSS, 1998), p. 143.

5. On this point, see Sergei Rogov, "Analysis: The Results Are Pitiful, but There Is a Way Out: Three Years of Trial and Error in Russian Foreign Policy," *Nezavisimaia Gazeta*, December 31, 1994, pp. 4–5, in *FBIS* (Central Eurasia), January 26, 1995, p. 10; and Aleksei Arbatov, director of the Geopolitical and Military Forecasting Center, "Rossiia: Natsional'naia bezopasnost' v 90e gody," *Mirovaia Ekonomika i Mezhdunarodnye Otnosheniia*, no. 7 (1994), pp. 5–15. On China's rise and Russia's decline, see Sherman Garnett, "Russia's Illusory Ambitions," *Foreign Affairs*, March/April 1997, p. 69.

6. Vladimir Abrimov, "The Foreign Ministry Hopes That the CIS Will Greet the New Year Without Bloodshed: Russia's Diplomats Are Reluctant to Step on the Same

Rake," *Segodnia*, December 16, 1994, p. 3, in *FBIS* (Central Eurasia), January 12, 1995, p. 6.

7. A. N. Krasnov, *Po ostrovam dalekogo Vostoka. Putevye ocherki nedeli* (Saint Petersburg: 1895). I am indebted to Evgenii Plaksen for calling my attention to this memoir.

8. Igor Rogachev, "Russia-China: The Principles and Parameters of Partnership," *Far Eastern Affairs*, no. 2 (1997), p. 26; Li Fenglin, "The Historic Choice of the Peoples of Our Two Countries," in *Far Eastern Affairs*, no. 2 (1997), p. 36. Igor Rogachev is the Russian ambassador to the PRC and Li Fenglin is the Chinese ambassador to Russia.

9. Vilia Gel'bras, "Kitaiskii Vopros Rossii," draft for publication in Carnegie Moscow Center Study, 1999, p. 6.

10. The debate took place in the pages of *Harbin Shizhi*, published by the Harbin city government. See Thomas Lahusen, "A Place Called Harbin: Reflections on a Centennial," *The China Quarterly*, June 1998, p. 408.

11. On the need to integrate the Russian Far East into Russia's Asia policy, see M.L. Titarenko and A.V. Ostrovskii, "Zakliuchenie," in *Rossiiskii Dal'nii Vostok*, p. 212.

12. Michel Tatu, "The Washington-Moscow-Beijing Triangle," *International Affairs* (Moscow), vol. 45, no. 2 (1999), pp. 64–65.

13. Song Yimin, "Sino-Russia, Russia-US, Sino-US Relations and Interaction among the Three," English translation of an article published in *Guoji Wenti Yanjiu*, no. 3 (1997), p. 19. For a Chinese analysis of the history of the triangle, see Guo Shuyong and Niu Jusheng, "70 niandai sulian he 90 niandai Eluosi guoji zhanlue huanjing ji dui Hua waijiao bijiao," *DongOuZhongYa Yanjiu*, no. 2 (1997), pp. 16–22.

14. On the impact of these challenges for the United States, see Michael Mandelbaum, "Westernizing Russia and China," *Foreign Affairs*, May/June 1997, pp. 85–89.

15. Lev Deliusin, "Vneshnepoliticheskie problemy Rossii na Dal'nem Vostoke, *Rossiia i Sovremennyi Mir*, no. 1 (1998), p. 78.

16. John Garver, "A Far Eastern Rapallo: The Post Cold War Russian-Chinese Strategic Partnership," *Far Eastern Affairs*, no. 1 (1998), pp. 55–56.

17. Sergei Rogov, "Russia as the Eurasian Bridge: Challenges of Russia's Integration into the World Community," Center for Naval Analyses, CIM 587/November 1998, p. 51.

18. Evgenii Bazhanov, "Rossiia kak velikaia derzhava (traditsii i perspektivy)," Institut Aktual'nykh Problem, Diplomaticheskaia Akademiia, Moscow, 1999, pp. 40–42; Oleg Davydov, "Russia's Foreign Policy in Transition," *Asian Perspective*, vol. 22, no. 1 (Spring 1998), p. 57.

19. See, for example, Aleksei Bogaturov, *Sovremennye teorii stabil'nosti i mezhdunarodnye otnosheniia Rossii v Vostochnoi Azii v 1970–90–e gg* (Moscow: Moskovskii Nauchnyi Fond, 1996), chapter 5; Dmitrii Trenin, *Kitaiskaia problema Rossii* (Moscow: Moskovskii Tstentr Karnegi, 1998), chapter 3.

Works Cited

BOOKS IN ENGLISH AND FRENCH

An, Tai Sung. *The Sino-Soviet Territorial Dispute*. Philadelphia: The Westminster Press, 1973.

Arbatov, Georgi. *The System*. New York: Random House, 1992.

Association of the Russian Far East and the Trans-Baikal et al., eds. *Investment Atlas*. Vol. 1. Khabarovsk: Far Eastern Office for Initiation and Expertise of the Investment Projects, 1999.

Barnouin, Barbara, and Yu Changgen. *Chinese Foreign Policy during the Cultural Revolution*. London: Kegan Paul International, 1998.

Baum, Richard. *Burying Mao*. Princeton, N.J.: Princeton University Press, 1994.

Bazhanov, Evgenii. *USSR-China in the Changing World*. Moscow: Novosti, 1989.

Besançon, Alain. *Origines intellectuelles du Léninisme*. Paris: Calmann-Lévy, 1977.

Bialer, Seweryn. *Stalin's Successors*. Cambridge: Cambridge University Press, 1980.

Blair, Bruce G. *The Logic of Accidental Nuclear War*. Washington, D.C.: The Brookings Institution, 1993.

Breslauer, George W., and Philip E. Tetlock, eds. *Learning in US and Soviet Foreign Policy*. Boulder, Colo.: Westview Press, 1991.

Brown, Archie. *The Gorbachev Factor*. Oxford: Oxford University Press, 1996.

Brown, Archie, ed. *Political Leadership in the Soviet Union*. Oxford: Macmillan, 1989.

Burr, William, ed. *The Kissinger Transcripts*. New York: The New Press, 1998.

Checkel, Jeffrey. *Ideas and International Political Change*. New Haven: Yale University Press, 1997.

Cohen, Stephen F. *An End to Silence*. New York: W. W. Norton & Company, Inc., 1982.

Colton, Timothy. *The Dilemma of Reform in the Soviet Union*. New York: Council on Foreign Relations, 1986.

Day, Alan J., ed. *China and the Soviet Union, 1949–84*. New York: Facts on File Publications, 1985.

Degras, Jane, ed. *Soviet Documents on Foreign Policy*. London: Oxford University Press, 1951.

Dittmer, Lowell. *Sino-Soviet Normalization and Its International Implications, 1945–1990.* Seattle: University of Washington Press, 1990.

Dobrynin, Anatoly. *In Confidence.* New York: Random House, 1995.

Duara, Prasenjit. *Rescuing History from the Nation.* Chicago: University of Chicago Press, 1995.

Dunlop, John B. *The Rise of Russia and the Fall of the Soviet Empire.* Princeton, N.J.: Princeton University Press, 1993.

Elleman, Bruce. *Diplomacy and Deception: The Secret History of Sino-Soviet Diplomatic Relations, 1917–1927.* Armonk, N.Y.: M. E. Sharpe, 1997.

Ellison, Herbert J., ed. *The Sino-Soviet Conflict.* Seattle: University of Washington Press, 1982.

Fingar, Thomas, ed. *China's Quest for Independence: Policy Evolution in the 1970s.* Boulder, Colo.: Westview Press, 1980.

Fleming, Peter. *News from Tartary.* London: Jonathan Cape, 1936.

Fleron Frederic J., Jr., Erik P. Hoffmann, et al. *Soviet Foreign Policy.* New York: Aldine de Fruyter, 1991.

Garthoff, Raymond. *Détente and Confrontation.* Washington, D.C.: The Brookings Institution, 1985.

Gati, Charles. *The Bloc That Failed.* Bloomington: Indiana University Press, 1990.

Gelman, Harry. *The Soviet Far East Buildup and Soviet Risk-Taking against China.* Rand R-2943–AF. August 1982.

Ginsburgs, George, and Carl F. Pinkele. *The Sino-Soviet Territorial Dispute, 1959–64.* New York: Praeger Publishers, 1978.

Goldstein, Judith, and Robert O. Keohane, eds. *Ideas and Foreign Policy: Beliefs, Institutions, and Political Change.* Ithaca, N.Y.: Cornell University Press, 1993.

Goncharov, Sergei N., John W. Lewis, Xue Litai, et al. *Uncertain Partners: Stalin, Mao, and the Korean War.* Stanford, Calif.: Stanford University Press, 1992.

Gorbachev, Mikhail. *Memoirs.* New York: Doubleday, 1995.

Gottlieb, Thomas M. *Chinese Foreign Policy Factionalism and the Origins of the Strategic Triangle.* Rand R-1902–NA, November 1977.

Griffith, William E. *The Sino-Soviet Rift.* Cambridge: MIT Press, 1964.

Harding, Harry, ed. *China's Foreign Relations in the 1980s.* New Haven: Yale University Press, 1984.

———. *China's Second Revolution.* Washington, D.C.: The Brookings Institution, 1987.

Hart, Thomas G. *Sino-Soviet Relations: Reexamining the Prospects for Normalization.* Aldershot, England: Gower, 1987.

Hersh, Seymour M. *The Price of Power,* New York: Summit Books, 1983.

Hewett, Ed. A. *Reforming the Soviet Economy.* Washington, D.C.: The Brookings Institution, 1988.

Hinton, Harold C. *The Sino-Soviet Confrontation: Implications for the Future.* New York: Crane, Russak & Company, Inc., 1976.

Hunt, Michael. *Ideology and US Foreign Policy.* New Haven: Yale University Press, 1987.

Jacobsen, David, ed. *Old Nations, New World.* Boulder, Colo.: Westview Press, 1994.

Jowitt, Ken. *New World Disorder: The Leninist Extinction.* Berkeley: University of California Press, 1992.

Kim, Ilpyong J., ed. *The Strategic Triangle.* New York: Paragon House Publishers, 1987.

Kissinger, Henry A. *The White House Years.* Boston: Little, Brown & Company, 1979.

Ladany, Laszlo. *The Communist Party of China and Marxism, 1921–1985: A Self-Portrait.* Stanford, Calif.: Hoover Institution Press, 1988.

Leong, Sow-theng. *Sino-Soviet Diplomatic Relations, 1917–1926.* Honolulu: University of Hawaii Press, 1976.

Leonhard, Wolfgang. *Three Faces of Marxism.* New York: Holt, Rinehart and Winston, 1970.

Li, Zhisui. *The Private Life of Chairman Mao.* London: Chatto and Windus, 1994.

Lieberthal, Kenneth G. *Sino-Soviet Conflict in the 1970s: Its Evolution and Implications for the Strategic Triangle.* Rand R-2342–NA, July 1978.

Linden, Carl. *The Soviet Party-State: The Politics of Ideocratic Despotism.* New York: Praeger Publishers, 1983.

Lynch, Allen. *The Soviet Study of International Relations.* Cambridge: Cambridge University Press, 1989.

MacFarquhar, Roderick, and John K. Fairbank, eds. *The Cambridge History of China.* Vol. 15. Cambridge: Cambridge University Press, 1991.

MacFarquhar, Roderick, ed. *The Politics of China,* 2nd ed. Cambridge: Cambridge University Press, 1997.

Medvedev, Zhores. *Andropov.* Oxford: Basil Blackwell, 1983.

Meisner, Maurice. *The Deng Xiaoping Era.* New York: Hill and Wang, 1996.

———. *Mao's China and After.* New York: The Free Press, 1986.

Mendelson, Sarah. *Changing Course.* Princeton, N.J.: Princeton University Press, 1998.

Mitchell, R. Judson. *Ideology of a Superpower.* Stanford, Calif.: Hoover Institution Press, 1982.

Oye, Kenneth A., Robert J. Lieber, and Donald Rothchild, eds. *Eagle Resurgent?* Boston: Little, Brown, and Company, 1987.

Paine, S. C. M. *Imperial Rivals: Russia, China, and Their Disputed Frontier, 1858–1924.* Armonk, N.Y.: M. E. Sharpe, 1996.

Palazchenko, Pavel. *My Years with Gorbachev and Shevardnadze.* University Park: Pennsylvania State University Press, 1997.

Petroff, Serge. *The Red Eminence*. Clifton, N.J.: The Kingston Press, Inc., 1988.

Quested, R.K.I. *The Expansion of Russia in East Asia, 1857–1860*. Kuala Lumpur: The University of Malaya Press, 1968.

———. *Sino-Russian Relations: A Short History*. Sydney: George Allen Unwin, 1984.

Richter, James G. *Khrushchev's Double Bind*. Baltimore: The Johns Hopkins University Press, 1994.

Rigby, T. H., and Bohdan Harasymiu, eds. *Leadership Selection and Patron-Client Relations in the USSR and Yugoslavia*. London: George Allen & Unwin, 1980.

Riker, William. *The Theory of Coalitions*. Westport, Conn.: Greenwood Press, 1984.

Robinson, Thomas W., *The Sino-Soviet Border Dispute: Background Development, and the March 1969 Clashes*. Rand RM-6171–PR, August 1970.

Robinson, Thomas W., and David Shambaugh. *Chinese Foreign Policy: Theory and Practice*. Oxford: Clarendon Press, 1994.

Ross, Robert S. *Negotiating Cooperation: The United States and China, 1969–1989*. Stanford, Calif.: Stanford University Press, 1995.

Rothenberg, Morris. *Whither China: The View from the Kremlin*. Miami: University of Miami, 1977.

Rozman, Gilbert. *The Chinese Debate about Soviet Socialism, 1979–85*. Princeton, N.J.: Princeton University Press, 1987.

———. *Mirror for Socialism*. Princeton, N.J.: Princeton University Press, 1985.

Segal, Gerald. *Defending China*. Oxford: Oxford University Press, 1985.

———. *The Great Power Triangle*. London: The MacMillan Press, 1982.

Shambaugh, David L. *Beautiful Imperialist: China Perceives America, 1972–1990*. Princeton, N.J.: Princeton University Press, 1991.

Shenfield, Stephen. *The Nuclear Predicament*. New York: Methuen, 1987.

Shevchenko, Arkady N. *Breaking with Moscow*. New York: Alfred A. Knopf, 1985.

Shlapentokh, Vladimir. *Soviet Ideologies in the Period of Glasnost*. New York: Praeger Publishers, 1988.

Snyder, Jack. *Myths of Empire*. Ithaca, N.Y.: Cornell University Press, 1991.

Soviet-Chinese Relations in a Changing World. Moscow: Novosti Press, 1989.

Staar, Richard F., ed. *Yearbook on International Communist Affairs, 1975*. Stanford, Calif.: Hoover Institution Press, 1975.

Steele, Jonathan, and Eric Abraham. *Andropov in Power*. Garden City, N.J.: Anchor Press, 1984.

Stephan, John. *The Russian Far East*. Stanford, Calif.: Stanford University Press, 1994.

Stuart, Douglas T., and William T. Tow, eds. *China, the Soviet Union, and the West*. Boulder, Colo.: Westview Press, 1982.

Sutter, Robert G. *Chinese Foreign Policy*. New York: Praeger Publishers, 1986.

Swearingen, Rodger, ed. *Siberia and the Soviet Far East*. Stanford, Calif.: Hoover Institution Press, 1987.

Tatu, Michel. *Le Triangle Washington-Moscou-Pékin et les deux Europe(s)*. Paris: Casterman, 1972.

Teague, Elizabeth. *Solidarity and the Soviet Worker*. London: Croom Helm, Ltd., 1988.

Tetlock, Philip, et al., eds. *Behavior, Society, and Nuclear War*. Vol. 2. New York: Oxford University Press, 1991.

Timmermann, Heinz. *The Decline of the World Communist Movement*. Boulder, Colo.: Westview Press, 1987.

Todorov, Tsvetan. *Genres in Discourse*. Cambridge: Cambridge University Press, 1990.

Ulam, Adam B. *Expansion and Coexistence: Soviet Foreign Policy, 1917–73*. New York: Praeger Publishers, 1974.

Urban, Joan Barth. *Moscow and the Italian Communist Party*. Ithaca, N.Y.: Cornell University Press, 1986.

Urban, Michael et al. *The Rebirth of Politics in Russia*. Cambridge: Cambridge University Press, 1997.

Visit of Mikhail Gorbachev to China, May 15–18, 1989. Moscow: Novosti, 1989.

Walt, Stephen M. *Explaining the Origins of Alliances*. Ithaca, N.Y.: Cornell University Press, 1987.

Westad, Odd Arne, ed. *The Rise and Fall of the Sino-Soviet Alliance, 1945–1963*. Stanford, Calif.: Stanford University Press, 1998.

White, Stephen, and Alex Pravda. *Ideology and Soviet Politics*. New York: St. Martin's Press, 1988.

Wich, Richard. *Sino-Soviet Crisis Politics*. Cambridge, Mass.: Harvard University Press, 1980.

Woodhead, H. G. W., ed. *The China Yearbook, 1924–5*. Tientsin, China: The Tientsin Press, Ltd., 1924.

Yang, Mayfair Mei-hui. *Gifts, Favors & Banquets: The Art of Social Relationships in China*. Ithaca, N.Y.: Cornell University Press, 1994.

Zagoria, Donald. *The Sino-Soviet Conflict, 1956–61*. Princeton, N.J.: Princeton University Press, 1962.

Ziegler, Charles. *Foreign Policy and East Asia*. Cambridge: Cambridge University Press, 1993.

Zimmerman, William. *Soviet Perspectives on International Relations, 1956–67*. Princeton, N.J.: Princeton University Press, 1969.

Zubok, Vladislav, and Constantine Pleshakov. *Inside the Kremlin's Cold War: From Stalin to Khrushchev*. Cambridge, Mass.: Harvard University Press, 1996.

BOOKS IN RUSSIAN

Admidin, Andrei, and Elena Devaeva. *Mezhdunarodnoe ekonomicheskoe sotrudnichestvo v Vostochnoi Azii*. Vladivostok: Dal'nauka, 1998.

Aleksandrov-Agentov, A. M. *Ot Kollentai do Gorbacheva*. Moscow: Mezhdurnarodnye Otnosheniia, 1994.

Bazhanov, Evgenii. *Dvizhushchie sily politiki SShA v otnoshenii Kitaia*. Moscow: Nauka, 1982.

———. *Kitai i vneshnii mir*. Moscow: Mezhdunarodnye Otnosheniia, 1990.

Berger, Ia. M. *Sotsial'nye protsessy v sovremennoi kitaiskoi derevne*. Moscow: Nauka, 1989.

Bogaturov, Aleksei. *Sovremennye teorii stabil'nosti i mezhdunarodnye otnosheniia Rossii v Vostochnoi Azii v 1970–90e gg*. Moscow: Moskovskii Nauchnyi Fond, 1996.

Borisov, Oleg [Oleg Rakhmanin]. *Sovetskii Soiuz i Man'zhurskaia revoliutsionnaia baza*. Moscow: Mysl', 1975.

———. *Vnutrennaia i vneshniaia politika Kitaia v 70e gody*. Moscow: Izd. Politicheskoi Literatury, 1982.

Borisov, Oleg, and B. T. Koloskov [Boris Kulik]. *K 30–letiiu KNR*. Moscow: Znanie, 1979.

Bovin, Aleksandr. *Nachalo Vos'midesiatykh*. Moscow: Izvestiia, 1984.

Brezhnev, Aleksei. *Kitai: ternistyi put' k dobrososedstvu*. Moscow: Mezhdunarodnye Otnosheniia, 1998.

Brutents, Karen. *Tridsat' let na Staroi Ploshchadi*. Moscow: Mezhdunarodnye Otnosheniia, 1998.

Burlatskii, Fedor. *Mao Tse-dun i ego nasledniki*. Moscow: Mezhdunarodnye Otnosheniia, 1979.

———. *Vozhdi i sovetniki*. Moscow: Izd. Politicheskoi Literatury, 1990.

Cherniaev, Anatolii. *Moia zhizn' i moe vremia*. Moscow: Mezhdunarodnye Otnosheniia, 1995.

———. *Shest' let s Gorbachevym*. Moscow: Progress, 1993.

Davydov, Iu. P., and V. S. Rudnev. *SShA: Regional'nye problemy vneshnei politiki*. Moscow: Nauka, 1971.

Gel'bras, Vilia, and Mikhail Nosov, et al. *Migratsionnaia situatsiia na Dal'nem Vostoke i politika Rossii*. Moscow: Carnegie Center, 1996.

Gorbachev, M. S. *Izbrannye rechi i stat'i*. Vol. 3. Moscow: Izd. Politicheskoi Literatury, 1987.

Gromyko, Anatolii. *Andrei Gromyko. v labirintakh Kremlia*. Moscow: IPO "Avtor", 1997.

Grozin, Andrei V., and Valerii N. Khliupin. *Natsional'naia bezopasnost' Kazakhstana: Problemy i perspektivy*. Moscow: Agent, 1998.

Ishaev, Viktor I., and Pavel A. Minakir. *Dal'nii Vostok Rossii: Real'nosti i vozmozhnosti ekonomicheskogo razvitiia*. Khabarovsk: DVO RAN, 1998.

Kapchenko, Nikolai. *Antikommunisticheskaia sushchnost' ideologii i politiki Maoizma*. Moscow: Znanie, 1976.

Kapitsa, Mikhail S. *Eskalatsiia verolomstva: Politika Pekina i Sovetsko-Kitaiskie otnosheniia*. Moscow: Znanie, 1970.

———. *Na raznykh paralleliakh: Zapiski diplomata*. Moscow: Kniga i biznes, 1996.

Krasnov, A. N. *Po ostrovam dalekogo Vostoka. Putevye ocherki nedeli.* Saint Petersburg: 1895.

Larin, Viktor. *Kitai i Dal'nii Vostok Rossii.* Vladivostok: Dal'nauka, 1998.

Lazarev, V. I. *Klassovaia bor'ba v KNR.* Moscow: Politizdat, 1981.

Medvedev, Roy. *Lichnost' i epokha. Politicheskii portret L.I. Brezhneva.* Moscow: Novosti, 1991.

Miasnikov, Vladimir. *Dogovornymi stat'iami utverdili.* Moscow and Khabarovsk: Russian Academy of Sciences and Priamurskoe Geograficheskoe Obshchestvo, 1997.

Ministerstva Inostrannykh Del. *Sbornik deistvuiushchikh dogovorov, soglashenii i konventsii, zakliuchennykh SSSR s inostrannymi gosudarstvami.* Vypusk 14. Moscow: Gosudarstvennoe izdatel'stvo politicheskoi literatury, 1957.

Mitrofanov, Aleksei. *Shagi do novoi geopolitiki.* Moscow: Russkii Vestnik, 1997.

Nekotorye problemy demarkatsii Rossiisko-Kitaiskoi granitsy, 1991–1997 god. Sbornik statei i dokumentov. Moscow: Nezavisimaia Gazeta, 1997.

Primakov, E. V., ed. *Mezhdunarodnye konflikty.* Moscow: Mezhdunarodnye Otnosheniia, 1972.

Savitskii, Petr, and Petr Suvchinskii, et al. *Iskhod k Vostoku.* Sofia: Balkan', 1921.

Sergeichuk, S. S. *SShA i Kitai: Isdanie vtoroe, dopolnenoe i ispravlennoe.* Moscow: Mezhdunarodnye Otnosheniia, 1973.

Titarenko, M. L., and O. V. Ostrovskii, eds. *Rossiiskii Dal'nii Vostok i Severo-Vostochnaia Aziia.* Moscow: Editorial URSS, 1998.

Trenin, Dmitrii. *Kitaiskaia problema Rossii.* Moscow: Carnegie Center, 1998.

Vitkovskaia, Galina, and Dmitrii Trenin, eds. *Perspektivy Dal'nevostochnogo regiona: Mezhstranye vzaimodeistviia.* Moscow: Carnegie Moscow Center, 1999.

———. *Perspektivy Dal'nevostochnogo regiona: Naselenie, migratsiia, rynki truda, Rabochii materialy, Vypusk 2.* Moscow: Carnegie Moscow Center, 1999.

Vladimirov, O. *Sovetsko-Kitaiskie otnosheniia.* Moscow: Mezhdunarodnye Otnoshenie, 1984.

Ziuganov, Gennadyi. *Geografiia pobedy. Osnovy Rossiiskoi geopolitiki.* AOA Saint-Petersburg Typography: Saint-Petersburg, 1997.

Zubakova, V. T. *Osnovnye aspekty Kitaiskoi problemy, 1969–75.* Moscow: Politizdat, 1975.

BOOKS IN CHINESE

Chen Hui. *ZhongE guanxi jishi.* Beijing: Chinese Academy of Social Sciences, Institute of East European, Russian, and Central Asian Studies, 1996.

Li Ke, and Hao Shengzhang. *Wenhua da geming de renmin jiefang jun.* Beijing: Chinese Communist Party History Materials Press, 1989.

Lu Nanquan, and Xue Jundu. *ZhongE maoyi guanxi.* Beijing: Chinese Academy of Social Sciences Press, 1999.

Zhou Wenqi, and Chu Liangru, eds. *Teshu er fuza de keti—gongchang guoji, Sulian he Zhongguo gonchangdang guanxi biannianshi*. Beijing: Hubei renmin chubanshe, 1993.

GROUPS OF ARCHIVAL DOCUMENTS

Moscow

Communist Party of the Soviet Union (CPSU) Central Committee Archives (TsK KPSS)

TsK KPSS, Fond 4, op. 15, 17, 19, 22, 24.

TsK KPSS, Fond 89, op. 8, 11, 21, 34, 42, 43, 82.

Khabarovsk

State Archives of Khabarovskii Krai, Party Archive of the Khabarovsk Krai committee of the CPSU

Fond p-35, op. 96, 100, 107, 110, 111, 112, 115, 117.

Washington, D.C.

Handwritten journals and diaries of Harry Robbins Haldeman, White House Special Files: Staff Member and Office Files: Harry Haldeman, Box 1; Richard M. Nixon Presidential Materials Staff at College Park, Md.

Pol 32–1 Chicom-USSR through Pol Affairs Rel Chicom-Viets, State Department Central Files 1967–69, Richard M. Nixon Presidential Materials, National Archives at College Park, Md.

White House Special Files (WHSF): Staff Member and Office Files (SMOF): Ronald Ziegler; Briefing Materials, Meetings with Heads of State, 1971–74 [Soviet Summit, May 1972], Soviet Viewpoint and Objectives; Box 37; Richard M. Nixon Presidential Materials Staff at College Park, Md.

AMERICAN DISSERTATIONS

de Berard Mills, William. "Sino-Soviet Interactions, May 1977–June 1980." Ph.D. diss., University of Michigan, 1981.

Bone, Jonathan. "Socialism in a Far Country: Development and Socioeconomic Change in the Russian Far East, 1922–1939." Ph.D. diss., University of Chicago, in progress.

Garrett, Banning. "The China Card and Its Origins: U.S. Bureaucratic Politics and the Strategic Triangle." Ph.D. diss., Brandeis University, 1983.

Gates, Robert Michael. "Soviet Sinology: An Untapped Source for Kremlin's Views and Disputes Relating to Contemporary Events in China." Ph.D. diss., Georgetown University, 1974.

Griffiths, Franklyn John Charles. "Images, Politics, and Learning in Soviet Behavior toward the United States." Ph.D. diss., Columbia University, 1972.

Kuchins, Andrew Carrigan. "Cognitive Change and Political Entrepreneurship: The Evolution of Soviet Policy toward China from 1976–1989." Ph.D. diss., The Johns Hopkins University, 1992.

Sandles, Gretchen Ann. "Soviet Images of and Policy toward China, 1955–1979." Ph.D. diss., University of Michigan, 1981.

Su, Chi. "Soviet Image of and Policy toward China, 1969–1979." Ph.D. diss., Columbia University, 1984.

JOURNALS

Full citations of all journal articles are listed in the chapter endnotes. These articles came from the following sources:

American, European, and English-Language Journals, Newspapers, and Media Compilations

American Political Science Review
Asian Perspective
Asian Survey
Asiaweek
Aussenpolitik (English edition)
California Slavic Studies
The China Quarterly
The Cold War International History Project Bulletin
The Current Digest of the Soviet Press
East Asia
Europe-Asia Studies
Far Eastern Economic Review
Foreign Affairs
Foreign Broadcast Information Service (FBIS)
Foreign Policy
The Harriman Institute Forum
The Hong Kong Standard
The International Herald Tribune
International Organization
International Security
Issues and Studies (Taipei)
Jamestown Monitor
Journal of East Asian Affairs

Journal of Northeast Asian Studies
The Military Balance
Le Monde
NBR Analysis
The New York Times
Open Media Research Institute (OMRI) Daily Report
OMRI Regional Report
Pacific Affairs
PlanEcon Report
Post-Soviet Geography and Economics
Problems of Communism
Problems of Post-Communism
Russian in Asia (RA) Report (Honolulu)
Radio Free Europe/Radio Liberty Daily Report
Radio Free Europe/Radio Liberty Newsline
Radio Free Europe/Radio Liberty Research Report
Radio Liberty
Review of International Affairs (Belgrade)
Russia and FSU Monitor
Strategic Survey
Soviet Union in the Pacific-Asian Region (SUPAR) Report (Honolulu)
Time
L'Unità
World Politics
Yearbook on International Communist Affairs

Russian Journals, Newspapers, Compilations, and Wire Services

Amurskaia Pravda (Blagoveshchensk)
Argumenty i Fakty
Aziia i Afrika Segodnia
Birobidzhanskaia Zvezda
Dal'nevostochnyi Uchenyi (Vladivostok)
Diplomaticheskii Vestnik
Interfax
ITAR-TASS
Izvestiia
Khabarovskie vesti
Kommersant
Kommersant-Daily

Kommunist

Kommunist Vooruzhennykh Sil

Komsomol'skaia Pravda

Krasnaia Znamia (Vladivostok)

Krasnaia Zvezda

Literaturnaia Gazeta

Mezhdunarodnye Otnosheniia (*International Affairs* in English translation)

MEiMO

Moskovskie Novosti (*Moscow News* in English translation)

Narody Azii i Afriki

Nezavisimaia Gazeta

Novoe Vremia (*New Times* in English translation)

Novyi Mir

Opasnyi Kurs

Partiinaia Zhizn'

Politicheskii Dnevnik

Pravda

Priamurskie Vedemosti (Khabarovsk)

Problemy Dal'nego Vostoka (*Far Eastern Affairs* in English translation)

Rabochii Klass i Sovremennyi Mir

Rossiia

Rossiia i ATR (Vladivostok)

Rossiia i Sovremennyi Mir

Rossiiskaia Gazeta

Rossiiskie Vesti

SShA

Segodnia

Sel'skaia Zhizn'

Svobodnaia Mysl'

Tikhookeanskaia Zvezda (Khabarovsk)

Utro Rossii (Vladivostok)

Vedemosti Verkhovnogo Soveta SSSR

Vek

Vestnik Ministerstva Inostrannykh Del

Vladivostok

Voennaia Mysl'

Voprosy Filosofii

Voprosy Istorii

Voprosy Istorii KPSS

Zavtra

Zolotoi Rog (Vladivostok)
Znamia

Chinese Journals, Newspapers, and Wire Services

Dangdai Wenxian
Dangdai Zhongguo Yanjiu
DongOuZhongYa Yanjiu
Eluosi Yanjiu
Guoji Jingji Pinglun
Guoji Maoyi Wenti
Guoji Shangbao
Guoji Wenti Yanjiu
Heilongjiang Jingji Ribao
Heilongjiang Ribao
International Trade News
Liaowang
Peking Review
Renmin Ribao (*People's Daily* in English translation)
Taipingyang Xuebao
Xinhua
Yuandong Jingmao Baodao

Index